BEDOUIN BUREAUCRATS

T0385990

BEDOUIN BUREAUCRATS

Mobility

and

Property

in the Ottoman Empire

NORA ELIZABETH BARAKAT

STANFORD UNIVERSITY PRESS
Stanford, California

Stanford University Press
Stanford, California

This book has been partially underwritten by the Stanford Authors Fund. We are grateful to the Fund for its support of scholarship by first-time authors. For more information, please see www.sup.org/authors/authorsfund.

Printed and bound by CPI Group (UK) Ltd, Croydon, CR0 4YY

Library of Congress Cataloging-in-Publication Data

Names: Barakat, Nora Elizabeth, author.
Title: Bedouin bureaucrats : mobility and property in the Ottoman Empire / Nora Elizabeth Barakat.
Description: Stanford, California : Stanford University Press, [2023] | Includes bibliographical references and index.
Identifiers: LCCN 2022035161 (print) | LCCN 2022035162 (ebook) | ISBN 9781503634619 (cloth) | ISBN 9781503635623 (paperback) | ISBN 9781503635630 (ebook)
Subjects: LCSH: Bedouins—Turkey—Politics and government. | Land tenure—Government policy—Turkey—History. | Real property—Turkey—History. | Central-local government relations—Turkey—History. | Turkey—Politics and government—1878-1909. | Turkey—History—Ottoman Empire, 1288-1918.
Classification: LCC DR572 .B18 2023 (print) | LCC DR572 (ebook) | DDC 956.1/015—dc23/eng/20220729
LC record available at https://lccn.loc.gov/2022035161
LC ebook record available at https://lccn.loc.gov/2022035162

Cover design: Gia Giasullo
Cover photos: (top) *Camp of the Banī Ṣakhr Bedouins: Tent of Sheikh Fawwāz,* 1906. Library of Congress, Prints & Photographs Division, LC-DIG-ppm-sca-38112. (bottom) *East of the Jordan and Dead Sea. General view of Kerak (Kir of Moab),* 1900–1920. Library of Congress, Prints & Photographs Division, LC-DIG-matpc-01692.
Typeset by Elliott Beard in Minion Pro 10.5/15

To my parents, Edward and Diana Cundy

CONTENTS

MAPS, FIGURES, AND TABLES

TABLES

NOTE ON TRANSLITERATION, DATES, CURRENCIES, AND MEASURES

This book contains transliterations of Ottoman Turkish and Arabic words and phrases into English. For Ottoman Turkish, I have transliterated using the modern Turkish equivalents. For Arabic, I have followed the transliteration system of the *International Journal of Middle East Studies*. For place names, I have adopted conventional contemporary English spellings (e.g., Mecca rather than Makka or Mekke). For individuals, I have adopted the spelling that most likely corresponds to the historical person's first language (e.g., Cemal Bey, Nahar al-Bakhit) while acknowledging the assumptions this entails. I have not used diacritics for proper names.

I have reported all dates mentioned in the historical texts I cite, converting lunar calendar (*hijri*) and solar (*rumi*) dates into the *miladi* (Gregorian) system even when the documents do not. For *hijri* calendar dates recorded in both Ottoman Turkish and Arabic sources, I have used the Ottoman abbreviation system:

> M: Muharrem/Muḥarram
> S: Safer/Ṣafar
> Ra: Rebiülevvel/Rabīʿ al-Awwal
> R: Rebiülahir/Rabīʿ al-Ākhir

Ca: Cemaziyelevvel/Jumādā al-Ūlā
C: Cemaziyelahir/Jumādā al-Ākhira
B: Receb/Rajab
Ş: Şaban/Shaʿbān
N: Ramazan/Ramaḍān
L: Şevval/Shawwāl
Za: Zilkade/Dhū al-Qaʿda
Z: Zilhicce/Dhū al-Ḥijja

The most widely mentioned currency in the eighteenth- and nineteenth-century Syrian interior was the Ottoman piastre (Arabic plural *qurūsh*, Turkish plural *kuruş*). In late nineteenth- and early twentieth-century court records from the province of Syria, reference is also made to Mecidi riyals, French liras, and Ottoman or British pounds. The following values are extracted from the imperial yearbook (*salname*) of the province of Syria from 1900:

	Mecidi riyal	French lira	Ottoman pound	British pound
Piasters	24	114	131.5	143

In the late nineteenth century, sharia court cases (from November 1897 and February 1902) indicate that monthly living expenses (*nafaqa*) of an adult individual in the interior district of Salt ranged between 50 to 120 kuruş.

In the majority of the texts under study, the unit of measurement used for agricultural land was the *donum*, equal to slightly less than one square kilometer (.939 km2) according to the "dunum" entry in Redhouse's *Turkish and English Lexicon*.

INTRODUCTION

IN OCTOBER 1879, Dawjan and Hamad al-Wiraykat, from the Wiraykat family of 'Adwan Bedouin, rode with their sons from their encampment in the region of Abu Nusayr southwest toward the town of Salt. They went to meet with a group of men who had come from the west, from the district capital of Nablus on the other side of the Jordan River, to register rights to land in the interior region where the Wiraykats camped and cultivated during the summer months. The path descended into a deep valley and then began a long climb to the elevated town. Hamad, Dawjan, and their entourage passed a few other Wiraykat encampments and farms, as well as lands controlled by their 'Adwani relatives, the Lawzis.[1] When they reached the outskirts of Salt in the early afternoon, they greeted the small Ottoman garrison stationed there and entered the district government's rooms at the center of town. A large group of 'Adwani men were already there, haggling over the land registration process. In the end, Hamad and Dawjan each registered separate plots of land in the region of Abu Nusayr northeast of Salt.[2]

The formulaic Ottoman land register that the day's work created listed the names of the places where individuals claimed land, the amounts of land they claimed, and, in some cases, the land's four car-

1

dinal borders. There is no evidence that the production of this 1879 register involved modern surveying techniques. No one stood on the land and demarcated borders with steel markers.[3] We have no record of the officials from Nablus actually visiting the Abu Nusayr region to survey the land in 1879. The borders were vague, often referring to the names of the holders of neighboring plots rather than to landmarks fixed in space. Dawjan al-Wiraykat's registrations listed no borders at all, and the imprecise toponyms and round numbers of units (donums) involved in both the Lawzi and Wiraykat registrations suggest a share-holding arrangement.[4]

Even so, the registers became the basis of something lasting. Ten years after this initial registration, Dawjan al-Wiraykat would use his 1879 title deed as collateral against a series of cash loans from a prominent merchant capitalist in the town of Salt.[5] Half a century later, during the British Mandate period in the 1930s, Hamad, Dawjan, and Hamad's son Ghishan al-Wiraykat mortgaged their land in the Abu Nusayr region to the Agricultural Bank in Salt for another series of cash loans.[6] Well over a century after that initial registration, in 2004, the Hashemite Kingdom of Jordan began a large-scale highway-building project with funding from the United States government. In the preceding years, the population of the city of Amman had swelled, first with Palestinians expelled from Kuwait and then with refugees of the American invasion and occupation of Iraq. The highway was meant to relieve the ensuing traffic congestion. Called "Jordan Street" (Shār' al-Urdunn), it was to cut directly through Wiraykat land, close to the regions Dawjan and Hamad registered in 1879. In response, two of Dawjan's great-grandsons joined fourteen other Wiraykat men and women in court in Amman in 2005. They demanded that the state, specifically the Public Works Ministry of the Hashemite Kingdom of Jordan, pay them compensation for losses in the value of the land their grandparents had registered around the town of Abu Nusayr, amounting to 121,389 Jordanian dinars, about USD 170,000. After a series of appeals, Dawjan's grandsons ultimately lost their case to garner a portion of the capital influx associated with the highway.[7] The case shows, however, that they had maintained their claims over land in the regions they registered, under the sovereign jurisdiction of three different governing regimes, for 150 years.

By registering land in 1879, and later entering the rapidly expanding Ottoman bureaucracy, Hamad and Dawjan al-Wiraykat contributed to fundamental transformations in the way people have understood, articulated, and contested their interrelated relationships to land and the state, not only in Jordan but across the Eastern Mediterranean, until today. The importance of the Ottoman registrations, and the conflicts over land that followed, lies partly in the fact that the British and French regimes in the post–World War I Eastern Mediterranean began where the Ottoman administration left off. They employed similar categories of land and population and built on preceding Ottoman institutions.[8] The 1879 registration, however, was also the centerpiece of an Ottoman attempt to include the landscape and the tent-dwelling inhabitants of the Syrian interior in newly coalescing forms of standardized imperial administration.

Prior to the 1870s, Ottoman lawmakers had focused their sovereign attention on the closely administered corridor of the pilgrimage route in the Syrian interior. Administering the pilgrimage engendered a wide network of lasting, multigenerational relationships with particular Bedouin groups in the surrounding regions, but the Ottoman regime had not attempted to directly govern the landscapes beyond the pilgrimage corridor or their inhabitants. Through a system of layered sovereignty, the imperial regime left everyday administration of land and other resources in the hands of Bedouin elites. In the 1860s and 1870s, in contrast, Ottoman lawmakers and officials looked to the Syrian interior as an outlet for capital, a ground for large-scale infrastructure projects, and a region of settlement for small-holding Muslim refugees. They shared this agrarian developmentalist vision with lawmakers, capitalists, and small-scale entrepreneurs in multiple imperial polities, responding to a booming and newly global grain market by focusing attention on landscapes they regarded, and defined through property law, as "empty."[9] After the global financial crisis of the 1870s, this moment of agrarian optimism shifted to one of anxiety.[10] For embattled Ottoman lawmakers in the aftermath of bankruptcy and loss of territory, the imperative to retain sovereignty over and develop spaces like the Syrian interior took on new urgency. In the 1890s and the first decade of the 1900s, the Ottoman government joined other imperial polities in attempting to fill landscapes they defined legally as empty, closely managing land and its human inhabitants and incorporating both into territorially bounded grids of administrative law.[11]

This book reveals the roles of Bedouin in these processes of Ottoman state transformation on local, imperial, and global scales. In the Syrian interior, a group of tent-dwelling men acquired positions as representatives of administratively defined "tribes," entering a standardized hierarchy of provincial governance in the late nineteenth century. These Bedouin bureaucrats used their growing political, social, and economic leverage to gain wealth and status and to maintain their communities' legal control over land. Their work was part of an uneven, contingent, and fundamentally unpredictable set of attempts to create administratively uniform and economically productive state space between the fiscal and territorial crises of the 1870s and the imperial disintegration of World War I. I use the term *state space* to describe the landscape within a territorially conceived and hierarchical administrative and judicial apparatus and a theoretically uniform and bounded grid of property relations.[12] Over the course of the nineteenth century, the Ottoman regime shifted from an imperial mode of governance crafted to manage human difference across a politically diverse landscape, in which layered forms of sovereignty were connected to both geographical space and human subjects, to a nation-state mode that aspired to standardize administration of juridically equal subjects within a bounded territory. In the final quarter of the nineteenth century, and especially after losses in the Balkans and a crippling fiscal crisis, Ottoman lawmakers saw potential in rural regions of the Eastern Mediterranean and Iraq that they had previously deemed marginal, aiming to both defend threatened Ottoman sovereignty in these regions and include them in an emergent imperial-national polity.

This book conceptualizes the Ottoman project of making territorial state space within a global context of polities attempting similar transformations from variegated imperial to standardized nation-state modes of governance. Global historians have recognized the similarities between increasingly aggressive imperial approaches to frontiers in the late nineteenth and early twentieth centuries, although this has largely been told as a story of European expansion. Many scholars have considered the expansion of settler "neo-Europes" like the United States and Australia within a comparative analytical frame.[13] In addition, multiple studies have noted the congruence between Russia's imperial expansion into Central Asia and Siberia in the late nineteenth and early twentieth centuries and the experience of "neo-Europes," especially the United States' expansion into western North America. The comparison between the Russian and American polities has been particularly useful because, in contrast to the late British or French empires, both expanded into contiguous regions populated by communities with whom they had long preexisting connections.[14] As Charles Maier has argued, "governing at home" was different when it came to territorial thinking about state-building, particularly in the realm of defining the legal status of settlers and the existing inhabitants of regions formerly deemed marginal.[15]

Ottoman attempts to expand direct administration, intensify resource extraction, and ensure territorial sovereignty and a loyal population in previously lightly governed regions like eastern Anatolia, the Syrian interior, and the Arabian Peninsula have not usually been placed in the same analytical frame as expanding contiguous empires like the American and Russian. Scholars have largely considered that by the late nineteenth century, the Ottoman state was contracting and defensive, not expanding.[16] Here, I draw on the American and Russian experiences to consider the Ottoman Empire within a framework of polities that embarked on making what Steven Hahn called "imperial nation-states" in the late nineteenth century.[17] In these contexts, lawmakers and officials attempted to integrate formerly lightly governed landscapes and their inhabitants into a more cohesive, standardized, and ultimately, if highly contested, national territorial landscape.[18] In the Russian, Ottoman, and American empires, attempts to transform "marginal" regions responded both to optimism around a global grain market and an aggressive and expansive British-centered global order in the decades preceding World War I. The Ottoman initiative to fill in spaces like the Syrian interior converged with the reconstructed US project of administrative expansion into the western plains and Russian initiatives in the Central Asian steppe to create state space under the firm control of a centralized administrative hierarchy.[19]

In particular, Ottoman legal expressions of "empty land" that privileged cultivation over other kinds of land use and state attempts to settle immigrants and refugees in regions deemed empty were remarkably congruent with the measures of other national-imperial polities. In the mid-nineteenth century, lawmakers in the Ottoman, American, and Russian regimes converged around evolutionary discourses of human productivity that privileged intensive cultivation in the determination of land rights and categorized existing populations as "nomadic" and undeserving of title because of their purportedly inefficient land use.[20] In the final decades of the nineteenth century, some Ottoman officials dreamed of large-scale refugee resettlement in the interior, considered confining Bedouin to well-defined territories and opening the interior to capitalist interests, and legally privileged settled cultivation in establishing increasingly exclusive individual property rights.

Making visible these convergences in imperial aspirations, administrative discourse, and law is important for deexceptionalizing the Ottoman experience and placing it in a wider global frame. But imperial aspirations are not the end of the story. A global perspective also illuminates the unique outcomes of these state-making projects in the Syrian interior and their deeply contingent nature. In particular, unlike many communities categorized as "nomadic" in other imperial polities and within the Ottoman Empire itself, Bedouin in the Syrian interior were able to maintain control over most of the land they had inhabited for generations well beyond the fall of the empire. While they lost some land to capitalist entrepreneurs and refugees, groups like the Wiraykat both maintained their seasonal mobility and increased their legal connections to the interior landscape in the final decades of Ottoman rule.[21] The major demographic shift to permanent settlement in the interior that Ottoman officials had envisioned in the 1890s did not occur until the mid-twentieth century, well after the fall of the empire and on terms no one in the late nineteenth century could have imagined. At the same time, men like Hamad and Dawjan al-Wiraykat took on important bureaucratic roles in the making of Ottoman state space alongside other middling and elite tent-dwelling Bedouin men.

What explains this unique outcome? As we will see, a set of historical relationships and circumstances enabled both elite and nonelite Bedouin men in the Syrian interior to maintain their communities' control over land by entering the expanding Ottoman bureaucracy. This process occurred on two levels: first, Bedouin elites in particular communities leveraged the political influence their ancestors had developed and maintained in the Ottoman administration of the pilgrimage route between Damascus and Mecca. These relationships became more complex and lucrative in the eighteenth century prior to imperial attempts to create territorial state space. Detailing these understudied and robust imperial networks complicates both Ottoman modernizers' and modern scholars' characterizations of the Syrian interior as a "tribal frontier" prior to the nineteenth century. *Bedouin Bureaucrats* presents late Ottoman attempts to create territorial state space as a renegotiation and intensification of existing forms of layered sovereignty rather than the "penetration" of an uncharted frontier. This renegotiation meant that elites within certain Bedouin communities with centuries of influence in the pilgrimage administration retained that influence despite Ottoman attempts at political and administrative standardization, maintaining their hold on increasingly valuable interior land.

On a second level, for Bedouin communities who did not have historical connections to the pilgrimage, a late Ottoman politics of administration that included them within aspirations of territorial state space was much more important. After the crises of the 1870s, Ottoman lawmakers constructed Bedouin as *potentially* productive Muslim subjects whose assumed political loyalty was important to sustain in sparsely populated regions like the Syrian interior. This position responded to anxieties about political loyalty and threatened territorial sovereignty that constituted a state of siege by the final quarter of the nineteenth century.[22] Expansive British, French, and Russian imperial practices—especially in forms of legal extraterritoriality that worked through protégés claiming immunities inside Ottoman borders—created thorny questions about the nature of imperial subjecthood, loyalty, and religious identity that deepened after the Russian-Ottoman war and the Treaty of Berlin.[23] When combined with the individualization of property rights in a nineteenth-century context of territorially conceived sovereignty, the perceived loyalties of landowners became newly politicized.[24] This was especially true in regions like the Syrian interior, which became a contested borderland and "spy-space" after the British occupation of Egypt in 1882.[25] This political environment constituted a significant barrier to capitalist expansion, as lawmakers attempted to close the land market to anyone whose loyalty they considered questionable.

The prioritization of political loyalty and the maintenance of sovereignty over aspirations to productivity created space for middling Bedouin bureaucrats to maintain land rights and participate in the politics of Ottoman administration.[26] Elite Ottoman statesmen considered Bedouin and other "tribal" populations analogous to Muslim refugees: they did not enjoy the privileges of cultivating, village-dwelling peasants in the new matrix of land rights, but they were potentially loyal, productive subjects. This construction undergirded administrative regulations and laws in the Syrian interior, but it also enabled men like the Wiraykats to bring the social struggles that the establishment of a private property regime precipitated into the Ottoman bureaucracy. In doing so, they left their mark on a constantly contested and unfinished project of modern state formation.

In the late nineteenth century, tent dwellers' encounters with a newly intrusive Ottoman administration created a different type of leader within their communities in Syria: the Bedouin bureaucrat. Men like Hamad and Dawjan al-Wiraykat, as headmen of administratively defined tent-dwelling communities, engaged in Ottoman bureaucratic practices across the encampments of the interior. Creating territorial state space entailed reaching every tent and house-dwelling inhabitant of the interior through theoretically standardized and rationalized practices of property registration, taxation, and dispute resolution. In the imagined state of codified imperial law, Bedouin headmen were the low-level officials meant to purvey state policy to their communities of subjects. Bedouin bureaucrats' quotidian performance of state power through the documentary processes of land registration, taxation, and adjudication increased their social and political influence both within the standardized Ottoman administration of the late nineteenth century and within their own communities.[27]

But Bedouin bureaucrats did not follow the playbook for administration laid out in minute detail in codified law. In particular, when Ottoman imperial land policy began to directly threaten Bedouin communities with dispossession, headmen turned their performance of state power on its head: rather than organizing their communities to collect taxes, they organized them to protest the settlement of refugees on land they regarded as their own, collected bribes for higher-level officials, and orchestrated prison escapes. Rather than integrating into the fundamental rural administrative category of the Ottoman agrarian imaginary, the settled village, they employed and maintained the "tribe" as a power field through which to contest and transform taxation, resource distribution, and state powers of adjudication.[28] Through their iterative performances of state power, Bedouin bureaucrats contributed to outcomes that were diametrically opposed to higher-level officials' visions and plans for the Syrian interior: ultimately, their tent-dwelling communities maintained much of their control over land without settling in villages. Into the twenty-first century, this control has taken two forms: on the one hand, state-sanctioned title deeds and, on the other, an informal market in unregistered land claimed for the state domain that both directly challenges central state attempts to monopolize the allocation of resources and complements and responds to state-sanctioned documentary forms of contract.[29]

Late Ottoman struggles over the governance of land and people established the terms for territorial state practice in Eastern Mediterranean landscapes for much of the twentieth century. By narrating the biographies of Bedouin involved in Ottoman administration from the eighteenth to the twentieth centuries, the contested administrative category "tribe" alongside the figure of the Bedouin bureaucrat, and the changing legal status of land in the Syrian interior, this book brings tent-dwelling populations to the center of a fundamentally unpredictable process of making state space. The formal land registration process in which Dawjan and Hamad al-Wiraykat took part was a foundational element of a broader imperial vision of transforming "empty land." It was also the beginning of a documented legal relationship between the Wiraykats and the lands of Abu Nusayr that lasted for more than a century.

TENT DWELLERS, AGRICULTURE, PROPERTY

This book explores the roles of individual men from five different communities—the al-Fayiz Bani Sakhr, the Kayid ʿAdwan, the Wiraykat ʿAdwan, the Manasir ʿAbbad, and the Fuqaha ʿAbbad—in the creation of Ottoman state space in the Eastern Mediterranean. Some, like the ʿAdwan communities, had been involved in wheat production for at least a century in the Syrian interior when Ottoman land registration began; others, like the Bani Sakhr, derived more of their livelihoods from camel herding and involvement in the pilgrimage administration. All of these communities lived in tents for at least part of the year, moved seasonally, and produced both agricultural and animal-based commodities in the late nineteenth century. Court and land registers show that alongside these activities, individual ʿAdwani, ʿAbbadi, and Bani Sakhr men played important roles in the daily bureaucratic tasks of establishing and maintaining a private property administration in the Syrian interior. Their contributions to the making of territorial state space necessitate a rethinking of durable assumptions about the fundamental incompatibility of mobile agropastoral practice, private property regimes, and modern administration in the Ottoman Empire and beyond.

Perhaps James Scott best articulated the idea that the modern state is the "enemy of people who move around" and that it creates social systems unilaterally "through its ability to give its categories the force of law."[30] Historical scholarship on the Ottoman Empire and the Eastern Mediterranean has also portrayed Bedouin, understood as nomadic and tribal, as external to reified state domains from diverse theoretical vantage points. Historians writing in the framework of modernization theory in the mid-twentieth century consistently depicted unruly and politically autonomous Bedouin as the fundamental obstacles to a nineteenth-century Ottoman modernization project.[31] In the twenty-first century, scholars approaching Ottoman reform through a lens of postcolonial theory transformed Bedouin from the spoilers of an apparently failed modernization project into the victims of an apparently successful one.[32] While employing sharply contrasting frameworks of the modern state, these studies shared assumptions about Bedouin communities as politically autonomous tribes inherently antagonistic to agriculture, private property, and bureaucratic institution-building.

The assumption that seasonally migrating, tent-dwelling agropastoralists like the Wiraykats were necessarily opposed to standardized administrative state-making has been closely related to two ideal types: the pastoral nomad and the segmentary tribe. Western European concepts of exclusive private property and enclosure influential throughout the colonized world employed an ideal of pastoral nomadism as their ultimate other.[33] In the work of John Locke and Adam Smith, nomads occupied stage two of a four-stage theory of human progress rooted in modes of subsistence: hunting and gathering, pastoral herding, farming, and, finally, commerce. Locke argued that by mixing their sweat with the soil to create something new, cultivators acquired exclusive rights to property, and Smith saw such property rights as the basis for law, judicial systems, and differentiated authority in society more broadly. While pastoral herders developed private property in animals, they did not have a connection to land meaningful enough to confer rights. For both Locke and Smith, the main empirical example of early evolutionary stages was Native Americans, whom Smith saw as consigned to the stage of hunting and therefore vulnerable to the "intermeddling" of the more advanced Europeans.[34] More complex versions of this evolutionist thinking entered historical scholarship mainly through the writings of Karl Marx and Max Weber, both of whom argued that mobile forms of land use and kinship-based political idioms were isolated phenomena of premodern societies that would necessarily disappear when urban forms of settlement and commerce spread.[35]

While the empirically tenuous nature of these evolutionist ideas has been understood for decades, their categories have exhibited remarkable staying power, especially in ideal types employed to describe communities inhabiting the rural areas of regions that came to be known as the Middle East. This is partly due to a voluminous twentieth-century anthropological literature that perfected the segmentary tribe as the political form nomadic societies took: autonomous, geographically isolated, and essentially egalitarian entities governed only by internal segmentary principles.[36] This discourse of unfettered tribes that Lila Abu-Lughod and others have so effectively deconstructed also enabled the idea of an isolated nomadic mode of production.[37] Scholars posited a hierarchical continuum of nomadic groups from the "pure" camel herders who visited villages and towns only rarely to the "mixed" sheep and goatherds more closely involved with settled life.[38] For people making a living herding livestock in the Eastern Mediterranean and Arabian Peninsula, agriculture became the ultimate mark of identity loss. Recent environmental history of the region has sometimes adopted the concept of a nomadic mode of production, positing nomads as a fixed, climatically determined historical element with the constant capacity, like locusts or sandstorms, to rise from the desert and threaten sedentary society.[39]

In contrast, this book contributes to a vein of social history and anthropology that has problematized assumptions about the social, economic, and political isolation and autonomy of tent-dwelling communities.[40] This scholarship has emphasized part-time agriculture that was not necessarily linked to permanent settlement, as well as myriad trade connections between communities spending more time on herding and those spending more time on agriculture.[41] The trajectories of tent-dwelling communities like the Wiraykats, who were involved in markets for both animal- and plant-based commodities in the nineteenth century, also illuminate the ways in which mixed uses of land created long-standing connections to particular landscapes. Other communities, like the Bani Sakhr, increased their agricultural production in direct response to the global wheat boom of the mid-nineteenth century. In the late Ottoman context, these connections to the landscape and to regional commerce framed Bedouin bureaucrats' active participation in the making of territorial state space.

At the same time, as a legal history, *Bedouin Bureaucrats* reveals the ways in which the nomadic tribe as an ideal type had specific historical effects in the administration of rights to property in the Ottoman context. Global historians have narrated the dispossession of populations defined as nomadic, imperfectly cultivating, or unproductive as a largely Anglo-American story that started in enclosure movements in sixteenth-century England and traveled to contexts of Anglophone white settlement and colonization worldwide.[42] An exclusionary discourse of agricultural productivity and improvement was hardly limited or endogenous to British and neo-British imperial contexts, however.[43] Between the seventeenth and nineteenth centuries, Ottoman officials developed similar ideas about the links between cultivation, exclusive individual property rights, and improvement. They envisioned an ideal landscape peopled by settled, cultivating smallholders with well-defined, easily taxable, and alienable rights to land. To achieve this, they created law codes mandating both the mass settlement of tent dwellers and the breakup of agricultural shareholding practices common in villages in Syria and beyond.[44]

The extent of the intent and implementation of a regime of individuated and alienable private property rights in the late Ottoman context has been the subject of some debate, and the legal constitution of individual property rights entailed references to both agricultural labor and tax payment.[45] But the emphasis on cultivation as the preferred form of labor for the establishment of individual prescriptive rights clearly privileged full-time agricultural land use and year-round, easily taxable village-based settlement. This legal construction of land rights represented a break from the vision of rural landscapes implied in fifteenth- and sixteenth-century Ottoman law—one involving many kinds of dwellings including both houses and tents, with many people involved in mobile and semimobile forms of part-time farming.[46] Explaining this historical shift, and especially its connections to changing Ottoman ideas about territorial sovereignty, requires a study of its own. The sketch here is preliminary, providing background to the story of Bedouin involvement in the creation of a private property regime in the Syrian interior.

Many scholars have demonstrated the deep influence of political theories most commonly associated with the fourteenth-century North African polymath Ibn Khaldun on Ottoman statesmen between the seventeenth and nineteenth centuries.[47] Like European scholars after him, Ibn Khaldun posited a fundamental juxtaposition between nomadic rural and urban settled communities. Whereas in evolutionist Lockean and Smithian thought, nomadic herders would eventually become settled agriculturalists and then graduate to commerce, in Khaldunian thought they would become city dwellers and create civilizations that would eventually decline and succumb to the external pressures of other nomadic communities.[48] Ottoman statesmen used Ibn Khaldun's ideas about the rise and decline of dynastic states to make sense of the relevance and power of mobile Turkic polities in medieval Muslim political formations, the institutional development of the Ottoman dynastic state in the sixteenth century, and what they perceived as the internal corruption of that state in the late sixteenth and seventeenth centuries.[49] These Khaldunian ideas of state formation took on increasing importance in the context of the political, environmental, and economic crises of the late sixteenth and early seventeenth centuries. In this period of heightened anxiety about imperial decline, the potential of actors understood as mobile (bandits and nomads) to dilute the state's bureaucratic power seemed more plausible.

It was also in this context of seventeenth-century crisis that Ottoman laws that attempted to regulate mobile pastoral practice and part-time farming in the empire began to shift. Fifteenth- and sixteenth-century Ottoman lawbooks and surveys convey diverse forms of rural land use, with part-time farming and seasonal mobility explicitly sanctioned and included in taxation schemes alongside settled year-round farming.[50] In the context of the seventeenth-century crisis, moves toward granting cultivating peasants more exclusive property rights were closely related to the ruling elite's perception of increasing rural mobility and the tax anxieties this mobility engendered. In Syria, a long-term change in official attitudes toward agropastoralism coincided with the uneven migration of large camel-herding Bedouin communities into the interior regions from the southern (Hijaz) and southeastern (Najd) regions. Aggressive attempts to relocate and settle particular groups, especially in the northern Syrian interior, were a response to the anxiety these migrations, along with rural unrest in Anatolia, precipitated.[51]

Khaldunian cycles continued to inform notions of Ottoman order among prominent statesmen during the Age of Revolutions at the turn of the nineteenth century.[52] But Tanzimat-era lawmakers also drew on Smithian ideas about progress and in some cases adopted the Ricardian idea of comparative advantage to argue that the Ottoman Empire should specialize in agriculture.[53] Nineteenth-century Ottoman iterations of Smithian economics marked a departure from Khaldunian cyclical thought. But evolutionist ideas about progress that centered cultivation as a crucial step in social development found precedent both in seventeenth- and eighteenth-century Ottoman anxieties about agropastoralism and in the early Islamic idea of property rights arising from the labor associated with cultivation, one that ruling elites had sidelined in the early modern period in order to maintain ultimate control over arable land.[54]

The gradual exclusion of part-time farming and pastoral land use from the realm of rights-generating labor in Ottoman legal thought followed. In the intrusive property reforms of the nineteenth century, embodied in the 1858 Land Code, the link between settled cultivation and individual rights to property became firmly entrenched in Ottoman law. While they implied greatly strengthened rights for cultivators, they also marked the exclusion of those who, according to the ideal-type categories of modern administration, did not cultivate. The mid-nineteenth century witnessed the first comprehensive Ottoman attempts to transform mobile tribes into settled villages across the empire in an effort to create a uniform state space.[55]

The connection between imaginaries of improved landscapes, legal definitions of individual and private property, and physical dispossession of local inhabitants was a global phenomenon in the nineteenth century.[56] Widespread imaginaries of a settled rural landscape made their way into Ottoman law and, in some cases, into experiences of enclosure and dispossession.[57] That Bedouin dispossession in the Syrian interior remained limited in the late Ottoman period was the result of local, regional, and global conditions constitutive of a particular politics of administration. The point that codified late nineteenth-century Ottoman property law can be mobilized to dispossess people whose historical connections to cultivation are considered tenuous has been quite salient in twenty-first-century Israel, where courts continue to reference the 1858 Land Code to dispossess Palestinian Bedouin families of the lands they have inhabited for generations.[58] In Israel, global, regional, and local contingencies have combined to render the existence on the land of Palestinian communities defined as Bedouin constantly precarious. In the late nineteenth-century Syrian interior, however, these contingencies enabled tent-dwelling Bedouin individuals both to acquire durable land rights and to participate in modern state formation. This outcome was closely related to the Ottoman Empire's status in the global "age of property."[59]

THE OTTOMAN EMPIRE IN THE AGE OF PROPERTY

Ottoman official attempts to create a uniform state space stretching across what was left of the empire's sovereign territory occurred in the aftermath of the crises of the 1870s. While the financial elements of these crises were felt worldwide, for the Ottoman government they manifested most clearly in the forms of state bankruptcy in 1875, losses of valuable territory in the Balkans in the 1877–78 Russo-Ottoman wars, and partial forfeiture of economic sovereignty in the establishment of the Ottoman Public Debt Administration.[60] These crises both created a sense of urgency about increasing state revenue and focused attention on the empire's remaining territory, including the highly contested regions of Syria and Iraq. As in other imperial polities, the project of making state space and its particularly national, territorial character took form during the intense interimperial competition of the late nineteenth century, especially in response to British financial and territorial expansion.[61]

Scholars of world history have long defined the Ottoman Empire as a peripheral zone of Western European—especially British, French, and German—capital expansion in the final quarter of the nineteenth century.[62] In Eric Hobsbawm's formulation of the "winners" and "losers" of the mid-nineteenth century that bifurcated the globe into zones of colonized and colonizer, weakened but still-sovereign spaces like the Ottoman Empire and Latin America were unquestionably in the "losers" chapter.[63] The Syrian interior and its inhabitants, in this bifurcated conception of world history, are relegated to the status of the periphery's periphery.[64]

This framework speaks a certain historical truth, especially from the perspective of British and French understandings of "the Eastern Question." It is crucial to recognize the limitations of Ottoman capacity to make state space in the late nineteenth century, especially in fiscal terms, not least because Ottoman lawmakers themselves were painfully aware of those limitations. Foreign-financed railroad construction, for example, in India as in the Ottoman territories, prioritized Western European over Ottoman prosperity, and as much as one-third of Ottoman revenue went to the financing of public debt.[65] But the Eastern Question narrative has also tended to obscure the historical significance of the Ottoman state-space project in the decades following the 1870s crises, especially in the realms of agrarian policy and civil law.[66] Court and land records, even those dealing with the Public Debt Administration, show that codified Ottoman law remained the referent for civil administration in the Syrian interior.[67] Ottoman lawmakers, like their American and Russian counterparts, sought to make imperial state space in competitive opposition to Britain's free trade hegemony before World War I. They struggled with questions of population, prosperity, and revenue that hinged on issues of labor, capital accumulation, and market creation.

These questions were shared among lawmakers in sovereign states across the nineteenth-century global context. Ottoman lawmakers looked to regions they had previously deemed marginal as underperforming spaces of potential in the context of making territorial state space in a competitive interimperial environment. They developed bifurcated visions of Syria in the mid-nineteenth century, reconstructing the interior as a neglected region in need of improvement in contrast to booming coastal towns like Beirut and Jaffa. After the 1870s crisis, they transformed landscapes outside the cultivated fields of settled villages from zones of part-time farming and grazing to "empty land," a phrase that took on new legal meaning owing to the empire's increasingly exclusionary private property regime. Ottoman officials employed both geographic imaginaries of improvement and a legal arsenal defining private property that were based on concepts of enclosure and exclusion after the 1870s. Historical shifts in agrarian policy were closely connected to concerns about territorial sovereignty.

The registration in which Dawjan and Hamad al-Wiraykat took part occurred during one of these shifts in Ottoman agrarian policy and governing practice. The 1879 process, through which 'Adwani men registered their rights to land on generous terms, came at the tail end of a period of agrarian optimism that Ottoman officials shared especially with their European and North American counterparts in the 1850s and 1860s. In both the Ottoman Empire and the United States, the mid-century global wheat boom encouraged capitalist entrepreneurs and cultivating producers to migrate to new regions and invest in agricultural production.[68] In the Balqa region of the Syrian interior, "pioneers" moved both from Palestine and Damascus into the Syrian interior to start plantation-style farming operations. These Ottoman pioneers treated local Bedouin, who were investing in larger-scale cultivation projects of their own, as landholders who deserved a share of their profits.[69] In the US context, the 1850s and 1860s witnessed large waves of migration, with contestations over the future political economy of the new territories west of the Mississippi, constituting one of the main immediate causes of the Civil War.[70] The American government bought up large amounts of territory in the western plains, forcing Native Americans onto what were still comparatively expansive reservations.

Migration into the western plains and the Syrian interior took different forms and occurred at vastly different scales. The combined populations of Minnesota, Kansas, and Iowa grew from two hundred thousand to more than one million in the 1850s, and Nebraska and the Dakotas would experience similar growth in the 1870s and 1880s.[71] While no comprehensive statistics have been compiled, migration to the southern Syrian interior consisted of a handful of monied families and a few thousand small-scale cultivators in the 1850s and 1860s.[72] Imperial laws in both contexts, however, are testaments to midcentury agrarian optimism and global competition, especially for European migrant cultivators construed as productive.[73] The American government issued the Homestead Act in 1862, promising immigrants plots of land and government assistance while promoting the future political economy of western territories as free soil.[74] This law would be the basis for the claims of thousands of migrant families for decades afterward. The Ottoman government issued an extremely encouraging immigration law in 1857, promising new immigrants tax-free land grants and government assistance with agriculture.[75] The 1858 Land Code, which transformed the rights of cultivators of state land from usufruct to alienable ownership that could be mortgaged, should also be read in this context of encouraging agricultural expansion.[76] This optimism among capitalists, officials, and expectant cultivators, and the impending competition over land it signaled, helps explain what motivated Dawjan, Hamad, and 331 other Bedouin men to obtain title deeds to land in October 1879. Viewed through a broader lens, both the 1857 immigration law and the 1858 Land Code fit into a global context of imperial land grants encouraging agricultural expansion.[77]

If optimism reigned among "pioneers" and imperial lawmakers across these agrarian spaces in the 1860s, anxiety replaced it after the fiscal crises and territorial losses of the 1870s, resulting in newly exclusivist and competitive imperial stances toward land that coalesced in the following decades. By the 1890s, officials of the Ottoman land administration, in particular, began to employ a logic of "empty land" in support of wealthy investors attempting to secure full land rights. Land officials imagined empty land in terms of the legal categories of the Land Code, in combination with an intensified discourse of improvement, to legitimize declaring the Syrian interior's desert fringe as an exclusive state domain in contradistinction to other local claims and auction it to investors. This move would have transformed Bedouin in the interior and elsewhere from business partners into wage-earning renters. This was the kind of policy followed in the United States, where the government began aggressively administering the plains region as landed property during this period. The American regime mandated exclusive individual registrations for Native American household heads and declared the leftover reserved land as state domain for sale to investors.[78]

Scholarship on Ottoman agrarian policy has focused largely on the social question, but debates among lawmakers were closely linked to the creation and maintenance of territorial sovereignty.[79] In Ottoman Syria, unlike in the American West, the exigencies of interstate competition curtailed investors' search for cheap wheat. Land officials' campaigns to sell "empty land" to capitalists met with fierce resistance from other Ottoman agencies. Their quarrel was related, first and foremost, to interimperial competition over territorial sovereignty. The question of Ottoman sovereignty in the Syrian interior became much more fraught after both the loss of territory in the Balkans and the British occupation of Egypt, which transformed the southern, arid regions inhabited by tent dwellers in Syria into a contested borderland. In this new political climate, in which questions of religious identity, nationality, and loyalty were closely intertwined, Ottoman officials in Damascus and Istanbul became increasingly skittish about the nationalities and religious identities of people owning land in the region. They constantly expressed concern about the politics of land speculation, specifically investors selling the titles to empty land they acquired at auction to foreign interests.

In this context, Ottoman officials in the Ministry of the Interior and the Damascus governor's office began drawing up technocratic plans for the development of the interior. They aimed to match "empty" land to productive, industrious, and loyal population groups. These initiatives targeted Muslim refugees displaced from the Russian Empire most specifically as ideal subjects.[80] But they also included Bedouin, if they were willing to settle in villages in the right places. These officials also lobbied to shield the land of the interior from capitalist investors. Their concerns about potential ownership of land by foreigners ultimately led to an imperial decree banning auctions of empty land in the Syrian interior in the mid-1890s, in line with a similar policy in Iraq.[81] These bans were a significant check on the expansion of capital into the Syrian interior at the turn of the twentieth century.

These technocratic Ottoman approaches to land, population, and ethnic and religious identity after the 1870s were remarkably similar to Russian attitudes toward the settlement of peasants from the interior in the southern steppe regions. While Russian peasants had migrated into the Kazakh steppe illegally throughout the nineteenth century, the legalization of such migration, the 1890s establishment of the Resettlement Administration, and the Stolypin land reforms of the first decade of the twentieth century transformed migration and land distribution into a technocratic initiative.[82] The project of "channeling . . . ethnic Russians to the empire's peripheries" responded to the same anxieties about building a loyal borderland population that Ottoman officials experienced. Like their Ottoman counterparts, Russian officials in the Resettlement Administration were concerned with productivity, and they aimed to match population to a fund of "empty land" in a process of state management.[83] In both contexts, officials looked for legal avenues to justify claiming empty land—that is, land used by agropastoralist groups understood as underproductive—for the state domain and reallocating it to industrious peasants.[84]

In the Hamidian period, territorial loss and Great Power attempts to sponsor both foreign protégés and nationalist separatist movements inside the empire combined with new doctrines of private property to produce increasingly exclusionary imperial policy. From the 1890s onward, the agrarian policy of the highest Ottoman officials moved closer to technocratic approaches to population and territory that prioritized excluding communities whose political loyalty was deemed questionable from landownership in borderland regions over capitalist expansion. This exclusionary policy was an important element in making territorial state space, and it culminated in violent creations of "empty land" in the form of the Armenian Genocide and the population exchanges of the early Republican period.[85] The creation of territorial state space through a private property regime and an aggressive definition of state domain after the crises of the 1870s laid the groundwork for these violent removals of population from bordered landscapes.[86] This policy shift responded to the rising anxieties of interstate competition, anxieties that overrode the desires of land officials to increase the capacity of local coffers through alliances with capitalists no matter their religious or national affiliations.

Even as the exigencies of interstate competition fueled anxieties about the political loyalties of particular communities, they also framed Ottoman officials' attitudes toward Bedouin as potentially productive and loyal Muslim subjects of national state space. Unlike in the Central Asian steppe under the Russian Empire, the spaces Bedouin inhabited were not reconstructed as Ottoman "colonies" and excluded from standardized imperial administration.[87] This inclusion in contiguous state space, combined with the ultimately limited nature of immigration into the interior, granted Bedouin men the demographic leverage both to participate in Ottoman administrative governance and to maintain control over much of their land throughout the tumultuous decades following the 1870s crises. Their participation had lasting effects both on the process of state formation and on the internal political economy of Bedouin communities themselves.

BEDOUIN BUREAUCRATS

In the decades after registering land in Abu Nusayr, Dawjan al-Wiraykat entered the lowest rungs of the Ottoman provincial administration as a headman of the Wiraykat community. In the vision of standardized rural administration set out in imperial codified law, the headman was the "access point" linking the provincial government to villages and town quarters for purposes of property administration, taxation, and dispute resolution.[88] This administration, fully elaborated after the crises of the 1870s, aimed to fit every Ottoman individual and every piece of land into a uniform and seamless state space. Men like Dawjan al-Wiraykat and his sons after him entered this bureaucratic space as headmen of administratively defined "tribes." The social and political influence they gained from these subordinate bureaucratic positions enabled them to maintain Wiraykat control over land in the interior, both through their involvement in land registration and through organizing resistance when Ottoman politics of "empty land" became untenable.

Why conceptualize tent-dwelling men like Dawjan al-Wiraykat, his sons, and others who occupied the position of headman as "bureaucrats"? The lives of Bedouin headmen did not resemble a Weberian ideal type: they did not report to any office from nine to five to scribble among uniform "bureaus."[89] Their positions were at least nominally elected, not appointed, and it is not clear if they drew a regular salary. Rather, I use the term to draw attention to Bedouin participation in and complex contributions to an administrative system and property regime defined and legitimated by claims to rationality and standardization. The world-historical comparisons that undergirded Weber's theory of bureaucracy denied the coeval nature of his ideal, the Prussian railway administration, and the Ottoman fiscal and land administrations at the turn of the twentieth century.[90] But Weber and late Ottoman lawmakers inhabited the same world. Rational administration was the shared solution to the immensely unsettling developments of the long nineteenth century: in the Ottoman case, the privileging of the ideal of "order" (*nizam*) extended from the "new order" military (*nizam-i cedid*) in the late eighteenth century to the "reordered" state administration (*tanzimat*) of the 1840s to the "courts of order" (*mahakim-i nizamiye*) of the 1870s.[91]

By becoming headmen, Bedouin entered a theoretically standardized hierarchical system that purported to be rational, procedural, and comprehensive: a system that aimed to create a "state effect." Administrative categories that theoretically applied across the empire were a crucial part of this state effect. The expansion of bureaucracy into the Syrian interior in the late nineteenth century meant that social struggles over land and wealth became articulated in reference to these administrative categories. These struggles took place in part through iterative performances of a property regime involving formulaic land deeds, judicial procedure, and tax assessment practices.

Michael Lipsky's analysis of "street-level bureaucrats" helps articulate my understanding of the iterative work Bedouin bureaucrats performed in the interior. Lipsky argues that low-level public servants like welfare agents, teachers, and police "mediate aspects of the constitutional relationship of citizens to the state" through their everyday interactions.[92] Lipsky's description of street-level bureaucrats' quotidian encounters with citizens of a twentieth-century welfare state is useful for imagining Bedouin headmen's work on projects like tax relief, avoiding foreclosure, and taking disputes to court with the subjects of their administratively defined communities in the nineteenth-century encampments and villages of the Syrian interior. Men like the Wiraykats performed this system with its forms and calculations in the tent-dwelling communities of the interior, even if they often signed the forms with their fingerprints and took time off from managing their herds to participate in tax collection.

Unlike Lipsky, however, I imagine the work of Bedouin bureaucrats not as "mediation" between a stable, external state and its citizens but as a daily performance of power that created a state in encampments and villages that looked quite different from the standardized administrative edifice that imperial and provincial legislators imagined. The quotidian performances of Bedouin headmen and other subordinate officials both changed the meaning of administrative categories and had a profound impact on which categories remained salient both in official understandings of the interior population and in the distribution of resources. In particular, Bedouin bureaucrats embedded the "tribe" into rural administration as a standardized population category alongside the village. In tandem with their social and political influence, men like Dawjan, Hamad, and their sons also increased their material wealth through their roles in the Ottoman bureaucracy. Their new status shifted the political economy within their own communities, prompting a new kind of contestation over resources and political representation conducted in terms of the administratively defined "tribe." These struggles unfolded in reference to, and simultaneously shaped the meaning and boundaries of, the tribe as a power field bounding struggles over taxation, land registration, and adjudication.[93]

Likewise, when Ottoman officials began challenging Bedouin communities' land rights with land grants to refugees in the final decade of the nineteenth century, Bedouin headmen began using the political influence and tactics they had gained through quotidian performances of the state to organize their communities in multiple forms of resistance. Some of these practices, especially the collection of bribes for superior officials, mimicked the calculative and distributive tactics of tax collection and took explicit advantage of the political and social connections headmen had gained in the town-based bureaucracy. They also used the cross-community connections they had built as Bedouin bureaucrats to violently resist refugee resettlement on a wider scale. Rather than treating the state as a fixed entity, therefore, I use district-level court and land records to reveal Bedouin headmen's participation in the practice of modern state formation, sometimes in direct opposition to the visions and plans of higher officials. These activities affected both the categories of rural administration and its outcomes.[94]

Lipsky's category of "citizen" was also highly unstable in the late Ottoman context. Through struggles over property and revenue conducted in terms of standardized administrative categories, the line between Ottoman subjecthood and citizenship came to be drawn in interior encampments. Whereas Ottoman subjecthood was defined by Ottoman nationality, male subjects with immovable property registered in their names acquired rights to become and vote for a wide range of provincial positions, on councils and as headmen, as members of a new administrative category: "men of property." The stakes of this category and its connections to political participation were high, because councils at the various levels of the provincial administrative hierarchy had extensive powers especially in the realm of determin-

ing land rights in the late nineteenth century.[95] Court cases show that
struggles over tax and land distribution in encampments were also
struggles over the political inequalities that discrepancies of wealth,
especially in land, had come to confer. These struggles drew a line
between two groups: property-owning Bedouin headmen with a voice
in local elections and the political processes that followed, on the one
hand, and Bedouin without those privileges whose claims pushed the
boundaries of the administrative categories that defined their tax obligations, on the other. This division can productively be thought in
terms of a line between citizens and subjects.[96]

In the past two decades, anthropologists and historians have highlighted the political roles of communities involved in herding and
part-time agriculture as empire-makers and mobile aristocracies.
In particular, this scholarship has revealed the territorial power and
dynamics of Central Asian and North American polities that existed
alongside, in both collaboration and tension, more well-known historical empires.[97] This scholarship, however, has focused largely on the
premodern and early modern periods. Pekka Hämäläinen's work on
Native American "kinetic empires" in the eighteenth and early nineteenth centuries, for example, has emphasized the rupture point that
the making of state space in 1870s America implied.[98] The account presented here draws on the insights of this scholarship but extends over
the rupture point of the late nineteenth century to explore the roles of
seasonally migrant, tent-dwelling men in the building of a governing
apparatus that aimed for bureaucratic standardization.

The late 1870s moment of administrative state-building and land
registration in the Syrian interior constituted a profound shift in relations between Bedouin communities inhabiting its landscape and
the Ottoman state. But contrary to their own modernist discourse of
rupture, Ottoman officials did not attempt to create homogeneous
state space in a previously untouched and isolated "tribal frontier."
Chapter 1 shows that in the eighteenth century, partly in response to
migrations of large camel-herding communities into the Syrian interior, the provincial administration in Damascus used tax-farming revenue to increase efforts to provision and secure the pilgrimage route to

Mecca.[99] In the process, they drastically expanded an existing practice of providing annuities to Bedouin groups, establishing long-term hereditary contractual agreements with particular elites and communities that lasted into the twentieth century. The chapter presents a model of layered sovereignty to describe the relationship between an overarching and geographically amorphous Ottoman "sphere of submission" and Bedouin leaders' everyday administrative control over parts of the interior landscape. Outside intensively cultivated regions, this form of governance created a network of alliances with loyal elites in the interior, aiming to provide security for trade and pilgrimage routes rather than comprehensively govern population and landed property. This network became much thicker in the eighteenth century. Through their work with the pilgrimage administration, leaders of specific camel-herding communities like the Bani Sakhr would acquire political privilege that proved crucial when the Ottoman regime moved to expand and standardize territorial governance in the late nineteenth century.

In the Syrian interior, Saudi expansion at the turn of the nineteenth century, the Egyptian interregnum of the 1830s, and the reestablishment of Ottoman rule in the 1840s were key moments in the transformation of this alliance-based form of governance. Chapter 2 shows that the unrest of the Egyptian period created opportunities for tent-dwelling elites whose wealth was based more in the trade and management of agricultural and pastoral products than in camel herding. Leaders of the 'Adwan community, in particular, accumulated notable wealth in the context of the global wheat boom of the mid-nineteenth century, prompting elites from camel-herding communities like the Bani Sakhr to increase their own involvement in agriculture. The rising wealth and power of 'Adwani elites and the promise of expanding wheat production fueled Ottoman officials' midcentury visions of a prosperous agrarian economy. These aspirations combined with city-based merchant capitalists' ambitions to extend intensive and uniform administrative governance to the interior in the late 1860s.

Chapters 1 and 2 use a variety of archival sources, chronicles, poetry, travelogues, and consular reports to place Ottoman reformers' claims that they were entering an untamed frontier into a global perspective of aggressive imperial expansion. Chapters 3, 4, and 5 shift to the sources that the Ottoman project of making state space in the interior produced: court cases, land registers, and imperial investigations. These provide a granular account of transformations focusing on one interior locale: the Balqa subprovince and the Salt district in contemporary Jordan. During the late nineteenth century, Ottoman governance shifted from a pilgrimage-based administration to one intrusively governing land conceived as property. New ways of governing the interior after the 1870s crisis represented a renegotiation of existing relationships with Bedouin communities like the Bani Sakhr and the 'Adwan, conducted in reference to standardized imperial law. But the administration also aspired to comprehensive connections with every tent dweller and village dweller, creating relationships with communities like the 'Abbad that had not been involved with the Ottoman administration previously. This Ottoman policy move to include the Syrian interior and its tribes in an emergent standardized state space, while also marking them as in need of improvement, enabled the rise of a group of Bedouin bureaucrats.

Chapter 3 shows that in the tent-dwelling reaches of the Syrian interior, implementation of this uniform system depended on the participation, and ultimately the day-to-day administrative labor, of Bedouin bureaucrats like Dawjan al-Wiraykat and his sons. Court and land records from the interior district of Salt illuminate the contributions of these men in the making of Ottoman state space. Dawjan al-Wiraykat's entry into the Ottoman bureaucracy built on his preexisting presence in regional wheat, barley, and clarified butter markets that credit relations with prominent town-dwelling capitalists sustained. His new connections to the paper-based circulation of imperial power also granted him a place in the Ottoman bureaucracy.[100]

Bedouin headmen's work as street-level bureaucrats in the encampments of the interior enabled them to enter the circles of town-dwelling merchant capitalists who dominated the administrative councils governing interior districts in reference to imperial codified law. Chapter 4 delves into the contradictions of this new kind of bureaucracy in the

1890s and 1900s, when Bedouin communities began to openly resist Ottoman reallocations of land they regarded as theirs to refugees. The social and political influence that men like Dawjan al-Wiraykat had accumulated with both Ottoman officials and powerful town-based merchant capitalists helped them navigate the violent conflicts that ensued.[101] Bedouin bureaucrats quickly translated the networks they had built through tax collection and court duties into organizing their communities to resist dispossession. They defended community rights when the government, defining the land they inhabited and used as "empty," tried to settle refugee communities in their midst. More subtly, Bedouin bureaucrats maintained an unofficial market in land that remained unregistered owing to imperial decisions to limit registration in an exclusively-conceived "state domain." The unofficial market Bedouin communities administered was "noncompliant" in the sense that it challenged the foundations of the state's exclusive claim both to state domain and to allocate land rights, but it also appropriated and complemented documentary forms of state sanction.[102] The persistence of this unofficial market in unregistered land into the twenty-first century is one of the most salient reflections of Bedouin communities' long-term contributions to an uneven and contingent modern land administration.

Whereas Chapter 4 shows the ways in which Bedouin bureaucrats problematized and reshaped land administration, Chapter 5 delves into their participation in the administration of resources and people. In particular, the active participation of Bedouin bureaucrats as headmen of "tribes," a category that had no place in uniform provincial governance as it was imagined in the 1860s, cemented its salience as a fundamental tool for the distribution of resources in the twentieth century. Court records from the late nineteenth century show that the tribe, as a population category within state space, became the bounding framework for contestations over resource distribution within administratively defined tent-dwelling communities.

Chapter 5 argues that ultimately, these contestations were about the nature and scope of Ottoman citizenship. The juridical equality of Ottomans had been a central pillar of standardized administration since the 1850s. But tax and administrative law limited participation in new forms of provincial politics, especially the right to vote in and stand for elections of governing council members and headmen, to property-owning, taxpaying men. These regulations created the figure of the "man of property" in the late Ottoman political context, men who had unique claims to the fullest political rights Ottoman citizenship offered.[103]

In terms of their wealth and proximity to Ottoman governing institutions, Bedouin bureaucrats became men of property, but nonelite tent dwellers could only aspire to their wealth and political status. In this emergent context, nonelite tent dwellers contested the prerogative of increasingly wealthy headmen to serve as their "access points," especially regarding the distribution of tax burdens within their communities. These contestations occurred within the administrative framework of the tribe that delineated political representation within tent-dwelling communities. During the second constitutional period (1908–14), the tribe embodied the contradictions of an Ottoman administration determined to reach individuals but deeply and historically intertwined with collectivities and their leaders.[104]

My conclusion explores the legacies of Bedouin bureaucrats' participation in Ottoman processes of modern state formation during the Faysali and British and French Mandate periods following World War I in the Syrian interior. In the immediate aftermath of the war, regional governments under the jurisdiction of the Faysali regime in Damascus increasingly regarded themselves as political and administrative reference points. This rural political empowerment undergirded the persistent interior resistance to colonial rule embodied in interlinked anticolonial revolts across the interior after British and French Mandate regimes proclaimed sovereignty in the early 1920s. The colonial regimes aimed to sever rural-urban connections that enabled wide-ranging resistance, especially through reifying and juridically isolating the "nomadic tribe," in hopes of containing the nationalism that they saw as a town-based phenomenon. This juridical bifurcation, creating a separate legal regime for those defined as "nomadic Bedouin," constituted a break from Ottoman imperial nation-building efforts that assimilated tribes into standardized village-based administration.

In contrast, British and French agrarian policy followed Ottoman precedent in leaving large swaths of land beyond zones of settled cultivation in a contested state domain. As in the late Ottoman period, much of the Syrian interior remained under the everyday administrative control of Bedouin communities until investor interest, refugee crises, or state-led development projects created drives to register land.[105] Under these conditions, a market in unregistered plots of land under elite Bedouin administration has persisted, sometimes until the present.[106] This land market and the contestations it continues to precipitate are one of the lasting legacies of the ever-unfinished project of making Ottoman state space.

1 BEYOND THE TRIBAL FRONTIER

IN SEPTEMBER 1718, Qaʿdan al-Fayiz, a leader of the al-Fayiz family of the Bani Sakhr, made his way north with an entourage of thirty men toward the fortress of Muzayrib, one hundred kilometers south of Damascus. They rode through the shrubby plain past small villages and came upon the tents surrounding the fortress. At this time of year, just two months before the Festival of Sacrifice that marks the end of the pilgrimage, Muzayrib became a giant tent city. It was filled with men and women from Bulgaria, Anatolia, and Crimea, all on their way to Mecca. In Qaʿdan's entourage were men carrying dried yogurt, clarified butter, and rounds of wool to sell in Muzayrib's bustling market—a "sea of humanity," as the Ottoman traveler Evliya Çelebi mused when he passed through the tent city in the late seventeenth century.[1] The main reason Qaʿdan had come to Muzayrib, however, was to meet with the Ottoman governor of Damascus, who had set up shop in the fortress in his capacity as the director of the Damascus-Mecca pilgrimage administration.[2]

The makeshift offices of the pilgrimage administration were crowded. Qaʿdan greeted men he recognized on all sides, many of whom he counted as distant family members. At the front, Qaʿdan took his seat next to the Ottoman governor of Damascus, flanked by leaders of the powerful 'Anaza confederation. These leaders and the men in their armies competed for valuable pastureland and political influence in the southern Syrian interior. They were also corecipients of lucrative Ottoman subsidies distributed in exchange for the peaceful passage of pilgrims between Damascus and Mecca.

Qa'dan came to the office of the governor to collect cash in the name of men from his father's and grandfather's generations in the al-Fayiz line of the Muha Bani Sakhr. Qa'dan's elder relatives had carved space for themselves in the pilgrimage bureaucracy in the opening decade of the eighteenth century, passing their influence to the sons, cousins, and nephews who carried their names. Qa'dan collected a total of 427 piastres in the names of thirty-two men.[3] Some of the payments were installments in ongoing subsidies he had received in cash and coffee in the preceding months. Later that day, he would host a feast at the al-Fayiz tent at the edge of the Muzayrib tent city, where he would begin to redistribute the money collected from the Ottoman governor. This feast was both a celebration of the pilgrimage and a governing tactic: the tent city was one of the only places Bani Sakhr leaders converged at the same time each year. Beyond the mundane redistribution of subsidies, it was also a chance for the al-Fayiz, the leading Bani Sakhr family, to showcase their wealth and hospitality in proximity to their 'Anaza competitors. News of the sheep and goats slaughtered for such meals would travel through the Muzayrib tent city, charting and broadcasting the wealth and power of the Bani Sakhr in the Syrian desert.

Through the lens of Qa'dan al-Fayiz and the Bani Sakhr, this chapter uncovers the roles of Bedouin communities in transforming Ottoman governance in the Syrian interior between the sixteenth and eighteenth centuries. The Bani Sakhr and 'Anaza competed for regional influence and lucrative Ottoman offices in the pilgrimage administration within a broader context of commercial expansion and elite wealth accumulation in Syria and across Eurasia.[4] As Bani Sakhr and 'Anaza communities began to dominate the regions around the Damascus-Mecca pilgrimage route in the late seventeenth century, the Ottoman pilgrimage administration based in Damascus expanded.[5] The Damascus administration directed increasing agricultural revenue to the pilgrimage, and the Ottoman subsidies to Bedouin groups living around the pilgrimage route grew exponentially. The registers documenting these subsidies constituted Ottoman knowledge production about Bedouin communities' members and internal political structures that was unprecedented in its detail. At the same time, Bedouin elites became more invested in Ottoman sovereignty in the Syrian interior and northern Hijaz through their pilgrimage-related duties and subsidies in the eighteenth century. Their descendants maintained influence in the pilgrimage administration, acquiring political leverage that shaped the process and outcomes of making Ottoman state space in the late nineteenth century.

This chapter complicates near-ubiquitous descriptions of the Syrian interior, the region surrounding the northern part of the pilgrimage route between Damascus and Mecca, as a "tribal frontier" before the reforms of the late nineteenth century.[6] The idea of a tribal frontier has obscured the long-standing relationships between Ottoman state institutions and prominent Bedouin communities that were crucial to the eventual outcome of the aggressive territorial state-space-making project of the late nineteenth century that the latter chapters of this book document. By leaving these long-term relationships only vaguely understood, historians have allowed Ottoman modernizers' claims that they were entering an "empty land" in the late nineteenth century to stand, eliding the long history of Bedouin contributions to state formation in the interior.

In turn, descriptions of an interior region in which Bedouin sovereignty was effective and Ottoman sovereignty was "nominal" in the seventeenth and eighteenth centuries have been important for claims about the coloniality of the Ottoman regime's attempts to make state space in the nineteenth.[7] These debates have elided the particular ways in which Bedouin communities' historical involvement with the pilgrimage administration both complicated Ottoman claims of modern rupture in the nineteenth century and fundamentally shaped the outcome of the imperial regime's attempts at territorial state-making. In this chapter, I lay the foundation for tracing these historical connec-

36   BEDOUIN BUREAUCRATS

tions between the pilgrimage administration in Syria and Bedouin communities inhabiting the landscape around the pilgrimage route. This foundation allows me to present the attempts to make state space in the nineteenth century that later chapters describe as a transformation of existing relationships rather than the penetration of a tribal frontier.

The idea of nominal Ottoman sovereignty in a tribal frontier relies on a definition of and aspiration to uniform territorial sovereignty that was hardly universal before the nineteenth century.[8] Recent histories of territory and territoriality, most focused on Western Europe, have emphasized the geographically uneven and multiform nature of state sovereignty after the Treaty of Westphalia. These histories have also noted the persistent intertwining of territorially focused forms of sovereignty and those built on human alliances. Although ideas about "personal sovereignty" would become legitimizing tropes, especially for European colonial occupation of Africa in the late nineteenth century, they were common across Eurasia throughout the period under study. With these interventions into the history of territory in mind, the Ottoman regime's practice of focusing direct administration on "nodes and corridors" like the pilgrimage route in variegated geographical regions including mountains, marshes, and deserts beyond zones of intensive agriculture was quite typical of early modern imperial polities.[9]

In contrast to historical descriptions of nominal sovereignty associated with a tribal frontier, this chapter employs a framework of layered sovereignty to describe the entangled regional power of Bedouin elites like Qaʿdan al-Fayiz and the imperial power of the Ottoman provincial regime.[10] In the newly conquered province of Damascus, Ottoman lawmakers extended a detailed fiscal system allocating village-based agricultural tax revenue to regional elites in exchange for military service in the sixteenth century. I refer to this system as "administrative sovereignty." It was an Ottoman form of direct rule implemented in varying forms throughout the empire and consisted of detailed claims to regulate people's relationships to the cultivated landscape and its revenue that were expressed in bound registers.[11] Outside the environs of cultivated, settled villages in the Syrian interior, Ottoman claims to sovereign power rested on shifting human alliances with Bedouin elites. Within their spheres of influence, these elites held administrative sovereignty; most important, they regulated land use and revenue distribution. But Bedouin elites also competed with each other for Ottoman offices and subsidies associated with the pilgrimage route. These offices were an important source of wealth and political authority in the interior.

The system of Ottoman offices and subsidies associated with the pilgrimage formed a matrix of human alliances that defined the boundaries of Ottoman sovereign claims in the interior beyond the direct administration of cultivated landscapes. I refer to this type of sovereignty as the "sphere of submission"—a rough translation of the term *ṭāʿat al-dawla*, which more precisely translates to "submission to the state." I use the term *sphere* to gesture to the way elites described leaving (*khurūj ʿan*) and returning to (*rujūʿ ila*), or being inside (*dākhilīn fī*) or outside (*khārijīn ʿan*), a state of submission. These descriptions lent a spatial character to the idea of submission to the imperial state, but it was a figurative and mobile spatial character that moved along with human elites. While inside the sphere of submission, Bedouin elites exchanged political loyalty to the Ottoman sultan for privileges.[12] In the ideal world of early modern imperial governance, the sphere of submission ensured the safety of the pilgrimage route, as well as its provisioning and upkeep, in exchange for subsidies. For Bedouin elites, the sphere of submission constituted one among many sources of wealth and authority in the interior. Elites' practice of leaving and reentering this figurative space rendered the sphere of submission unstable and precarious.[13] But especially in the eighteenth century, the sphere of submission became a much more complex, variegated, and lucrative affair that involved thousands of Bedouin men.

An increasingly complex network of human alliances defined the sphere of submission. That network, however, was deeply connected to physical spaces through the human communities it involved. The Bani Sakhr and ʿAnaza communities extended forms of Ottoman sovereignty into their spatially defined spheres of influence that surrounded the pilgrimage route. The layered sovereignty that emerged created a distinct politics of administration in the Syrian interior in the eighteenth century. This politics included concepts like *dira*, referring to the landscape in which particular Bedouin groups controlled resources and enjoyed political influence, and *khuwwa*, the protection tax that Bedouin elites levied on subordinate tent- and village-dwelling communities in the Syrian interior, the Arabian Peninsula, and Iraq. *Dira* also sometimes referred to the ability to regulate passage through a particular landscape.[14] The concept of *dira* differed in important ways from modern notions of territory: the boundaries of *dira*s were highly fluid, and the term did not entail commodification of landed property.[15] But *dira* remained a deeply spatially rooted form of political connection to particular landscapes and their inhabitants.[16]

The sharp interstate competition of the late eighteenth century, especially the globalized British-French rivalry and Russian expansion, hardened political boundaries across Eurasia and the Americas.[17] This competition took different forms within the Ottoman Empire; in the Syrian interior, the rise of the Saudi state, followed by Mehmed ʿAli's insurgent regime, initiated a profound crisis in the Ottoman sphere of submission. The competition these entities represented precipitated a more territorially defined relationship between the Ottoman state, the tent-dwelling inhabitants of the Syrian interior, and its semiarid landscape. The process of making territorial state space eschewed and denied earlier forms of layered sovereignty that combined spatial and human-alliance-based forms. Even so, the human alliances of the sphere of submission would leave their mark on the territorial state space of the late nineteenth century.

LAYERED SOVEREIGNTY IN THE EARLY MODERN SYRIAN INTERIOR

By the time Qaʿdan al-Fayiz arrived in Muzayrib to collect cash and coffee from the Damascus governor's administration in the early eighteenth century, the Ottoman Empire had claimed sovereign control over the landscape stretching from Damascus to Mecca for two hundred years (see map 1.1). The pilgrimage route snaked through an arid interior region in which access to water was a crucial deciding factor for the viability of human and nonhuman life.[18] The route lines the western edge of a vast triangle of land between river systems: the Jordan to the west, the Barada to the north, and the Tigris/Euphrates to the east. Between these river systems, human settlements clustered around more precarious water sources like wells and springs that ebbed and flowed in accordance with extremely variable annual rainfall. On average, the northern part of the landscape surrounding the pilgrimage route received more rain, meaning more wells, springs, and shrubby vegetation that sustained livestock. Past the fortress of Maʿan, four hundred kilometers south of Damascus, people and animals entered a landscape in which wells, oasis settlements, and seasonal encampments provided sustenance for communities on the move, whether Bedouin, merchants, or pilgrims traversing the landscape between Damascus, Baghdad, and Mecca.[19]

MAP 1.1. The Syrian interior and the Arabian Peninsula, showing eighteenth-century pilgrimage forts extracted from subsidy registers.

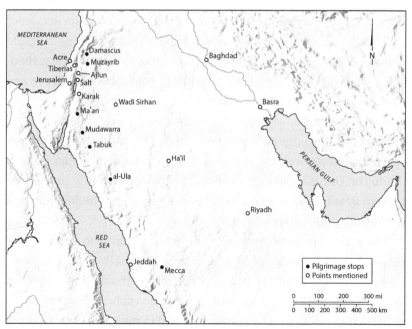

Prior to the Ottoman conquest, a number of political dynasties vied for influence in this interior region. Especially in the cultivated regions of the northwest corner of the Syrian interior, just over the Jordan River from Palestine, these dynasties built bases in fortified settlements like Hisban and Karak and enjoyed formal ties with the Mamluk administration based in Cairo.[20] Some of these dynasties had military bases in highland fortresses; others worked mainly from desert-based encampments and oasis settlements.[21]

After defeating the Mamluk dynasty in 1516, the Ottoman regime encountered this interior landscape as an aspirational sovereign power. The regime established a fiscal and military system that projected sovereignty over the interior landscape east of the Jordan River in two main ways. The first, based on fiscal surveys that divided the local population into taxpayers, on the one hand, and receivers of tax revenue, on the other, was an Ottoman form of administrative sovereignty honed over centuries of rule in the more well-watered landscapes of the Balkans and Anatolia, which also built on preceding Mamluk fiscal systems. General lawbooks of the fifteenth and sixteenth centuries, as well as particularized lawbooks, those drawn up for each province at the time of conquest and periodically revised, outlined the details of this order.[22] Second, the Ottoman regime distributed offices to create a matrix of human alliances that carried Ottoman sovereignty, theoretically, over the length of the pilgrimage route south to Mecca and through arid interior regions all the way to Baghdad. Through these alliances, the regime attempted to protect pilgrims en route to Mecca and distribute its largesse in the holy cities. This sphere of submission was a form of sovereignty that relied on officeholders' pledges of loyalty to the Ottoman sultan; as such, it was an inherently precarious but important form of imperial influence residing in mobile humans rather than built villages fixed in space.

These two layers of sovereignty—detailed claims to regulate the distribution of agricultural surplus among imperially recognized military men in cultivated and geographically identifiable landscapes, on the one hand, and a more spatially amorphous sphere of submission, on the other—overlapped and intermingled in multiple ways, but they rested on different obligations and expectations. In a few small sub-provinces of the newly established province of Damascus in the north-west corner of the Syrian interior, Ottoman administrative sovereignty rested on the cultivating village as the foundational unit of population. The creators of this system assumed that households inhabiting villages and their environs would produce enough food to both subsist and pay, in the form of taxes, agricultural surplus to men who held grants to collect those taxes in exchange for military service to the Ottoman regime. In the decades after the Ottoman conquest of Syria in 1516, the regime embarked on a detailed survey project of agricultural regions that produced a household-level list of village-dwelling taxpaying households, on the one hand, and grant holders who were authorized to collect those taxes, on the other. In more thickly populated locales, like Jerusalem and Damascus, the Ottoman regime also established courts, records of which provide a sense of how this list-based system actually functioned.[23] In the Syrian interior, where there are no records of sixteenth-century courts, the lists of taxpayers and tax receivers drawn up in a few subprovinces in the 1530s were a sovereign claim, the daily implementation of which is difficult to examine.[24] The surveys are useful, however, for understanding the spatial elements of that claim because they consist of named household entities organized into productive villages carrying toponyms, some of which survived throughout the Ottoman centuries. Imperial and provincial lawbooks and fiscal registers from the sixteenth century also describe the types of land use and revenue collection that were permissible to tax. In this sense, they have much to say about the ways in which people used, inhabited, and moved over the land.

How far into the interior did this detailed order of administrative sovereignty reach, and how did it address communities that did not live in villages or use land primarily for cultivation? Map 1.2 shows how twentieth-century geographers visualized the ways in which these registers produced a spatial representation of power in the southern-most interior subprovinces that the Ottoman regime surveyed. Using toponyms in the tax registers that survived into the twentieth century, the geographers attempted to represent the boundaries of Ottoman

MAP 1.2. The spatial extent of late sixteenth-century Ottoman fiscal registers. Map adapted from Wolf Dieter Hütteroth and Kamal Abdulfattah, Historical Geography of Palestine, Transjordan and Southern Syria in the Late 16th Century (Erlangen: Fränkische Geographische Ges., 1977), 5.

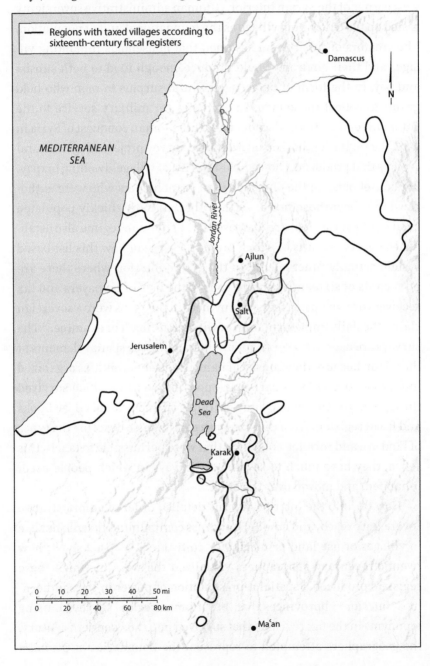

Regions with taxed villages according to sixteenth-century fiscal registers

MEDITERRANEAN
SEA

Damascus

N

Jordan River

Ajlun

Salt

Jerusalem

Dead
Sea

Karak

0 10 20 30 40 50 mi

0 20 40 60 80 km

Ma'an

administrative sovereignty by sketching lines around these named places.

In the sixteenth century, however, the boundaries of Ottoman administrative sovereignty captured in fiscal registers were not conceptualized as fixed lines on a map but rather referred to particular kinds of land use. Much of this land use was seasonal or changed from year to year. Although the fiscal system clearly rested on the population category and agricultural produce of the village, its drafters also attempted to regulate a more variegated world, including particular instructions for taxing the land use of communities not included in lists of cultivating village dwellers (*reaya*). Sixteenth-century lawbooks and fiscal registers named and organized tent-dwelling communities: the general lawbooks included instructions for taxing tent-dwelling "walkers" (*yörük*) in the Balkans and Anatolia, while the registers for the Syrian interior used the ethnonym *arab* to refer to Bedouin communities in the 1530s. These lawbooks divided both *yörük* and *arab* communities into subgroups using the categories *taife* and *cemaat*.[25] Sixteenth-century lawbooks and fiscal registers allowed grant-holding military men to tax both the livestock holdings of these tent-dwelling communities and their part-time farming between and on the edges of villages. Furthermore, they outlined a specific tax category and method for collecting surplus from productive farms that were named but had no permanent inhabitants (*mazraa*).[26]

How did this system of administrative sovereignty envision the relationship between communities that did not inhabit year-round village settlements and the landscape? The fiscal registers for the sub-provinces of the interior connected tent-dwelling Bedouin to particular named settlements in the sense that their taxes were allocated to a specific military man's revenue, the rest of which came from taxes assessed on the agricultural produce of fixed settlements. As a population category, however, the lawbooks specifically distinguished between village-dwelling cultivators and tent-dwelling Bedouin by anticipating the latter's seasonal mobility. In the tax register of the subprovince of Ajlun in the Syrian interior, communities designated as *arab* were to pay fixed taxes for their livestock holdings and their

use of summer and winter grazing grounds. When *arab* engaged in agriculture, they were to pay a reduced farm fee and a tithe on whatever
crops they produced. Through the spatial category of the uninhabited
farm and the human category of the tent-dwelling part-time farmer,
sixteenth-century Ottoman law anticipated and deemed permissible a
certain level of transhumance among an identified segment of the population. These laws were part of a wider-ranging imperial system in
which particular tent-dwelling communities were assigned obligations
particularly suited to seasonal mobility: to work in mines, provide military service, or to provision a military campaign with supplies.[27]

A community named "Bani Sakhr," of which Qaʻdan al-Fayiz's
family was a part, is listed in these sixteenth-century tax registers.
It is difficult to discern their relationship with the al-Fayiz, however,
because the latter only enter the documentary record in the early eighteenth century.[28] But the description of the Bani Sakhr in the sixteenth-
century fiscal registers for the subprovince of Ajlun is a good example
of the general laws' vision of part-time farming: the register specified
that the Bani Sakhr livestock tax went to a particular military man's
office (*amir liva*) but that if the Bani Sakhr cultivated the land, they paid
a proportional tax (tithe) on their agricultural revenue to whichever
military man was assigned to collect revenue from the farm or village
in which they cultivated.[29] In the subprovince of Ajlun, the tithe on cultivation counted for about 10 percent of the total tax taken from communities defined as tent-dwelling and mobile (*tevaif-i urban*), including
the Bani Sakhr, in the 1530s; the other 90 percent was assessed on
livestock.[30] Some groups in the tax register, identifiable only with the
name "*Arab* x,"[31] were associated exclusively with particular farms and
taxed for their cultivation but on uninhabited farmlands (*mazraa*) in
which specific settled households were not listed.[32] In a register from
the subprovince of Marj Bani ʻAmr, west of Ajlun, Bani Sakhr families
were listed as cultivating in two such uninhabited farms.[33]

The sixteenth-century surveys therefore recorded a high level of
detail concerning tent-dwelling groups, including them in the fiscal
system by categorizing their tents as households and taxing them both
for livestock production and part-time farming on arable land. Be-

cause settled villages were their foundational topographical category, however, these surveys also revealed the spatial limits of this detailed claim to administrative sovereignty. The concept of land "outside the register" (khārij al-daftar/haric az defter), elaborated both in imperial tax law and provincial fiscal registers, was one such limit. As an administrative construct, this phrase referenced a comparative temporal rather than spatial distinction: revenue-producing units that had not appeared in previous surveys were noted as being "outside the register," meaning that they were additions to the previous register but that the tax-collecting military man had added them through legal means. Because they refer to topographical units, however, they also imply a spatial border to the regions treated in the register, gesturing toward a landscape of other potential locations remaining outside.[34]

The general lawbooks of the late fifteenth and early sixteenth centuries also assumed that there were Ottoman sovereign lands beyond the geographical zones of intensive cultivation. In particular, the law imposed limits on where tax-collecting military men could collect revenue. The lawbooks insisted that revenue-producing units in tax registers (defters) were the only basis of legitimate taxation. Lands used for pasture, wood collection, or other "empty" (hali) areas that were not registered could not be taxed: the general lawbooks specifically warned against this practice.[35] To allocate revenue from these places outside the boundaries of their administrative sovereignty, officials had to add them to the register and specify who would lawfully receive their surplus. In addition, twentieth-century geographers who parsed sixteenth-century tax registers noted that there were some uninhabited farms on the desert fringe in the southern part of the subdistrict of Hebron that were not attached to villages but were, rather, part of the "wild land" (tābiʿ al-barrīya).[36] This was another gesture to the landscape lying outside the surveys' geographical scope that remained less legible to Ottoman officials, even as the registers listed Bedouin moving between that landscape and the cultivated zones of the register in some detail.

The lawbooks' legitimation of livestock raising and part-time farming in the sixteenth century reflected both the importance of pastoral land use across Ottoman landscapes and the political power of entities involved in pastoral production. In Anatolia, the Ottoman administration was concerned with securing the loyalty of powerful tent-dwelling communities in the context of an ongoing war over people and landscapes with the Safavids.[37] In Syria, the power of groups involved in herding who inhabited the environs of the pilgrimage route linking Damascus and Mecca, a newly acquired pillar of Ottoman legitimacy across the empire, also necessitated legal recognition of this type of land use.[38] Accordingly, the survey registers both recorded and implicitly sanctioned mobile grazing and part-time farming practices, producing a variegated but interconnected vision of the cultivating landscape.

Outside this geographically limited realm of administrative sovereignty focused on the northwest corner of the Syrian interior, the Ottoman regime extended its reach south both through constructing new forts along the pilgrimage route from Damascus to Mecca and through establishing a network of alliances with officeholders.[39] Agreements with officeholders demanded loyalty to the Ottoman sovereign in exchange for delegated administrative sovereignty. For example, the regime maintained the office of sharif of Mecca, making agreements with the elite Meccan families who claimed descendance from the Prophet Muhammad and competed fiercely for the right to protect the holy cities of Mecca and Medina. These sharifian families had a wide network of political alliances with the Bedouin communities inhabiting the Hijaz region of the western Arabian Peninsula, alliances that stretched east across the Najd plateau to Baghdad and the Persian Gulf. The Ottoman regime did not draw up fiscal registers for subprovinces in Hijaz: that level of local administration was left to the sharifs themselves.[40]

The Ottoman regime also employed a system of offices adopted from the Mamluks and closely connected to the administration of the pilgrimage itself. The regime extended the historical office of the Arab Emirate (*imārat al-'arab*) that Mamluks had used to grant legitimacy to Bedouin dynasties inhabiting the semiarid regions of Syria and Iraq with political ties to the Cairo regime.[41] As the locus of imperial sovereignty shifted from Cairo to Istanbul, the Damascus provincial administration became the more important center of pilgrimage organizing. Another key office was the Directorate of the Pilgrimage, usually granted to a military man with tax-collection privileges in the province of Damascus in the sixteenth century.[42] These offices entailed lucrative subsidies and the ability to distribute money and responsibilities to a network of regional elite allies tasked with provisioning and protecting the pilgrimage route.

In the late sixteenth century, two different factions of the tent-dwelling Mufarija community competed for the offices of the Arab Emirate and the Directorate of the Pilgrimage.[43] Although they did not appear in the fiscal lists of the tax surveys, the Mufarija gained power and wealth in the fertile plains of Hawran to the north of Ajlun subprovince over the course of the sixteenth century, slowly pushing the group that had dominated the region, the Sirhan, east toward the valley that came to hold their name (Wadi Sirhan).[44] The leader of the Sardiyya community of the Mufarija, Salama bin Fawwaz, gave his nickname to the Jughayman fort in the northern Hijaz on the pilgrimage route.[45] By the mid-seventeenth century, the pilgrimage administration had transformed the office of the Arab Emirate into a new title, Shaykh of the Syrian Bedouin (*shaykh al-shām / Şam urban şeyhi*),[46] and the office was firmly in the hands of the Sardiyya Mufarija family.[47]

Competition for Ottoman offices was only one element of the wider conflict between the Sardiyya, the Sirhan, and other regional dynastic families who vied for political influence in the Syrian interior. Access to pasture and the right to collect surplus from cultivating villages, both included and excluded from Ottoman fiscal lists, were the other main elements of this competition. In the first half of the seventeenth century, the Sardiyya assumed not only the pilgrimage-related office of Shaykh of the Syrian Bedouin but leadership of the local political confederation "the people of the North" (*ahl al-shimāl*).[48] In loose geographical terms, "the North" referred to the northwest part of the Syrian interior bordered by Damascus in the north, Karak in the south, the Jordan Valley in the west, and Wadi Sirhan in the east, including the regions of Hawran, Ajlun, Balqa, Wadi Sirhan, and Karak (about thirty thousand square kilometers). "The people of the North" contrasted with "the people of the South" (*ahl al-qiblī*) inhabiting the region of the pilgrimage route between Maʿan and Medina.

The designation "people of the North" appears nowhere in Ottoman fiscal registers. The term referred to an interior politics that existed before and outside the boundaries of Ottoman administrative sovereignty. Like the concepts of *dira* and *khuwwa*, "people of the North" was a spatial referent that described a regional mode of administrative sovereignty in regions beyond the reach of Ottoman fiscal registers.[49] Ottoman offices, both those related to the pilgrimage route and the official permission military men held to collect taxes in the fiscal system, were therefore only one source of authority and legitimacy in the sixteenth-century Syrian interior. Men like Salama bin Fawwaz of the Sardiyya enjoyed Ottoman permission to collect taxes and held offices related to the pilgrimage administration. But the Sardiyya also had wide-ranging military power to collect surplus from communities that did not show up in fiscal registers. In fact, many of the military men who held the rights to collect agricultural tax revenue in the subprovinces of Damascus were regional magnates with extensive political networks that predated the Ottoman conquest. These networks were crucial to buttressing Ottoman sovereign claims in the region at its inception in the early sixteenth century. Until the mid-seventeenth century, dynastic families like the Bani Haritha (Turabays) and the Ghazzawis whose influence predated the Ottoman conquest usually held the military tax-collecting offices in the interior subprovinces of Marj Bani ʿAmr and Ajlun.[50]

From this perspective, detailed sixteenth-century Ottoman lawbooks and fiscal surveys appear as contested claims to regulate a regional political situation that predated the conquest and to fit it into imperial modes of administration.[51] Ottoman lawbooks constructed the collection of taxes outside of carefully drafted fiscal lists as unlawful. Beyond the geographic reach of fiscal registers, however, well-connected leaders like Salama bin Fawwaz had the power to decide who could collect which surplus from whom: the basis of administrative sovereignty. The precarity of Ottoman sovereign claims in the interior comes through in the fiscal registers themselves. The record specifically mentions that some communities of one powerful Bedouin group in the region, the Bani Mahdi, were "in rebellion" at the time of the 1596 survey and refused to pay any taxes at all.[52]

At the same time, drawing a line around the spatial referents of the fiscal register and labeling the regions falling outside that line a "tribal frontier" is both insufficient and imprecise. The Sardiyya were active competitors for Ottoman-granted rights to collect taxes within the fiscal system and direct the pilgrimage route, both lucrative offices. But they also enjoyed influence far beyond the regions mentioned in Ottoman tax registers, subjecting subordinate Bedouin and oasis communities to demands for protection tax. Through Sardiyya elites, in other words, the spatial concept of Bedouin *dira* and the carefully delineated Ottoman fiscal registers became intertwined. To Bedouin military men, Ottoman offices were a particularly lucrative option among multiple sources of political authority and wealth in the Syrian interior. Their pledges of submission to the Ottoman sultan were therefore inherently conditional but also significant. This precarious and shifting system of human alliances, rooted in unpredictable humans rather than enduring named landscapes, defined the Ottoman sphere of submission that reached beyond fiscal registers into the "wild land" of the interior.

This combination of spatially rooted imperial fiscal registers and human alliances alongside claims to *dira* constituted a landscape of layered sovereignty in the sixteenth century. As in other early modern empires, the Ottoman regime created a corridor of direct administrative sovereignty along the pilgrimage route, embodied in its forts, through the interior.[53] But a system of human alliances extended less intensive and spatially rooted claims to Ottoman sovereignty into the regions surrounding this corridor, forming a "sphere of submission" that moved, along with human communities, over the landscapes of the North. In the seventeenth century, following waves of rural unrest in Anatolia and changing demographics in Syria, the contours and terms of these layers of Ottoman sovereignty began to shift.

STRUGGLES OVER THE NORTH

In the seventeenth century, the inhabitants of the lands of the North witnessed two interlinked transformations. The first was the incremental northern migration of large camel-herding Bedouin groups from Najd, most notably Bani Sakhr and 'Anaza communities, who eventually claimed the landscape around the northern part of the pilgrimage route as their *dira*. The second was a series of Ottoman reforms that disempowered local military dynasties, rerouted provincial agricultural surplus toward the Damascus treasury, and enabled distribution of extensive subsidies to Bani Sakhr and 'Anaza elites in exchange, theoretically, for a peaceful pilgrimage route. These dynamics dismantled the influence of previously dominant military dynasties, changed the terms of administrative sovereignty in cultivated regions, and created enduring links between the Ottoman regime and the Bani Sakhr and 'Anaza communities. Although contested, these links would endure for two centuries.

The migration of Bedouin communities from Najd and Hijaz into the North has often been associated with drought in Najd in the late seventeenth century. But because the migrations were incremental, nonlinear, and stretched across the seventeenth and eighteenth centuries, parsing their causes and effects is complex.[54] The early stages of these migrations were probably one impetus for a series of provincial reforms at both ends of the pilgrimage route that grand vezirs and provincial governors from the Köprülü family initiated in the second half of the seventeenth century. These reforms were also part of the wider dynamics of "crisis and transformation" encompassing Ottoman attempts to recover from the protracted period of rural unrest across Eurasia at the turn of the seventeenth century.[55]

In Damascus, imperial and provincial officials transformed the long-standing revenue-collecting privileges of local military dynasties that the fiscal system had sustained into tax farms that rerouted agricultural surplus to Damascus-based military men (Janissaries). Eventually, the revenue from these tax farms went directly to the provincial treasury.[56] A simultaneous transformation occurred in the

sphere of submission: first military men, and later provincial governors of Damascus themselves, took on the office of the Directorate of
the Pilgrimage (Amīr al-Ḥajj).[57] These measures aimed to consolidate
revenue and political power in the hands of reforming Ottoman governors, especially those associated with the Köprülü vezirial regime.[58]

The Köprülü administration also focused energies on the other
end of the pilgrimage route. In Mecca, Ottoman delegation of administrative sovereignty to the sharifian dynasty had defined the sphere of
submission in Hijaz since the early sixteenth century, but competition
among different branches of the dynasty had become increasingly violent.[59] The Ottomans concentrated on the Red Sea city of Jeddah, the
main port of entry for the grain that sustained Mecca and Medina,
especially from Egypt.[60] In the 1670s, in an attempt to influence the balance of power between sharifian families and increase direct Ottoman
influence in Mecca, the Köprülü-appointed governor of Jeddah clashed
with the prominent Meccan sharif Saʿd bin Zayd, who fled to exile in
1671. As in the province of Damascus, Bedouin communities in Hijaz
were closely involved in these conflicts—the Harb community, from
which the Bani Sakhr are sometimes said to be descended, sheltered
Saʿd bin Zayd from the Ottoman authorities as he fled Hijaz.[61]

To certain prominent men in the Bani Sakhr and ʿAnaza communities, the balance of power in the interior regions stretching from
Damascus to Mecca must have looked like it was swinging decisively in
favor of the Ottoman dynasty at the height of the Köprülü period in the
1670s. Qaʿdan al-Fayiz's father, Dabis al-Fayiz, moved north with his
community, the Tawqa of the Bani Sakhr, leaving the region surrounding al-Ula north of Medina where they had established bases during
the preceding century. In the late seventeenth century, they headed for
the more fertile Balqa region between Karak and Ajlun.[62] The Tawqa
followed another Bani Sakhr community, the Khuraysha, under the
leadership of first Muhammad and then Sulayman Khuraysha. Oral
histories recorded in the twentieth century that charted these migrations do not describe the Tawqa and Khuraysha joining kin groups already inhabiting the North, but they may have been in contact with
descendants of the Bani Sakhr recorded in the sixteenth-century tax

registers described above.[63] Around the turn of the eighteenth century, the al-Fayiz Tawqa, the Khuraysha, and other Bani Sakhr and ʿAnaza families were able to decisively displace the Sardiyya from their position of prominence in the lands of the North.

In these recorded oral histories, the conflict that ensued between the Bani Sakhr and the Sardiyya when the Bani Sakhr entered the Sardiyya's northern *dira* revolved around control over their most valuable assets: horses and camels. Bani Sakhr oral history related that the Sardiyya leader al-Mahfuth al-Sardi tried to claim his political superiority over Dabis al-Fayiz and Sulayman al-Khuraysha by demanding a valuable horse from them. When they refused, the enmity between the groups grew. The Khuraysha and Tawqa were able to overcome the Sardiyya, who were purportedly much more numerous and had many more mounted horsemen, with a forward-attack and ambush strategy. They sent a delegation of fifty horsemen to attack al-Mahfuth al-Sardi's camp east of the pilgrimage route, then led the counterattacking force to a place where the rest of the community's armed men were lying in wait. In this way, they dealt a decisive blow to the Sardiyya community, claiming northern pastures as their *dira* and thereby living there tax-free.[64]

In his detailed anthropological analysis of Nabati poetry, Saad Sowayan has analyzed the way these oral histories trade in repetitive motifs and move between "history and mythology."[65] Still, he argues, especially read together, they can provide valuable information about the lived experience of migration from the Arabian Peninsula. The Bani Sakhr story of equine glory is quite similar to those told by other communities who clashed with the Sardiyya over the right to inhabit pasture and collect revenue from groups they considered subordinate in the North in the late seventeenth century: the Wuld ʿAli and Hassana communities of the ʿAnaza. These groups, known to have been the southern neighbors and enemies of the Bani Sakhr in Hijaz, began spending summers in the North in the seventeenth century as well. ʿAnaza lore regarding their own confrontation with al-Mahfuth al-Sardi in the southern Syrian interior is quite similar to that of the Bani Sakhr, involving al-Sardi's attempt to "borrow" a horse from the Yaʿish

Hassana family of 'Anaza, Hassana refusal, and an eventual pitched battle that the newcomers won decisively.[66] 'Anaza orators also made use of a common story of sending a scout to the Syrian region of Busra, near Damascus, to make narrative sense of the group's migration: in these stories, which the 'Anaza's Shammari enemies also told, the scout returned from Syria with a bag bursting with plants, boasting of the rich pastureland to be had around Busra and encouraging his kinsmen to migrate.[67]

Revolving around great men, these stories obscure, but sometimes provide glimpses into, the complex internal political economies that produced a slow and nonlinear migration to the North. The material and social grounds on which the Sardiyya, and then the Bani Sakhr and 'Anaza, claimed influence in the North are subtle in these stories. They contain fleeting references to collection of protection taxes (*khuwwa*) from subordinate communities cultivating and grazing animals within dominant groups' geographical spheres of influence. In one narrative, the Sardiyya leader (al-Mahfuth) attempted to collect fees from the Bani Sakhr and 'Anaza in exchange for their use of the North's pasture.[68]

These battles between Bani Sakhr, 'Anaza, and Sardiyya men occurred outside the fiscal system of Ottoman administrative sovereignty. But beyond their attempts to gain unfettered and untaxed access to pastureland, Bani Sakhr and 'Anaza men also challenged Sardiyya leaders' influence in the fast-changing pilgrimage administration. The decisive blow to Sardiyya power in the North came not with a battle over camels, horses, or pasture but with their loss of pilgrimage-related privileges.[69] By the start of the eighteenth century, after a series of dramatic battles that left both an Ottoman governor and the Sardiyya leader holding the office of Shaykh of the Syrian Bedouin (Kulayb bin Fawwaz al-Sardiyya) dead, the Sardiyyas' position in the sphere of submission became much more precarious.[70] One of Dabis al-Fayiz's most effective tactics for displacing the Sardiyya from the pilgrimage administration involved undermining their reputation as able protectors of the route by attacking the caravan himself, with the spoils from the attacks also enriching his community.[71] Bani Sakhr campaigns against the Sardiyya in the North focused on the revenue and influence Ottoman offices in the pilgrimage administration conferred. These offices seemed up for grabs in a period of political and fiscal transformation at the turn of the eighteenth century.

The northward migration of camel-herding communities was entangled with the overhaul of the pilgrimage system in ways that are yet to be fully understood.[72] But this migration also contributed to transformation in the modes of administration of cultivated, settled regions of Ottoman administrative sovereignty in the Syrian interior. In the final decade of the seventeenth century, the Köprülü vezirial regime embarked on another major initiative: the settlement of herding communities from eastern Anatolia in the northern Syrian interior (north of this chapter's North).[73] Reşat Kasaba has linked these efforts to a general Ottoman rejection of mobility in response to the hardening of state borders in post-Westphalia Europe.[74] In the Syrian interior, however, the settlement initiative also aimed to shift regional demographics in response to the influx of Bedouin communities from Najd and Hijaz, especially the 'Anaza who moved farther and farther north in the late seventeenth century.[75]

Beyond the targeted settlement initiative in northern Syria, there are indications that the changes in administrative sovereignty that occurred in various ways across the empire in the seventeenth and eighteenth centuries made the kind of part-time farming and movement in and out of village communities described above more complex. The tax-farming contracts that replaced revenue grants to military men entailed greater levels of administrative sovereignty for tax farmers, who were also expected to increase productivity in the regions they oversaw. At the same time, the tax-farming system entailed greater autonomy for village dwellers to allocate tax burdens within their own communities.

Ottoman jurists began to address the rights of the "people of the village" (*ahali-i karye*), imagined as an exclusive group, to allocate lumpsum tax burdens among themselves and exclude "outsiders" (*ecnebi*), in the seventeenth century.[76] Mundy and Smith argue that, at the same time, in the absence of detailed registers articulating property rights, jurists "sought to interpret the cultivator's right as arising from labor invested in the plough lot, not simply from possession."[77] Lawbooks of the late sixteenth and seventeenth centuries also indicate a hardening of the boundaries between settled and nomadic communities, outlining a clear vision for how tent dwellers could "throw down their tent poles," permanently integrate into settled communities, and engage in more intensive cultivation.[78] Combined, these regulations suggest that the part-time farming and movement in and out of village communities apparent in sixteenth-century registers became more precarious in a context of expanding tax farming. These were important precursors to the agrarian reforms of the nineteenth century, which wrote pastoral practice out of the rural landscape in much more aggressive legal terms.

TIGHTENING THE SPHERE OF SUBMISSION

At the beginning of the eighteenth century, the struggle over pasturelands, animals, and political power in the North centered on the pilgrimage administration and the expanded system of subsidies it came to entail. Through their claims to both the sharif of Mecca and the governor of Damascus, Bani Sakhr men like Sulayman al-Khuraysha and Dabis al-Fayiz inaugurated more than a century of generous and stable subsidies from the Damascus pilgrimage administration to thousands of beneficiaries in their wider tent-dwelling communities. This enhanced subsidy system was the Ottoman administration's attempt to guarantee that Bedouin communities, especially those who had come to dominate the North over the preceding century, would remain in the sphere of submission, protecting pilgrims from attack on the long stretches between military forts on the pilgrimage route. This system created unprecedented official knowledge about the internal political economy of the Bani Sakhr and 'Anaza communities while becoming their main source of cash-based revenue.

As I have noted, Bedouin groups like the Sardiyya had been receiving subsidies to protect the caravans throughout the period of Ottoman sovereignty over the pilgrimage routes to Hijaz. Faroqhi notes that the subsidies to Bedouin inhabiting the landscapes around the Damascus and Cairo caravan routes came from their respective provincial treasuries and that the Damascus route subsidies constituted a substantial portion of the provincial budget by the late seventeenth century.[79] The first specific mention of allocations to Bani Sakhr Bedouin is in a register from 1672. In this register, the amounts earmarked for the Mufarija Sardiyya leaders Salama bin Rabbah and Hamdan bin Rashid dwarfed the amounts allocated for the Bani Sakhr.[80] The 1672 register is also the earliest that specifies individual allocations within Bedouin groups rather than the totals distributed to each community. Individual names were a new level of granular knowledge of tent-dwelling communities connected to the pilgrimage administration as its revenue and political power became concentrated in Damascus.

In 1703, leading Bani Sakhr men concluded an agreement with Sharif Saʿd bin Zayd, who had reentered the sphere of submission after returning from exile to serve his second and longest term as sharif of Mecca.[81] Qaʿdan al-Fayiz's father, Dabis, alongside Sulayman al-Khuraysha and other leaders, agreed to take on new responsibilities in the pilgrimage administration in return for exponentially increased annuities. A 1718 register of Bedouin subsidies divided the individual allocations into sections based on when they were first agreed on. This register preserved the history of each community's fortunes in the pilgrimage administration (see figs. 1.1, 1.2). The register tells a story of dramatic increase in Bani Sakhr allocations from 1,131 piastres in 11 individual allocations in 1674 to 26,344 piastres in 910 allocations in 1703. Records of ʿAnaza allocations chart a similarly exponential increase in the early eighteenth century, followed by relatively stable allocations into the early nineteenth century.[82]

The 1703 agreements were part of a wider consolidation of the pilgrimage administration in the hands of the Damascus governor.[83] The list of allocations referred to claims made by Bani Sakhr individuals directly to Sharif Saʿd bin Zayd. The language used for these claims (temessükat) implies that the structure of allocations resulted from a process of consultation between the sharif and tent-dwelling leaders.[84] The redirection of funds from regional dynasties with revenue col-

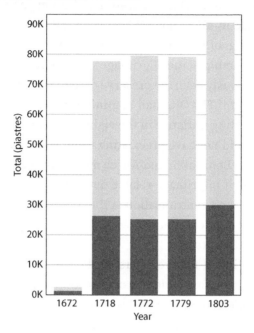

FIGURE 1.1. Subsidies paid to the Bani Sakhr (dark grey) and ʿAnaza (light grey) communities, 1672–1803. Source: BOA.EV.HMK.SR defters 192 (1672), 825 (1718), 2221 (1772), 2422 (1779), 3207 (1803).

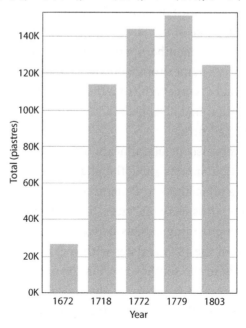

FIGURE 1.2. Total subsidies paid to Bedouin, 1672–1803. Source: BOA.EV.HMK. SR defters 192 (1672), 825 (1718), 2221 (1772), 2422 (1779), 3207 (1803).

lection privileges to the Damascus administration enabled this exponential increase in allocations.[85] Five years after these agreements,
in 1708, the office of the governor of Damascus merged with that of
the main directorship of the pilgrimage administration (*Amīr al-Ḥajj*),
which had previously been the preserve of regional military dynasties
like the Sardiyya.[86] The Ottoman administration also embarked on a
second fort-building initiative in the eighteenth century, adding forts
in regions that did not have preexisting water sources.[87] The detailed
registers of 2,457 Bani Sakhr and ʿAnaza men who received subsidies in
exchange for their pilgrimage-related duties were part of the pilgrimage administration's centralization at the provincial level and its role
as the fiscal and political centerpiece of the Ottoman province of Syria
in the eighteenth century.

A close reading of four registers of allocations to Bedouin—from
1718, 1772, 1779, and 1803[88]—demonstrates how the provincial pilgrimage administration conceptualized power within and formed relationships with the tent-dwelling population inhabiting the regions around
the route. The registers begin with offices established in the sixteenth
and seventeenth centuries, including the Shaykh of the Syrian Bedouin
and offices associated with the protection and provisioning of specific
forts. In 1718, the office of the Shaykh of the Syrian Bedouin was recorded in the names of members of the Mufarija Sardiyya community,
but the community's name drops from the 1772 and 1779 registers.[89] By
1803, the office had disappeared from the register altogether, indicat-
ing that the position had disappeared along with the prominence of
the Sardiyya in the North.

All five registers also include allocations for the protection and provisioning of particular forts along the pilgrimage route. It is in these
sections that the allocations to Bedouin look most like payments in
exchange for spatially specific services, like transporting barley to the
Muzayrib fort or providing camels between al-Ula and Damascus.[90]
A note included in the 1803 register with regard to payments to the
Kurayshan family in the southern Syrian town of Maʿan, initiated in
the 1780s, illuminates the nature of these deals: brothers from the
family would receive allocations only if they avoided internal conflict

and corruption and fulfilled their duties, with a threat of violence to their father and descendants if they went astray. The note refers to written agreements (*sanadat*) between the family and the provincial government that laid out these conditions and specifies that the money for the allocations would be taken from the provincial treasury.[91]

In terms of the totals paid out, as well as page space, detailed individual allocations to the Bani Sakhr and 'Anaza communities dominate the registers after 1703. These allocations were not specifically tied to any conditions in the register. Unlike the money earmarked for the Shaykh of the Syrian Bedouin, the subdivision of money allocated to the 'Anaza and Bani Sakhr was quite specific, listing the amounts claimed by hundreds of individual beneficiaries in each subcommunity within these larger entities. Under each allocation, the registers include the name of the (always male) beneficiary, followed by the amount of money allocated to him, and the name of the person or people who actually received the money, or sometimes commodities, "in hand." While the names of those who received money or commodities changed from register to register, the name of the beneficiary of the allocation remained the same throughout the eighty-five years covered by the four registers. The registers therefore consistently included the names of some of the main contenders for power along the Hajj route at the turn of the eighteenth century: Dabis al-Fayiz and Sulayman al-Khuraysha of the Bani Sakhr, Milhim Mizyad of the Hassana, and Sha'il Tayyar of the Wuld 'Ali.[92] Through their negotiations with the sharifs of Mecca and the Damascus governors at the turn of the eighteenth century, these men transformed the governance of the pilgrimage corridor, inaugurating stable subsidies paid in their own names that endured into the nineteenth century.

In outlining a durable structure of allocations, the registers created detailed imperial knowledge about Bedouin communities. Using different sizes of script, they expressed a hierarchical system of communal categories through which the Ottoman administration understood Bedouin politics and attempted to create alliances, using information they gleaned from the claims of the beneficiaries themselves. The largest script size expressed the name of the larger community, "*urban* x," like *urban* Bani Sakhr or *urban* ʿAnaza. These large groups of *urban* were subdivided into *taifes* whose names appeared in smaller script, which included ʿAnaza communities like Hassana and Wuld ʿAli. *Taifes* were further subdivided into *al*s, an Arabic term for extended family. In terms of community size, the *al* was the closest parallel to the *cemaat* of sixteenth-century tax registers; each register after 1703 listed between thirty-nine and forty-one Bani Sakhr *al*s.[93] Each *al* included a list of individual men, presumably the prominent household heads of that particular extended family, who were each assigned a specific allocation in Ottoman piastres (see fig. 1.3).

The registers' organization of Bedouin individuals in the Syrian interior followed the same general rules as the organization of space. The categorical resemblance between the fixed status of topographical villages in the sixteenth-century tax registers described in the first section of this chapter and the human beneficiaries of allocations recorded in the pilgrimage administration registers is striking. When new allocations were added for a specific extended family (*al*) or individual in the registers, these were conceived as having earlier been "outside the defter" (*haric az defter*) in the same way that administrators added new revenue-producing villages to their lists.[94]

Especially in the final quarter of the eighteenth century, the registers also demonstrate that fiscal authorities conceived of the apportionment of subsidies to Bedouin in similar terms as apportionment of tax burdens within settled, cultivating communities. The development of new apportionment strategies followed two broad transformations in eighteenth-century fiscal practice: lump-sum tax collection from bureaucratically designated communities like villages and districts, and a shift from fixed-rate taxes on produce like the tithe to apportioned taxes like the *avarız* extraordinary levies, which were collected by dividing village and town populations into separate taxpaying categories and apportioning the predetermined amount to be collected among them.[95] The fiscal practice for redistributing tax burdens to account for economic and demographic changes within particular communities was called the *tevzi*, or apportionment, system.[96] Both

FIGURE 1.3. Political structure of the Bani Sakhr Bedouin community represented in script sizes in a portion of a subsidy register: A, Taife-i urban Bani Sakhr (The Bani Sakhr taife of Bedouin); B, Al Muha min Bani Sakhr (The Muha al of the Bani Sakhr); C, Individual beneficiary name, amount, and name of person who received the subsidy. Source: BOA.EV.HMK.SR 2221, p. 62 (modified).

the 1718 and 1772 registers of allocations to Bedouin include lists of "additional" payments to prominent Bani Sakhr, Wuld 'Ali, and Hassana *al*s. Beginning in 1779, the register referred to this extra distribution among Bedouin leaders as a formal apportionment, or *tevzi*.[97] The use of this term to refer to the apportionment of subsidies in a similar manner to its usual tax-related usage implies that fiscal officials conceived of the Bedouin communities of the pilgrimage route regions as an administrative unit within which a consistent principle of apportionment needed to be maintained.

When he lived with 'Anaza communities in the early nineteenth century, John Lewis Burckhardt insisted that they were fiercely egalitarian, with the leaders expected to redistribute the cash and commodities they received from outside sources like the Damascus pilgrimage administration.[98] The registers themselves, however, do not evoke an image of an egalitarian community. Among individuals within groups defined by the register as extended families (*al*s) and among extended families within larger tent-dwelling communities (*taife*s), the structure of allocations to Bedouin for protecting and provisioning the pilgrimage route was highly stratified. The register divided the Bani Sakhr *taife* into forty-one *al*s in 1718. Among these, allocations to the Muha/al-Fayiz Bani Sakhr *al* dwarfed all others, with the Muha receiving 3,265 piastres in seventy-eight separate allocations in 1718 and steadily climbing to 7,493 piastres in ninety-two allocations in 1803. Within these communities, the distribution was also stratified among individual named beneficiaries and those receiving cash, the latter named in only 35 percent of allocations. Qa'dan al-Fayiz himself is the best example of this: in 1718, he collected 404.5 piastres in portions of twenty-seven of the seventy-eight Muha allocations, pocketing at least 12 percent of the community's total subsidy.[99]

It is not easy to understand what these amounts meant in terms of purchasing power in the eighteenth-century interior, as the most detailed price data has been gleaned from urban court records.[100] Increases in subsidies over the course of the eighteenth century probably responded to inflation. Burckhardt discussed prices and living expenses with the 'Anaza communities he lived with in 1810 and estimated that the annual expenses of a Bedouin family came to around seven hundred piastres in the early nineteenth century, with major expenses including wheat (two hundred piastres), barley for the family's horse (one hundred), clothing for the family (two hundred), and luxuries like coffee, tobacco, and lambs (two hundred). Whether or not Qaʿdan al-Fayiz distributed all he had in various shows of hospitality, Burckhardt was adamant that the pilgrimage subsidies were ʿAnaza shaykhs' most important revenue source, and the same was likely true for the Bani Sakhr.[101]

In the first decade of the nineteenth century, the German naturalist Ulrich Seetzen recorded an account of the subsidy register that he heard from his Damascene guide, whom he identified as J. Milky (Mulki?). Milky told Seetzen that the "grand list" governing the distribution of the Bedouin subsidies contained the names of "all the shaykhs and even several simple Arabs" and that it "exactly marked" the share that each individual could claim. Milky described the gathering of men at the Muzayrib fortress to receive allocations each year, as well as some of the negotiations that occurred: first, he claimed the Damascus governors undervalued the currency in which they calculated the allocations so they could pocket the difference, increasing the annual shares of particular shaykhs so as to "buy their silence" in this exploit. Second, Milky asserted that prominent shaykhs often brought the Damascus governors valuable horses in exchange for the names of their sons being added to the list.[102]

The eighteenth-century subsidy system represented an unprecedented level of Ottoman involvement with the inhabitants of the interior. The system responded to new regional realities, especially the migration of Bani Sakhr and ʿAnaza communities and their political weight beyond cultivated regions. In attempting to forge wide-ranging alliances with hundreds of Bani Sakhr and ʿAnaza tentholds, officials in Damascus and Mecca produced detailed knowledge about these communities that changed the form of human-alliance-based governance in the interior. The subsidy system was not based on a territorial conception of space. The only toponyms the registers mentioned were the forts along the pilgrimage route. But the system represented a much more elaborate set of relationships with Bedouin communities, communities with close ties to the landscape of the North.

Despite these detailed efforts, the "grand list," like the fiscal registers of the sixteenth century, remained Ottoman sovereign claims that tell us relatively little about the political situation on the ground. In the mid-eighteenth century, the Bani Sakhr became involved in increasingly violent regional competition over tax-farming contracts and Ottoman offices. In this climate of interstate competition in which expanding Western European empires increasingly set the terms, maintaining political influence in the North came to involve a complex triangular exchange of cash, commodities traded on a widening scale, and weapons. This dynamic, combined with increasing pressure on the amorphous borders of the sphere of submission, pushed early modern Ottoman spatial politics to a breaking point.

COMMERCIAL EXPANSION AND REGIONAL AND IMPERIAL RIVALRIES

Through vying for the cash subsidies of the pilgrimage administration, the Bani Sakhr entered a commercial configuration involving cash, agricultural commodities such as coffee and wheat, and firearms.[103] This expanding regional commerce revolved around tax-farming magnates who built their fortunes on Mediterranean and Red Sea trade.[104] Many of these magnates were connected to agents of increasingly dominant British and French imperial projects, which competed with each other for commercial influence on a global scale that included the Eastern Mediterranean, especially in the coastal regions of Palestine and Egypt.

The tax-farming magnates' commercial-imperial competition created intricate trade and military networks that stretched into the interior. Bani Sakhr elites were increasingly involved in competition among these magnates that rendered the sphere of submission volatile, culminating in their devastating attack on the pilgrimage caravan in 1757.[105] But the Bani Sakhr's lasting relationship with the Ottoman administration was not severely tested until the expansion of the Saudi state, which was the first political entity with universalist claims to challenge Ottoman sovereignty in Hijaz and the Syrian interior since the sixteenth century. Saudi expansion changed the stakes of leaving the Ottoman sphere of submission, offering a distinct and local alternative to Ottoman sovereignty.[106] At the same time, the Saudis' intrusive fiscal practice heralded a new practice of territorial governance in the North. In the end, the Bani Sakhr cast their lots with the Ottoman administration, setting the stage for their roles in more direct territorial governance in the nineteenth century.

Economic historian Şevket Pamuk has described the mid-eighteenth century as a period of peace, stability, and commercial expansion across the Ottoman Empire.[107] Beyond the maritime trade over the Mediterranean and Red Seas, there are indicators of increasing overland trade in the empire's interiors.[108] The Bani Sakhr and ʿAnaza participated in the regional consolidation of the Ottoman piastre through receiving tens of thousands of coins in pilgrimage subsidies each year, moving the currency decisively into the markets of the Syrian and Arabian interiors.[109] The pilgrimage administration also increased Bani Sakhr and ʿAnaza participation in the expanding trade of luxury commodities. In the pilgrimage subsidy register from 1718, 111 of 2,601 total allocations included payments in coffee as well as cash.[110] The practice of paying Bedouin in coffee demonstrates the pilgrimage administration's connections to the commercial world of the Red Sea and Hijaz, where overland trade of Yemeni coffee was closely connected to the provision of grain to Jeddah, Mecca, and Medina from Egypt.[111]

While Pamuk suggests that decades of interimperial peace created an environment for commercial expansion prior to the Russo-Ottoman wars that began in the 1760s, elite wealth accumulation and its close connections to a burgeoning European weapons industry also increased the stakes and lethality of conflicts over Ottoman offices in the long term. In the eighteenth century, the practice of delegating administrative sovereignty to regional elites through tax-farming contracts intensified. These contracts included the responsibility not only to collect and deliver revenue but also to build fortifications, monitor agriculture and commerce, and generally administer the district of the tax farm. Regional magnates' wealth and power hinged on their ability to enforce monopolies on the internal sale of valuable commodities like cotton and wheat through acquiring tax-farming contracts that functioned as Ottoman administrative offices. In particular, magnates on the Syrian coast traded Syrian agricultural commodities for cash and firearms from French merchants. Bedouin elites used pilgrimage subsidies to buy firearms and other commodities from them in turn.[112] At the same time, the political influence Bani Sakhr elites acquired in the pilgrimage administration in the eighteenth century set the stage for their political influence in the North, eventually in the form of titled landed property, that they consolidated in the late nineteenth century and sustained after the fall of the Ottoman regime.[113]

Priya Satia has argued that the British weapons industry of the eighteenth century, fueled by virtually continuous and increasingly lethal wars between Britain and France, were an important driver of the Industrial Revolution.[114] The trade of agricultural commodities for weapons between Ottoman tax farmers and French merchants on the Syrian coast illustrates the ways in which commodity production in the Eastern Mediterranean, Ottoman fiscal practice, and a wide network of commercial and political connections stretching into the interior contributed to the building of a global economy increasingly focused on French, and later British, demand. This dynamic would only increase in the nineteenth century, and its effects on Ottoman sovereignty were multilayered. At the regional level, increasing trade provided new opportunities for tax-farming elites to consolidate wealth, weapons, and widening spheres of influence.

Changes in the alliances between regional elites with tax farming privileges and Bedouin communities in the interior were one complex effect of shifts in an increasingly global economy. In particular, a consolidated currency and growing firearms trade distinguished these eighteenth-century networks from their sixteenth-century iterations.[115] Whereas sixteenth-century Ottoman orders mandated the confiscation of arrowheads from Bedouin in Syria, the eighteenth-century fortresses along the pilgrimage route were fitted with gun turrets.[116] Burckhardt offered estimates of "matchlocks" spread across the population of the Arabian Peninsula and the North in the early nineteenth century.[117] The spread of firearms in the seventeenth and eighteenth centuries increased the stakes of conflicts between commodity magnates and shifted the balance of power among Bedouin communities in the North. The pilgrimage administration became a more prominent, though certainly not the only, route to political power in the Syrian interior.

The first of these tax-farmer-cum-monopolists in the North was from a Bedouin family based in Palestine: Zahir al-'Umar al-Zaydani. Beginning in the 1740s, when members of the Zaydani family obtained tax-farming contracts for fiscal units in Galilee (Rama, Shafa 'Amr, and Safad), Zahir al-'Umar rapidly expanded his influence over northern Palestine and eventually the port of Acre.[118] His ability to direct trade with the French in Acre partly fueled his power, military force, and wealth, because he monopolized the sale of cotton and wheat produced in the interior to particular French merchants at prices he had the regional power to set.[119] Zahir al-'Umar built his regional cotton mini-empire on networks of alliances that stretched across the Jordan River into the Syrian interior. His sons vied for the right to administer the subprovince of Ajlun in the North, especially in the second half of the eighteenth century.[120]

These networks precipitated increasing violence because Zahir al-'Umar traded the cash crops he acquired through tax farming for weapons from French merchants, which he could then redistribute or sell to his allies, including the Bani Sakhr and other Bedouin groups.[121] The rise of elite tax farmers with wide-ranging networks of alliances cemented links between agricultural production and tax farming, commodity monopolies and wealth accumulation, and competitive and wide-ranging regional violence that lasted until the mid-nineteenth century across both coastal and interior Syria.

Both Zahir al-'Umar and his successor, Cezzar Ahmed Paşa, became more involved in the politics of the Syrian interior as grain production increased in the late eighteenth century. Zahir al-'Umar sent a military campaign to the town of Salt in the Balqa region just west of the pilgrimage route around 1760, attempting to assert direct control over grain-producing communities.[122] Cezzar Ahmed Paşa created a vast operation for grain provision based on his control of tax farms, first in the province of Sidon and eventually over the entire southern Syrian region.[123] Increases in recorded advances on tax farms for Ajlun, to the north of Salt, suggest that grain production was expanding all over the Syrian interior, stretching across the Jordan River, during Cezzar Ahmed Paşa's tenure.[124]

Both Zahir al-ʿUmar and Cezzar Ahmed Paşa faced fierce regional competition, especially from the al-ʿAzm family, which dominated the governorate of Damascus in the eighteenth century. Bedouin groups were closely involved in conflicts between these factions as armed military forces.[125] Although this competition focused on revenue-producing agricultural regions, it also involved the pilgrimage, stretching into the interior geography of the North. By the mid-eighteenth century, the fusion of the governorship of Damascus and the directorship of the pilgrimage was a major element of the prestige of al-ʿAzm governors, and they spent at least three months of each year collecting revenue from the environs of the North to support the pilgrimage and accompanying the caravan to Hijaz.[126] Governors of Damascus controlled the timely distribution of subsidies, and the registers show that they exercised increasing control over the names and amounts on the "grand list" in the late eighteenth century.[127]

If the governors of Damascus held significant sway over the list, the Bani Sakhr and ʿAnaza, the main Bedouin groups in the pilgrimage administration, retained the power to leave the sphere of submission and attack the pilgrimage caravan, dealing sometimes-fatal blows to the prestige of particular governors. There are indications that the Bani Sakhr were actively involved in the conflict between Zahir al-ʿUmar and the al-ʿAzm governors. Asad Paşa al-ʿAzm's successor, Husayn al-Makki, neglected the annual subsidies to Bedouin altogether in 1756.[128] In 1757, Qaʿdan al-Fayiz planned a spectacular attack on the pilgrimage, first isolating the caravan by attacking the relief force that met it on its return to Damascus from Mecca and then inflicting hundreds of casualties and looting extensive property.[129] The spoils of the Bani Sakhr attack were purportedly sold in Acre, connecting the event directly both to Zahir al-ʿUmar and the competition for political power and wealth across eighteenth-century Syria.[130]

The 1757 attack was certainly a blow to Ottoman prestige in Syria and Hijaz. The Bani Sakhr's ability to mount such a devastating assault revealed how the interlocking dynamics of wealth accumulation and the spread of firearms sustained cycles of violence. By the 1770s, however, Bani Sakhr elites were back in the sphere of submission with much the same weight in the distribution of subsidies that they had enjoyed before the 1757 attack.[131] Like other rebellions in the Syrian interior, the Bani Sakhr's attacks on the pilgrimage aimed to carve permanent space within the Ottoman sphere of submission that would ensure a steady revenue stream rather than a fundamental shift in the existing political order.

Increasingly violent competition over political influence and commerce, however, did challenge the viability of the sphere of submission at its foundations. In particular, provincial magnates' influence over commodity markets and production in the Eastern Mediterranean heralded the possibility that they could transcend the layered system of Ottoman sovereignty entirely, as Mehmed ʿAli would a few decades later in Egypt. Although figures like Cezzar Ahmed Paşa and Mehmed ʿAli were closely linked to the British-French rivalries undergirding zones across increasingly global spheres in the late eighteenth century, interstate competition in the form of Saudi expansion constituted the most immediate crisis of the Ottoman sphere of submission in the North. The Saudi enterprise was a direct challenge to Ottoman legitimacy in Hijaz, southern Iraq, and southern Syria. In the interior region of the North, the rapid expansion of the Saudi emirate began a decisive shift both in the stakes of membership in the Ottoman sphere of submission and its approach to the landscape as sovereign space.

As the Saudi emirate consolidated influence in the Arabian Peninsula in the second half of the eighteenth century, first ʿAnaza, and later Bani Sakhr, tent dwellers walked a thin and politically precarious line between diametrically opposed Ottoman and Saudi spheres of influence. While professing adherence to the Wahhabi faith and the Saudi dynasty, they continued to collect annual subsidies from the pilgrimage administration.[132] By the late eighteenth century, part of their subsidy revenue was likely going toward the payment of Saudi annual taxes. The eighteenth-century Saudi state is often remembered for its rapid expansion and devastating violence, but it also created an income-based revenue administration with salaried tax collectors for each of its districts.[133] While tax assessment and collection continued to rely on community-based knowledge, this administration represented a concerted effort to cut through existing Ottoman networks of tax administration in Hijaz and the North.[134]

The tightrope the Bani Sakhr walked between Ottoman and Saudi influence probably began to fray in 1805, when Saudi forces occupied Mecca and began complicating Damascus pilgrimage operations.[135] It is not entirely clear how this development affected annual subsidies to Bedouin, but Saudi pressure on the North was also increasing during this period.[136] In 1809, when the usually feuding governors of the provinces of Sidon and Damascus united to defend Damascus against a major Saudi campaign, Sulayman Paşa, governor of Sidon, called on Qaʿdan al-Fayiz's son Saʿd as part of a group of regional military commanders marching from Palestine to Muzayrib.[137] The long arm of the relationship the Bani Sakhr had built over decades with the Damascus pilgrimage administration eventually superseded any affinity their leaders may have had for the Saudi enterprise. That Sulayman Paşa included Saʿd Qaʿdan in his missives and viewed al-Fayiz troops as weighty enough to include in the mobilization against Saudi expansion also indicates the extent to which Bani Sakhr power had spread over the interior regions of the North in the eighteenth century.

The expansion of Saudi influence into northern Hijaz may have increased the Bani Sakhr's numbers in the North by providing the final motivation for those families who remained in al-Ula to move in the direction of Karak. Three years after the Saudi raid, when Burckhardt traveled through Syria, he reported Bani Sakhr forces systematically expelling all of their local rivals, attempting to impose a monopoly over the revenues of the North. He heard that they had entered the region quite recently, as a response to the tightening Saudi administration in Hijaz.[138] In the defining moment of the crisis of Saudi expansion, in other words, the Bani Sakhr chose to cast their lots with the Ottoman sphere of submission, asserting their role as prominent inhabitants of the North's pastures and cultivated regions throughout the nineteenth century.[139]

RETHINKING THE TRIBAL FRONTIER

In the midst of World War I, the Damascene scholar 'Izz al-Dīn Tanūkhī began a journey into the Syrian interior, fleeing imminent Ottoman arrest in Aleppo. He took the Hijaz Railway to the Balqa stop and headed for a Bani Sakhr encampment near the village of Zarqa. When he arrived, he found that he had just missed Haditha Khuraysha, a descendant of Sulayman, who was on his way to collect his pilgrimage annuity, now from the provincial capital of Damascus rather than the fortress of Muzayrib.[140] Haditha Khuraysha continued a practice that had endured since the late seventeenth century. That he left for Damascus to collect his annuity just as his encampment welcomed a Damascene dissident fleeing Ottoman arrest demonstrates both the enduring interconnections between urban and rural politics and the legacies of the sphere of submission in the modern period.

The framework of the autonomous tribal frontier has leaned heavily on models of Ottoman state decentralization that tend to flatten the seventeenth and eighteenth centuries into a long period of provincial neglect. In contrast, the Bani Sakhr's trajectory implies a sustained period of tightening of the sphere of submission in the early eighteenth century followed by a distinct crisis in the late eighteenth century. Commercial expansion and wealth accumulation entailed increasingly violent elite competition over revenue and political influence, often expressed in competition over Ottoman offices and tax farms. The interconnected circulation of commodities, cash, and firearms both exacerbated this violence and raised the specter of an internal rebellion aimed at a more robust form of provincial autonomy beyond the existing structure of Ottoman offices. Mehmed 'Ali's transformation from a successful cotton-monopolist provincial governor to a separatist rebel epitomizes this crisis in the sphere of submission.[141]

The late eighteenth century was a period of intensified interstate competition, revolution, and new forms of bordered territorial sovereignty on a global scale.[142] In the Eastern Mediterranean, French campaigns in Egypt and Palestine were one aspect of this competition, but it was Saudi expansion that pushed the sphere of submission to its breaking point in the Syrian interior. The Saudi state's attempts to establish regionally based and intrusive forms of governance paved the way for both Mehmed ʿAli's administration and the reinstated Ottoman provincial regime to implement similar measures in the Syrian interior in the nineteenth century. Competition over the landscapes of the North rendered the layered sovereignty that had characterized Ottoman governance in the interior region much less tenable.

The Ottoman constellation of fiscal registers, forts, and networks of elite revenue recipients became tightly interwoven in the eighteenth-century Syrian interior. These agreements referenced alliances with human elites, not geographical referents, and they implicitly left much of the daily practice of rural administration to ʿAnaza and Bani Sakhr elites. They also left many large tent-dwelling communities in the Syrian interior entirely outside the sphere of submission. But their increasing level of detail, naming thousands of beneficiaries, reveals that the network of human alliances forming the Ottoman sphere of submission became much thicker in the eighteenth century. The registers show that layers of "personal sovereignty" existed at varying levels of complexity, intertwined in the Ottoman case as they were elsewhere with territorial governance. The registers were an important precursor to moves in the mid-nineteenth century to comprehensively enumerate interior communities as uniform and comparable tribes and connect them to specific geographical regions and to specific plots of land in an attempt to create territorial state space.

The long-standing and lucrative connections between Bedouin elites and Ottoman officials detailed in this chapter also had an impact on the internal political structures of Bedouin communities themselves. The framework of a tribal frontier has obscured this impact, positing an isolated and autonomous "tribal society" prior

to nineteenth-century reform. Bani Sakhr and ʿAnaza elites certainly
maintained a level of regional autonomy. Like other provincial elites
in the Ottoman context, they had wide-ranging powers of wealth distribution and adjudication within their encampments and regions of
influence. But the political influence and revenue they derived from
their positions in the sphere of submission formed an indispensable
element of their local authority.[143]

While the Saudi and Egyptian administrations violently discarded
some existing structures of local authority in the early nineteenth
century, others remained intact.[144] The work of Dabis al-Fayiz and his
descendants to build a lasting position in the sphere of submission still
held resonance two centuries later. At the same time, as we will see,
the attempts of the reconstituted Ottoman administration to include
the interior in standardized forms of administration simultaneously
worked through and attempted to transform preexisting relationships
with provincial elites, who maintained their status as purveyors of
knowledge about tent- and house-dwelling families, their wealth,
and their connections to the landscape even as their ranks grew and
changed.

Excavating the history of Bedouin communities' roles in Ottoman
governance before the Tanzimat era reveals the highly political nature
of modernizers' claims that they were encountering the Syrian interior for the first time in the second half of the nineteenth century.
Alongside their imperial counterparts elsewhere, Ottoman lawmakers
would move to commodify and more intensively govern regions they
had deemed economically marginal in the late nineteenth century.
In the name of capital expansion, immigrant and refugee settlement,
and borderland security, lawmakers and officials would gloss over
their previous agreements and connections with the inhabitants of
regions that they saw with new eyes, as full of productive potential.
Likewise, Ottoman land officials who portrayed the Syrian interior as
an uncharted and empty frontier peopled "only by wandering nomads"
and ripe for commodification and refugee settlement ignored the
long-standing legacy of Bedouin groups' service to the pilgrimage and

presence in Ottoman administration. While these imperial claims of modern rupture were hardly unique on a global level, in the Ottoman case they would prove particularly difficult to sustain. After a century and a half of deep engagement with the sphere of submission, Bedouin communities would prove adept at navigating and remaking modern bureaucratic structures and channeling them to fit the politics of the North.

2 COMMERCIAL CAPITAL IN THE SYRIAN INTERIOR

IN APRIL 1853, DHIYAB AL-HUMUD, shaykh of the 'Adwan, left his Balqa encampment near the town of Salt with a small entourage of relatives and rode down the well-trodden, precipitous paths to the Jordan Valley below. On the way, they passed their wheat fields, greeting the 'Adwan men who guarded laboring slaves. As night fell, they reached the Jordan River and set up camp on its banks. The next morning they rode through the cool dawn mist up the winding road toward Nablus. When they arrived, Dhiyab al-Humud made his way to the Ottoman buildings in the center of the city to address the Nablus Advisory Council. Because of his commercial deals with Nabulsi merchant capitalists and involvement in the city's politics, he knew he had the ear of the 'Abd al-Hadi family, who controlled the council.[1]

The council clerk recorded al-Humud's statement: he had recently learned that a group of horsemen from the 'Abbad tribe (*'ashīra*), from the Salt region on the East Bank of the Jordan River, had crossed to the Nablus region and attacked villages on the Mediterranean coast, stealing livestock and burning buildings and fields. Dhiyab al-Humud also heard that the horsemen had been telling the villagers they attacked that they were in fact from his own ʿAdwan group. He had come to assure the council, the representative of Ottoman authority in Nablus, that he and his group (*jamāʿatuhu*) were completely loyal to the Ottoman government and would not dream of participating in such activities. He claimed that the ʿAbbad, however, who were outside the exalted Ottoman state's sphere of submission (*khārijīn ʿan ṭāʿat al-dawla al-ʿalīya*), made a habit of attacking villages across the Jordan River. Both the ʿAdwan and the ʿAbbad were "foreign Bedouin" (*ʿurbān aghrāb*) in the area and unknown to the local villagers. The ʿAbbad could easily claim that they were from the ʿAdwan, both so that what they stole would not be taken back from them and to tarnish Dhiyab al-ʿAdwan's good reputation with the Ottoman authorities. Dhiyab al-ʿAdwan insisted that he and the ʿAdwan only used such attacks to discipline the villagers of the Ajlun region east of the Jordan, who were also outside the Ottoman sphere of submission. He concluded with the claim that these disciplinary measures were in accordance with his orders from the Ottoman government.[2]

Dhiyab al-ʿAdwan communicated with the Nablus Advisory Council in the language of the sphere of submission. He claimed administrative sovereignty in the Balqa and Ajlun regions of the Syrian interior and attempted to deflect blame for a violent attack by distinguishing his followers from the rebellious ʿAbbad. This chapter charts Dhiyab al-ʿAdwan's rise to wealth and influence in the Syrian interior in the mid-nineteenth century in the context of a newly global wheat market, his imprisonment and exile at the hands of an increasingly intrusive Damascus administration in the late 1860s, and his return to a transformed administrative landscape in the Syrian interior. In many ways, Dhiyab al-ʿAdwan's story is similar to those of other regional magnates who maintained complex relationships with the Ottoman regime, including the Bani Sakhr leader Qaʿdan al-Fayiz described in chapter 1.

Dhiyab al-ʿAdwan's methods for deriving value from the landscape were profoundly different from Qaʿdan al-Fayiz's, however. The ʿAdwan herded sheep rather than camels, meaning that their migrations were much shorter. They relied on pastoral production and part-time agriculture for their livelihoods, and they were not involved in the pilgrimage administration. Whereas chapter 1 followed the Bani Sakhr over a landscape stretching 775 kilometers (480 miles) from al-Ula to Damascus, this chapter zooms in on the political economy of a region one-tenth that size, the Balqa, where the ʿAdwan claimed administrative sovereignty. Furthermore, while the Bani Sakhr's involvement in the pilgrimage administration furnished close ties to Damascus, Jeddah, and Mecca, the ʿAdwan, whose *dira* straddled the Jordan River, were firmly oriented toward Nablus, Hebron, and Jerusalem. Following his father and grandfather, Dhiyab al-ʿAdwan engaged in agricultural production in the interior, and his connections to merchants in Palestinian cities linked him, his elite cousin-rivals, and their extended households to emerging global commodity markets in the mid-nineteenth century. Their competitive haggling over agricultural land as a legal asset "with a peculiar kind of value that is related to a prospective pecuniary yield" undergirded their status as investors in an age of commercial capital in that period's Syrian interior.[3]

In this chapter I trace the fortunes of Dhiyab al-ʿAdwan to elaborate three main arguments. First, in the eyes of most mid-nineteenth century observers, and within the framework of the Ottoman sphere of submission, ʿAdwani leaders held administrative sovereignty within increasingly bordered landscapes in the Balqa. Since at least the late eighteenth century, ʿAdwani cousin-rivals divided land in the Jordan Valley and the Balqa plains among themselves and developed well-known, if constantly contested, borders with their neighbors, most importantly the Bani Sakhr. These borders became more important in the wake of the Egyptian occupation of Syria, when Bedouin elites began sending commodities across the Jordan River in response to demand in Palestinian ports linked to a newly integrated global grain market. In the context of the mid-nineteenth-century grain boom, ʿAdwani leaders began treating these well-trodden landscapes as profit-generating assets: they exploited sharecropping and enslaved labor, collected taxes from cultivating village communities, and created a contract-based system for escorting European travelers through the "Holy Land." These activities created substantial wealth, generating

visible inequalities within 'Adwani communities. At the height of his
power and influence in the 1850s, Dhiyab al-'Adwan and his close male
relatives acted as merchant capitalists in their own right, especially
through their involvement in the grain boom experienced across Eurasia and the Americas.[4]

Second, the mid-nineteenth-century Syrian interior, and to a certain extent the Syrian provinces more broadly, were legally complex
spaces in relation to imperially sanctioned individual and collective
land rights. While the Ottoman regime began implementing a title-
deed scheme in regions closer to Istanbul in the 1840s, this process
did not begin in the Syrian interior until the late 1860s. As grain prices
rose and competition over land increased in the hinterlands of Nablus
and Jerusalem, town-based merchant capitalists began consolidating
usufruct rights to agricultural land in sharia courts, and some began
looking further afield toward the interior. In 'Adwan country, the closest sharia court was a day's ride away over difficult terrain. Bedouin
leaders, however, made land deals with enterprising merchant capitalists from towns to the Balqa's north and west outside of court. Such
out-of-court contracts were common across Syria, and they followed
the requirements of Islamic legal procedure in the absence of a judge.[5]
The basis of these deals was the shared understanding that particular Bedouin elites controlled particular pieces of land and deserved a
share of the profits of new agricultural ventures.

Third, this regional land market and noticeable regional wealth
accumulation, especially Dhiyab al-'Adwan's, brought the Ottoman administration in Damascus into 'Adwan country in the late 1860s, first
with a military campaign and then with a permanent district in the
form of a garrison force, a court, governing councils, and a treasurer.
The potential tax revenue of the Balqa region motivated Ottoman officials, while town-based merchant capitalists to the region's west and
north sought easier and cheaper access to interior land as the environment around Nablus and Damascus became more competitive. Usurp-
ing administrative sovereignty in 'Adwan country was the first step
toward making unified Ottoman state space amenable to both faraway
capitalist interests and revenue collection. The creation of permanent

Ottoman districts in the interior marked the end of the politics of the sphere of submission. This transformation signaled a profound shift in the status of leaders like Dhiyab al-ʿAdwan, whose position was thereafter conceptualized within the "tribe" as a standardized bureaucratic category that gained new meaning in the process of making territorial state space in the 1870s.

Dhiyab al-ʿAdwan's story also illuminates changing Ottoman official attitudes toward mobile pastoralism, part-time farming, and rural political leadership in the mid-nineteenth century. The reconstruction of the Ottoman imperial state after the Mehmed ʿAli secession crisis included new laws that articulated a uniform vision of "tribes" (aşiret) settled on winter grazing grounds in the 1840s. Aşiret became the singular residual term for rural populations existing outside villages during this period, flattening communities like the Bani Sakhr and the ʿAdwan that were diverse in size, political power, and everyday livelihood into a single administrative category. At the same time, these laws articulated an Ottoman agrarian imaginary that envisioned the future disappearance of aşirets through their transformation into settled villages.[6] The 1858 Land Code, which granted alienable, exclusive usufruct rights to individuals in settled cultivating communities, complemented this agrarian imaginary of an orderly, cultivating, village-based landscape. The 1859 Title Deed Regulation and the 1864 and 1871 Provincial Administration Regulations peopled this ideal rural landscape with administrative entities, also focused on village communities, that would implement property regulations, taxation, and population management. These laws, along with immigration policies aiming to increase the rural population, embodied a sense of agrarian optimism and confidence that the landscape and its diverse inhabitants would fit into universally applicable legible, loyal, and easily taxable categories. In short, they began to articulate a vision of uniform Ottoman state space that excluded pastoral practice, part-time farming, and rural mobility.

In extending standardized administrative practice into the Syrian interior, Ottoman officials joined other nineteenth-century empires attempting to incorporate "frontier" regions with populations deemed problematic, especially because of their mobility, in the nineteenth century.[7] In many of these contexts, optimistic agrarian imaginaries responded to a shared environment of high grain prices in a newly integrated global market, optimism around prospects for cultivation-based peace and prosperity, and a concurrent privileging of intensive, settled farming over part-time cultivation and pastoral practice. Immigration laws friendly to foreign farmers in 1857 and the Land Code of 1858 codified the Ottoman vision of a standardized, smallholding, private-property-based future. Like the American West and the Kazakh steppe, the Syrian interior was linked to the newly integrated global wheat market through its commercial connections to faraway coastal cities, and the high grain prices of midcentury enhanced agrarian optimism.[8] But Ottoman officials in the Syrian interior shared the challenges of plural legal frameworks for determining land rights, on the one hand, and growing settler and capitalist interest, on the other.[9] Like their counterparts in other imperial polities, Ottoman lawmakers' attempts to transform and standardize agrarian property relations as a fundamental element of imperial nation-making responded to a complex and multilayered existing property regime.

In the Syrian interior, as elsewhere, Ottoman modernizers legitimized their violent usurpation of Bedouin leaders' administrative sovereignty with narratives of an unproductive and lawless interior. These narratives denied the histories of imperially sanctioned administrative sovereignty, commercial connections between towns and their extended hinterlands, diverse forms of labor exploitation, and long-standing connections to the Ottoman state that this chapter and the previous one outline. These denials were indispensable for reformers' project of ensuring that capitalist expansion in the interior conformed to emergent Ottoman norms and benefited the imperial treasury, and they have dominated narratives of both state formation and the history of capitalism in the Eastern Mediterranean since. This chapter presents these narratives as a legitimizing discourse, revealing an interconnected region prior to the establishment of state space, the linkages of which would continue to leave marks on modern state formation in the decades to follow.

THE 'ADWAN IN THE NORTH

The Bani Sakhr's eighteenth-century world revolved around camel-herding, the pilgrimage administration, long-range migration, and balancing Saudi expansionism with loyalty to the Ottoman order. The 'Adwan, in contrast, were deeply involved in the agricultural worlds of the North. While stolen horses and military maneuvers sometimes appear in recorded 'Adwani oral histories, they also trade in the liberation and betrayal of cultivating peasants. 'Adwani history is grounded in the politics of households, providing glimpses into dynamics of labor distribution within the community, especially around axes of gender and slavery. Furthermore, while these histories are full of movement, they describe a more detailed and spatially limited geography than those of the Bani Sakhr and 'Anaza. These stories focus squarely on the Jordan Valley and the Balqa plateau that overlooks it. Recorded 'Adwani oral histories make sense of the broader dynamics of monopolist magnates in Palestine and their competition with Ottoman governors in the late eighteenth century, 'Adwani competition and collaboration with the Bani Sakhr in the early nineteenth century, and the years of Egyptian rule over Syria in the 1830s. These themes set the stage both for Dhiyab al-'Adwan's wealth accumulation during the global wheat boom of the mid-nineteenth century and the Ottoman regime's forced expansion of administrative sovereignty into the North.

———

In the seventeenth century, two brothers fled Iraq, following caravan routes to Mecca, after a dispute over the murder of one of their relatives. They crossed over the pilgrimage route, through the lands of the Sardiyya, and headed southwest, entering the fertile landscape of the Jordan Valley controlled by a group called the Mahdawiyya. For reasons unknown, they stopped in a place called Jabal Samik, in the elevated plains of the Balqa region overlooking the valley. One of the brothers had a son named 'Adwan, whose name became attached to this new family in the North. By the mid-eighteenth century, 'Adwan's sons and grandsons had displaced the Mahdawiyya, securing 'Adwani control over the Jordan Valley and Balqa plains, some of the most fertile lands of the North.[10]

In 'Adwani oral histories recorded in the nineteenth and twentieth centuries, the opportunity to displace Mahdawi leaders from the Jordan Valley came in the form of a peasant revolt. A prominent Mahdawi leader, Jawda al-Mahdawi, had reportedly been exacting egregious amounts of revenue, in agricultural products and animals, from the cattle and vegetable farmers in the Jordan Valley. The situation became untenable when Jawda al-Mahdawi both humiliated men who had come to perform annual labor on his estate and tried to marry a woman from the village of Fuhays near Salt in the hilly region of the Balqa overlooking the valley. The aggrieved cattle farmers and desperate Fuhaysis knew that 'Adwan men had recently lost a relative in a violent fight with Jawda al-Mahdawi, and they went to them for help. 'Adwan's grandsons used this opportunity to unite the 'Adwan and the villagers against Jawda al-Mahdawi, staging a "bloody celebration" for the marriage in Fuhays at which an 'Adwan surprise attack took down much of the Mahdawiyya leadership. The Mahdawiyya scattered in the region of Beysan west of the Jordan Valley, migrating as far as contemporary Lebanon.[11]

If 'Adwan's grandsons displaced Jawda al-Mahdawi as regional strongmen, they did not transform the Balqa's political economy; rather, the 'Adwani leadership became the beneficiaries of agricultural surplus and peasant labor in place of the Mahdawis. In the mid-eighteenth century, as Zahir al-'Umar extended his influence west of the Jordan River, their sons, first cousins named Kayid, Salih, and Qiblan, divided the lands of the Jordan Valley among themselves. The oral history of the 'Adwan from the mid-eighteenth century onward revolves around struggles between these men over divisions of land, political influence, and the wealth derived from agricultural surplus. These conflicts focused on two contiguous regions that the 'Adwan migrated between in the eighteenth and nineteenth centuries: the "wadi," meaning the Jordan Valley north of the Dead Sea, an intensely humid and fertile region where they camped in the winter, and the "shifa," the hilly plateau and surrounding rain-fed plains of the Balqa two thousand feet above where they camped during the hot summer months (map 2.1). During the 150 years after 'Adwan and Nimr's victory over the Mahdawiyya, the wadi and the shifa came to be known as the lands of the 'Adwan, a discrete subregion of the North. Although its borders were certainly contested, both by the Bani Sakhr and "the people" of villages unhappy with 'Adwani leadership, it formed a cohesive region dotted with landmarks bearing 'Adwani names throughout the nineteenth century, some of which survive today.[12]

Beginning with Zahir al-'Umar's tenure in the mid-eighteenth century, the agricultural surplus of the wadi and the shifa became part of the wider power struggle between Acre-based commodity monopolists and Damascus-based Ottoman governors that I explored in chapter 1. Zahir al-'Umar's attempts to tax the North were a turning point in the struggles between 'Adwani cousins. Zahir al-'Umar sent a military force to attack the 'Adwan in the 1760s. In the conflict that ensued, one prominent 'Adwani cousin took advantage of the fractious politics of that era and called on the governor of Damascus for assistance against both Zahir al-'Umar and his cousin who was attempting to take over his lands in the valley, inviting another military contingent to the North. In the oral histories recorded in the nineteenth and twentieth centuries, the provincial politics explored in chapter 1 play secondary roles to the power struggles between 'Adwani elite cousins and their contested relationships with the village, town, and tent dwellers of the North, whom they attempted to subordinate. The story of the "Ziyadna" (Zahir al-'Umar's family) campaign, recorded in the early twentieth century, focuses on a castle on the hilltop of the town of Salt, the largest permanent settlement in the North. After the Damascus and Ziyadna military contingents retreated, the "people of the Balqa" purportedly threw the 'Adwani cousins out of the castle, tired of the violence and tax demands they had brought on the region.[13]

These struggles likely continued under Cezzar Ahmed Paşa, although he is not as prominent in 'Adwani lore as the Ziyadna. Despite the difficulties coastal magnates faced in redirecting agricultural production toward the coast, there are indications of increasing agriculture in the valley in the broader context of commercial expansion

MAP 2.1. The spatial extent of 'Adwan country in the late 1870s. Based on the map titled "Portion of Eastern Palestine" accompanying C. R. Conder, Survey of Eastern Palestine (London: Committee of the Palestine Exploration Fund, 1889).

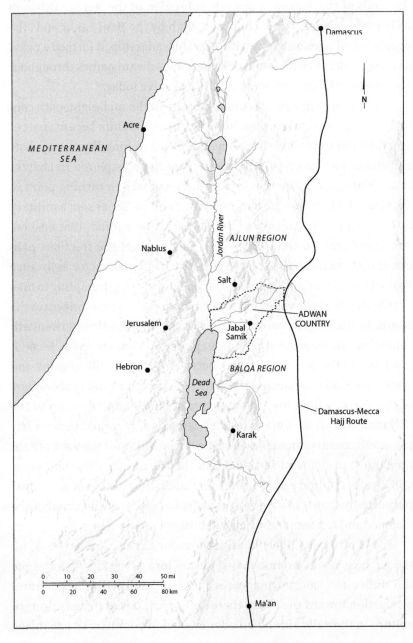

in Palestine and the Eastern Mediterranean. An inscription that late nineteenth-century travelers deciphered on one fort in the valley, surrounded by wheat mills, states that it was built by a prominent 'Adwani cousin, Dhiyab, in 1773.[14] The closest available tax-farm data, from the region of Ajlun to the north of 'Adwan country, also shows sharp increases in value in the late eighteenth century.[15]

It seems that during this period, 'Adwan country, and the town of Salt in particular, developed a regional reputation as a refuge, especially from expansive taxation and later conscription, projects that would endure until the late 1860s. The steep ascent from the wadi to the shifa and hilly terrain around Salt certainly played a role. While Saudi expansion was a major challenge to Bani Sakhr administrative sovereignty in the interior and the Ottoman sphere of submission more broadly, and Saudi campaigns reached far to the north of 'Adwan country, there is no record that the 'Adwan or the inhabitants of Salt ever paid Saudi taxes.[16]

Even so, Bani Sakhr elites did begin to challenge the 'Adwan for the rich agricultural surplus of the wadi and the shifa soon after they ejected the Mahdawiyya, demanding protection payments from villagers in 'Adwan country as they consolidated control of the North in the eighteenth century.[17] After the conflicts with Zahir al-'Umar and the governor of Damascus, an 'Adwani cousin who was not directly involved in these struggles, Nimr al-'Adwan, assumed leadership of 'Adwan country at the turn of the nineteenth century. Nimr al-'Adwan soon became both a celebrated warrior-poet and a central figure in mediating the community's complex relationship with the Bani Sakhr.

Nimr al-'Adwan's poetry and regional fame provide an unusually detailed glimpse into the uneasy coexistence of the Bani Sakhr and the 'Adwan in the early nineteenth-century North, as well as the political economy of 'Adwani tentholds. His poetry narrates two tragic love stories with prominent Bani Sakhr individuals: a woman from the Khuraysha family, Wadha, with whom Nimr fell in love and married, and his close friend 'Awad al-Fayiz, Dabis al-Fayiz's grandson and Qa'dan's great-nephew. Nimr and Wadha's love story is exemplary: they met at a well, a gathering place and site for risky intercommunity flirtation.[18]

Nimr's love for Wadha was so great that he laid aside certain patriarchal social mores, privileging her, declining to marry anyone else until she died, and becoming consumed by grief after her death.[19] While the historical Wadha probably died of illness, the tragic stories and poems include one in which Nimr kills Wadha himself, mistaking her for an intruder trying to steal the prized horse tied to his tentpole.[20]

Nimr's marriage to Wadha occasioned much closer ties between his 'Adwani community and her Khuraysha community, even if they were sometimes at war while they were married. Whenever Wadha left the 'Adwani dominions to visit her family, a sense of their spatial boundaries with neighboring Bani Sakhr lands was reinscribed.[21] Their marriage set the stage for Nimr's close friendship with the prominent Bani Sakhr leader 'Awad al-Fayiz. 'Awad al-Fayiz was the heir to Qa'dan al-Fayiz's allocation and position in the pilgrimage administration: in 1803, he collected four hundred piastres in pilgrimage allocation payments in Dabis al-Fayiz's name.[22] When Nimr bin 'Adwan quarreled with his 'Adwani cousin-rival Humud al-Salih, he went to stay with 'Awad al-Fayiz, an arrangement facilitated by his marriage to Wadha and his reputation as a prominent horseman and poet.

Nimr's poetry and the stories that explicate it crescendo around two tragedies: his falling out with 'Awad al-Fayiz and harrowing journey back to his 'Adwan kinsmen from the lands of the Bani Sakhr at the height of summer, and the death of his beloved wife, Wadha.[23] The ends of Nimr bin 'Adwan's relationships with both Wadha and 'Awad al-Fayiz exemplify the conflict and cooperation between the Bani Sakhr and 'Adwan communities that would continue throughout the nineteenth century, punctuated by violent confrontations and prominent intermarriage. This is a history of struggle over the landscape of the North, but it also narrates the Bani Sakhr's long-term and uneven shift from a camel-herding community migrating long distances along and over the pilgrimage route between summer and winter and deriving their livelihood from livestock and the pilgrimage administration to a more localized community heavily invested in agricultural production, and eventually ownership of commodified land, on the fertile plains of the shifa.

Beyond disputes over land and its surplus, the stories of Nimr bin 'Adwan also furnish glimpses into 'Adwani political economy, especially how people who were considered genealogical outsiders were integrated into everyday operations through the social structure of the tenthold. Alongside the political importance of intercommunal marriage, the tenthold was a mechanism for organizing the labor of both slaves and hired shepherds. In the early nineteenth century, these narratives cast slavery as a domestic and paternalist arrangement central to household labor, patriarchal gender relations, and hospitality. In one prominent story, while Nimr was away in Nablus, the domestic slave in charge of his tent's coffee service, Rashud, approached Wadha and asked her for a kiss. When Nimr returned and Wadha told him what happened, he exiled Rashud, providing him with animals and cash as he banished him from the wadi and the shifa (the 'Adwani dominions).[24] The stories describe tentholds living and moving in units centered on men and their genealogically defined families, in addition to economically and socially dependent and enslaved men and women from outside those families. They describe dependent and enslaved women performing inner-facing work like cooking and childcare in Nimr and Wadha's tent, while dependent and enslaved men performed hospitality functions and cared for animals.[25]

These stories also mention Nimr's close connections with merchant families in Nablus and Damascus. They do not provide details about the material substance or extent of these connections. They depict Nimr as an unusually educated man, and his salons with figures like Musa Tuqan of Nablus, whom he visited multiple times in the early nineteenth century, are narrated as part of his ability to move between the cultural worlds of town and desert.[26] It is highly likely, however, that there was a commercial basis, either in trade in the barilla ash for making soap or possibly wheat, to this relationship.[27]

In the second decade of the nineteenth century, under unclear circumstances, Nimr bin 'Adwan lost the leadership of the 'Adwan to his cousin Humud al-Salih. Humud died shortly thereafter, and his son Dhiyab, whose 1853 petition to Nablus authorities opened this chapter, rose to prominence among the 'Adwan. This shift in internal 'Adwani politics precipitated a deterioration in the 'Adwan's relationship with the Bani Sakhr. By 1812, the Bani Sakhr had pushed the 'Adwan north into the hills of Ajlun, asserting their control and right to collect surplus over the more intensively cultivated western plains of the Balqa and the Jordan Valley.[28] The 'Adwani interregnum in the wadi and the shifa and the Bani Sakhr's preoccupation with the pilgrimage route and Saudi expansion made space for a new alliance of local tent dwellers, the 'Abbad, to take shape in 'Adwan country during this period.[29] As evidenced in Dhiyab al-'Adwan's petition that opened this chapter, the 'Abbad would become important rivals to 'Adwani hegemony in the following decades.

This period in Ajlun in the 1810s may have created the social ties necessary for Dhiyab al-'Adwan to claim the authority he mentioned in the same Nablus petition. Soon after, however, he had returned to the wadi and the shifa, successfully pushing the 'Abbad west of the Jordan River.[30] The 'Adwan and Bani Sakhr restored their alliance in the face of a common enemy in the early 1830s: Ibrahim Paşa's campaign and eventual conquest of Syria from Adana to Hijaz. For the inhabitants of the interior, the most striking rupture of the Egyptian period was the sustained presence of an army that ranged in size from twenty-five thousand to ninety thousand troops.[31] This army required transportation, food, lodging, and men, resources that Ibrahim Paşa increasingly tried to find in Syria rather than transporting from Egypt.[32] Ibrahim Paşa's forces targeted the Bani Sakhr and 'Anaza beginning in 1832 as part of their attempt to requisition camels for the army. While 'Anaza factions stalled, the Bani Sakhr rejected this new role outright and sustained multiple military attacks in the 1830s.[33] The 'Adwan and other communities in the Balqa came to the Bani Sakhr's aid, and Dhiyab al-'Adwan spent most of the decade in prison in Homs, north of Damascus.[34]

The Egyptian period in Syria has been widely regarded as an important turning point in the history of the Eastern Mediterranean.[35] Aided by a large army and a chain of command referring to Cairo, the administration sought to implement many of the reforms that the Ottoman regime had only attempted closer to its own capital, especially direct tax collection and conscription. These measures concentrated on urban centers west of the Jordan River and around Damascus, but they stretched into the interior regions of Ajlun and Hawran, targeted other rural regions like Bilad Bishara, and reached in largely punitive forms to the towns of Salt and Karak in the interior.[36] The administration of revenue also shifted, with power becoming concentrated in city councils that would live on after the departure of the army. These councils generated important shifts in local power relations, with families like the ʿAbd al-Hadis in Nablus gaining lasting power over the distribution of tax-farming contracts and local judicial councils.[37] But because the establishment of city councils depended on a settled population of two thousand or more, none of these changes were implemented east of the Jordan River.[38] Like the Ottoman provincial regime before it, the Egyptian regime focused direct administration on settled, cultivated regions.

At the same time, the Egyptian moment was transformative because of the widespread and collective rebellions precipitated by intrusive tax collection and, especially, attempts at conscription. Tax revolts had already escalated around Syria in the 1820s, but conscription added a new layer of frustration, especially among village-based cultivators and tent-dwelling Bedouin.[39] During the Egyptian period, a trend of rebellion starting in rural areas and spreading into cities that would continue for more than a century coalesced. In this context, the southern interior regions, especially around the castles of Salt and Karak, continued to harbor rebel leaders, peasants, and Bedouin fleeing military retaliation. These processes knit house-dwelling villagers and extended-hinterland-dwelling Bedouin closer together and created new relations of subordination between villages and Bedouin groups extracting surplus in exchange for protection.[40]

Ibrahim Paşa's anger over the Bani Sakhr's refusal to offer up their camels to the Egyptian military effort seems to have become something of an obsession, as wave after wave of rebellion ensued across Syria. The multiple campaigns against the Bani Sakhr and thousands of lost animals must have been devastating.[41] The sustained military attacks on the Bani Sakhr also gave the ʿAdwan a chance to reestablish

their authority in the wadi and the shifa, collecting surplus from cultivators, moving animals and people freely, and directing new agricultural operations. With the restoration of Istanbul's sovereignty in 1840,
Dhiyab al-Humud returned to 'Adwan country triumphant.

The long-term consolidation of 'Adwani influence in the wadi and
the shifa followed patterns of governance and social life similar to
those I described in chapter 1: while the Ottoman sphere of submission loomed in the background, Nimr al-'Adwan and his cousin Dhiyab
al-Humud presided over the use of land and labor, as well as the distribution of surplus in the early nineteenth century. In fact, because
the 'Adwan were not involved in the pilgrimage administration, their
contacts with the Ottoman regime operated mainly through their relationships with other families and communities, especially the Bani
Sakhr and the Tuqan family in Nablus. In 'Adwan country, administrative sovereignty meant authorizing which people could move over the
landscape. It also referred to the military power necessary to collect
agricultural surplus, construed as protection fees, from cultivating village communities, less powerful tent-dwelling groups, and, depending
on the political climate, the prosperous town of Salt. When Dhiyab
al-'Adwan returned to the wadi and the shifa in 1840, these conditions
were beginning to shift.

WHEAT, VIOLENCE, AND AGRICULTURAL "PIONEERS" IN MID-NINETEENTH-CENTURY SYRIA

Dhiyab al-Humud came home to an increasingly competitive commercial environment in the 1840s. New activity in port cities and a widening and lucrative wheat market undergirded disputes over land across
the Eastern Mediterranean in the 1840s and 1850s.[42] Like their counterparts around Nablus and Damascus, Dhiyab al-'Adwan and his cousins
found new ways to convert their contested control over the Balqa landscape into wealth. According to the divisions of land they developed in
the late eighteenth century, they employed multiple means of labor exploitation to increase agricultural production in response to merchant
demand, rising grain prices, and violent competition over land and tax

revenues in more populated regions. From an imperial perspective, their intensified use of 'Adwan country for part-time agriculture occurred in a liminal legal environment prior to both the 1858 Land Code and the establishment of Ottoman courts and administrative bodies in the interior. But this environment operated in reference to a widely shared Islamic legal tradition with forms of contract shared across the extended hinterland and a broad understanding that Bedouin groups exercised administrative control in the interior. These shared understandings framed lasting agreements between Bedouin leaders and enterprising "pioneer" merchant investors. In partnership, Bedouin elites and town-based merchants invested in land as capital, setting up large-scale farming operations in the interior for producing and exporting wheat and barley.

The increasing merchant activity on the Mediterranean coast in the 1840s was linked to the novel integration of a global grain market, with events and policies affecting prices almost simultaneously from Liverpool to Jaffa.[43] While the British regime's forced termination of monopolies from the Levant Company to Mehmed 'Ali Paşa's operations in Egypt set the stage for larger numbers of British merchants to set up shop in eastern Mediterranean ports, the globally integrated nature of this market was a new phenomenon. Economic historians regard the repeal of the British Corn Laws in the mid-1840s as a major turning point in the creation of an integrated wheat market that connected regions like the Syrian interior, along with the American West, to industrializing England.[44]

In Syria, rising prices of agricultural commodities and growing communities of coastal merchants precipitated the attempts of urban magnates like the 'Abd al-Hadi family in Nablus to consolidate control over increasingly valuable agricultural land, labor, and produce in the 1840s and 1850s. Urban magnates in Nablus, Jerusalem, and Damascus vied for offices that conferred rights to control tax revenue. This competition involved violent coalition building and wealth accumulation, on the one hand, and attempts to gain legal sanction for expanded rights over land and its produce, on the other. Coalition-building strategies focused on political and economic relationships that stretched across networks of villages and encampments in extended hinterlands. These long-standing networks, often expressed in credit contracts, enabled the moving of agricultural surplus, whether in wheat, cotton, olive oil, or the barilla ash used to make soap, to the cities.[45] Such commercial networks and alliances, strengthened and extended during the period of sustained regional rebellion against Egyptian rule, were crucial in determining political power and military potential across a wide region stretching across the Jordan River and Jordan Valley into the interior.

Nimr al-ʿAdwan's close relationship with Musa Tuqan of Nablus in the 1810s was one such long-standing alliance between Bedouin elites in the interior and commercial magnates in Palestinian cities. Nimr's cousin, Humud, may have cultivated a relationship with the Tuqans' rival, Husayn ʿAbd al-Hadi, as a way to amass wealth and political power in contradistinction to Nimr. By the 1840s, Humud's son Dhiyab had created a strong alliance with the ʿAbd al-Hadi family, whose support for the Egyptian regime had strengthened its political and economic status in Nablus and the extended hinterland.[46] Despite his claim that his followers were "unknown" to the settled communities of Palestine's Mediterranean coast in his 1853 petition to the Nablus Advisory Council, Dhiyab al-ʿAdwan and his extended family and followers were particularly involved in the increasing conflicts over political power and agricultural land in the regions around Nablus.[47] Dhiyab al-ʿAdwan's 1853 petition that opened this chapter was probably orchestrated in concert with the then-governor of Nablus, Mahmud ʿAbd al-Hadi, to deflect attention from criticism for ʿAdwani attacks on coastal villages that the ʿAbd al-Hadis may have themselves encouraged. Similar accusations of ʿAdwani fighters attacking the same villages reached Istanbul later.[48]

At the height of the violence around Nablus in 1858, Dhiyab al-ʿAdwan came to the aid of the ʿAbd al-Hadis in opposition to the Tuqan; the most detailed historian of the conflict describes the "prince" of the ʿAdwan (Dhiyab) and his army systematically looting the property of those villagers loyal to the Tuqans from Galilee to the Mediterranean coast.[49] These conflicts, and Dhiyab al-'Adwan's ability to sway their outcome, represented the height of his attempts to accumulate political and economic influence in a sharpened competition with other rural leaders in tents and villages across the Eastern Mediterranean.

Alongside this violent coalition building, the 'Abd al-Hadis also attempted to consolidate control over land and surplus through legal means: they began buying up usufruct rights to agricultural land in the Nablus sharia court, obtaining records of their purchases in the form of sharia-court-issued rulings (*hujjas*) that documented the court's verification of each transaction, including bordered descriptions of the land involved.[50] The sharia court registers for Damascus contain transactions in usufruct right to agricultural land that follow the same pattern and documentary form.[51] These transactions in usufruct rights over rain-fed, state-owned agricultural land were novel: sharia courts regularly handled transactions involving privately owned property like houses, irrigated fields, and urban plots, and they issued *hujjas* documenting these transactions. But usufruct rights over arable lands subject to the tithe, the backbone of Ottoman agricultural revenue, were the prerogative of tax-farming land administrators according to imperial law.[52]

This increasingly widespread practice of transacting in usufruct rights to rain-fed agricultural land in Syrian sharia courts using *hujjas* (*hüccuc-ı şeriyye*) alarmed Ottoman officials and reached the agenda of the Ottoman Supreme Council of Judicial Ordinances in Istanbul in the early 1850s.[53] While an 1847 law had inaugurated a new title-deed (*tapu*) system for usufruct rights in agricultural land across the empire, the provincial regimes in Sidon and Damascus had not yet implemented this law. In a broader sense, the legal status of agricultural land in Syria had been a subject of debate among jurists since the Ottoman conquest.[54] The Supreme Council understood the sharia courts' practice in the 1850s in reference to this three-centuries-old debate, implying that both jurists and Ottoman subjects who transacted in land in sharia courts were adopting a minority position among Syrian and Egyptian legal scholars that claimed agricultural land in Syria was in the same legal category as alienable irrigated land near town centers (mülk)—that is, that cultivators were its full owners and could buy and sell their rights through sharia court transactions as they pleased.[55]

The Supreme Council issued a decree that reiterated the legal position ascendant in Istanbul, that the land had long ago reverted to state ownership, and that cultivators in Syria had to pay fees and taxes to obtain title deeds ensuring their continued usufruct rights.[56] They also needed the approval of an official of the land administration; a sharia court ruling (ḥujja/hüccet), this decree implied, was not sufficient as legal proof of sale of usufruct right. Jurists in Syria would debate the legality of this practice of sharia court judges issuing hujjas for sales of agricultural land in the 1860s, with continuing evidence of imperial and provincial-level concern and attempts to ban the practice.[57]

At issue was both the central state's ability to develop a birds-eye view of property administration in the empire, in particular to ensure that agricultural land in Syria did not fall into foreign hands, and the payment of relevant taxes and fees. It is not clear if subjects like the ʿAbd al-Hadis using the sharia court, or the judges who sanctioned sales, were actually asserting full ownership of land; the hujjas they obtained usually used legal terminology implying the transfer of usufruct right, not simple sale as with fully owned mülk property. There was also no title deed office in Damascus or Nablus to visit during this period. But the new practice of registering transactions in usufruct rights over agricultural land in the Nablus sharia court in the 1850s demonstrates the ʿAbd al-Hadis' desire both to expand their holdings and to obtain some form of imperial legal sanction confirming that expansion.[58]

The legal complexity in Nablus was compounded in the interior, where the closest sharia court required at least a day's journey over difficult terrain. Even so, just as the ʿAbd al-Hadi family consolidated its control over the Nablus hinterland in a context of rising commodity prices in the 1840s and 1850s, Dhiyab al-Humud and other tent-dwelling leaders consolidated their control over the Balqa plateau (the shifa) and the ultrafertile Jordan Valley (the wadi). Between Dhiyab al-Humud and his cousins, land division kept to the basic outlines of the agreements forged between their grandparents in the late eighteenth century in the time of Zahir al-ʿUmar.[59]

Within these spheres of territorial influence, Dhiyab al-ʿAdwan converted his control over the landscape into increasing revenue in two main ways in the 1840s after he returned from his prison term in Hama. First, he continued to collect agricultural surplus from villages in exchange for protection, threatening to tax by force if villages did not comply. Second, he employed slave labor for agriculture.[60] While little is known about the origins of these slaves or their numbers, ʿAdwani leaders told visitors to the region at midcentury that they were Nubians purchased at markets in the Hijaz.[61] Travelers to the region recorded seeing plastered holes in the ground for storing grain all over ʿAdwan country in this period.[62] We know relatively little about how much of the grain surplus Dhiyab al-ʿAdwan moved out of ʿAdwan country for sale. There is evidence, however, that grain from the region east of the Jordan River responded to demand in Palestine during a period of intensified export as early as 1850.[63]

ʿAdwani leaders also transformed their consolidated control over the interior landscape into revenue in the mid-nineteenth century by developing a contract-based system for offering protection to foreign travelers, especially European Christians interested in the biblical archaeology of ʿAdwan country and the North more broadly. Dhiyab al-ʿAdwan generally left the duty of actually guiding travelers to his cousins, especially Qiblan and ʿAbd al-ʿAziz al-ʿAdwan, but he often made an appearance in travelers' tents and surely took a cut of the revenue.[64] In the 1850s, these were documented contractual relationships concluded in Jerusalem, sometimes in the presence of the British or French consuls, depending on the travelers' nationality, with different travelers comparing guiding and protection prices and sometimes attempting to circumvent the ʿAdwan monopoly.[65]

The increased presence of European travelers in the interior and the budding ʿAdwani tourism operation further illuminate the politics of layered sovereignty in the mid-nineteenth-century interior. European travelers often complained that Ottoman official permission did not protect them from threats of violence and Bedouin tolls. They

used this point to argue, sometimes supported by the statements of ʿAdwani and other leaders, that the ʿAdwan were completely independent
of Ottoman sovereignty, a claim historians have often taken at face
value.[66] But for Ottoman officials, merchants from towns in Palestine
and northern Syria, and villagers from rural Palestine who traveled to
the interior, violence in ʿAdwan country was predictable and usually
manageable through agreements with local leaders. To be sure, the absence of a permanent Ottoman military force in the interior, let alone
an Ottoman court, meant that travel, work, and settlement occurred
on ʿAdwani terms. As explained in chapter 1, the ʿAdwan leadership
held *administrative* sovereignty in the wadi and the shifa in an environment of layered imperial sovereignty. This administrative sovereignty
was similar to tax farmers' and other privileged elites' control over
everyday operations throughout the empire. This limited the ability
of Europeans, whom ʿAdwani elites saw as sources of wealth, to move
through the interior and access its wealth, and their frustration fueled
their claims about Ottoman lawlessness.[67]

But merchants from Palestine and Syria had a different experience
of the interior. This point is clearly evidenced in the decisions of a
few merchants to build on their existing commercial connections and
move there beginning in the 1850s and 1860s, later styling themselves
as "pioneers."[68] The violent competition over land and resources in
Palestine and northern Syria were probably the main motivations
for merchants in Nablus, Jerusalem, and Damascus attempting to
expand their portfolios to look to the interior as a potential zone of
cheap commodities, especially grains.[69] Beginning sometime in the
mid-1850s, family firms located in these cities began moving into the
Balqa region, and in the 1860s they began setting up large-scale farming operations.

The best-documented of these ventures is the Abu Jabir operation,
centered in the village of Yaduda, forty kilometers southeast of the
town of Salt. Salih and Ibrahim Abu Jabir moved to the interior from
Jerusalem initially in the early 1850s, using connections they had developed through their involvement in the barilla ash trade with the
ʿAdwan and the ʿAwazim, another Balqa community. In his detailed

family histories, Raouf Abujaber describes the close links between Salih Abu Jabir and urban merchants in Damascus who invested in grain production in the Hawran plains of the northern interior. He hypothesizes that these Damascus contacts and tax-eager Ottoman authorities encouraged Salih to invest in wheat farming in the Balqa region, which he apparently did around 1860.[70] While this is certainly likely, the other dynamic motivating Salih was his growing connection with Bani Sakhr magnate Rumayh al-Fayiz, who was willing to provide him with land through a contractual partnership to start a plantation-farm operation. In the Abu Jabir family narrative, the agreement between Salih and Ibrahim Abu Jabir, on the one hand, and Rumayh al-Fayiz, on the other, stipulated that the Abu Jabirs would till the land around the village of Yaduda, paying all expenses, including labor, and would remit half of the harvest to Rumayh, as well as half of the land, retaining the other half of the land for themselves.[71]

Original copies of this agreement are not available to researchers. But the existence of a relatively typical cocultivation contract that formed the basis for a long-standing, if highly contested, farming operation in the interior more than a decade before the establishment of courts, land offices, or a permanent military force is instructive. First, the legal form of this contract was similar to cocultivation (*mugharisa*) contracts certified in courts in cities like Tripoli at the time but for fully owned irrigated properties like gardens.[72] This was more than simply an extension of the Ottoman order into the interior, however, because such profit-sharing agreements were common not only in the well-protected Ottoman domains but also in oasis towns across the Arabian Peninsula, where the Ottoman legal order, at least in terms of everyday administration, was quite distant.[73] These contracts had long pre-Ottoman roots in Islamic legal contexts, exemplifying the blurred boundaries of customary, Islamic, and Ottoman law in the broader region between the Mediterranean and the Indian Ocean. These blurred boundaries meant that even in the absence of an Ottoman court to certify the agreement between the Abu Jabirs and Rumayh al-Fayiz, they drew from a mutually intelligible and specific set of legal tools to complete their contract.

The stipulation of the contract implying that Rumayh al-Fayiz agreed to the long-term Abu Jabir acquisition of land at Yaduda is somewhat unique, especially for rain-fed land.[74] It may have reflected an assumption on the part of Rumayh al-Fayiz that Salih and Ibrahim Abu Jabir would be useful partners because of their ability to access agricultural labor from Palestinian villages. Although much less documented, an influx of Palestinian and Egyptian peasants into the Balqa coincided with the migration of investors, with peasants becoming sharecroppers on farms like the Yaduda operation and new Bani Sakhr farms to its south, around the village of Umm al-Amad, as well as on ʿAdwan-controlled farms in the Jordan Valley. This peasant migration involved at least eight thousand cultivators during the 1850s, some of whom were forcibly returned to their villages in Palestine by the Ottoman administration in the 1860s.[75]

Scholars have defined the increased agricultural production in the Syrian interior as precapitalist because it did not employ the new technologies so important to transformations of labor-capital relations, especially in North America.[76] As recent critics have pointed out, however, these judgments tended to define capitalism as an endogenous national-imperial developmental state rather than a global process that necessarily combined different modes of production and labor relations.[77] In the nineteenth century Syrian interior, increasing trade linkages entailed a new focus on land as a vehicle for investment and wealth accumulation, a process that was closely related to calorie-rich grains fueling laboring bodies in industrial Europe. The sustained focus on grain export of the 1850s and 1860s was a new phenomenon in the interior, embodying the region's contribution to an expanding global wheat market.[78] This involvement entailed labor-based migration, new levels of capital accumulation among investors, and new ways of organizing human bodies to reap as much wheat and barley as possible from the land. In other words, the global wheat market entailed deepening processes of commercial capitalism in the interior. The midcentury plantation farming efforts were, by all accounts, extremely successful. Other investors joined Salih Abu Jabir in the 1870s, many of whom he counted as family members or acquaintances.[79] Bani

Sakhr shaykhs, who Mustafa Hamarneh argued formed a "new landed aristocracy" during this period, also joined in exploiting the opportunities for profit that grain production entailed.[80]

In most existing accounts, this shift in the way people derived value from land could only take place once direct Ottoman administration provided the "security" necessary for market expansion and investment. The implication of this argument is that such investment was impossible in the insecure decades that preceded Ottoman direct rule. This position obscures the social and economic interconnectedness of the coastal northern and interior regions at midcentury and especially the shared legal constructs that enabled those connections. The location that Salih and Ibrahim Abu Jabir chose for their farm in the 1860s, before the establishment of an Ottoman garrison or land administration, sits directly on the border dividing Bani Sakhr and 'Adwan lands, only ten kilometers from Jabal Samik, the site where 'Adwani ancestors first camped when they migrated from Iraq in the seventeenth century. Contemporary reports also reference power-sharing agreements between the 'Adwan and the people of the town of Salt, which sat in the middle of 'Adwan country, including stipulations that 'Adwani fighters disarm when they entered the town.[81]

These borders and power relations were contested and could change quickly, especially since they do not seem to have been directly connected to wider imperial systems of tax-farming contracts and court orders. But they demonstrate the salience of Bedouin administrative sovereignty in the absence of a permanent Ottoman presence, as well as a widespread consensus that Bedouin controlled distribution of the landscape's resources in the context of layered sovereignty in the nineteenth century. The shared respect for contracts following widely accepted Islamic legal norms provided the legal framework for a world "bound together by obligation."[82] Until the late 1860s, this legal framework operated in and through the administrative sovereignty of Bedouin elites and their complex connections to an Ottoman sphere of submission. Rather than enabling investment per se, the imposition of direct Ottoman rule stripped the 'Adwan of administrative sovereignty, rerouting agricultural surplus from elites like Dhiyab al-'Adwan to the

Ottoman treasury and creating opportunities for faraway capitalists to expand their profiles.

TRIBES TO VILLAGES:
THE OTTOMAN AGRARIAN IMAGINARY

In the aftermath of the Mehmed ʿAli secession crisis, imperial lawmakers in Istanbul drafted comprehensive agrarian reforms that formed the centerpiece of the policies known as the Tanzimat. Over the following three decades, a succession of declarations and codified laws articulated a uniform and standardized vision of Ottoman state space. This vision included a specific agrarian imaginary that was shared across multiple imperial polities in the mid-nineteenth century: a rural population of unruly "tribes" transformed into settled, orderly villages; individual holders of transactable land rights paying taxes directly to the imperial treasury through village-based bureaucratically sanctioned intermediaries; and a hierarchical system of provincial governance, including representative councils down to the village and town quarter as basic units.[83] In the aftermath of the Egyptian "troubles," as Ottoman officials often referred to them, these reforms were not immediately piloted in the Syrian interior. It would take local initiatives, not least the growing wealth of Dhiyab al-ʿAdwan and increasing interest in the Balqa as a space of capitalist investment, to bring Ottoman officials with newfound developmentalist aspirations into the interior. These aspirations entailed both a discursive amnesia with regard to Ottoman governance prior to the Egyptian interregnum and a related construction of the interior as a wild space in dire need of improvement. These discourses legitimized the usurpation of ʿAdwan and Bani Sakhr administrative sovereignty, paving the way for a state-sanctioned and directly administered land market and the rerouting of agricultural surplus from Bedouin elites to the Ottoman treasury.

Reşat Kasaba has documented the increasingly hostile attitude of Ottoman administrators toward rural mobility in the nineteenth century.[84] Lawmakers argued for the fiscal importance of settling mobile tent dwellers in the early days of the Tanzimat, in the programmatic decrees that the newly convened Supreme Council of Judicial Ordinances (*Meclis-i Vala*) drafted in the 1840s.[85] One of these decrees, issued to the Anatolian provinces in 1844, illustrates the way midcentury lawmakers envisioned rural mobility as interrelated with broader issues identified as problematic for standardized administrative sovereignty, especially with regard to revenue collection. Council members aimed to incorporate tribes (*aşiret*s) into the emerging system of administration-by-bureaucrats, to marginalize tax farmers, and to consolidate the village as the singular unit of rural governance.

The 1844 decree is striking in that it refers to communities moving between winter and summer grazing grounds in a uniform fashion as *aşiret*s and even suggests appointing an "Aşiret Minister." The decree recognizes the multiplicity of lifeways included in this emerging population category of *aşiret*s,[86] describing a wide range of patterns of rural mobility. Some of this lingering diversity is apparent in Dhiyab al-ʿAdwan's 1853 petition that opened this chapter, in which he described the ʿAdwan as both an *ʿashīra* and a *jamāʿa*, the Arabic equivalent of *cemaat,* one of the multiple terms discussed in the previous chapter that Ottoman officials used to categorize and tax communities they understood as tent-dwelling and noncultivating prior to the mid-nineteenth century. But these terms were increasingly collapsed into *aşiret* during the Tanzimat period. *Aşiret* became an Ottoman equivalent for the English term *tribe* as a residual category for rural communities whose mobility and administrative sovereignty posed challenges to modernizing reformers.[87] Accordingly, while standardizing the category "tribe" across diverse populations in Anatolia, the decree simultaneously envisioned its erasure. The decree ordered that tribes should settle on their winter pasturing grounds and emphasized that they should be governed "like the rest of the local inhabitants" (*ahali-i saire misillü*).[88] While making exceptions for climactic conditions that necessitated traveling to summer pasturing grounds to maintain livestock health, the decree unequivocally prohibited traveling across provincial lines. Such travel would mean that the administration of tribes would fall under the authority of numerous officials, rendering efficient taxation, policing, and census efforts impossible.

The text also emphasized the need to bring tribes and the lands they inhabited under the umbrella of the developing rural bureaucracy and marginalize "leaders and influential people" (*vücuh ve zi-nüfuz*) who had become invested in their mobility. The decree implied that certain wealthy tax farmers, possibly those invested in fees for summer and winter grazing grounds, would stand to lose if tribes whose revenues they collected settled in one location and entered regular village administration. In the 1840s, Istanbul-based lawmakers construed the settlement of tent dwellers as part of the bitter struggle over tax revenue—that is, agricultural surplus—in the empire's rural provinces. In Syria, men like Dhiyab al-ʿAdwan were the "leaders and influential people" benefiting from the physical and political distance of the existing Ottoman system of layered sovereignty. In short, the extension of the category "tribe" was an integral part of the effort to usurp the administrative sovereignty of ʿAdwani and other tent-dwelling elites in multiple regions of the empire.

There is extensive evidence of the attempted and uneven implementation of the 1844 decree, including in the province of Aleppo, the changing borders of which reached into the Jazira region in the 1840s and 1850s.[89] Aggressive reforms in the southern interior were much more limited during this period.[90] An attempt to establish a district centered in the village of Irbid in the Ajlun region in the early 1850s was short-lived.[91] In the early 1860s, after sectarian violence in Mt. Lebanon and Damascus precipitated foreign intervention, the regime began appointing "foreign"—that is, nonlocal and often native-Turkish-speaking—officials at lower levels of administration in Syria. In Nablus, the violence of the 1850s and Dhiyab al-ʿAdwan's triumphant sweep of villages in Palestine culminated with a provincial military campaign against his allies, the ʿAbd al-Hadis. After that campaign, the governorship of the city was held exclusively by "foreigners."[92] One of these "foreigners," Hulu Paşa, launched a concerted effort to change the balance of power in the interior from his base as governor of Nablus, imprisoning Dhiyab al-ʿAdwan and other prominent Bedouin leaders. While Hulu Paşa's reputation as a ruthless "Turkish" official lives on in the interior, his project seems to have been limited to collecting back taxes in the 1860s.[93]

An initial articulation of the southern Syrian interior as an underdeveloped landscape full of productive potential came with a troika of high-level Ottoman reformers—Ahmed Cevdet, Midhat, and Mehmed Raşid Paşas—who were appointed to provincial governorships in Aleppo, Baghdad, and Damascus respectively in the 1860s and early 1870s. Their appointments were part of a new attempt by the central government in Istanbul to extend administrative governance beyond Aleppo to the interior regions of Syria, Iraq, and the Arabian Peninsula. Before their appointments in Syria and Iraq, these men were involved in drafting a new series of imperially universal, codified laws that outlined their vision of transforming the landscapes that mobile tent dwellers inhabited into a productive countryside full of settled cultivators living in villages. Most important, this countryside would be subjected to a private property regime governed by individual ownership, exclusive land use, and universal tax obligations.

Alongside the 1844 decree on the settlement of tribes, the 1858 Land Code and 1859 Title Regulation provided the scaffolding for this midcentury imperial agrarian imaginary of an orderly village-based and settled countryside. With these two laws, legislators like Ahmed Cevdet Paşa also outlined imperial prerogatives for determining increasingly valuable land rights in an environment of contrasting claims that they believed produced conflict and confusion in Syria. The Land Code and the Title Regulation differ from earlier Ottoman lawbooks in their vision both of population and ideal forms of rural land use. Whereas sixteenth-century laws made space for rural mobility and part-time farming, codified law from the second half of the nineteenth century envisioned the rural population using agricultural land composed exclusively of village-based farmers (*ahali*). The part-time farming and seasonal movement in and out of cultivated areas that had been an important element of sixteenth-century Ottoman law was no longer expected or sanctioned in the late 1850s.

Furthermore, while the "people of the village" had been a recognizable category of rural administration since the seventeenth century,
in the Land Code they became an even more bounded and exclusive
group.[94] Not only were the people of the village authorized to use
common grazing grounds inside and outside the village's boundaries,
but they could prohibit others from doing so (Article 97). The code
included detailed instructions for how many animals could graze in
these areas (Article 99). It also empowered titleholders to prohibit
others from trespassing on their lands, although customary rites of
passage were to be respected (Articles 11 and 12). Beyond this oblique
reference to rites of passage, neither tent dwelling nor herding-and-
grazing practices were explicitly mentioned in the 1858 Land Code.
No longer were tent dwellers' use rights to winter or summer grazing
grounds to be recorded in special registers: by the 1850s, tent dwellers
themselves were outside the official register and external to the vision
of Ottoman state space.

One of the Land Code's most transformative elements was its creation of a pathway to individualized legal ownership over land that,
while still expressed in the language of usufruct (*tasarruf*), moved
much closer in the rights it conferred to fully alienable and mortgage-
able fee simple title.[95] For the people of the village, the path to such a
title entailed producing a previous record of right to usufruct (*tapu*) or
showing that they had been in control of and cultivating a particular
piece of land for at least ten years, implying prescriptive right (*hakk-ı
karar*). Because the new title system had not been implemented in Syria
before the Land Code, it was the latter provision for prescriptive right
that became most important in subsequent land registrations. If a
person wanted to register land and could not prove prescriptive right,
they would have to pay the land's market price (*bedel-i misil*) to the
treasury, effectively buying a piece of state-owned land.[96] With these
provisions, the Land Code outlined the type of rural production—full-
time, settled cultivation—that would be privileged in determining title.
Part-time farming or the use of arable land for grazing were not to
denote prescriptive right.

The exclusion of part-time farming and mobile pastoralism implicit in the Land Code aligns with both the 1844 settlement decree in Anatolia and the attempts to encourage, and sometimes to force, the permanent settlement of tent dwellers in the mid-nineteenth century that Kasaba, Gratien, and others have detailed.[97] The Provincial Administration Regulations of 1864 and 1871 provided much of the administrative infrastructure for the agrarian imaginary of an orderly, settled countryside embodied in midcentury codified law. The Provincial Administration Regulation, which Midhat Paşa had been instrumental in drafting and piloting in the Balkans, aimed to extend direct Ottoman administration in a standardized fashion into the empire's highly diverse countrysides. While laying out a hierarchical, centralized, and standardized form of rule across diverse Ottoman human and geographical landscapes, lawmakers also attempted to formalize and codify forms of community-based governance, especially around processes of revenue collection, that had developed in the Ottoman realm since the sixteenth century.[98] These local bodies, reformulated as councils reaching from the provincial level down to the district and village, were to form the connection between individual Ottoman subjects and the higher levels of government in matters ranging from population to tax assessment and revenue to property relations to public security.[99]

In rural regions, one of the Provincial Administration Regulation's most important stipulations was the formalization and privileging of the position of the headman (*muhtar*) as the elected representative of administratively defined village and town-quarter communities.[100] The Ottoman regime institutionalized the office of the headman (*muhtarlık*) in Istanbul in the late 1820s. Initially, headmen were responsible primarily for policing population movements in a period of increased migration to urban areas.[101] When Sultan Mahmud II issued orders generalizing the election of headmen in villages throughout the Anatolian countryside in the 1830s, the position also acquired important fiscal responsibilities.[102] These regulations were part of a set of reforms aiming to sideline provincial Ottoman magnates (*ayan*) who had built

regional mini-empires out of the wide-ranging powers of local administration lifetime tax farms entailed in the eighteenth century.[103] Along
with local religious leaders, headmen were a community-based, in-
expensive solution for the lack of a bureaucratic revenue-collection
administration with direct ties to villages and town quarters.[104] Musa
Çadırcı's research in court records in Anatolia found that the office
was part of an effort to redistribute the former duties of provincial
magnates in particular districts, especially with regard to taxation.[105]

Locally sourced headmen were not necessarily the first choice of
an emergent bureaucratic cadre in Istanbul in the 1830s and 1840s.
Many Ottoman lawmakers preferred creating a salaried revenue-
collection administration with direct ties to individual payers, and
they attempted to do so in the 1840s. But salaried bureaucrats faced
challenges accessing revenue from villages and town quarters that
had administered their own payments in distribution (tevzi) for generations during the age of lifetime tax farming, and initial attempts
faced declining revenues and tax revolts.[106] In contrast, the headman
was to participate in, not replace, the village- and town-level councils managing the distribution of tax burdens.[107] The office's potential
integration into these existing tax-farming structures is perhaps one
reason it survived, unlike the salaried tax collectors (muhassils) of the
1840s, into the twentieth century. The office of the headman privileged
and maintained the village as a bounded unit. This unit consolidated
over decades of local administrative sovereignty in an environment
of lifetime tax farming, and the official Ottoman agrarian imaginary
both privileged and reified that long-term consolidation.

The midcentury programmatic reforms also envisioned important
roles for village headmen in land registration and transactions. The
Title Regulation of 1859, which accompanied the 1858 Land Code, stipulated that when someone wanted to sell usufruct rights over land,
they must first obtain a certificate (ilmühaber) from the headman of
their village or town quarter, who would attest to their uncontested
usufruct rights over the land in question and refer the title deed to the
provincial council and treasury official for verification and modifica-
tion.[108] This regulation preceded the establishment of an imperial land

administration, so it left the verification of land deeds to provincial councils. But headmen would retain their roles as "access points" responsible for verifying local property relations for decades to follow.

In the 1860s and 1870s, Midhat Paşa and his colleagues refined, restricted, and programmatically outlined the position of the village headman in the Provincial Administration Regulations. According to the 1864 law, elected headmen organized in councils were to distribute tax burdens and coordinate government tax collection among their constituents, administer local guards and watchmen, monitor cleanliness and hygiene, facilitate agricultural production, and settle disputes within the boundaries of the law (this last power would be rescinded with the development of the nizamiye court system in the late 1870s). The drafters of the Provincial Administration Regulation envisioned the headman as an intermediary for communicating with local communities: the headman was to relay the content of imperial laws to his constituents and inform the authorities of events in their jurisdictions.[109]

The village headman's many duties demonstrate Ottoman modernizers' stakes in standardizing rural settlement in villages in the nineteenth century. None of these regulations, with the exception of the 1844 decree specifically referring to rural settlement, mentioned the "tribe" as a unit of administration. The mobile, tent-dwelling lifestyle that the tribe represented to Ottoman lawmakers was not part of the new ideal landscape. These relentlessly future-focused regulations captured lawmakers' conviction at midcentury that the empire's prosperity depended on an agrarian landscape of productive, settled villages. The village community and its elected headmen would be the key to a smoothly functioning property administration, revenue collection, and secure population. As the 1844 regulation articulated, the first step toward realizing this goal involved eliminating those local leaders who benefited from the status quo of regional forms of administrative sovereignty. In the Syrian interior, transforming tribes into villages meant undermining men like Dhiyab al-ʿAdwan. In the late 1860s, the developmentalist governor of Syria, Mehmed Raşid Paşa, planned to do just that.

MAKING A DISTRICT IN THE INTERIOR

In 1866, not long after his experiences in Adana and just after his appointment to the governorship of Aleppo, Ahmed Cevdet Paşa toured
the Hama hinterland with the new governor of Damascus, Mehmed
Raşid Paşa. The two men strategized about how to increase revenue
collection in the interior regions of the Jazira, Hawran, and Balqa.
Their main concern was ousting Bedouin (*urban*) who were collecting
agricultural surplus from villages, meaning that some villages were
double-taxed and some failed to remit any surplus to the treasury. They
planned to establish a mobile detachment to tour the interior regions,
as a show of force.[110] In a request he submitted to the Supreme Council
in Istanbul after the harvest and tax-collection season the following
year, Ahmed Cevdet Paşa discussed his initiative with Mehmed Raşid
Paşa. In his request, he drew a clear distinction between the "desert"
(*çöl*) and the "settled and cultivated regions" (*mamure*). He maintained
that because of the mobile force he and Mehmed Raşid Paşa had established, the Bedouin had not been able to collect the surplus in the Dayr
al-Zor region during the summer of 1868. He asked the central government for funds for hybrid camels (*hecinler*), which he maintained were
easier to train for missions involving firearms, known to terrify and
immobilize mules (*esterler*). Finally, Ahmed Cevdet Paşa articulated his
sweeping visions of a productive interior landscape in northern Syria,
writing that in the "roughly 100-hour-space between Aleppo and Baghdad" the land was very fertile and prime for development (*imara*).[111]

This growing developmentalist mood among Ottoman lawmakers
and officials certainly included Mehmed Raşid Paşa, who was a younger
protégé of Ahmed Cevdet's. But Mehmed Raşid Paşa also focused on
the interior's existing grain surplus. In the early days of his governorship in Syria, which began in 1866, Mehmed Raşid Paşa had developed
a reputation for favoring prominent Damascus grain merchants who
wanted to buy up land in Hawran.[112] These men, the counterparts of
the ʿAbd al-Hadis in Nablus, were attempting to expand their control
over the grain-producing hinterlands south of the city, pushing mid-
size entrepreneurs like the Abu Jabirs further afield in the process. For

Mehmed Raşid Paşa, the potential revenue of ʿAdwan and Bani Sakhr dominions presented a way to appease Hawrani elites displaced by the increasing power of Damascus grain merchants, reinforcing the status of the southern interior as an extended hinterland of both Nablus and Damascus markets.[113] A firmer hold over the Balqa would satisfy both challenges of future revenue and distribution concerns in the present.

At the same time, the precipitous rise of wealth and influence of the "prince of the Balqa," Dhiyab al-Humud, led Mehmed Raşid to initiate a military campaign into ʿAdwan country in the spring of 1867. After his run-in with Hulu Paşa, Dhiyab al-Humud definitively left the Ottoman sphere of submission and began building a local power base that challenged the changing provincial administration. One of his allies was ʿAqil Agha, another prominent Bedouin magnate based in northern Palestine who had been entering and exiting the Ottoman sphere of submission, holding Ottoman official titles and serving in the military forces of Ottoman governors in Acre, for his entire professional career.[114] Dhiyab al-Humud and ʿAqil Agha united in their frustrations with Hulu Paşa's intrusive campaigns and responded by attacking their mutual rivals in Nablus villages, stealing livestock, destroying property, and killing people.[115]

Reports such as these certainly contributed to Mehmed Raşid Paşa's resolve to lead a military campaign into ʿAdwan country. But the more immediate impetus was a plea for assistance from Dhiyab's cousin Kayid Abu ʿUrabi, who had allied with the ʿAbbadi leader Kayid al-Khitalayn and a prominent merchant from the town of Salt, Husayn al-Sabah.[116] In local oral histories, these three men went all the way to Istanbul to entice the Ottoman military to launch a campaign against Dhiyab al-ʿAdwan. In the eyes of many in the interior, including his Abu ʿUrabi cousins from the ʿAdwan, Dhiyab al-ʿAdwan's wealth, influence, and claims to control the landscape and surplus of the interior had become egregious. Their rapidly changing commercial environment notwithstanding, many ʿAdwani elites continued to view the Damascus administration as a resource. The Ottoman military could help cut Dhiyab al-ʿAdwan down to size as it had many bloated magnates before him: there was no reason to think that this particular military campaign would lead to a much more lasting shift in local and regional politics.[117]

Mehmed Raşid Paşa spent the summer of 1867 on campaign in Hawran and Balqa, basing his operations in Muzayrib and organizing a major southern campaign with the assistance of Ruwalla and Wuld ʿAli troops and ʿAdwan guides.[118] In the report he wrote to Istanbul a month after the Balqa campaign, Mehmed Raşid Paşa was triumphant: he recalled that "even during the Egyptian tumult," Ibrahim Paşa had entered the Balqa region with his entire army and succeeded in accomplishing nothing beyond destroying the Salt castle after a month-long siege. He presented his Balqa campaign as a way to redeem the Ottoman administration in Damascus from the stain of the Egyptian "troubles," a period that Ottoman subjects often invoked to symbolize chaos, misrule, and lack of confidence in Ottoman sovereignty.[119]

Mehmed Raşid Paşa claimed that Dhiyab al-ʿAdwan had consolidated his control over the entire territory of the Balqa and was expanding across the Jordan Valley into the Tiberias region. Despite his claim that Dhiyab al-ʿAdwan's operation was impeding agricultural practice in the region, he expressed his understanding of Dhiyab al-ʿAdwan's relationship to the landscape as that of a landowner with transferrable usufruct rights (*tasarruf*), in the language of the 1858 Land Code.[120] Furthermore, with the help of their guides, Kayid Abu ʿUrabi and Kayid al-Khitalayn, the campaign seized an extraordinary amount of grain, held in secret ʿAdwan storage sites all over the North.[121]

In his report on the campaign, Mehmed Raşid Paşa expressed his sense of moving into an unsettled zone ripe with potential. Stopping in the Roman ruins of Jerash on his way south, he marveled at the extensive architecture, musing that the city "must have been extremely organized and developed." It was surrounded by fertile and highly productive land, he mused, but because of the attacks and oppression of Dhiyab al-ʿAdwan, no permanent settlement was to be found: the people were engaged in agriculture, but they were living in tents. For Mehmed Raşid Paşa, as for his reformist colleagues, a more productive and well-administered landscape with surplus flowing to the Damascus administration rather than Balqa-based leaders was easy to imagine.

Mehmed Raşid Paşa described arriving in the town of Salt after obtaining pledges of loyalty and obedience from some of the Bedouin communities in the Balqa and sending soldiers to fan out over the landscape and find Dhiyab al-ʿAdwan. His soldiers cornered a wounded Shaykh Dhiyab in a difficult-to-access hideout south of Salt that "no Ottoman official had ever visited." For all of Mehmed Raşid Paşa's claims that he was entering uncharted territory, the 1867 campaign ended in a negotiated settlement concluded by the Ottoman regime's most dependable ally in the interior, Fandi al-Fayiz, heir to the Bani Sakhr influence in the pilgrimage administration described in chapter 1. Al-Fayiz negotiated safe passage for Dhiyab al-ʿAdwan in 1867, guaranteeing that he would "never set foot in the Balqa again." This new iteration of the long-standing but unstable ʿAdwan–Bani Sakhr alliance produced the marriage of Dhiyab's daughter ʿAlia and Fandi's son Sattam in the early 1870s.[122]

The agreement reached between Dhiyab al-ʿAdwan and Mehmed Raşid Paşa in August 1867 speaks to the ongoing dynamics of the sphere of submission even in a campaign focused on an imagined future of exclusive administrative sovereignty. In his report, Mehmed Raşid Paşa described Fandi al-Fayiz as the "fighter" (hamledar) of the pilgrimage, implying that he was a trustworthy ally of the Ottoman state in the Balqa. Talha Çiçek's findings about the participation of Wuld ʿAli fighters in Mehmed Raşid Paşa's Balqa campaign further illustrate the importance of the politics of the sphere of submission and the historical ties between the Damascus regime and particular Bedouin groups.[123] The Bani Sakhr and Wuld ʿAli communities each played central roles in protecting the pilgrimage route, and both were closely tied to the Ottoman administration through extensive networks of subsidies.

Mehmed Raşid Paşa would enter the Balqa once again in 1869, after reports that Dhiyab al-ʿAdwan had never left the region and Fandi al-Fayiz himself had exited the Ottoman sphere of submission, protesting Mehmed Raşid Paşa's policy of selling Hawran land under Bani Sakhr control to Damascus investors and asserting his right to collect taxes from villages north of the Zarqa River.[124] In the 1870s, with the stationing of a regular Ottoman garrison in Salt and the establishment of a regular tax administration, the agricultural surplus of the North was finally diverted from 'Adwani and Bani Sakhr elites to the Damascus treasury.

Dhiyab al-'Adwan spent the next eighteen months in detention in Nablus before being sent into exile in Cyprus. Like so many fallen magnates, he was able to return to Nablus two months later, and he eventually made his way back to 'Adwan country, possibly as part of a deal between his son 'Ali and Mehmed Raşid Paşa. Ten years after Mehmed Raşid Paşa's second campaign, in 1879, an Ottoman census in the Balqa listed Dhiyab al-'Adwan as one of the wealthiest men in the region.[125] He received a stipend from the Damascus administration, taken from his own confiscated wealth, until his death in 1890.[126] His son 'Ali continued a prominent career in the Balqa, also receiving an Ottoman stipend, and his grandson Sultan led an important revolt against the British-Hashemite occupation of the region in 1923.[127]

In a long view of the history of the Syrian interior, Dhiyab al-'Adwan was one of the last local leaders who negotiated his relationship with the Ottoman imperial state in terms of a loosely defined and highly contested sphere of submission. In the decades that followed his exile to Cyprus, he would remain prominent in the wadi and the shifa albeit within a new context of Ottoman administrative governance that reached much further into the everyday lives of 'Adwani families. The initiation of that intrusive form of governance across the landscapes of Syria, Iraq, and the Arabian Peninsula responded to local exigencies and struggles over political power, the landscape, and its surplus. But the novel attitude of officials like Mehmed Raşid Paşa toward land and population in the Balqa also referenced imperial, and larger global, trends. Ottoman reformers' visions of a productive interior landscape both reflected and reproduced imperial policies that privileged intensive, year-round cultivation over other kinds of land use.

Modernizing Ottoman officials' attitudes toward the Syrian interior reflected the amnesia of modern state-making.[128] Even as Mehmed Raşid Paşa claimed that Ottoman officials had never before ventured into the remote lands of the North, he relied on the Ottoman pilgrimage administration's allies in the region, the al-Fayiz elites of the Bani

Sakhr, to complete his mission. The interregnum of Egyptian rule was rhetorically useful for these men: having lost sovereignty over Syria for almost a decade, they could claim a new start, one in which Ottoman governance would look markedly different. This chapter has focused on the space between the claims of Ottoman modernizers and lived experiences in the Syrian interior, a landscape that Ottoman officials increasingly inhabited themselves. Even as Mehmed Raşid Paşa's campaigns fit into a reformist imperial discourse of rupture, they also responded to an environment of commercial expansion in Syria that local leaders, including Dhiyab al-ʿAdwan, had exploited to become rich. Dhiyab al-ʿAdwan's growing wealth, built on the labor of politically and socially subordinate cultivators, wage laborers, and slaves in the Balqa and rooted in control over land, garnered the attention of enterprising merchant capitalists like the Abu Jabirs, who saw the interior as ripe for investment. It also frustrated his cousin-rivals within the ʿAdwan, who allied with other tent- and town-based leaders to invite the Ottoman military force in Damascus to cut Dhiyab al-ʿAdwan down to size.

Like Native American groups in North America, the activities of ʿAdwan and Bani Sakhr leaders in the mid-nineteenth century can be conceptualized as "shape-shifting"—especially for the Bani Sakhr, who took the opportunity that high grain prices and arable land presented to become much more involved in agriculture than before.[129] Descriptions of Dhiyab al-ʿAdwan's ostentatious consumption in the mid-nineteenth century also imply an increasingly elite, exclusive, and commodified character of access to land and the potential of that access to generate wealth. Alongside the ʿAbd al-Hadi and Abu Jabir families, Dhiyab al-ʿAdwan and his cousins and al-Fayiz elites contributed to an environment of commercial capitalism in the interior, treating land as an asset for pecuniary gain. The notion of shape-shifting, however, reminds us that this deepened iteration of commercial capitalism in the mid-nineteenth century North was not a fundamental step in a teleology but rather a long and nonlinear process of balancing different kinds of land use, including cultivation and pastoral practice.

The dissonance of agricultural production and tent dwelling did trouble a certain teleology of progress for Ottoman modernizers like Midhat Paşa, however. In the interior, this teleology undergirded their narratives of an underdeveloped provincial landscape. The increasingly apparent potential for wealth generation that engendered this dissonance brought the Ottoman administration into the interior in the late 1860s. Dhiyab al-ʿAdwan's rivals could not have predicted that their plea for assistance to Ottoman authorities to cut him down to size—a common use of Ottoman military force as a resource in regional political disputes in the eighteenth and nineteenth centuries—would lead, this time, to the permanent establishment of Ottoman direct rule in the interior. Only in hindsight does the formal district that Mehmed Raşid Paşa's military campaigns left behind in the Balqa region emerge as the first step in making Ottoman state space, a contingent process that would be contested and reformulated at every turn.

The regulations framing Mehmed Raşid Paşa's vision of the development of the interior reviewed in this chapter embody the mood of agrarian optimism shared across numerous imperial spaces in the mid-nineteenth century. Alongside the Land Code, the Ottoman government issued an extremely encouraging immigration law in 1857, promising new immigrants tax-free land grants and government assistance with agriculture.[130] These legal frameworks provided the administrative basis for granting land to immigrants constructed as productive. At the same time, these regulations demonstrate a willingness to deny existing populations constructed as unproductive historic land rights.

In this chapter I have emphasized that Bedouin leaders and the town-based merchant capitalists who settled in the interior prior to the extension of direct imperial governance shared a legal space and built their early relationships on mutually recognizable forms of contract. In one sense, this shared space was a "middle ground" similar to that described by scholars of the Russian and American imperial contexts to describe the pre-state-space encounter between actors of different sovereign and legal contexts, especially in the commercial realm.[131] It is difficult, though, to characterize the legal frames of reference of merchants and Bedouin as two separate entities between which a middle ground was necessary. The Islamic legal tradition informed both Bedouin and Ottoman forms of property administration and constituted another coterminous lived experience that modernizing claims of underdevelopment and the need for improvement denied. This shared legal space and "intellectual infrastructure" of familiar forms of contract, one that stretched across the Arabian Peninsula to the Indian Ocean world,[132] would prove extremely important when Ottoman officials intensified their attempts to transform the interior landscape into state space by implementing a private property regime.

Imperial modernizers' shared visions of agrarian prosperity at midcentury were important, but they were not the end of the story. For one thing, the global financial crisis of the 1870s would transform a general mood of agrarian optimism into a desperate scramble to increase agricultural productivity and tax revenues, especially in the Ottoman case, in the final quarter of the century. More fundamentally, the conflict between the programmatic plans of Istanbul-based modernizers and the complex experiences of the interior became sharper during the process of making a directly ruled administrative district in 'Adwan country in the 1870s and 1880s. The next chapter turns to this process.

3 PRODUCING TRIBES AND PROPERTY

IN SEPTEMBER 1894, RUFAYF AL-WIRAYKAT, his paternal cousin Minakid, and five relatives left their encampment in the neighborhood of Abu Nusayr, north of the village of Amman, and rode to the town of Salt. They passed a few other Wiraykat encampments and farms, as well as lands owned by their 'Adwan relatives, the Lawzis.[1] When they arrived in Salt, they headed for the "foreign quarter" (*maḥallat al-aghrāb*), where most of the town's merchants lived. Over the preceding two decades, Salt had become a bustling district capital, with two Ottoman courts, various governing councils, a land and tax administration, and a permanent military force. The town had also become the second home of a growing group of enterprising commercial capitalists who had moved to the interior from Nablus, Jerusalem, and Damascus since the 1860s, looking for cheap wheat and plentiful land.

For Rufayf and Minakid al-Wiraykat, September was a busy period of drawing up contracts with these merchants before the Wiraykats moved their families and belongings to the Jordan Valley for the winter. Rufayf and Minakid were heirs to the Wiraykat family wheat-production operation on lands around Abu Nusayr that Minakid's

PRODUCING TRIBES AND PROPERTY   117

father, Dawjan, had registered with the Ottoman authorities in the late 1870s. The year 1894 had been a good one for Wiraykat wheat, and Rufayf and Minakid, the leading landowning men in the family, were constantly fielding requests from merchants in Salt who wanted to buy the next season's wheat in advance.

The tax collector in Salt, Habib Effendi, had also noticed the Wiraykats' prosperity. Rufayf al-Wiraykat, who was the elected headman (*mukhtār*) of the Wiraykat tribe (*'ashīra*), had promised to bring his relatives to Salt and stop by Habib Effendi's house to pay the annual taxes on their wheat fields before the family left for the Jordan Valley for the winter. They had agreed on how to parcel out the tax burden beforehand: each of the seven leading Wiraykat men would pay in proportion to how much land he managed. Rufayf's first paternal cousin, Minakid, who was the wealthiest man in the family, had agreed to cover for the 238-piastre tax burden of two of his relatives as a loan. They settled the tax debt in the shaded courtyard in front of Habib Effendi's house.[2]

Rufayf and Minakid told this story years later, when the debt they contracted that day became the subject of a court case. Their story of lending to their relatives, as headmen of the Wiraykat community, to cover taxes on land and produce illustrates the intertwinement of taxation and credit among tent-dwelling communities in the late nineteenth-century interior. It also demonstrates the deep entanglement of Wiraykat men both with the regional grain market and the newly established permanent Ottoman administration. The tax administration Habib Effendi represented was a foundational element of the Ottoman regime's attempts to claim administrative sovereignty and establish territorial state space in 'Adwan country: registering its land, trees, and built environment to individual owners and taxpayers; adjudicating disputes in locally based courts; and enforcing daily, continuous submission to the Ottoman order with a permanent military force. In the 1870s and 1880s, Ottoman officials attempted to shift the role of the imperial regime in the interior from that of a distant sovereign of a sphere of submission to that of a local administrator. In this period, Ottoman governing councils and courts became involved in, and came to frame, struggles over district-level resources and political legitimacy in reference to imperial law in a highly contested and constantly shifting practice of administrative sovereignty.

This chapter examines the construction of an Ottoman district in the heart of ʿAdwan country in the aftermath of Mehmed Raşid Paşa's 1867 and 1869 campaigns. The participation of middling Bedouin men like Rufayf and Minakid al-Wiraykat in this project of making and maintaining state space in the 1870s and 1880s precipitated important changes in leadership structures within Bedouin communities, the ʿAdwan included. In the eighteenth and early nineteenth centuries, powerful shaykhs, like Qaʿdan al-Fayiz and Dhiyab al-Humud, who moved in and out of the Ottoman sphere of submission were the main links to Ottoman governance in the Bedouin communities among which they wielded power. While their work was vital to administration, especially regarding the pilgrimage, their participation in governance, and ultimately their submission to the Ottoman order, was intermittent, seasonal, and fundamentally unpredictable. In contrast, the 1880s witnessed the rise of a group of Bedouin bureaucrats whose influence was intimately intertwined with the mundane administrative processes of governing landed property.

Through these processes, midlevel leaders in Bedouin groups that had not been directly involved in Ottoman administration previously, including some ʿAdwan communities and their rivals, the ʿAbbad, became party to the daily practices of modern state formation. These men took on legally standardized positions as headmen, entering a bureaucratic hierarchy that, on paper, reached all the human communities living in the empire. The headman was the linchpin of modern Ottoman governance at its lowest levels, responsible for coordinating tax collection, policing, and verifying control over land in his community toward creating a property register. Through assuming this bureaucratic office, particular Wiraykat men acquired social and material capital in the late nineteenth century, carving space for themselves in the Ottoman administration alongside the more spectacular power of Dhiyab al-ʿAdwan and his son ʿAli.

Rufayf and Minakid al-Wiraykat's entry into provincial governance was closely intertwined with their long-term involvement in
southern Syria's agricultural commodity markets. In the 1870s and
1880s, both Ottoman officials and merchant investors, who were
sometimes the same men, dealt with Rufayf and Minakid as agents
of their community's surplus wheat, barley, and clarified butter for
purposes of tax and trade. The Wiraykats were involved in long-term
debt relationships with particular town-based merchant capitalists,
who consistently bought their products through various types of
credit contracts, which sometimes included land as collateral. Many
litigants enforced these contracts in the Salt sharia court established
in 1869, a venue that the growing community of town-based merchant
capitalists from Nablus, Damascus, and Jerusalem dominated. The
sharia court and the merchant families who dominated its activities
continued the preexisting practice of recognizing Bedouin as the primary holders of alienable rights to arable rain-fed land in the interior
that was common before the establishment of a permanent district
administration.

This market for land and agricultural commodities, structured by
private contracts concluded in houses and tents and sometimes enforced in the sharia court, served the needs of interior tent and town
dwellers.[3] It did not provide Ottoman officials or faraway capitalists
with a birds-eye view of property relations, whether for investment
purposes or for efficient taxation. In the late 1870s, in the aftermath of
fiscal and territorial crisis, prominent Ottoman reformers described
Syria as a region split between a bustling coast and an underdeveloped, lagging interior. For these modernizers, the most important
marker of the interior's unacceptable state was the large number of
local inhabitants who continued to live in tents, and the most important remedy was a comprehensive and standardized property and tax
administration along the lines of the Provincial Administration, the
Land Code, and related codified laws. The fiscal crisis of the 1870s increased reformers' motivation to swiftly enable the interior to realize
what they saw as its revenue-producing potential.

To realize these visions of prosperity and tax revenue, some high-level reformers continued to promote the militarized settlement campaigns of midcentury that had attempted to erase tent-dwelling communities, categorized as tribes, from the rural landscape in Adana and elsewhere.[4] But the plan that prevailed in the Syrian interior responded to the exigencies of state-making in a context of territorial loss and heightened interimperial competition, one in which the imperative to maintain a loyal, viable population mitigated plans for militarized settlement. The solution that emerged in the late 1870s was to encourage settlement by allocating land to individual tent-dwelling Bedouin as members of administratively defined tent-dwelling tribes without using military force to settle them in villages. The implementation of this policy maintained the tribe as a foundational category of rural administration even as midcentury codified law had erased it from future visions of the provincial order.[5]

As individual members of administratively defined tribes, then, men from the 'Adwan and 'Abbad communities registered rights to rain-fed agricultural land and received title deeds in the interior in the late 1870s and early 1880s. Despite their documented participation in grain markets, however, and unlike their village-based counterparts, tent-dwelling individuals did not register rights to land based on long-standing possession and use, inheritance, or previous purchase. Rather, they registered land at the pleasure of the state, by order of imperial decree. This easily rescinded privilege corresponded with Ottoman officials' image of a population neatly bifurcated between settled "village inhabitants" (ahali) and tent-dwelling "tribes" (aşiret). Even though many tribes were involved in part-time farming, they were not judged deserving of labor-based property right over the lands they inhabited. Rather, the first land commissions granted them title as a means to encourage them to become village inhabitants. The category "tribe" retained the meaning it had acquired in midcentury legal codes, as a residual administrative category marking tent-dwelling communities as in need of improvement within a totalizing project of making state space.

For men like Dawjan al-Wiraykat and his sons and nephews, however, the employment of the tribe as an administrative category within a comprehensive system of land allocation and tax collection presented an opportunity to gain power, both social and material, over processes of resource distribution. In the Salt district, tribes and their representative headmen became the means for codifying the land rights of tent-dwelling Bedouin communities without requiring that they live in houses, give up their herds, and enter village administration, even within a legal framework that clearly privileged village dwelling and exclusive cultivation. Dawjan al-Wiraykat's sons entered the Ottoman bureaucracy, deepening their ties with merchant capitalists and Ottoman officials (who were often the same men) through daily processes of negotiating tax burdens, signing off on property transactions, and witnessing in Ottoman courts.

Through these processes, headmen like the Wiraykats became the face of the transformed Ottoman state in their communities. They were responsible for the everyday processes that constituted daily interactions with a state that claimed through codified law to be distant and impersonal just as its governing technologies, most notably those involving standardized paper forms, became ever-present in the lives of the inhabitants of the interior.[6] Dawjan's sons became bureaucrats in the sense that they straddled a dividing line between state and society that they were meant to maintain and perform.[7] This integration of Bedouin representatives into the newly standardized administrative hierarchies of Ottoman state space was an important, and unique, element of Ottoman governance in the interior as land registration expanded.

Land registration, in the Ottoman context as elsewhere, responded to new official anxieties about the productivity and availability of land. In the Ottoman context, these concerns were related in particular to the fiscal crises of the 1870s and to an influx of Muslim refugees after the Russo-Ottoman war, leading officials to think in terms of land's scarcity rather than its abundance.[8] The land registration efforts in the Balqa responded to these twin imperatives, which became increasingly interrelated: expanding the productivity of land deemed underutilized and settling destitute Muslim refugees who were constructed as both politically loyal and potentially productive.

Creating a settled, productive landscape was surely one goal of land registration, but in the Balqa region this goal was mitigated by the imperative to avoid rural unrest.[9] Ottoman lawmakers included Bedouin in the process of land registration without forcing them to settle in villages because they needed to maintain their political loyalty and physical presence in a territorially understood context of siege. In the Syrian interior, these imperatives added up to a policy of development through administrative inclusion. The precarious status of Ottoman sovereignty in the increasingly competitive interimperial context of the late nineteenth century therefore set the stage for the emergence of Bedouin bureaucrats. High-level Ottoman officials may have preferred forced settlement, but they had neither the political nor the material capital to carry out such a policy in the 1880s. What emerged was a construction of Bedouin as potentially loyal Muslim subjects whose membership in "tribes" marked them as in need of improvement.

Within this global context, which afforded them comparatively wide opportunities for state-making, the men who became Bedouin bureaucrats played crucial roles in maintaining their communities' control over land and developing new ways of performing the Ottoman state as street-level bureaucrats. Their willingness to assume this role was by no means a foregone conclusion, a point emphasized by other Bedouin communities' rebellion against Ottoman attempts to tax and survey. The choices of men like Minakid and Rufayf al-Wiraykat to enter the expanding Ottoman bureaucratic order had long-standing impact, both on the trajectory of property relations in the interior and on the political status of the communities they claimed to represent within a modern state context.

STATE SPACE IN THE NORTH

The establishment of a district in the Balqa region of the Syrian interior followed a wider pattern of bureaucratic expansion in the Ottoman Empire during the Hamidian period.[10] In the aftermath of Mehmed Raşid Paşa's campaigns into the southern Syrian interior and Dhiyab al-ʿAdwan's exile, the Damascus administration set up a permanent, year-round Ottoman military presence in the Balqa region of the Syrian interior for the first time, as well as a formal district (*kaza*) based in the town of Salt. The structure of the new district followed the general outline of the 1864 Provincial Administration Regulation reviewed in chapter 2. Reflecting the long-standing ties between the southern interior and central Palestinian cities, the new district was made subordinate to the subprovince (*liva/sancak*) based in Nablus and included a district governor, a treasurer, a sharia court, and a town council tasked with the administrative and judicial duties outlined in the Regulation.[11]

The composition of these early governing entities reflected the changing social makeup of the interior, especially the town of Salt, in the 1870s. During that decade, declining wheat prices, competition over land proximate to cities, and close ties to the Ottoman regime motivated an increasing number of capitalist investors to move east and south, especially from Nablus, Jerusalem, and Damascus. By the 1880s, these town-based men dominated the councils and sharia court in the town of Salt.[12] Like Salih Abu Jabir before them, these merchant capitalists viewed Bedouin as the owners of interior land and the main agents in distributing its agricultural surplus. Building on the commercial expansion of the mid-nineteenth century, merchant capitalists initially entered the interior on the terms of its existing tent- and town-dwelling inhabitants.

Following the Provincial Administration Regulations, town-based councils formed the backbone of provincial governance in the interior. The initial composition of these councils in Salt reflected the political situation at the time of Mehmed Raşid Paşa's military campaigns in 1867 and 1869. Dhiyab al-ʿAdwan's rivals who accompanied the Ottoman military force into the southern interior took on important roles in this new administration. Kayid Abu ʿUrabi, Dhiyab al-ʿAdwan's cousin-rival who accompanied Mehmed Raşid Paşa's campaign in 1867, served on the judicial council in the early years of the administration. The ʿAbbadi and Salti men he had worked with to sideline Dhiyab al-ʿAdwan also held council seats. Salih Abu Jabir, the "pioneer" merchant capitalist introduced in chapter 2, served on the judicial council into the

1880s. Other members of these councils were mainly luminaries of the town of Salt whose families had lived there for generations.[13]

In the late 1870s and 1880s, increasing numbers of merchant capitalists from Nablus, Jerusalem, and Damascus joined the Abu Jabir family, and they began to dominate town-based district governance. These families did not leave detailed accounts of their migrations to the interior, but their movement coincided with a widespread agricultural crisis in Syria. In the late 1860s, wheat prices in Syrian ports had already begun to fall in the face of competition from Indian and postbellum American grains. In the first half of the decade, conditions of drought, hunger, and a cholera epidemic precipitated a provincial fiscal crisis that mirrored the wider imperial bankruptcy of 1875.[14] In a context of heightened competition and falling prices, men who had benefited from the wheat boom of the 1840s to the 1860s in the hinterlands of Nablus and Damascus looked for cheaper sources of produce from farther afield to maintain profit. The Damascus administration's campaigns against Dhiyab al-'Adwan, and the establishment of courts and councils that these capitalists were used to dominating in Damascus and Nablus, was an added incentive; Mehmed Raşid Paşa's campaign had responded, at least in part, to the interests of merchants in Hawran looking to extend their influence south.[15]

In these early years of district-making, the sharia court established in 1869 was the main imperial venue regulating property relations. Like the sharia courts in Nablus and Damascus that had been established much earlier, the Salt sharia court issued *hujjas* that litigants could use as proof of sales and credit agreements. Sharia courts had been the backbone of Ottoman provincial governance prior to the state-space-making reforms of the nineteenth century: the Tanzimat regulations of the 1840s, the Land Code, and the Provincial Administration Regulations. Establishing a sharia court was a basic element of creating an Ottoman district, meaning that this new court in Salt was a crucial element for incorporating the interior into the older form of administrative sovereignty described in chapter 1. And as I noted in the previous chapter, sharia courts were important arbiters of local property relations in cities like Nablus and Damascus in the mid-nineteenth century.[16] In Syria, sharia courts had mainly regulated and sanctioned transactions in fully owned (*mülk*) land within towns or in their immediate "green belts" of irrigated and rain-fed orchards and gardens.[17] In the context of the grain boom of the mid-nineteenth century, however, transactions in usufruct rights of state-owned rain-fed land had become much more common in urban sharia courts across Syria, transactions expressed and recorded through shar'i *hujjas*.[18]

The earliest surviving records of the Salt court date to the 1880s, but the activities they recorded probably represent the court's work in the first decade after its 1869 establishment as well. These records show an institution busy with property transactions and debt agreements following contractual forms and evidentiary procedures typical of sharia courts established much earlier in larger Syrian towns and cities.[19] The sharia court records show that the practice of transacting in usufruct rights to rain-fed, state-owned land within particular Bedouin communities' spheres of influence (*dira*) was well-established in the interior prior to the establishment of a land administration. The court gave interior inhabitants like the Wiraykats, as well as the merchant capitalists with whom they transacted, new ways to make claims on land they controlled, that land's agricultural produce, and the credit that merchant capitalists brought into the interior. The court also provided documentary evidence of those claims in the form of standardized legal documents, *hujjas*. Table 3.1 and the accompanying figures (3.1– 3.3) depict the distribution of types of transactions in three volumes of Salt sharia court transactions that produced *hujjas* in the 1880s.[20]

The analysis summarized in table 3.1 and figures 3.1–3.3 demonstrates that most of the property transactions concluded in the sharia court in the 1880s involved houses, shops, and irrigated orchards and gardens in the town of Salt and its green belt. These transactions followed historical patterns of property transactions involving fully owned (*mülk*) greenbelt land in regional sharia courts. But the 1880s court cases also included a significant number (thirty-nine) of transactions in rain-fed, state-owned, agricultural land. In 95 percent of these transactions involving rain-fed land, people identified as Bedouin tent dwellers were the sellers or the mortgagers of the property in ques-

TABLE 3.1. Property transactions in the Salt sharia court, 1881–1889

Type of transaction	Number of transactions
Final sales	214
Temporary sales	102
Loans with property as collateral	76
Total property transactions	392

Source: Salt sharia court records, Center for Documents and Manuscripts, University of Jordan, Amman, Jordan, vols. 1–3, 1881–89.

FIGURE 3.1. Final sales by property type. Data extracted from Salt sharia court records, vols. 1–3.

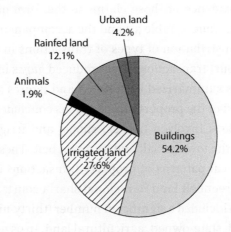

FIGURE 3.2. Temporary sales by property type. Data extracted from Salt sharia court records, vols. 1–3.

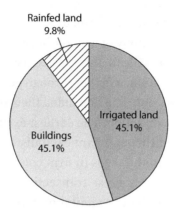

FIGURE 3.3. Loans by type of collateral. Data extracted from Salt sharia court records, vols. 1–3.

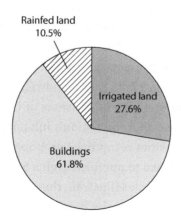

tion. These transactions show the ways in which the new sharia court provided legal legitimacy to a preexisting market in usufruct rights to land in the Syrian interior.

Sharia court procedure, following Islamic jurisprudence (*fiqh*), privileged the knowledge of adult men by sanctioning property transactions based on the testimony of upstanding male witnesses.[21] These witnesses attested to the seller's uncontested use or ownership rights over the property in question, whether through purchase, inheritance, or long-standing possession, and appended their signatures to the resulting record of the transaction. The earliest existing cases from the Salt sharia court depict the merchant capitalists who relocated from Nablus and Damascus in the 1870s in firm control of the court as recurrent witnesses.[22] Many of these transactions referenced previous sales concluded outside of court, similar to the cocultivation contract Rumayh al-Fayiz concluded with Salih Abu Jaber around 1860.[23] The court formalized transactions that were common in the interior before its establishment and in preexisting Ottoman sharia courts in Syrian cities, bringing these contracts into a state-sponsored Ottoman forum and documenting them with the signatures of a sharia court judge (*naib*) and prominent community-based witnesses.

Like Salih Abu Jabir before them, sharia court judges and the local merchant capitalists they relied on as witnesses and purveyors of local knowledge constructed tent-dwelling Bedouin as the original holders of transferrable usufruct right over the region's land. The sharia court records detailing land transactions, as well as reports of other out-of-court agreements, suggest both that tent-dwelling communities had a well-developed understanding of divisions of land within their *dira*s among individuals and that the region's inhabitants as well as newcomer merchant investors recognized and operationalized these divisions when they wished to purchase rights to land in the new Balqa subprovince.[24] Two examples illustrate these points. In autumn 1883, the sharia court recorded two sales between a merchant named Khalil Effendi al-Hasbani and men from the Manasir 'Abbad community of tent dwellers in the region of Marj Sikka.[25] The court record described this land as being in the "subdivision" (*maqsam*) of the seller, Nimran bin Muhammad al-Salim of the Manasir. Also in August 1883, Nikola Effendi Shalhub, a Damascene merchant living in Salt, bought land from ʿAli Rashid Abu Wandi of the Abu al-Ghanam in Khirbat al-Taym on behalf of a merchant in Jerusalem from the Abu Suwan family.[26] These were significant amounts of land at significant prices: the Abu al-Ghanam sale was for one thousand Mecidi riyals (twenty-four thousand piastres). These sales imply not only that "subdivisions" of land rights were agreed on within and among Bedouin communities but also that both the sharia court, as an institution represented by its judge, and the enterprising merchant capitalists who dominated its daily proceedings recognized these agreements as sufficient for issuing a formal record of the transfer in the form of a *hujja*.

In the 1880s, the court accepted diverse forms of evidence for the right to sell land. In the Abu al-Ghanam sale, Rashid Abu Wandi provided two witnesses to attest to the fact that he was acting as the agent (*wakīl*) for the entire Abu al-Ghanam tribe.[27] In the Manasir sales, the court proceeded on the weight of local witness testimony, including that of Nikola Shalhub, the agent who bought land from the Abu al-Ghanam. These evidentiary practices also applied to tent dwellers' use of land as collateral for credit. Eugene Rogan has documented how the sharia court facilitated the extension of capital especially from Jerusalem, Nablus, and Damascus into the interior through the legal mechanisms of temporary and final land sales, loans with property as collateral, and forward-purchase (*salam*) contracts of the main commodities produced in the interior: wheat, barley, and clarified butter.[28] While litigants did sometimes present written deeds to buttress their claims to the property in question, the sharia court often proceeded on witness-backed claims of long-standing use or inheritance without requiring written evidence.

Early sharia court records in Salt reflected the construction of legal identity on the terms of the 1869 Ottoman Nationality Law and the Provincial Administration Regulations. Each *hujja* identified each litigant's name, religion, nationality, and place of residence, sometimes also specifying a previous place of residence—especially for merchant capitalists who had recently relocated from Damascus, Nablus, or Jerusalem.[29] In this last element of formulaic identification, the court also distinguished between village, town, and tent dwellers in the district of Salt. Bedouin were defined as "tent dwellers" (*sukkān al-khiyam*), as "'*arab*," or sometimes as both. The court records also located each individual within a legally defined community, usually an "'*ashīra*" (tribe) described as "inhabiting the environs of the town (*qaṣaba*) of Salt." Town dwellers were identified by their town quarter (*maḥalla*), while others were identified as inhabiting particular villages (*qarya*).

For the Hanafi Islamic legal procedure followed by sharia courts, these descriptions were important for identifying particular people as male or female adult individuals capable of completing legal transactions—that is, of sound mind and majority status. But these identifications also reflect the divisions outlined in codified law, especially the Nationality Law of 1869, which defined Ottoman subjecthood in contradistinction to foreigners, and the Provincial Administration Regulations, which outlined administrative hierarchies, including villages and town quarters.[30] The inclusion of "tribe" as a formal population category for communities of tent dwellers inhabiting the environs of the town of Salt is striking, and I will return to this point below.

While these descriptions reflect the increasing imperative to document the interior population precisely in the 1880s, such identifications of collective membership did not carry legal weight in property transactions in the sharia court. When a Wiraykat man wanted to obtain a *hujja* from the sharia court for a land sale, he did not need a Wiraykat representative to attest to his ownership of that land; rather, in accordance with Islamic jurisprudence, any upstanding member of the wider community could attest to his right to sell, although the testimony of juridical males was stronger than that of females.[31] Merchants based in Salt could attest to the character of Bedouin sellers and the community knowledge of land use inherent in the sale, even if the seller was described as being from a Bedouin community, and vice versa. While the records reflected existing descriptions of community boundaries in the interior, property administration was not legally tied to those boundaries in the sharia court. In fact, the Provincial Administration Regulation's population categories were not even enough to prove identity in the sharia court setting: the court continued to require upstanding community witnesses to confirm that people were who they said they were.[32]

This *fiqh* and local-community-based evidentiary system, sanctioned by a provincially-appointed sharia court judge, undergirded a market for houses, gardens, and shops in which bounded plots of rain-fed agricultural land were both commodified with particular monetary values and transformed into collateral for credit during a period of rapid commercial expansion in the interior. This market, however, did not provide a comprehensive list of land rights either for Ottoman officials concerned about maintaining imperial sovereignty and fiscal viability or distant capitalists like Abu Suwan, who transacted in usufruct rights through an agent in Salt. There was no centralized provincial or district-level register documenting the claims of *hujja* holders within a defined space that a distant landowner could attempt to enter or state officials could monitor; rather, the system relied on verified witness testimony to establish the right to transfer land rights. Furthermore, this market in usufruct rights to rain-fed agricultural land was a threat to fiscal order because sharia court transactions and their resulting *hujja*s were not linked to any external tax or land register regulated by officials of central state agencies. As concerns over foreign influence in the Syrian interior increased in the 1880s and 1890s, this court-based land market could also have been perceived as a threat to imperial sovereignty. While the identification procedures described above were partly meant to regulate foreign property ownership, they did not make such ownership easy to monitor.

As we saw in chapter 2, governing bodies in Istanbul had been expressing anxieties over sales of rain-fed, state-owned land in sharia courts using *hujja*s (*hücec*) since the early 1850s. In 1878, the head judge in Damascus issued an order to sharia court judges all over the province of Syria to stop issuing deeds of sale of usufruct rights to state-owned land.[33] For the central and provincial governments, knowledge of a sharia-court-based land market was another incentive to establish land-registration commissions and branches of the property administration, asserting that the "essence" (*raqaba*) of the land was in the treasury's hands and that the central state alone had the right to allocate rights to it.[34]

This early documentary evidence of property relations in the interior shows transactions that built on existing legal understandings of rights to land, fitting them into the terms of the Land Code and the Provincial Administration Regulations. The transactions documented in the sharia court records were intensified versions of the property relations of the earlier nineteenth century, when men like Nimr al-ʿAdwan provided Nablus-based merchants like Musa Tuqan with commodities produced in the North. The migration of merchant capitalists to Salt gave them more direct access to interior commodities, especially grain, but a wider swath of tent-dwelling men also gained access to credit. The sharia court was the main venue for these transactions, providing litigants with state-sponsored documented contracts, and these contracts recognized Bedouin communities as the owners and agents of interior land. Recognizing the cohesion of this sharia-court-based land market is important because it provided the documentary forms and basis for an enduring trade in land using *hujja*s even after the establishment of an official property registry, a process documented below. Still, sharia court records did not provide a birds-eye view, a "grid," of the tax status of interior land or its availability for sale. This lack of a grid was problematic both for Ottoman officials with developmentalist aspirations and for faraway capitalists without extensive social connections in the interior. We turn now to their concerns.

BIFURCATING THE PROVINCE OF SYRIA: DOCUMENTING VILLAGES AND TRIBES IN THE INTERIOR

Ten years after Mehmed Raşid Paşa's campaign and the establishment of a district in Salt, a group of Ottoman reformers retrained their attention on the Syrian interior. In the late 1870s, with the empire's fiscal and territorial losses clear, the imperative to improve spaces deemed underdeveloped in order to simultaneously increase revenue and ensure the population's loyalty took on new urgency. These reformers articulated an understanding of Syria as a province bifur-cated between an advanced coastal region, on the one hand, and an underdeveloped interior with a mobile, tent-dwelling population ill-equipped for reforms, on the other. They debated plans for settling tent-dwelling communities based on officials' growing experience with settlement campaigns elsewhere in the empire in the preceding decades. The concept of an underdeveloped interior and debates over its improvement introduced the employment of "tribe" (*ashira/aşiret*) as a standard category for organizing rural populations, alongside "vil-lage," to the Syrian interior. This category became the basis for admin-istering all tent-dwelling groups in the region. These modernizers also set the stage for the establishment of a formal property administration along the lines of the Land Code in the 1880s and 1890s, one that would register land to tent dwellers on the basis of their affiliation with a represented tribe.

In 1879, in the immediate aftermath of imperial bankruptcy and territorial loss, the prominent reformer Midhat Paşa returned to Syria in an attempt to save both the empire and his own career.[35] In January 1879, he submitted a lengthy report to Istanbul with recommendations regarding the administration of Syria.[36] He envisioned rural advance-ment through the instrument of civil administration and went on to propose the implementation of the 1864 Provincial Administration Regulation, which he had helped draft and pilot in the Balkans, as a decisive rupture in the progress of both the province of Syria and the entire empire.

In his report, Midhat Paşa claimed that the uneven pace of admin-istrative reform across the province of Syria had created a distinct gap in the habits of the local people and their social development. He saw a clear difference between the political state and aptitudes (*istida'at*) of the people in the coastal areas, especially Mount Lebanon, which had come under special administration after the conflicts of 1860, and those of the interior subprovinces. These interior subprovinces—Hawran, Jabal Druze, Hama, and Balqa—"remained in a state of disor-der and lack of administration, with impermanent places established by desert-dwelling Bedouin."[37] Midhat Paşa viewed what he described

as the special privileges leaders of Bedouin groups and particular religious communities received as among the most important reasons
for this bifurcation between the coast and the interior. The provincial
administration could not leave these neglected regions as they were:
the imperative to collect more revenue was crucial. The first step
toward a more legible, taxable interior, he argued, consisted of property surveys and more regularized and intrusive taxation practices.[38]
Standardization would transcend uneven development and erase the
history of special exceptions Bedouin and others had come to expect.

Midhat Paşa's report on the province of Syria did not discuss methods for settling Bedouin, although he had direct experience with militarized settlement schemes during his governorship of Iraq in the
early 1870s.[39] He did discuss his views on settlement in an 1879 letter
to the Council of State in response to a proposal of the governor of
Jerusalem to settle forty thousand to fifty thousand Bedouin by creating villages in the Gaza subprovince of southern Palestine.[40] Midhat
Paşa viewed Gaza as "potentially as fertile as Hawran," and he held
the Bedouin population of the region responsible for scattering the
settled inhabitants (*ahali*) and leaving the land unused. But Midhat
Paşa's experience in Iraq had shaken his overall confidence in settlement schemes. He noted that such projects had been in place for two
to three decades but that a high percentage of those who settled returned to tent dwelling quickly. He found what he saw as an insistence
on mobile, tent-dwelling practice confounding, claiming that fear of
conscription and Bedouin's innate love of living in tents were the underlying reasons. He mused that "if someone is born in a tent and for
forty or fifty years lives under a tent breathing the fresh air, he will not
want to leave it for the best-built house or building."[41]

Despite his concerns over entrenched exceptions to standardized
rule, Midhat Paşa proposed a ten-year exemption from conscription
until Bedouin communities were comfortably settled, and he advocated granting them the choice to continue living in tents as long as
they would register and own land, citing situations in Iraq in which
such tent dwellers were "considered settled inhabitants." Midhat Paşa
had reservations about this exception, since it would not produce the

"benefits of civilization and settlement," but he saw a compromise as preferable to tent dwellers remaining entirely outside the Ottoman administrative grid, their landscapes refuges for rebels.

Midhat Paşa's plan for the gradual settlement of tent-dwelling groups was hardly palatable to all high-level Ottoman lawmakers in Syria in the crisis environment of the late 1870s. In October 1878, Kamil Paşa, then governor of Aleppo who had gotten his start in administration in Hawran under Mehmed Raşid Paşa[42] and would serve as Grand Vezir in the 1890s, submitted a proposal to Istanbul to create a province on the eastern side of the Jordan, centered on the ancient Roman capital of Amman.[43] Kamil Paşa insisted that Bedouin leave their tents, arguing that if they refused, they should be pushed deeper into the desert, where hunger and thirst would make them recognize the state's superior power and force them to settle. To speed up this process, he suggested that officials destroy any tents they saw or fire a few shots over them. Kamil Paşa also suggested forcing Bedouin to stop breeding "millions of useless camels" and to switch to smaller livestock.[44] He envisioned settled Bedouin cultivating rice between the Dead Sea and Lake Tiberias so as to end the need for American and Genovese rice imports. Kamil Paşa was also one of the first Ottoman officials to recommend settling immigrants in the southern interior in five-hundred-household communities, claiming there was too much land in tent-dwelling hands for effective use.

Midhat and Kamil Paşas represented two ends of a political spectrum with shared underlying assumptions: the Syrian interior was in need of improvement, and tent-dwelling Bedouin were both the main obstacle and potential solution to that project. The work of a man on the spot in the Balqa, Mehmed Yusuf Bey, illustrates how these assumptions affected the crafting of everyday policy in the interior. In 1877, the governor of Syria issued an order to carry out property surveys across the Balqa subprovince. In preparation, Mehmed Yusuf Bey, a career official in the provincial administration in Damascus,[45] prepared a detailed report including military and civil recommendations, statistics on crime, and a list of prominent "men of property and influence" (*sahib-i emlak ve heysiyet*) across the districts of the subprovince from Nablus to Karak.[46] While he surveyed the entire subprovince in his report, including Nablus and its surrounding villages, he devoted most of his recommendations to the Salt district east of the Jordan River in the interior, which he saw as most in need of development because of the continuing dominance of tent-dwelling populations there. His report shows that Midhat Paşa's perception of a province between a developed coast and an underdeveloped interior, separated by dwelling type, was widespread among modernizing officials in the 1870s.

Mehmed Yusuf Bey began his report with a vision of militarized settlement similar to what Kamil Paşa had proposed: because most of the inhabitants of Balqa subprovince were "rebellious Arab tent dwellers," the towns of Salt and Karak needed sizable military forces to back up Ottoman officials' efforts. He argued for allocating "empty" (hali) lands to cooperative tribes in "appropriate places and according to their desires" and exiling the leaders of noncooperative ones, concurring with Midhat Paşa's assertion that certain populations in Syria had been spoiled by years of concessions. Like Midhat Paşa, Mehmed Yusuf Bey saw Bedouin leaders as benefiting from the various types of titles and offices they had obtained while simultaneously transgressing Ottoman rule, describing the politics of the sphere of submission rather eloquently. He advocated a bureaucratic style of governance that transcended the politics that had sustained men like Dhiyab al-'Adwan, 'Aqil Agha, and Fandi al-Fayiz in preceding decades.

Echoing Mehmed Raşid Paşa's sentiments in the 1860s, Mehmed Yusuf Bey argued that considering the size of the region and its fertility, evidenced by the ancient ruins dotting the landscape, these interior districts should have been some of the most productive in the empire. If the Bedouin of the region could be brought to submission and settled, he argued, these regions would be a prime source of revenue. Mehmed Yusuf Bey's recommendations were extensive. Beyond settling Bedouin on carefully allocated state lands and exiling the troublemakers among them, he also advocated founding a school, a branch of the Ottoman Bank, and a post office in the district of Salt.

Mehmed Yusuf Bey also had recommendations for reforming the judicial system and property administration in particular. He argued that the deputy judge presiding over the sharia court was overstretched and was handling cases that were clearly in the jurisdiction of the civil court system that he was not qualified or legally authorized to settle. He also recommended establishing a unified office that would deal with matters of property and taxation. In a detailed description of the activities of these officials, he articulated the importance of an integrated grid of property administration and taxation:

> The imperial land administration will send its officials to a village, and they will document the following scenarios: plots of land with unclear borders, land that is abandoned [metruk] and empty [hali], and land whose owner has died. They will document transfers of this land to others through sale or inheritance, and identify land that is left to the state and can be sold at auction. These officials will also register the transfer and ensure that the property tax [vergi] information has been updated. . . . When their work is complete, no one will be able to deny the validity of the register or the treasury's tax claims.[47]

This description of the work of an integrated survey office and property administration highlights the two main goals of the entire operation: identifying "empty" land that the treasury could sell at auction—that is, land on which there were no existing claims—and integrating land and tax registers in a comprehensive manner so as to increase their local authority. Mehmed Yusuf Bey articulated the importance of a property grid for the establishment, sustenance, and legitimacy of the state domain. His argument for the future integration of survey and taxation procedures gestures to a more confused present in which many did try to deny the validity of the registers in regions that had undergone survey, complicating the state's claim to be the ultimate arbiter of property right. Like Midhat Paşa, Mehmed Yusuf Bey saw the inclusion of the subprovince in the standardized administration of the well-protected domains as key to the uplift of both its landscape and the people who lived there.

Mehmed Yusuf Bey's description of the population of Balqa subprovince also reflected his sense of a population divided between settled villages and tent-dwelling tribes. For the section of his report on

the Nablus hinterland, Mehmed Yusuf Bey neatly fit the population
into the categories of the Provincial Administration Regulation, listing
the names of prominent men in thirty-seven villages (*karye*) organized
into ten counties (*nahiye*). For the interior district of Salt, however, he
listed the men of property in the town of Salt itself and added a section
on "Balqa tribes" (*Balka aşairi*)|, including estimates of the number of
tents and armed horsemen each tribe included. This list is sketchy,
with round numbers, missing data, and confusion between similar
names. It is, however, one of the earliest attempts to conduct a comprehensive census of the region's human inhabitants, one that included
every community represented as a standardized tribe comparable to
other tribes in a chart. The list included three levels of wealth, with
the major shaykhs of the Bani Sakhr, the Bani Hassan, and the 'Adwan
(Dhiyab al-'Adwan and his son 'Ali) in the first category, followed by
less prominent groups, as well as estimations of the populations and a
report on the tax payments of each group (see table 3.2).

Mehmed Yusuf Bey's report reflects both Ottoman officials' understanding of the Balqa region in the late 1870s and their blueprint for
transforming it. This blueprint responded to a growing sense of crisis
and urgency in the immediate aftermath of bankruptcy and loss of
territory in the Balkans. Where Ahmed Cevdet Paşa had articulated a
vague and sweeping vision of green space in the Jazira region in 1866,
by 1879 Midhat Paşa and Mehmed Yusuf Bey were advocating for roads,
post offices, and shaykhs-turned-bureaucrats in landscapes ranging
from Gaza to Balqa. Mehmed Raşid Paşa's invocation of lost Roman
glory to evidence the region's productive potential in 1867 became
standard in reports on the interior during this period, strongly evoking
a simultaneous French discourse of a Roman golden age and potential improvement in Algeria.[48] As Mehmed Yusuf Bey argued, the first
step toward realizing these goals would be gridding the interior, creating the birds-eye view of property relations necessary for prosperity
under the central Ottoman state's firm guidance.

TABLE 3.2. Tribes (aşiretler) in the Salt district of Balqa subprovince

Name	Number of tents	Population	Number of horsemen	Number of weapons	Tax comments
Bani Hassan	500	6,000–7,000	300	1,000	Paid tithe and sheep tax, not military
'Ajarma	300	1,500	50–60	700	Paid tithe and sheep tax, not military
Da'ja	200	–	30	100	Paid tithe and sheep tax, not military
Abu al-Ghanam	700	–	150	500	Paid tithe and sheep tax, not military
'Abbad	700–800	4,000	–	–	Paid tithe and sheep tax, not military
Mashalkha	100	–	–	–	Paid tithe and sheep tax, not military
Saqqar	200	–	–	–	Paid tithe and sheep tax, not military
Ghazzawiya	100	–	–	–	Paid tithe and sheep tax, not military
'Adwan	350	–	120	300	Paid tithe and sheep tax, not military
Bani Sakhr	700–800	–	400	1,000–1,500	Paid sheep and camel taxes
Hanahna	50	–	5–10	30–40	Paid sheep and camel taxes
Masa'id	50	–	–	–	Paid tithe and sheep taxes
Salit and Hajaya	300	–	–	–	none
'Arab al-Hawarith*	30	–	–	–	–
Jaramna*	15	–	–	–	–
Jarnid*	15	–	–	–	–[†]
Bani Hamida	300	–	–	–	none[†]

Source: BOA.Y.PRK.UM 2/7, 2 N 1296/20 August 1879, pp. 5–6.

*These names are impossible to verify in the original table.

[†]The original table includes a note explaining that the Bani Hamida did not pay any taxes because they had not submitted to Ottoman authority. They were in a state of "unsubmission" or disobedience (adem-i itaatta dahi bulunduklar).

IMPLEMENTING THE OTTOMAN AGRARIAN IMAGINARY

Land registration according to the dictates of the Land Code and the Title Regulation began in Salt district in 1879, soon after the reports of Kamil Paşa, Midhat Paşa, and Mehmed Yusuf Bey, as part of a comprehensive effort to survey the cultivated regions of Syria.[49] These registrations institutionalized the Land Code's assertion that officials of the Ottoman land administration, not local elites or *hujja*-issuing sharia court judges, had the power to distribute rights to agricultural land. In the decade after these initial registrations, the title deeds they produced, as well as a new reliance on community leaders with the state-guaranteed power to administer property relations, became more common, first in sharia court–based transactions and later in a new office of the property administration. Through these novel processes of regulating property relations, the tribe—as an administrative entity with an elected headman as its state-sanctioned representative (*muhtar/mukhtār*)—took on new meaning in the interior in the 1880s and 1890s. To examine these processes, I return to the story of Dawjan al-Wiraykat and his agnates, who rose to prominence among the ʿAdwan through the intertwined processes of state-controlled property administration, the institutionalization of the tribe, and the office of the headman.[50]

Dawjan al-Wiraykat and his brother Hamad, Rufayf al-Wiraykat's father, received their first Ottoman titles to land in the 1879 registration. An official of the land administration in Nablus, accompanied by a commission, recorded 513 individual registrations among 332 men from the ʿAdwan and ʿAbbad tribes (described in the register as the "ʿAdwan aşireti" and the "ʿAbbad aşireti"). The process began in October 1879, two months after Mehmed Yusuf Bey issued his report on the Balqa's population and recommendations for improvement. Dawjan and Hamad's registrations were typical: they each registered two hundred donums of land, Dawjan in Marj Lahim and Hamad in neighboring Wasiya. Both plots were in the vicinity of Abu Nusayr, south of the town of Salt. Hamad's son Ghishan also registered land.[51] The registrations reflected existing patterns of political influence and wealth among ʿAdwani men in the 1870s: the only individual who reg-istered large plots of land, ten times as much in total as Dawjan and Hamad, was Dhiyab al-ʿAdwan's son ʿAli, who was receiving a regular salary from the provincial government by 1879.[52] Among all registra-tions completed in October 1879, the average plot size was 251 donums. Ninety plots of land were registered among more than one individual, with two one-thousand-donum plots divided among eight men.[53]

These initial registrations codified existing patterns of land use and control that had already enabled land sales to capitalist investors in and out of sharia courts in the preceding decades. Unlike those private and court-sanctioned contracts, however, registration according to the 1859 Tapu Regulation provided a grid, a mappable list that claimed to comprehensively collate all the claims in these particular communi-ties. In contrast to the sharia court system and existing understand-ings between merchant capitalists and tent dwellers managing land and agricultural production in the interior, these land registrations did not construct Bedouin as the historic holders of usufruct right to the land they registered. The Land Code stated that local inhabitants could receive title to land for which they held existing usufruct right by showing they had cultivated the land and paid taxes for ten years. This was the stipulation for "prescriptive right" (hakk-ı karar), which also exempted those who could prove long-standing and uncontested use, possession, and tax payments from paying the treasury the market price (bedel-i misil) of the land in exchange for title.[54]

Mehmed Yusuf Bey's census, completed two months before the Balqa registrations began, stated that many tent-dwelling groups, including the ʿAdwan, had been paying tithes on their agricultural produce in Balqa subprovince. But just as Mehmed Raşid Paşa had ignored ʿAdwani wheat production in his categorical descriptions of the interior population as "wandering Bedouin" in 1867, Ottoman law-makers did not regard Bedouin communities' part-time farming as a foundation for prescriptive rights to land. Rather, Dawjan, Hamad, and other would-be titleholders listed as members of the ʿAbbad and ʿAdwan tribes were granted rights to land at the pleasure of the state, not as legal usufruct holders like their village-dwelling counterparts.

The land registrations among tribes in Salt district relied on the legal force of an 1877 provincial order that granted land administrators the power to waive the normally assessed tax on the land's value (harc-ı mu'tad). Hamad and Dawjan al-Wiraykat did not present written evidence or witness testimony to show that they were cultivating the land they registered or that they had paid tithes on their produce in accordance with the Land Code's requirement for prescriptive right. Rather, they registered their land and received title on the force of a provincial decree.

In general, the 1879 registrations followed the politics of administration that Midhat Paşa had advocated during his short tenure as governor of Syria: tent dwellers would acquire title to land without being required to settle in permanent homes or take up full-time agriculture. Their newfound, title-based attachment to land would encourage them to give up migration without the use of military force.[55] The reports of Midhat Paşa, Kamil Paşa, and Mehmed Yusuf Bey on the Syrian interior in the late 1870s, all of which urged the settlement of tent dwellers, were not particularly specific regarding where they should settle. Midhat Paşa, in reference to the landscape he confronted in Gaza and his efforts in Iraq, discussed "appropriate places" (münasib yerleri), while Mehmed Yusuf Bey envisioned them settling "in empty spaces as they liked" (diledikleri mahall-i halilerde).[56] Kamil Paşa, who was more focused on destroying tents and disposing of camels, did not address the problem at all. Their proposals were in line with the Land Code: while village dwellers were to register lands they had cultivated previously with prescriptive right, tent dwellers, who according to the bifurcated vision of the rural economy did not cultivate, were to be granted "appropriate" land at the pleasure of the state, similar to land grants to refugees. Modernist Ottoman lawmakers did not conceptualize Bedouin land rights in terms of their historic use of or connection to the land for grazing and part-time farming.

Why did Dawjan and Hamad al-Wiraykat take part in the Ottoman land registrations that began in 1879, especially one that implicitly denied their historic land rights? This is an important question to consider, not least because historians have consistently argued, with very little evidence, that peasants and pastoralists resisted land registration in Syria and Iraq because of fears of taxation and conscription.[57] While Dawjan and Hamad al-Wiraykat did not leave narrative explanations for their actions, it is possible to trace what they did with their title deeds to lands near Abu Nusayr after they received them, if perhaps only partially. The sharia court remained the main state-sanctioned venue for property transactions throughout the 1880s, before the establishment of a permanent branch of the property administration in Salt.[58] During this period, Dawjan, Hamad, and other smallholders used the title deeds they obtained in the 1879 registration as one way among many to claim control or ownership over land in order to sell it for cash or use it as collateral to obtain credit. In short, the title deeds became a new way to convert control over land into value.

The sharia court records show that Dawjan and Hamad were able to profit both materially and politically from their legal ownership of land in the Balqa in the 1880s and that their sons Minakid and Rufayf expanded their wealth after they died. Both Dawjan and Hamad were heavily involved in managing wheat production. Eight years after the initial land registrations in Salt, in 1887, Dawjan al-Wiraykat used the land he had registered as collateral against a forward-purchase contract of wheat with two prominent Salt-based merchants, Raghib Shamut and Dawud Mihyar. The merchants provided cash, and Dawjan pledged to have wheat from his fields delivered to them after threshing at the end of the growing season. Attached to Dawjan's contract was a mortgage agreement: if Dawjan did not provide the promised wheat, the merchants would gain control of two pieces of agricultural land that he claimed he farmed and had usufruct rights over.[59] One of these pieces of land was listed in Dawjan's name in the 1879 land registration; the other was not.[60] A year later, Dawjan completed another mortgage of the same land to the same urban merchants. This time, rather than registering a forward-purchase contract, Dawjan sold usufruct rights over rain-fed land that he had inherited from his father to Shamut and Mihyar temporarily for a period of seven months, at the end of which he was obligated to repay the loan.[61]

One motivation to acquire land titles may have come from new-comer but locally based merchant capitalists like Shamut and Mihyar, who dominated the town councils and sharia courts that produced most of the region's state-sanctioned documentary evidence of prop-erty right. Dawjan and Hamad al-Wiraykat and their sons after them moved surplus wheat, barley, and clarified butter to these merchants through credit arrangements similar to ones used in the long-standing relationships between merchants in Nablus and peasants in the vil-lages surrounding the city.[62] Like these earlier credit relationships, merchants like Mihyar and Shamut may have been using landed col-lateral to tie commodity agents like Dawjan al-Wiraykat more closely to their own accounts in what had become a competitive credit market in the interior. In other words, the mortgage market may have been aimed more at the control over surplus than the control over land or other kinds of property. A number of scholars have argued that even though the Land Code created clear legal paths to mortgage and fore-closure, merchant capitalists were reluctant to face the social upheaval that dispossession would have entailed and were eager to maintain existing relations of production.[63] This conclusion depends ultimately on a fuller sense of property relations across the Eastern Mediterra-nean in the late Ottoman period. As we will see in chapter 4, the Land Code's creation of conditions for the dispossession of those deemed unproductive would become most clear in the form of settlement and projected settlement of both Jewish and Muslim Circassian refugees.

Even if foreclosure remained relatively rare, Ottoman authorities regarded the extensive lending activities of Shamut, Mihyar, and other newcomer capitalists to the region with suspicion. Mehmed Yusuf Bey had warned in 1879 specifically against the spread of what he described as highly usurious lending in the Balqa, recommending the establish-ment of a branch of the Ottoman Bank in Salt to provide an alternative credit source for cultivators.[64] Indeed, Dawjan al-Wiraykat's successive mortgages to Dawud Mihyar and Raghib Shamut in the 1880s could have signaled that he was entering a cycle of debt and likely to lose his landed property. This was probably the outcome for some tent dwell-ers. Sharia court records preserve both records of tent dwellers acting

as wage-earning laborers and probate inventories of capitalist estates with small, geographically scattered plots presumably acquired
through foreclosure.[65]

The trajectory of the Wiraykats seems to have been different,
however. Dawjan and Hamad's sons were able to use their increasing
access to credit to accumulate capital of their own, eventually becoming small-time creditors. It is not clear when exactly Dawjan died, but
in the 1890s and early 1900s his son Minakid became one of the wealthiest men in the Wiraykat community. Minakid Dawjan al-Wiraykat was
one of the few men from the district of Salt described as a producer
of commodities, whether tent- or village-dwelling, who managed to
become a creditor at the close of the nineteenth century. Beyond lending to his relatives to cover their tax burdens, Minakid also became a
creditor in the commercial realm in the early twentieth century, lending wheat and cash to other members of the Wiraykat through the
same legal mechanism, the forward-purchase (salam) contract, that
his father began borrowing with in the 1880s.[66]

Alongside their moneylending activities, Dawjan al-Wiraykat's sons
maintained their roles as producers, or managers of commodity production, in the local markets for wheat, barley, and clarified butter.[67]
They also increased their landholdings in the vicinity of Abu Nusayr.
In 1904, four of Dawjan's sons registered land with the land administration established in 1891 in Salt.[68] Hamad's four sons also appear
in the surviving records performing similar registrations.[69] In 1912,
Minakid's brother Sulayman cashed in on some of their land, selling
to a local villager and a resident of Salt for close to eighteen thousand
piastres.[70] In the absence of a surviving probate inventory for any
Wiraykats, it is impossible to know how significant these lands were
to the family's assets, but the sums they gained through selling of land
were significant for the period.

Holding land with title deeds in the terms of the 1858 Land Code
was one way among many that Dawjan and Hamad al-Wiraykat, and
their sons after them, transformed their preexisting influence in the
environs of Abu Nusayr into wealth in the new and rapidly changing
institutional and political context of Ottoman state space in the Syrian

interior. Taking part in the grid-making property registrations of the late 1870s and early 1880s, they used their title deeds to collateralize and sell land in their control. In the 1890s, modes of land administration in the interior shifted again, and Dawjan and Hamad's children were able to take on new roles in the Ottoman provincial bureaucracy that enabled them to maintain control over land as a site of wage labor, a source of commodities, and, increasingly, a carrier of wealth. These new roles entailed performances of state power that enhanced their social as well as material capital, acquired and maintained through the increasingly standard category of the "tribe."

LAND, HEADMEN, AND TRIBES

The Wiraykat family's rising commercial influence was surely related to their control of fertile land in the Abu Nusayr region and their ability to manage wheat production and sale. But it was also entangled with their position as officially sanctioned leaders within the Wiraykat community. Minakid and Rufayf al-Wiraykat were part of a new group of midlevel rural leaders distinct from the high-level shaykhs of the preceding period like Dhiyab al-ʿAdwan. This new group of men took on the lowest position in the bureaucratic hierarchy laid out in the Ottoman vision of provincial administration expressed in codified law in the 1860s and 1870s: that of the headman. Therefore, it was not only merchant capitalists who managed to take advantage of their positions in new governing bodies to gain social influence and material wealth. The uneven process of surveying the interior Balqa region also precipitated the rise of a group of Bedouin bureaucrats who derived power and influence chiefly through their close connections to the expanding Ottoman bureaucracy. The trajectory of the Wiraykat family, the sons of Dawjan and Hamad al-Wiraykat, illustrate the dynamics of this new group of Bedouin bureaucrats. Their ability to use commercial connections with merchant capitalists to accumulate wealth was closely connected to their roles in the process of making Ottoman state space.

The role of the headman became prominent in the process of codifying patterns of land distribution in the mid-1880s. The property transactions preserved in the sharia court's *hujja*s provide the earliest evidence of the election of headmen among local communities in Salt and the importance of this office to the process of determining property rights. In sharia court transactions from the early 1880s, people evidenced their legal right to sell rights to agricultural (*miri*) land by stating that they had been in uncontested control of the land "since time immemorial," that they had inherited their land rights, or that they had bought them either in or out of court. As I have noted, for the sharia court, these statements in conjunction with witnesses verifying the honesty and integrity of the person claiming control of the land were sufficient to complete a sale, and the witnesses could be any upstanding members of the district community.[71] In the mid-1880s, however, sellers began referencing certificates ('*ilm wa khabr*) signed by the headmen (*mukhtār*) of their communities (villages, town quarters, and tribes) to support these claims and record land sales and mortgages.[72] In the sharia court, such written evidence was not necessary or sufficient, although it may have reduced the price of credit.

In contrast to sharia court practice in sanctioning land transactions, when a regular branch of the imperial land administration (*defter-i hakkani*) was established in Salt in the early 1890s, individuals were required to present official certificates from their community headmen to establish prescriptive right (*hakk-ı karar*) to the land in question. The land administration office followed the dictates of the 1859 Title Regulation as well as the Provincial Administration Regulation, both of which elevated the office of the headman, quite closely. The 1859 Title Regulation mandated that certificates from headmen attesting to an individual's uncontested control over land for at least ten years were the standard requirement for establishing prescriptive right to land. Based on their undisputed cultivation of the land for ten years, individuals were entitled to a title deed after payment of taxes and fees, not the land's market price. Legally, headmen had the responsibility to acknowledge an individual's land rights that were generated by historic use.[73] If this acknowledgment was missing, the individual would have to buy the land from the treasury for full market price in order to obtain a title deed. The headman's role in legally determining rights to property, as well as obligations to the treasury, was therefore central.

While the initial 1879 land registration did not recognize Bedouin potential to show prescriptive right, once a regular property adminis-tration was established in Salt in the early 1890s, Bedouin individuals could register land with prescriptive right. But like village and town dwellers, they needed the approval of the designated headmen of their administratively defined communities to sign off on the transaction. When Dawjan al-Wiraykat's sons registered lands in Abu Nusayr in 1904, they proved their prescriptive right through showing certificates from the headman of the Wiraykat tribe and approval from the Salt ad-ministrative council.[74] As the case of Minakid and Rufayf al-Wiraykat that opened this chapter shows, headmen were also the "access points" of the Ottoman treasury, represented by the town-dwelling Habib Effendi, to the agricultural surplus of encampments. That case, in which Minakid and Rufayf demanded repayment of loans they had contracted with their relatives at tax time, exposed the tensions the institution of the tax-collector-headman created. Rufayf al-Wiraykat's relatives returned to court a week later, claiming that Rufayf had never delivered their payment to the tax collector, so they did not owe him anything.[75] Rufayf's defense revealed rifts among the Wiraykats: he said he had a long-standing quarrel with his cousins, to the point that he had left the Wiraykat encampment to stay with his more distant relatives, the Nimrs.[76]

Beyond their central roles in processes of property administration, headmen like Rufayf al-Wiraykat in Salt were also mainstays at the sharia court, providing testimony, verifying witnesses, and perform-ing many of the same services otherwise controlled by the merchant investor community discussed above.[77] By the mid-1880s, headmen were well established as the main points of contact between tent-dwelling communities and the mushrooming Ottoman administration in Salt. These headmen took on foundational roles in the developing property administration by certifying the control of their constituents over land as a legal foundation for both sale and mortgage in the terms of the 1858 Land Code.

Midhat Paşa's politics of administration advocated for treating tent dwellers "like the rest of the settled inhabitants" even if they did not move into permanent houses and take up full-time agriculture. These policies provided part of the context for the contested rise of a group of Bedouin headmen who played crucial roles in everyday processes of allocating land rights, distributing tax burdens, and ensuring rural security among tent-dwelling communities. While Bedouin headmen did not have seats on the town-based governing councils dominated by merchant capitalists, their work was crucial to the daily performance of Ottoman power in communities residing in encampments and villages across the Syrian interior in the final decades of Ottoman rule.

The other important element of the late Ottoman administrative context was Mehmed Yusuf Bey's categorization of the interior as a juridical town (Salt) surrounded by juridical tribes. The election of headmen like Minakid and Rufayf as the access points for tent-dwelling encampments cemented the "tribe" ('ashīra/aşiret) alongside the village as a foundational category of rural administration in the Syrian interior, while fundamentally changing the political structure within tent-dwelling communities themselves. In Salt, the defining of tribes as administrative units for which headmen were elected meant that leaders of communities who camped seasonally or year-round within the district, and not only "paramount shaykhs" like Dhiyab al-'Adwan, were granted these important powers with regard to the daily performance of Ottoman power. Because of the lack of Ottoman census figures at the level of detail necessary for the period, it is difficult to make this argument quantitatively, but based on Mehmed Yusuf Bey's 1879 figures and later counts, headmen were elected or appointed for tribes of five hundred to one thousand tent-dwelling people.

Headmen were the key players in tent-dwelling groups in terms of everyday Ottoman administration beginning in the 1880s. In his review of Transjordan's social and economic history, Tariq Tell argues that a "local administrative elite" emerged from "the tribal aristocracy and the larger merchant landowners" in the Balqa region in the Hamidian period.[78] This notion of the Ottoman bureaucratization of a "tribal aristocracy," and their simultaneous transformation into large landowners in the wake of the 1858 Land Code, is not confined to the southern Syrian interior.[79] As in other areas of the empire, many of the elites whose families established their influence in the eighteenth and first half of the nineteenth century prospered.[80] Dhiyab al-Humud's son 'Ali retained his Ottoman salary, registered a large amount of land in his own name, and obtained an Ottoman title, and the descendants of Fandi al-Fayiz of the Bani Sakhr created expansive plantation farms and became directors of the subdistrict of Jiza, south of the Balqa, some attaining the title of paşa.[81]

The outcome of direct Ottoman administration in communities like the 'Adwan was much more complex and multilayered, however. It was not only the "tribal aristocracy," such as Dhiyab al-'Adwan and his sons, who gained administrative positions and land through involvement in the emerging modern bureaucracy. The Hamidian reforms also created the administrative framework for the rise of a group of lower-level tent-dwelling leaders like Minakid and Rufayf al-Wiraykat, who registered smaller amounts of land and became Ottoman headmen. For groups like the 'Adwan and 'Abbad, middling headmen would become much more important for completing the administrative requirements of participation in commerce and governance in the Balqa region as the Hamidian period progressed. For the 'Abbad and other groups who had not enjoyed good relations with the Ottoman authorities or pilgrimage-related posts prior to the 1870s, the expansion of the bureaucracy entailed in making state space signaled their first entry into Ottoman administrative positions. During an interview in the late 1980s with anthropologist Andrew Shryock, an elderly man from the 'Abbad Duwaykat community expressed the importance of this shift in Ottoman relations with Bedouin in the Salt district. Duwaykat described how previously there were only a few shaykhs, but after the time of his father in the early twentieth century, "every clan had its own *mukhtar*. . . . Nowadays everyone is a shaykh. Now, there is a shaykh in every house. Before, there was only one, two or three."[82]

Existing historiography has portrayed the establishment of modern Ottoman administration in the Balqa as detrimental to the livelihoods of tent-dwelling Bedouin. By the mid-1880s, Bedouin were no longer involved in the governing councils controlled by bureaucrats introduced above, who were largely merchant financiers. But men like Rufayf Wiraykat gained significant power within their communities by registering land, negotiating tax burdens, and participating in key roles in court. Furthermore, Minakid Dawjan's activities as a creditor show that the Wiraykats were able to profit materially from their positions in the new Ottoman administrative apparatus, becoming, along with other families of *mukhtars*, a "middling group" with close ties to sites of production: encampments, fields, and grazing grounds. In the Ottoman bureaucracy, headmen were the street-level bureaucrats who performed the Ottoman state in everyday life.[83]

TROUBLE ON THE HORIZON:
VIOLENCE AND "EMPTY LAND" IN THE 1880s

Readings of the records of the sharia court and land registers in the interior produce a fairly linear narrative of the formation of state space along the lines that Midhat Paşa and Mehmed Yusuf Bey envisioned. These archives demonstrate that lawmakers integrated the region's landscape and population into the categories of codified law with increasing detail, adding particular categories like the "tribe." But petitions to various government agencies in Istanbul tell a more complex story about the contestations this process of bureaucratic expansion and attempts at standardization engendered at their outset. While codified imperial regulations provided a language for engagement between encampments and the various arms of the extending administration, the outcomes of Ottoman attempts to create state space in the interior remained fundamentally precarious and unpredictable.

First, while particular 'Adwan and 'Abbad leaders gained political capital from their connections to the Ottoman regime, other tent-dwelling Bedouin groups completely rejected the imposition of Ottoman administrative sovereignty. Some groups, like the Bani Hamida, whose *dira* lay south of 'Adwan country toward Karak, did not take part in the 1879 land registration at all. In the late 1880s, a provincial commission attempted to survey the wealth of the Bani Hamida tent-dwelling community between Salt and Karak. Bani Hamida leaders rejected the survey, refused to pay livestock and property taxes, and eventually led an armed confrontation against the Ottoman gendarmes.[84]

After the confrontation, a group of headmen from the district of Salt sent a telegram to the Ottoman Grand Vezir in support of the provincial commission's work. They cited the large size of the Bani Hamida community (seven hundred tents), and stated that they owned seven villages (khirba) and wide swaths of land.[85] The telegram asserted that the Bani Hamida had been rejecting tax payments for a long time and that their lands had become a refuge for criminals from surrounding regions. Signed by nineteen headmen and three shaykhs of ʿAdwani and ʿAbbadi communities, as well as town-dwelling Saltis, the telegram congratulated the Ottoman administration for "bringing the Bani Hamida into submission"[86] by forcing them to pay two thousand Turkish liras in taxes for their animals.[87] The telegram claimed that the Bani Hamida had often attacked the peaceful, taxpaying communities to their north in and around Salt, and that many families had left their homes because of Bani Hamida aggression. Now, these families were able to return to "their original homelands" (awṭānihim al-aṣlīya). The headmen used the language of the sphere of submission, drawing a clear red line between their own taxpaying, upstanding communities of Ottomans and the Bani Hamida community of "bandits" (ashqīya).

On a broad level, the confrontation with the Bani Hamida and their absence from the processes of making state space also shows the indispensability of headmen as "access points" during this initial period of surveying the interior.[88] The inability of Ottoman officials to forge alliances with leaders of the Bani Hamida and other communities meant that the comprehensive state-space-making project remained fundamentally incomplete. The headmen's letter implies that creating strong alliances with the ʿAbbad and ʿAdwan in the interior through promoting their middling leaders as headmen may have precluded the regime's ability to access the Bani Hamida from the start, rendering the project of making state space both incomplete and embedded in local politics from its inception.

Indeed, the telegram shows the ways in which 'Adwani, 'Abbadi, and Salti men holding the office of headman claimed stakes in the district-level politics of surveying and taxing property holdings in the early Hamidian period and made the contested and sometimes-violent process of making state space their own. In the 1890s and early 1900s, 'Adwani and 'Abbadi headmen would continue to bring the social struggles of the interior into bureaucratic circles, most notably in terms of conflict over land. These conflicts emphasized the tensions between the entry of some Bedouin groups into the Ottoman bureaucracy, on the one hand, and Ottoman officials' ability to deny Bedouin land rights based on the Land Code's privileging of continuous cultivation, on the other.

This fundamental tension in Ottoman policy was apparent from the inception of the process of surveying interior land in the 1880s. The earliest land registrations in the interior part of the Balqa subprovince included two villages of Christian farmers, Rumaymin in 1879 and Fuhays in 1881, who settled year-round on land they had been cultivating seasonally from Salt. They registered the land with prescriptive right. In 1880, however, when a community of Christian settlers supported by the Latin Patriarchate, as well as the French and British consuls in Jerusalem, moved to the region of Madaba south of Salt from Karak, Midhat Paşa used the Land Code to dismiss the claims of Sattam al-Fayiz of the Bani Sakhr, Fandi al-Fayiz's son, on grounds that he had not registered the land, cultivated it, or paid his taxes.[89] This was an early example of the way the Land Code, which privileged full-time cultivation, could be used to deny prescriptive right to people using land for grazing or other purposes, especially when settlers with foreign support wanted to register the same land.

Midhat Paşa's correspondence from this period shows that he saw a conflict with the Bani Sakhr as the lesser of two evils; so insistent were the British and French consuls in Jerusalem about the urgency of granting Karaki Christians land in Madaba that he was afraid his failure to do so would invite foreign intervention.[90] The conflict over Madaba presaged dynamics to come—a sense of land scarcity and the transformation of the Syrian interior into a contested interimperial borderland especially after the British occupation of Egypt.

Once again, Midhat Paşa's ruling was not the end of the story: Bani Sakhr communities would violently contest Christian settlers' rights to the land around Madaba throughout the Ottoman period, especially during summer months when they crossed into the arable plains from the lands beyond the pilgrimage route.

These conflicts over land settlement and allocations anticipated struggles over land allocations to refugees that were already becoming clear in other parts of the empire.[91] The first groups of Circassian refugees displaced for the second time from Bulgaria, Serbia, and Romania arrived in ʿAdwan country in 1878 and 1880, but they did not make a lasting impression on local officials. Mehmed Yusuf Bey did not include them in his census, and foreign observers doubted that their settlement in Amman would survive.[92] In the decades to follow, however, land grants to refugees would become a major point of contention between Bedouin bureaucrats and Ottoman officials, complicating the roles of these men as "access points" and street-level bureaucrats in their tent-dwelling communities.

In February 1913, after Minakid al-Wiraykat's death, his children and siblings visited the property administration office in Salt to confirm their inherited rights to four pieces of land and a garden.[93] The entry in the property register is a prime example of the way various governing entities in Salt worked together to determine property right. Minakid's heirs first had to present a document certifying his death and their rights as inheritors issued by the sharia court. They also had to present a document from the headman of their tribe (whose name is not provided in the records), certifying that Minakid had indeed held usufruct rights over the land in question. The property administration office performed an on-site investigation and adjusted the borders listed on the title deeds, and this entire procedure was approved in two separate decisions of the administrative council in Salt. Finally, the parts of the land Minakid himself owned were split between his three sons and three daughters, and new deeds reflecting the change in borders were drawn up for his offspring showing the land that remained in their control.

In some cases, the land the Wiraykats registered around Abu Nusayr stayed in the family into the twenty-first century. The ability of the Wiraykats to maintain control over land was closely related to the social and material capital of men like Rufayf and Minakid, who were intimately involved with Ottoman administration in the region. Even though Ottoman lawmakers across the political spectrum favored the settlement of tent dwellers in permanent houses as the foundation of their vision of an orderly and productive countryside, the politics of administration of the 1880s allowed for the entry of headmen from sections of tent-dwelling tribes into the bureaucracy. Neither Minakid nor Rufayf al-Wiraykat reported to an administrative office, and we do not know the extent of their literacy. They did not conform to an understanding of bureaucracy that rests on salaries and appointments; however, while maintaining control over land, they established and performed Ottoman power on a daily, consistent basis in Bedouin encampments throughout the region: collecting taxes, relaying information, and, perhaps most important, sanctioning landownership. More broadly, Minakid and Rufayf al-Wiraykat's position was distinct from that of previous intermediaries like Dhiyab al-'Adwan because they performed the Ottoman state at its lowest and most mundane levels precisely at the moment when that state began to claim its distance from social life through standardized, codified law. Like other subordinate officials of the late nineteenth and early twentieth centuries, prominent Wiraykat men straddled a line between state and society that was increasingly conceptually delineated in law but required constant maintenance and reproduction in practice.[94]

Wiraykat bureaucrats' work both maintained control over land and performed Ottoman state power through a unique set of administrative categories for governing the Balqa region that would endure beyond the Ottoman period. By making territorial state space in the form of the Salt district, the tribe became a "collective identity . . . in relation to a larger national whole."[95] This category served to render all of the interior's human inhabitants living within increasingly important Ottoman borders legible in a modular, standardized, and

countable form with particular attributes. It also marked an imperative shared among imperial lawmakers on a global scale to transform
populations deemed underproductive into loyal, cultivating, and taxpaying potential citizens of cohesive national-imperial polities. This
shared imperative reflected the global political economy inhabited by
the Ottoman, American, and Russian empires in the 1870s and 1880s:
an environment of financial crisis, loss of optimism in global grain
markets, and growing interimperial competition.[96]

In this vein of interimperial competition, it is crucial to recognize
the extent to which the establishment of an imperial property administration along the lines of the 1858 Land Code and 1859 Tapu Regulation
was connected to concerns about imperial sovereignty.[97] This was especially true in the Syrian interior, where the process of building a property administration occurred largely in the 1870s, in the aftermath of
territorial losses to the Russian Empire, and the 1880s, when the British
occupation of Egypt was a proximate threat to Ottoman territorial sovereignty. This concern with sovereignty is visible in the sharia court's
identification of the nationality of every property owner, which was
especially important when it came to land increasingly conceived as
territory. It was also important, however, for the imperative to move
transactions in agricultural land out of sharia courts and into a property administration that would allow state officials to monitor landownership on the more comprehensive scale that registers allowed.

The Ottoman move to integrate the Syrian interior into what officials saw as a more developed coastal administration built on the long
history of social and economic ties between these regions and Bedouin
communities' participation, especially in the administration of the pilgrimage. As this and previous chapters have detailed, this history included a widely shared set of legal instruments that structured capital
expansion in the interior prior to direct Ottoman administration. This
shared history enabled the extension of Ottoman state space because
the legal forms on which it built were already quite familiar in the interior. Ottoman officials and Bedouin bureaucrats worked from shared,
if contested, Islamic legal traditions for governing property relations.

As we will see in chapter 4, Bedouin bureaucrats' inclusion in Ottoman administrative bodies would become important when remaining tensions inherent in codified Ottoman attitudes toward legal nomads became more difficult to sustain in the 1890s and 1900s. In these decades, pressure to identify "empty land" to create land grants for Muslim refugees, to sell land to speculating capitalists, and to support state development projects increased. These tensions complicated the positions of Bedouin bureaucrats as the access points of an aggressive and intrusive Ottoman administration. Their efforts to defend and maintain their communities' rights to traverse, pasture, and cultivate the interior landscape would continue to affect the shape of Ottoman state space in the early twentieth century.

4 BUREAUCRACY IN CRISIS

EARLY ON A FRIDAY MORNING in May 1907, Nahar al-Bakhit, head-man of the Manasir ʿAbbad *aşiret*, left his camp in Marj Sikka, east of the town of Salt. He headed west, toward the village of Ayn Suwaylih. Chechen refugees had established Ayn Suwaylih the year before on land granted by the Ottoman property administration.[1] On a hill over-looking the village, he found the encampment where a large meeting was set to take place. The encampment was bustling with men from all over the Salt district. Nahar al-Bakhit greeted his colleagues from other ʿAbbadi communities, as well as the leaders of the ʿAdwan and the Bani Hassan, whose *dira* was north of Salt. A few townsmen from Salt and villagers from Fuhays were also at the meeting. Most of the men were armed, some with Martini rifles smuggled from British-occupied Egypt.[2] Nahar al-Bakhit had recently obtained one of these rifles, and he checked it frequently as he greeted his colleagues.

Even for Nahar al-Bakhit, who often worked with other communities in Salt district in his official Ottoman capacity as headman of the Manasir, this meeting was extraordinary. The ʿAbbad, ʿAdwan, and Salti townspeople often quarreled over the district's resources, espe-cially its land. But on that Friday morning they had a common enemy.

The meeting had been called because of a fight between Bedouin and Chechen refugees that had left a Bedouin man seriously wounded. The fight was over rights to use land: the Chechens had stopped the Bedouin, who were trying to graze their sheep on land near Ayn Suwaylih that the Chechens had planted with wheat. On hearing of the quarrel, the leaders of the local Bedouin groups had decided to meet to discuss the issue of refugees claiming control over land they regarded as theirs.

Later that Friday afternoon, more than two thousand Bedouin and townsmen from Salt descended on the Chechen refugee village of Ayn Suwaylih and began shooting into windows and doors.[3] According to the report of the Ottoman county governor, Cemal Bey, the "wretched" (*biçargan*) refugees were "slaughtered like sheep" (*koyun gibi boğazlarak*) with eleven refugees killed and fifteen seriously wounded. But the Chechens were also armed and fought back, inflicting similar casualties on the Salti side. The battle lasted until after dark. The Chechens were victims of a major theft: the entire contents of twenty-eight houses were reportedly stolen, as well as all the village's livestock.[4]

The violence that Bedouin groups, led by headmen, initiated in Ayn Suwaylih was a direct response to past and potential dispossession. The mounting conflicts over land in the Syrian interior that the 1907 attack and its aftermath exemplify point to a crisis in the Ottoman process of making state space in the early twentieth century. This crisis was closely related to the regime's far-reaching attempts to overhaul registration and taxation of land and people that began in the 1860s and accelerated after the fiscal and territorial losses of the 1870s. As envisioned in imperial legislation, by the 1890s, registration and taxation of Balqa resources relied heavily on rural headmen like Nahar al-Bakhit. Like other headmen and low-level Bedouin officials, Nahar al-Bakhit benefited from his connections to the Ottoman administration, gaining social connections both in his community and among Ottoman officials through his daily activities as a bureaucrat—collecting taxes, verifying land transactions, and serving as a witness in court. But al-Bakhit also became the official representative of a community suffering from an Ottoman land policy that increasingly viewed land controlled by Bedouin as "empty" and available for reallocation to refugees, like the ones in Ayn Suwaylih in the 1890s. This chapter relates how headmen like Nahar al-Bakhit shifted from organizing Ottoman tax collection to organizing resistance against Ottoman land policy in the final years of Hamidian rule.

The threat of dispossession that refugee resettlement represented politicized property relations in the Syrian interior in a way that initial processes of land registration had not. The Land Code and its amendments strengthening the rights of creditors to foreclose on individually owned property intensified existing debt relationships between merchant capitalists and Bedouin communities, but numerous scholars have recognized the limited nature of foreclosures during this period across Greater Syria.[5] For example, Mundy and Smith argued that "Ottoman administration did not detach the object, 'land,' to which individual rights were registered, from the social forms of its mobilization in production" and that the "Ottoman empire did not bow down to the holy grail of private property until the very end of the century."[6]

How, and on what terms, did the relations of individual property established in the Land Code become linked with enclosure and dispossession in the late Ottoman Syrian interior?[7] In this chapter I argue that this linkage coalesced when Ottoman officials began conceptualizing the landscape of the Syrian interior as an empty space in an environment of threatened territorial sovereignty. While the organization of the landscape into individually owned registered plots rested on the legislations and survey projects reviewed in the previous chapter, this concept of territory was closely related to the crises of the late 1870s and their aftermath.[8] This perception coalesced into policy in the Syrian interior in the 1890s, as myriad pressures converged on the region: an influx of refugees constructed as productive, loyal cultivators who were promised grants carved from "empty land" and a new land administration primed for reallocation; increasing interest from distant capitalists, including Zionist financiers aiming to found a Jewish colony who also employed concepts of productive refugees; and the British occupation of Egypt in 1882, which rendered the identity, loyalty, and intentions of landowners in the interior, now a contested imperial borderland, a new source of anxiety. Plans to build a railway along the pilgrimage route only increased this sense of concern over who owned the region's land.[9] In short, in the 1890s, the new private property regime enabled officials and faraway capitalists to legally realize their imaginaries of the interior as an "empty" space for potential development, whether in the form of refugee resettlement, a Jewish colony supported by foreign capital, or infrastructural projects.

This convergence of pressures sparked a debate among Ottoman officials about how to administer the interior. On one side of the debate were newly installed officials of the imperial land administration, who favored allocating the lands Bedouin inhabited to investors as fast as possible to increase treasury revenue, both from the initial sales of state land and from subsequent taxes. On the other side were high-ranking Ottoman officials in Istanbul who argued that opening the region to unregulated investment carried the threat of foreign intervention, as agents of both Zionist and British interests seemed to be scouting for land. These officials favored settling groups perceived as loyal, usually refugees but potentially Bedouin, in small plots surrounding the planned railroad route and in other strategic locations. While this debate revealed differences among Ottoman authorities' visions of the future of Syria, it also indicated how the range of official understandings of property relations in the empire had changed in the 1890s. Both sides of the debate shared an aggressive understanding of legally unused land as state domain. This understanding contrasted sharply with earlier ideas about state ownership, in which the Ottoman state had been a distant allocator of land's use and revenue while retaining control over its "essence" (raqaba). In the 1890s, land officials came to regard the Ottoman treasury as a privileged competitor for landownership among smallholders and capitalists: state domain became the state's private property.[10]

As competition over land increased, the space for recognizing the historic rights of populations categorized as tent-dwelling members of tribes shrank. At the imperial level, Bedouin came to occupy the same legal position as refugees: potential recipients of land grants at the state's pleasure.[11] This was a distinctly different position from those categorized as cultivating villagers, who deserved legal rights to land based on their historic use and residence. Officials on all sides of debates over agrarian policy shared one assumption, forged over centuries of transformation in Ottoman land legislation: pastoral land use, part-time farming, and tent dwelling were not to produce rights to land that were increasingly understood as exclusive, alienable, and inheritable. The implementation of this position through allocation of lands the ʿAbbad, ʿAdwan, and other groups used for grazing and part-time farming to refugee families prompted the Ayn Suwaylih attack. The 1907 events, and others like them, responded to a widespread Ottoman official position that the rights to land of Bedouin tribes, categorized administratively as bounded rural communities not engaged in cultivation, were expendable.

A faction of Ottoman reformers advocating an "empty land fund," largely from the Ministry of the Interior, dominated the debate over the future of the Syrian interior in the end, limiting registration and sale of the land Bedouin inhabited. Limitations on the registration and sale of the interior landscape were an important and underrecognized structural reason for tent-dwelling groups' ability to maintain quotidian control over land and avoid dispossession or confinement to particular spaces in both Syria and Iraq. In other regions of the empire, especially Anatolia, the convergence between imaginaries of landscape improvement and the legal privileging of both cultivation and perceived political loyalty produced widespread enclosures, large-scale plantation farming, and dispossession of local populations.[12] In Palestine, despite legal regulations on Jewish land purchase, registration of the landscape under individual names enabled highly contested sales of land controlled by Zionist investors and the dispossession of peasants and Bedouin from the 1890s onward.[13] The outcome on Syria's desert fringe, however, was different. Bedouin groups maintained much of their control over land going into World War I.

To be sure, claims of state domain that posited the land administration as the sole allocator of unregistered land within bounded Ottoman territory rendered this control more precarious. But limitations on the sale and registration of much of the interior meant that Bedouin communities retained a great degree of administrative sovereignty over unregistered land. Continuing disputes in sharia courts that referenced out-of-court land deals suggest that the *hujja*-based land market described in chapter 3 endured after the establishment of a register-based title administration. In the twentieth century, scholars from Jordan to the Euphrates Valley in Syria found Bedouin communities selling unregistered land in the state domain to incoming refugees and investors with *hujja*s. Omar Razzaz has theorized these practices in terms of "semi-autonomous noncompliance" because of the ways they simultaneously complement, build on, and fundamentally challenge central state power.[14] The endurance of a *hujja*-based land market utilizing the historical "bonds of obligation" forged in centuries of sharia court transactions embodies the deeply uneven outcomes of the state-space project in the interior.[15]

Part of the decision to limit land sales in the interior and retain land for an exclusively conceived state domain had to do with wide-ranging suspicions over the ability of imperial land officials to extract themselves from local politics in their determinations of which land was "empty." These determinations rested firmly on local knowledge curated by district-level governing councils dominated by locally based merchant capitalists who were also deeply involved in land markets. As in other regions that imperial polities transformed into state space in the late nineteenth and early twentieth centuries, anxieties over the capacity and potential corruption of the agents of land administrations, seen as in league with local capitalists, were a fundamental feature of processes of registration and reallocation.[16]

In this chapter, I use the imperial investigation following the attack on Ayn Suwaylih to show how the process of creating state space in the Syrian interior rendered the idea of a bureaucratic, centralized state existing over and above society that reformers attempted to maintain with intricate codified laws impossible to realize. The investigation's findings about Nahar al-Bakhit's activities after the Ayn Suwaylih attack illustrate this point. Through his daily performances of state power as a Bedouin headman—collecting taxes, registering land rights, and witnessing in court—Nahar al-Bakhit had developed close ties with soldiers, treasury officials, and civil administrators. In prison after the attack, he used these connections, as well as his ability to organize his community, to orchestrate a large-scale bribery attempt and prison escape. Beyond performing quotidian state power as a street-level bureaucrat, Nahar al-Bakhit straddled a blurry line between the imperial state and the everyday lives of its subjects, as well as activities deemed legal, like taxation, and illegal, like bribery.[17] For modernizing imperial officials, he and other Bedouin headmen exemplified the ever-unfinished and fundamentally unpredictable process of making state space.

More broadly, the imperial investigation shows how attempts to create state space had thickened the web of ties among the communities in the interior, including Ottoman officials. In particular, the social struggles attending reallocation of land rights occurred *within* the expanded bureaucracy.[18] The imperial investigation, guided by a body of codified law that aimed to translate district-level conflict into a detached and standardized set of forms toward a lawful and predictable resolution, ended in frustration. There was no external formulaic solution to the problem of land allocations in an environment of individual ownership and threat of enclosure; the unsettled and locally entangled nature of modern state power was there from the bureaucratic start.[19] At the same time, the investigation highlights the importance of Bedouin bureaucrats' place at the table in the complex web of district-level land politics. Their inclusion as headmen of tribes in regular district administration meant that they, too, developed the social ties necessary to participate in the making, and the outcome, of imperial state space.

CREATING EMPTY LAND

The violent attack Nahar al-Bakhit led was an escalation of Bedouin communities' conflicts over land use with the Chechen refugees of the village of Ayn Suwaylih. It came after almost two decades of tension between inclusion of tribes in standardized administration and political empowerment of their headmen, on the one hand, and the potential denial of land rights to members of administratively defined tribes that were embedded in Ottoman codified law, on the other. In the 1870s and 1880s, this tension was somewhat muted as the new administration developed a policy of registering land to Bedouin communities tax-free to encourage them to settle. In the 1890s, however, the tension around a policy of granting Bedouin land rights "at the pleasure of the state" rather than in recognition of their historic use rights precipitated increasingly violent conflict in the interior.

The reasons for this intensifying tension operated at a number of scales, from the local and regional to the imperial and global. First, in the 1890s, officials began to explicitly articulate the potential for the resettlement of refugee Circassians, who had lost their homes in the Balkans after the Treaty of Berlin, in the Syrian interior. Many Ottoman officials argued that the interior region could accommodate tens of thousands of industrious settlers. This potential seems to have driven the establishment of a permanent office of the Imperial Land Registry (*Defter-i Hakkani Nezareti*), which issued title deeds in the town of Salt beginning in 1892. One of the first actions of this new office was completing initial land registrations to Circassian communities, some of which had already been inhabiting the region for more than a decade. The imperative to settle refugees may also have played a role in the establishment of a new subprovince with its capital in Karak in 1895, a proposal that had been discussed periodically over the previous ten years.[20]

These registrations followed the stipulations of the 1857 promise of land grants to immigrants: the refugees received land free of charge, paying only taxes and fees, but they could not sell it for twenty years.[21] Even so, the optimism underlying land grants to immigrants had dissipated by the 1890s: loss of territory and the influx of refugees prompted the Hamidian administration to restrict immigration.[22] By the 1880s and 1890s, Ottoman commissions were scouting out "empty land" all over the empire for the settlement of refugees.[23] In short, because of the profound political shifts of the 1870s, in the 1890s the issue of refugee resettlement became linked to a perception of land scarcity in many parts of the empire.

Alongside these perceptions, many Ottoman officials saw the settlement of refugees as the most straightforward solution to developing the Syrian interior, which they still did not see as living up to its
productive potential. The former head of the Imperial Land Administration in Damascus, Mehmed Sirri Bey, estimated in the early 1890s
that the Balqa region's fertility, evidenced by its "gigantic" (*cesim cesim*)
Roman-era ruins, could easily support fifty thousand refugees. He saw
ruins of olive presses and wells as clear evidence that the land was
fertile and would produce "very nice grains."[24] For many of these officials, Bedouin could also join in this prosperous future if they agreed
to settle down and establish villages.

Settlement of refugees and Bedouin in villages of smallholding individuals was not the only possible future for a productive southern
Syrian interior, however. Capitalist investors also became more interested in the region in the 1890s. Some of these investors were men
looking to make up for profit losses in the depression of the 1870s and
1880s, including merchant capitalists and agents of Zionist financiers
scouting locations for a potential Jewish colony. The British Christian
Zionist Laurence Oliphant proposed buying one million acres in Balqa
subprovince from the Ottoman state to found a juridically autonomous
self-governing colony in 1880. In his travelogue, *The Land of Gilead*, Oliphant explained that the Syrian interior reminded him of the British
Northwest Province, suggesting that the government develop reservations for the local Bedouin, whose small-scale agricultural pursuits
he deemed as inefficient and useless as those of Native Americans. He
envisioned Bedouin becoming a captive labor force for a productive
Jewish colony.[25]

Despite the convergence between Oliphant's vision of Bedouin laboring on large plantations and that of some Ottoman officials, Kamil
Paşa in particular, the Ottoman Council of Ministers rejected Oliphant's proposal because they thought the self-governing colony he
proposed sounded like a "state within a state" (*hükümet bir hükümet
içinde*).[26] The debates around Oliphant's proposal reveal Ottoman lawmakers' growing struggle to balance the imperative to attract capital
to develop landscapes they thought needed improvement, on the one

hand, and the sharply articulated links between foreign capital and threats to Ottoman sovereignty, on the other.[27] The question of whether to support a Jewish colony encapsulated a contradiction for Ottoman officials all the way up to the sultan: how to encourage capital infusion into the Eastern Mediterranean without opening it to foreign intervention? This conundrum coalesced in the aftermath of the 1875 Ottoman bankruptcy when Oliphant made his proposal. A decade later, amid rising controversy over foreign control of the Ottoman public debt, it had become an even more salient issue.[28]

The tensions between encouraging capital accumulation and avoiding foreign intervention also increased in the Syrian interior after the British occupation of Egypt in 1882. The spatial proximity of this new British foothold focused anxieties over how to maintain Ottoman sovereignty with aggressive imperial neighbors if the land market were completely open. Within this context, the issue of Zionist financiers continued to animate officials in Syria. When the Ottoman government rejected official proposals to establish a Jewish colony east of the Jordan River, and eventually banned land sales to Jews in the entire region, financiers like Baron Edmund de Rothschild adopted a tactic of "infiltration": obtaining land through third-party sellers.[29]

In 1893, the governor of Syria, Rauf Paşa, wrote to his superiors in the Ministry of the Interior in Istanbul expressing concerns about these attempts. He focused on the conduct of officials of the new imperial land registry across the interior, in the Syrian subprovinces of Balqa, Hawran, and Hama, as well as in parts of the neighboring provinces of Beirut and Jerusalem. He wrote that officials of the land administration were claiming that wide swaths of land in these subprovinces were legally "unused" (*mahlul*) so that they could claim them for the state treasury and sell them to local capitalists at low prices. These local capitalists would purportedly then sell the land to foreign interests, including "Rothschild's agents" (*Rothschild'in vekilleri*), for much higher prices, funneling some of the profits to the land officials as kickbacks in return.[30]

Rauf Paşa's letter indicates a deep mistrust of local land officials and suspicion that they were acting in league with local capitalists, a suspicion that only grew among higher-level Ottoman statesmen in the following decades. But Rauf Paşa also emphasized more complex problems with defining the legal status of the interior's land. To legally auction "the routes of Bedouin," officials were using a category of the Land Code, *mahlul*, which provided both the main pathway for the state treasury to reclaim land that had previously been registered to titleholders and an important limitation on individuals' exclusive rights to land under the Land Code. If titleholders let cultivation of registered land lapse for three years, they forfeited title and would have to buy their titles back from the treasury at market price (*bedel-i misil*). If they declined, land officials could sell the rights to the land at auction (Article 78). Similarly, if titleholders died without heirs, including female heirs as of the 1840s,[31] the state could seize and resell their title deeds at auction. Rauf Paşa complained that land officials were using the *mahlul* category inappropriately, not for land recently registered and left fallow but for land that had been "empty and uncultivated for a very long time" (*kadimden hali ve muattal*) and that constituted "the routes of Bedouin" (*urbanın cevelangahı*). In other words, land registry officials were attempting to expand the area of land that they could legally sell to local investors, who could then resell it to capitalists whose ties to foreign interests were not always known to local officials. Rauf Paşa objected to the aggressive attempts of officials to claim "the routes of Bedouin," expanding state domain in a way that ultimately compromised Ottoman sovereignty in the interior.

There was another category of the Land Code that Rauf Paşa may have thought was more appropriate for such land: *mevat*, describing land far enough from population centers that if someone stood on the edge of the cultivated and inhabited region and yelled loudly, their voice would not be heard. This land could be "opened" with the permission of local land administrators, implying that those who wanted to work the land would have to buy its title from the treasury (Article 103).[32] In the 1860s, an amendment to the Land Code stipulated that those who "opened" such land through investment could obtain title *gratis*.[33] The *mevat* category was in fact being used in other parts of the empire, including Palestine, to justify the auction and development of "empty land," especially in marshy areas not formerly considered habitable because of malaria.[34] With *mevat* land, however, officials were only to distribute free title to those who showed investment and maintained cultivation. The categorization of land as *mahlul* instead of *mevat* was therefore a win-win situation for both land registry officials and investors wishing to obtain title, either for large-scale farms or for speculation: investors got a transferable title to land without having to make an initial investment beyond the land's price, and land officials got kickbacks and the auction price for the treasury.

The central response to Rauf Paşa's warning letter about the dangers of foreign infiltration in Syria if large swaths of land were put up for open auction was swift: in July 1893 an imperial decree banned all sales and auctions of *mahlul* land in the two provinces of Syria and Beirut, as well as the Jerusalem special county.[35] In pinpointing these three administrative areas, the imperial decree covered the regions of an extended "Holy Land," stretching as far east as the Hajj route and as far north as Hama. The ban reflected not only fears about Zionism and other foreign threats, however, but also a profound distrust of district-level officials of the Imperial Land Registry, a mistrust Rauf Paşa referred to clearly but that also pervaded the highest levels of Ottoman governance.[36]

Ottoman officials from the district to the imperial levels would argue about this ban for the remainder of the Hamidian period. On one side of the debate were officials like Rauf Paşa, the Ottoman Minister of the Interior, and some members of the Council of State in Istanbul. These officials favored the ban, which they considered similar to a ban on sales of *mahlul* land instituted in Iraq a decade earlier. In their eyes, such bans enabled careful identification and allocation of empty land in the state domain to loyal, cultivating, taxpaying smallholders. Bedouin, provided they transformed from mobile tribes into settled villages, were candidates for this type of state-directed land registration. The preferred candidates, however, were Muslim Circassian refugees, who were seen as particularly loyal to the Ottoman cause.

These officials were highly concerned about the potential consequences of open land auctions in the Syrian interior without thorough knowledge of the identity and intentions of bidders. Rauf Paşa laid out clearly the dangers of auctioning "the routes of Bedouin" to the highest bidder: if the government made no effort to ensure the loyalty of those buying Syria's land, it could easily fall into the hands of encroaching foreign interests. While Rauf Paşa emphasized growing worries over Zionists, officials were also increasingly concerned about Christian magnates with potential ties to the British government gaining control of land so close to the border with Egypt. These officials framed refugee and Bedouin settlement as an opportunity. Rauf Paşa maintained that the routes of Bedouin were becoming more valuable as transportation routes reached them and that sooner or later Bedouin would be enticed to settle near the projected Hijaz railroad project. If interior land was carefully allocated to loyal Bedouin and refugees, Ottoman sovereignty and interior prosperity would be simultaneously possible across the province of Syria.[37]

On the other side of the debate over the Syrian interior were officials of the Imperial Land Registry. In general, their representative, the minister of the Registry, argued that the government should sell the routes of Bedouin at auction to whoever had the most money to buy the land, benefiting the treasury both from the sale price and from the ensuing taxes on land and produce. Promarket land administrators in Syria spent the decade after the 1893 ban on auctioning "empty and unused" (hali ve mahlul) land advocating for its recension or revision. Osman Paşa, Rauf Paşa's successor as governor of Syria, articulated the logic of their promarket position in a letter to the Ministry of the Interior in October 1894. He argued that the most important threat to Ottoman imperial interests in Syria, Beirut, and Jerusalem was not that empty land would fall into the hands of foreign interests but that local cultivators would deprive the provincial treasury of much-needed revenue.[38]

Land registry officials explained this reasoning in legal terms: if they were not allowed to auction mahlul land and it was not immediately allocated to refugees, the people of the villages and towns neighboring that land would take de facto possession by gradually extending the borders of their cultivation illegally. If they cultivated the land for ten years before formal title was issued, they would be able to claim prescriptive right in court. According to the Land Code, a successful claim of prescriptive right would give the "encroaching" (*tecavüz*) farmers the right to obtain a title deed to the land free of charge—that is, without paying its market price to the treasury. If the land was auctioned, however, it would go to the highest bidder, with its sale price going directly to the treasury. The treasury would then be able to collect the property and tithe taxes from the new owner on an annual basis. Leaving the land *mahlul* therefore meant not only risking the land's sale price but losing annual tax revenue.

Osman Paşa's arguments and their repeated corroboration by land officials illustrate one logical conclusion of the Land Code in the post-crisis context of the 1880s and 1890s. The Imperial Land Registry pitted the state against cultivators, envisioning the treasury as a competitor for the right to sell agricultural land to wealthy buyers at auction rather than losing it to local cultivators squatting on land outside the boundaries of their title. By the 1890s, the prescriptive rights stipulated in the Land Code for cultivators had become increasingly problematic for local land administration officials hoping to gain wide profit margins for the treasury, as well as to line their own pockets through auction of off-the-grid land to wealthy investors. Beyond their interest in self-enrichment, they imagined a new kind of state domain in which the treasury would act as a competitive, asset-investing capitalist interest in its own right.

In 1904, the Financial Department of the Council of State weighed in on the debate over the Syrian interior, supporting the promarket property officials in Syria and lauding their commitment to increasing treasury revenue. The Financial Department argued that property officials should auction the land that was not to be allocated to refugees and Bedouin quickly so that the treasury could benefit from its sale price and future tax revenues. The Financial Department pointed out, however, that some land that property officials had designated as *mahlul* might be sold at very high prices at auction, and the local administration should therefore take this into consideration in deciding which lands to allocate to refugees and Bedouin. Lands for such allocations were to be expendable and not particularly valuable, with value tied directly to the fertility of the land's soil and its available water resources.[39] In effect, the Financial Department proposed creating reservations for Bedouin and refugees and selling off the "extra" land to wealthy investors.

But the dreams of Laurence Oliphant, the Imperial Land Registry, and the Financial Department of creating reservations in the Syrian interior were not to be realized: in July 1905, the Grand Vezir's office slammed the door on the debate over the future of the Syrian interior,[40] declining to lift the ban on auction or sale of any *mahlul* land in the region. The Grand Vezir's office expressed continuing doubt regarding the integrity of land officials and noted the lack of plans for immediate allocation of the land to refugees and Bedouin. Of course, imperial legislation only went so far, and there is extensive evidence that land sales continued in spite of the ban. Even so, the ban surely affected potential attempts to create large estates in the interior, whether on the part of Ottoman or foreign capitalists.

This debate illustrates important shifts in the way Ottoman officials envisioned the role of the state in land administration and an emergent concept of state domain in the final quarter of the nineteenth century. Officials of the imperial land registry were not the first to attempt to claim the land of the southern interior *mahlul*. In the 1860s, Mehmed Raşid Paşa had done the same with lands in Hawran that he wanted to sell to urban investors, and this may have been an important motivation for extending direct administration south into Balqa in the first place. The governor of Aleppo had employed a similar tactic in the 1850s.[41] In the 1890s, however, these attempts occurred in a context of perceived land scarcity and the ability, after the work of registration commissions in the 1870s and 1880s, to conceive of the totality of registered claims to rights over arable land in the province.

In this context, land registry officials did not see their role as distributing as many titles as possible to village dwellers willing to cultivate the land and pay taxes. Rather, they saw the treasury as a competitor against cultivators for the best agricultural land, with the

Land Code's stipulation of prescriptive right constituting a threat to the state's prerogative. This led to a newly aggressive stance in defining the state domain as space in which no other claims limited the state's right to define the preferred future of the landscape, whether it be capitalist investment, refugee resettlement, or large-scale development projects like the Hijaz Railway.

This position was one, but certainly not the only, way of interpreting the Land Code and related amendments, which enabled the registration of alienable land rights to individuals in reference to a comprehensive list of rights to land in particular geographical regions. Like earlier Ottoman land laws, the Land Code empowered officials to register title in tandem with the use of the land for agricultural production, mainly by smallholders. The aggressive stance of the "market faction" of officials from the imperial land registry and the financial department developed in the aftermath of the 1870s crisis and an environment of sharpened interimperial competition. These changed circumstances encouraged officials on both sides of the debate to use every possible plot of land in Syria and other provinces as productively as possible while ensuring that those controlling the land were loyal to the Ottoman cause. The debate over the Syrian interior therefore illustrates the interconnections of land policy and the fight for territorial sovereignty in Syria and elsewhere that characterized the Hamidian period.

For our purposes, the unarticulated assumption underlying both sides of the debate over the Syrian interior that "the routes of Bedouin" were empty state land is obvious. Rauf Paşa was not concerned that Bedouin rights were being usurped when he wrote to his superiors; rather, he was concerned that land registry officials were opportunistically using an inappropriate legal category to sell off state land and line their own pockets. Oliphant was most explicit: the only historic land rights to be considered in the event of a Jewish colony were those of the cultivators living in the town of Salt.[42] Like many other foreign and Ottoman observers, he saw Salt as an island of industrious settlement in a sea of tent-dwelling chaos. But in line with the broader position I articulated in the previous chapter, Bedouin were potential members of the loyal Ottoman polity if they would leave their tents, create village communities, and cultivate continuously.

MAPPING EMPTY LAND

The Ottoman Grand Vezir's preference for tightly planned land allocation in the Balqa reflected imperial officials' high level of anxiety around foreign agents and foreign intervention in late nineteenth-century Syria. This technocratic project of landscape and population engineering required extensive and detailed information about the land involved, and producing such information required support from district-level actors. Officials of the imperial land registry relied on local governing bodies to survey "empty land," especially district administrative councils. In the town of Salt and across the interior, merchant capitalists with deep interests in the emerging land market dominated these councils. The relationships between local capitalists and district-level land officials, in fact, prompted the accusations that land administrators were corrupt in the first place. This fundamental challenge to the vision of a self-regulating, politically detached, and predictable bureaucracy that central Ottoman lawmakers envisioned and attempted to create through codified law played out in multiple domains at the turn of the twentieth century. Bedouin bureaucrats were at the center of these challenges.

There were conflicts over land at district levels all over the empire but especially in regions with extensive unregistered land. These conflicts are clearly visible in the historical record of Balqa subprovince beginning in the 1890s, just as policies around land grants to refugees coalesced and began to be implemented. Concerns about grants of empty land to refugees united village, town, and tent dwellers in the district of Salt. In 1893, town dwellers in Salt petitioned the Ministry of Justice for assistance after the district governor allocated land in the vicinity of the town to Circassian refugees, obtaining a ruling returning the land to them.[43]

Similar district-level conflicts seem to have been common throughout the interior. But the debate reviewed above between promarket
officials and those concerned primarily about the maintenance of Ottoman sovereignty in defining Ottoman land policy produced an attempt
to comprehensively survey unregistered "empty and *mahlul*" land in
the interior in the late 1890s. In 1898, land officials clamoring for the
ban on auctioning *mahlul* land to be lifted claimed that more than one
million donums of land in the counties of Hama, Hawran, and Damascus, along with the southern district of Salt, were *mahlul*, urging
the Grand Vezir's office in Istanbul to conclude a settlement quickly.
The Grand Vezir's office, however, requested more information about
the land, including the amount of *mahlul* land in each administrative
district, the availability of water, and the arability of the soil. These
specific requests were similar to the information being collected for
empty land in other parts of the empire in the 1890s in preparation for
reallocation to refugees.[44] At the same time, considering the rumors
about the corrupt motives of property officials, the Grand Vezir's request for more information about the purportedly one million donums
of *mahlul* land in Syria can be read as a test of property officials' actual
knowledge of and ability to allocate the land in question.[45]

Based on this request, imperial land registry officials solicited reports from the ten districts on the fringes of the Syrian desert about
the location and size of *mahlul* lands in their territories. This process
stretched over eighteen months and produced a detailed list including
130 entries and a total of 1,407,135 donums.[46] In determining and prov-
ing the *mahlul*-ness (*mahluliyet*) of particular plots of land in order to
auction them, ministry officials depended entirely on district administrative councils. As was the case in Salt district, these local leaders
were often the same merchant capitalists, the Abu Jabirs, the Mihyars,
and the Shamuts, with whom land officials were accused of colluding.
These councils provided information about the details of the terrain,
borders, availability of water, and potential claimants to land in their
particular region. Table 4.1 shows the breakdown of the locations of
purportedly *mahlul* and empty land in Syria aggregated by district.

TABLE 4.1. Empty and unused (*mahlul ve hali*) land in the province of Syria (organized by district)

County	District	Number of locations	Total donums
Damascus (Şam)	Wadi al-Ajam	6	34,783
Damascus	Hasbaya	2	3,015
Hama	Hama	4	31,293
Hama	Homs	5	236,480
Hama	Salamiya	8	52,670
Hama	Hamidiya	7	10,912
Hawran	Ajlun	18	100,682*
Hawran	Busra al-Harir	8	18,000
Hawran	Daraa	14	331,900
Karak	Salt	58	587,400
Total	n/a	130	1,407,135

Source: BOA.BEO 1327/99496, 12 M 1317/11 Mayis 1315/22 May 1899, p. 6.
*Not including the thirteen locations in which property officials were unable to survey because the land was controlled by Bedouin.

The original list from which Table 4.1 is derived includes the county (*liva*), district (*kaza*), subdistrict (*nahiye*), village (*karye*), and specific location (*mevki*) of each piece of land, with the specific location usually being a locally used name for an area (which often survives today) rather than an official administrative category.[47] Map 4.1 shows 60 percent of the points on the original 1899 list, mapped onto a contemporary base map. The map, while it illustrates only those points that could be positively linked to contemporary locations using the geographical databases GeoNames and Google Maps, shows that the majority of the locations listed are on the desert fringe in contemporary Syria and Jordan, covering Ottoman districts from Hama in the north down to Salt, which in 1899 extended south of the town of Karak.

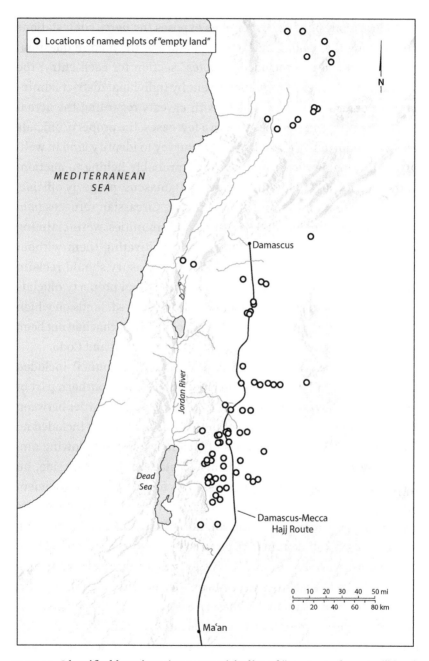

MAP 4.1. Identified locations (60 percent) in list of "empty and unused" land in the province of Syria. Locations extracted from BOA.BEO 1327/99496, 12 M 1317/11 Mayis 1315/22 May 1899, p. 6.

A close analysis of the list of plots exposes the fierce contestations surrounding the *mahlul* and "empty" nature of the land in question. The original list also included a "notes" section for each entry; the "notes" entries refer to the reports sent by individual district administrative councils and are replete with caveats regarding the actual emptiness of the land in question. In a few cases, the property officials used the opportunity presented by the survey to identify land in well-watered, valuable areas that they were probably itching to auction. In the district of Wadi al-Ajam, south of Damascus, property officials complained that immigrants from Amasya, Circassian refugees (*muhacirin*) from Rumeli, and Türkoman communities were claiming lands "without license" (*bila rühset*) and cultivating them without paying taxes; officials thus argued that the treasury should reclaim the land. In Hama, the administrative council and property officials included cultivated lands that were not yet registered, lands on which taxes were not being paid, and lands held collectively that had not been distributed to individual owners as stipulated in the Land Code.

In southern Syria, the district administrative council included eighteen pieces of land in the district of Ajlun, in the southern part of the county of Hawran, just south of the contemporary border between Jordan and Syria.[48] For thirteen of these locations, the list included no information at all besides names of locations and the following ominous note: "Because these lands are located on the desert side, on the routes of Bedouin, surveying them was found to require sufficient military force, and a detailed investigation was stalled." Of the points on the list, 44 percent fell in the southern district of Salt, comprising a reported 587,400 donums (41 percent of the land reported). These locations are clustered around the historic pilgrimage route and speak directly to Rauf Paşa's concern about the security of the projected Hijaz Railway project. Most of these areas are listed with nondescript borders that often refer only to other locations on the list or the Hajj route itself. The majority do not contain detailed descriptions, suggesting that the Salt administrative council's actual knowledge of the lands they claimed as empty and *mahlul* may have been tenuous. While they did not openly admit defeat, as they had on Ajlun's desert fringe, anyone looking at the report's pages of self-referential borders and locations with round numbers of donums would have questioned the process of making the list and which local reality it referred to.

The few exceptions to this norm were in the northern part of the Salt district near the town itself. In the area of Sahab and Salbud, east of the Circassian village of Amman, the list revealed a protracted court dispute between Egyptian immigrants who had settled on land allocated by imperial decree and a Salti investor, Hana Qa'war, who claimed he had previous rights to the land. Other entries illustrate the problems tent-dwellers' part-time farming could pose for property officials' claims of land as *mahlul*. In an area called Thahr al-Himar, near the Circassian refugee settlement of Wadi Sir, the compilers insisted that even though the Manasir were indeed cultivating four hundred donums of the five-thousand-donum area, "absolutely no farming" could be seen on the remaining area: it was "entirely" empty (*katiyen felahet görmeyerek hali bulunduğu*).

This list of empty land did not create the decisive effect in Istanbul that the property officials had hoped for. On the contrary, it highlighted their uneven knowledge of the landscape in Syria and the multiple local claimants to its "empty" lands. It also revealed how dependent they were on district administrative councils controlled by local elites, many of whom were known to be investing in land. In 1903, the Minister of the Interior expressed the distrust engendered by this situation, proposing to the Grand Vezir's office that an independent commission be formed, headed by an expert, to verify that the lands in the list provided were indeed empty and abandoned.[49] Not surprisingly, the Imperial Land Registry was against the formation of an independent commission to reassess the *mahlul* nature of the land in Syria included in the list prepared by its officers.[50] The Land Registry Minister's argument revealed the frustrations of land administrators: he claimed that no matter who was sent from Istanbul or Damascus to create a list of abandoned and unused lands in Syria, their work would depend on that of the local administrative councils. This was how the district property administration officials had drawn up the original list of *mahlul* lands, and any independent commission would not have another way to glean the local information necessary to make a new list. The property minister articulated the essence of modern bureaucracy's legibility problem: the detailed information required for intrusive, standardized governance was only obtainable through local inhabitants with multiple loyalties and interests.

The property minister's second argument against an independent commission was even more telling in terms of Ottoman bureaucrats' understanding of "empty land" and the rival claims of village and tent dwellers. He said that no matter how many commissions and councils verified the *mahlul* nature of any piece of land, there would still be people who would come forward with prescriptive claims in court when that land was auctioned, sold, or allocated to a particular group of refugees. Therefore, the only way to ensure that this land would be used for the purposes the central state wished was to override the courts by issuing an imperial decree ordering that they throw out all claims of prescription over the land in question, similar to a policy implemented in Iraq in the 1890s.

The property minister's response indicated not only that the property administration's claims that particular agricultural land was *mahlul* in order to auction it off were contested, but also that the existing legal system provided forums and structure for the claims of local cultivators and Bedouin to contest the registration of land to "newcomers," whether refugees or wealthy investors. The defensive tone of the list's entry for Marj al-Hammam described above, which insisted that the land in question was "absolutely empty," anticipated the kind of court claims the property officials were attempting to stave off. District property officials were in a complex position, not only because of their dependence on local knowledge but also because they had to address counterclaims from local inhabitants in court when they attempted to auction land or allocate it for various government projects. These counterclaims lengthened the process of allocating land to refugees or selling it to investors, all the while strengthening the claims of "encroaching" cultivators. The Grand Vezir's office, however, was unsympathetic, denying the request to quash court claims alongside the request to lift the ban on auctioning unused and abandoned land to private owners.

A full understanding of the details of these struggles in Salt and in many other late Ottoman locales is hampered by the lack of an existing accessible archive for the district Court of First Instance. By the 1890s, disputes over agricultural land had moved decisively out of the sharia court; in fact, in a few cases in Salt, the sharia court judge declined to issue a ruling because of the Court of First Instance's jurisdictional prerogative over cases involving state land.[51] In the late Ottoman judicial landscape, courts of first instance were the venue not only for land disputes but for challenging the administrative actions of Ottoman officials.[52] Contemporary Court of First Instance records from the town of Homs in northern Syria contain multiple cases in which cultivators challenge the decisions of land administrators (*tapu memurları*) to register land they claimed was in their control to other actors, often prominent merchant capitalists.[53] The correspondence described here implies that the Court of First Instance was an important venue for struggles over agricultural land across the Syrian interior and a forum in which to specifically challenge the decisions of land administrators.

The highly political nature of property officials' claims that land was unused and could be seized and sold by the state shines through in these details of disputes over land reallocation. They also show the increasingly aggressive and competitive stance of land officials in claiming land for the state domain. Without a full archive of the Court of First Instance, also established in Salt in the 1890s, it is difficult to ascertain the extent to which Bedouin litigants, like their cultivator counterparts farther north, attempted to reclaim land rights through the state-sanctioned legal system. But the records produced by the transformed civil judicial system do provide a glimpse into the dynamics of resistance to land reallocations in the early twentieth century. To understand those dynamics, we return to the story of Nahar al-Bakhit and the Manasir 'Abbad Bedouin who opened this chapter.

NAHAR AL-BAKHIT AND GOVERNANCE BY MUKHTAR

The career of Nahar al-Bakhit embodies the increasing tensions around land allocations in the interior district of Salt. In many ways, Nahar al-Bakhit's story is similar to that of Dawjan al-Wiraykat and his family detailed in the previous chapter. He became a headman of the Manasir sometime in the 1880s and was a mainstay in the proliferating sites of Ottoman administration thereafter: the sharia court, the administrative council, the Court of First Instance, and the treasury office.[54] But the political position of Nahar al-Bakhit's 'Abbad community in relation to the Ottoman administration in the mid-nineteenth century differed markedly from that of Dawjan al-Wiraykat's 'Adwan. Unlike the 'Adwan, the 'Abbad do not have a cohesive, singular origin story following the community over centuries.[55] Rather, they became a named and known confederation of distinct communities in the interstices of the power struggle between the 'Adwan and the Bani Sakhr in the first half of the nineteenth century. When Dhiyab al-'Adwan moved his operation north to Ajlun in the 1820s after a conflict with the Bani Sakhr, the 'Abbad were able to gain control of some of the lands in the shifa and the wadi, precipitating long-standing conflicts over land when Dhiyab returned. Dhiyab al-'Adwan referred to them as "bandits" in his 1853 petition to Ottoman authorities. In the mid-nineteenth century, 'Abbadi communities were marginalized in "'Adwan country," and one of their prominent leaders, Kayid al-Khitalayn, had been an eager participant in the effort to bring the Ottoman military into the region to cut Dhiyab al-'Adwan down to size.

For Nahar al-Bakhit's larger community, Damascus's activist policy aimed at the 'Adwan was a welcome change in the local balance of power.[56] More broadly, headmen from tent-dwelling communities like the 'Abbad, whose local influence in the Balqa was somewhat tenuous, benefited directly from the expansion of Ottoman governance in the region. New regulations, the increasing number of year-round Ottoman officials, and expanded revenue-collection processes necessitated the appointment of a government representative from each tribe. Therefore, headmen were semielected, semiappointed not only for the Manasir, the 'Abbadi group Nahar al-Bakhit led, but also for the Fuqaha, the Zuyud, the Jabra, the Nu'aymat, and other 'Abbadi communities.[57] This was similar to the way lower-level 'Adwan leaders like Dawjan al-Wiraykat benefited from Ottoman policy, but for the 'Abbad the context was different: through codified law, Ottoman reforms attempted a leveling of the playing field between midlevel leaders of the 'Abbad, the 'Adwan, and other local communities with longer histories of close connection to the administration, like the Bani Sakhr. Like the Wiraykat, these groups were similar in size to villages; local accounts estimate the Manasir to have included 117 households, or between six hundred and one thousand people, in the early twentieth century.[58]

The Salt sharia court records and land registers of the 1870s and 1880s show how Nahar al-Bakhit benefited from Ottoman bureaucratic expansion. We first meet al-Bakhit during the initial Ottoman registration of purportedly empty state-owned agricultural land in Salt to Bedouin. His name appears in a long list of people who were identified only as "from the 'Abbad tribe." In 1879, he and three other members of the Manasir registered a sizable three thousand donums (about 680 acres) of agricultural land in the Marj Sikka area of the Salt district in four equal shares. This registration, the largest among the 'Abbad, implied that al-Bakhit was already a powerful member of the Manasir in the late 1870s and that he joined a group of local Bedouin leaders who actively cast their lots with Ottoman administration.[59]

Al-Bakhit resurfaces in the sharia court records in August 1885, when Saltis were still buying and selling land rights. In one such land transaction, al-Bakhit was described as one of three "headmen of the 'Abbad," certifying in court that another member of the Manasir had control over a piece of land in the area of Marj Sikka necessary to sell it.[60] A few months later, al-Bakhit appeared in court again to transfer the use rights of five pieces of land in his own control to a merchant from Salt in exchange for eight thousand Ottoman piastres.[61] While the sizes of these pieces of land are not mentioned, the price indicates that they were significant. Al-Bakhit continued to participate in the land market in the 1890s when transactions moved decisively to the Land Registration Office. The land registers show that he bought a large plot from a fellow member of the Manasir in 1899 and then registered and sold a plot to Circassian refugees in 1902. In the latter transaction, al-Bakhit asserted his prescriptive right over the land in question, paying only the fees for the title deed to register land rather than its full price.[62]

Sharia court records from the first decade of the twentieth century show that as a headman, al-Bakhit performed myriad daily administrative duties for the Manasir. Many of these duties involved supporting their participation in the expanding market for agricultural commodities in the Salt region. In 1901 and 1902, al-Bakhit was named as defendant in four separate debt claims of merchants in Salt because he had acted as guarantor to members of the Manasir and Fuqaha sections of the 'Abbad on forward purchase (*salam*) contracts for wheat concluded between 1899 and 1902.[63] Starting in 1895, headmen also provided stamped certificates (*ilmühaber*) to members of their communities, attesting that they had the required control over particular pieces of land necessary to register it in their own names in the land office.[64]

Nahar al-Bakhit can also be seen defending the financial interests of members of the Manasir in the sharia court. In 1897, he testified as a witness in support of two Manasir women. The women, who may have been al-Bakhit's immediate relatives, claimed that they had given the Ottoman tax director in Salt cash for safekeeping. They complained that the tax director would not give them their money, and despite the director's protests, Nahar al-Bakhit's testimony, combined with that of another witness, was enough for the deputy judge to order that the cash be returned to the women.[65] This case is one small example of the complexities that could arise from the headmen's simultaneous loyalties to both his constituents and the royal treasury and the ways this office could sometimes benefit local groups at the treasury's expense.[66]

Administratively, Nahar al-Bakhit was a thriving member of a group of low-level bureaucrats whose rising power was linked closely to the expansion of the Ottoman bureaucracy in the southern Syrian interior in the 1880s and 1890s. His tenure as headman of the Manasir community of the 'Abbad tent dwellers in Salt was fairly typical of the group of Bedouin bureaucrats introduced in the previous chapter. He was involved in the expanding markets for land and agricultural commodities in Salt, as well as the Ottoman administrative and judicial apparatus regulating them. The sharia court and land records documenting these processes create the impression of a smooth incorporation of tent dwellers and other rural Ottomans into an expanding governing apparatus, one defined by its adherence to imperially applicable codified law, its rational and impersonal character, and its connections with juridically categorized village- and tent-dwelling Ottoman subjects. These records assert that the most difficult conflicts between tent-dwelling subjects and Ottoman officials were over small amounts of cash.

But Bakhit's involvement in the Ayn Suwaylih attack seriously complicates this smooth story of incorporation into a codified, rationalized, and expanded Ottoman administration. Even though he and other 'Abbad Bedouin participated in Ottoman land registration, they had been losing particular plots deemed unused or empty to government allocations to refugees since the early 1890s. Al-Bakhit was surely the recipient of myriad complaints from his constituents about ongoing conflicts with refugees. The sharia court case in which he testified for members of the Manasir against the district financial officer was only the tip of the iceberg in terms of the political complexities associated with being a headman in the early twentieth century. A decade after that case, Nahar al-Bakhit's relationship with the Ottoman authorities in Salt took a sharp turn for the worse. His movement from tax collector to prisoner illuminates the ways in which Bedouin headmen inhabited the edges of the always-incomplete process of making state space.

THE AFTERMATH OF THE AYN SUWAYLIH ATTACK

The Salt sharia court records and land registers provide momentary glimpses into Nahar al-Bakhit's administrative activities and land transactions in the southern interior in the last decades of the nineteenth century. Materials generated by Ottoman provincial and imperial investigations into the Ayn Suwaylih attack create a much more detailed narrative of his life during the summer months of 1907, when he began to use his ability to perform quotidian state power for a new purpose: rather than collecting taxes from the Manasir, he collected money from them to bribe Ottoman officials and secure the release of himself and his community from prison. These investigations were part of a broader inquiry into the conduct of the governor of Karak county, Cemal Bey. Cemal Bey was a civil servant who had moved among different locations in the Syrian interior for much of his career, presiding over increasingly sharp struggles over land. In fact, the investigation into his conduct concerned his tenure in Karak as well as his previous post in Hawran, to the north. While the investigation originated with the governor of Syria, Şukri Paşa, and was carried out by a special commission from Damascus, the Court of First Instance's nizamiye infrastructure and district-level staff both framed the investigation's procedures and assisted the committee's attempts to gather information. The documentation the investigation produced includes word-for-word depositions, letters of testimony from various figures in the interior, and detailed reports. Together, they tell the following story.

In the days after the Ayn Suwaylih attack in early May, Nahar al-Bakhit was taken into custody in Salt along with about sixty other 'Abbadi and 'Adwani men, as well as a few members of the Bani Hassan, a large tent-dwelling community attached administratively to the district of Ajlun (north of Salt), and townsmen from the nearby village of Fuhays. For Nahar al-Bakhit and his colleagues, the prolonged detention of so many of the leading men of the 'Abbad and 'Adwan in early summer, an important season for their agricultural projects just before harvest, would have been nothing short of disastrous. Once in prison, Nahar al-Bakhit quickly resumed his role as representative of the Manasir with the Ottoman authorities. Rather than collecting taxes or witnessing court cases, however, he aimed to secure the release of the men from his and other Bedouin communities from prison.

According to later depositions, Nahar al-Bakhit was at the forefront of an attempt by the imprisoned Bedouin, villagers, and townsmen to gather enough money from fellow prisoners and relatives to bribe

Ottoman officials, from the police and local military all the way up to the county governor, to secure their release as initial investigations into the Ayn Suwaylih attack began.[67] Al-Bakhit was well positioned to lead this initiative precisely because he had cultivated so many connections with local Ottoman officials through his work as headman of the Manasir. While in the Salt lockup, al-Bakhit met with a local military officer and reportedly gave him cash to pass on to the governor of Karak county, Cemal Bey.[68] Beyond trying to secure their release through bribes, the prisoners also attempted to escape from the Salt lockup repeatedly in May and June. In late June, Cemal Bey used their escape attempts to justify moving the seventy detainees 140 kilometers south to the Karak castle (fig. 4.1), ostensibly a larger prison facility and closer to his own headquarters.[69] This decision was even more disastrous for Nahar al-Bakhit and his fellow prisoners. Once in Karak, a twenty-four-hour ride on horseback from Salt, they would be effectively cut off from their family and business networks, and it would be extremely difficult to continue directing their affairs from inside prison.

After a journey on the newly opened Hijaz railroad from Amman to Karak, the prisoners were shown their new quarters: a section of the castle used as a grain warehouse for the military had been hastily emptied ahead of their arrival.[70] Cemal Bey was later criticized for ordering the soldiers to imprison humans in a space meant for supplies: while bigger than the lockup in Salt, the prison was damp, low-ceilinged, and had sewage problems that quickly got out of hand.[71] In subsequent depositions, al-Bakhit's fellow prisoners described how once in Karak, he began two projects as the unofficial leader of the detainees. The first involved gathering more money for the guards and police at the Karak prison from his fellow prisoners, as well as his relatives. Nahar al-Bakhit was used to collecting money from the Manasir community for taxes; the effort to raise cash for bribes involved the same kind of project. Prisoners available to give depositions later said they paid into the bribery effort on a sliding scale according to ability, and later accounts noted that each of the 117 households of the Manasir contributed a fixed amount, with the grand total sent to Cemal Bey in Karak.[72]

FIGURE 4.1. "East of the Jordan and Dead Sea: Crusader Fortification, Kerak." Photo by the photographer of the American Colony in Jerusalem, c. 1900–1920. G. Eric and Edith Matson Photograph Collection, Library of Congress. www .loc.gov/item/2019696904/.

Al-Bakhit reportedly met with a military official he knew to pass on the bribe.[73] In general, al-Bakhit's fellow prisoners described him as being on good terms with the prison officials; they said he left the prison when he wanted and could often be found playing cards with the guards and soldiers.[74] It seems likely that al-Bakhit used these opportunities outside to work on his second project: planning the escape of the Manasir and the other Ayn Suwaylih detainees from the Karak prison. Al-Bakhit reportedly befriended two poor men from the southern town of Ma'an who had been in the Karak prison before the Salti Bedouin and townsmen arrived, convincing them to widen a small window in a lower floor of the warehouse that al-Bakhit had identified, probably on his daytime jaunts outside the prison, as the perfect escape route. He promised them food, clothing, and by some accounts, wives, after the escape. Some of the other detainees described Nahar al-Bakhit in their depositions as a rich, well-known headman, a man to be listened to and believed. One of the prisoners who did not join in the escape effort testified that he had decided to stay behind specifically because he was afraid of Nahar al-Bakhit.

Using iron tools that al-Bakhit either bought in Karak or that his relatives gave him when they visited, the Ma'anis worked for twenty warm nights in late June and early July, dropping down to the lower floor and boring a hole that enlarged the small castle window enough for men to squeeze through.[75] When the hole was finished, Nahar al-Bakhit reportedly instructed a group of fifty men to squeeze through, lower themselves into the dry moat by rope, and run away.[76] At dawn on August 4, the officer on duty, who was sleeping outside the prison because the smell of sewage had become too much to bear, heard the sound of a man screaming in pain from behind the prison. He woke up his fellow officers and they went to see what had happened. To their reported horror, they found that fifty of the detainees had escaped. Their leader, Nahar al-Bakhit, had not survived; in an apparent fatal fall, he lay dead in the dry moat below the escape hole whose opening he had orchestrated.[77] For the Manasir 'Abbad community, it was the end of an era.

In the late 1980s, when anthropologist Andrew Shryock conducted interviews with 'Abbadi men in Amman as part of his ethnography, he heard the story of Nahar al-Bakhit's death from Haj Tawfik Ruwayij al-Duwaykat. Al-Dwaykat's story is very similar to the Ottoman record, with the colorful addition that Nahar al-Bakhit broke the rope the escapees used to lower themselves into the dry moat from the castle because he was overweight. Al-Duwaykat added that the "Turks" hanged six captured escapees in Karak, an event with no corroborating documentary evidence. Duwaykat also claimed that his father, whom he described as "an official in the Turkish government in Salt," had been in prison with al-Bakhit for his involvement in the Bedouin "war" with the Chechens but had not tried to escape.[78]

The story of Nahar al-Bakhit's death related here, based on the archival record preserved in Istanbul because of its importance to the prosecution of a county governor, also illustrates the ways in which oral histories and stories that are traded among interior communities enter the imperial archive. The stories of Nahar al-Bakhit's prison escape that Bedouin informants related to the investigative team sent to Karak draw on familiar motifs that recur in Nabati poetry and narrative in the Arabian Peninsula and the Syrian steppe. In particular, the stories about Nahar al-Bakhit draw on a motif of prison escape after a painstaking, protracted process of making a hole in the prison wall.[79]

The life and death of Nahar al-Bakhit illuminates the complexity of the role of the headman in late nineteenth-century Syria and beyond. While al-Bakhit benefited from his administrative position, his rise and that of his colleagues complicates narratives of smooth incorporation into a rationalized Ottoman bureaucracy. The Manasir 'Abbad whom al-Bakhit represented had benefited from expanded markets for land, commodities, and livestock in the interior. They were also victims, alongside other Bedouin, of confiscations of valuable agricultural land that the provincial administration designated as unused or empty. This tension created the phenomenon of a government-sanctioned headman orchestrating a violent rebellion against the government policy of settling Muslim refugees on land the Bedouin controlled and using abilities he had gained to perform state power in the Ottoman bureaucracy, as well as his connections with administrative and military officials, to orchestrate both bribery and a large-scale prison break.

Nahar al-Bakhit's story shows the way expansion of the Ottoman bureaucracy came to embody the social struggles of the rural interior, complicating the goals of the state-space project to create an autonomous entity with a birds-eye view.[80] Headmen were central to land registration, taxation, adjudication, and law enforcement. The everyday processes of making and maintaining state space—raising revenue, creating infrastructure, monitoring public security, and regulating resource allocation—depended on their quotidian activities. But their positions within the Ottoman bureaucracy also increased their ability to influence broader provincial and imperial policy. This was partly because of the personal connections they gained as Ottoman officials— with the military officers who accompanied tax collection tours, with the treasurers and financial directors who took their tax money, and with the land administration and courts that used their testimony to verify claims. Nahar al-Bakhit's story shows how the everyday, repetitive activities of modern bureaucracy in Salt district, in operation for nearly three decades by 1907, created a dense web of social ties among headmen, treasurers, career officials, and low-level military personnel, not to mention "ordinary" Ottoman subjects that the bureaucracy targeted as sources of revenue. In times of community crisis, this web could be used to challenge the state's expressed policy just as it was used to implement it.

BUREAUCRACY IN CRISIS: THE CEMAL BEY INVESTIGATION

The wider provincial investigation into Cemal Bey's conduct epitomizes what Ilana Feldman has described as the simultaneous efficacy and tenuousness of modern bureaucracies.[81] The investigation followed codified imperial procedure very closely and made use of new technologies dedicated to the pursuit of rational justice: forensic methods, word-for-word depositions, and a strictly hierarchical chain of command that created a voluminous amount of paper through its meticulous reporting on standardized forms.[82] These repetitive formalities were central to the civil court system's attempts to construct and present new, centralized procedure as above the realm of social practice and politics, an integral part of creating state space in the interior and all over the empire.[83] Even so, the dense web of social ties among salaried career officials, headmen, policemen, soldiers, and tent- and house-dwelling local inhabitants, a web the bureaucracy itself helped to sustain, proved extremely difficult for the men running the investigation to navigate.[84]

A team appointed by an official with the title "public prosecutor of the administrative council" carried out the provincial investigation into Cemal Bey's conduct in October and November 1907. As stipulated in the Provincial Administration Regulations, special investigative teams stepped in for accusations against members of the civil service but followed the same procedural regulations as the public prosecutors in the broader civil court system.[85] The administrative public prosecutor's team employed experts in their on-site investigations: in Karak, they used a report prepared by a local architect who visited the scene with the Karak nizamiye court officials the day after the escape to measure the hole made by the prisoners and estimate how long it had taken them to make and what tools they had used.[86] The team also questioned tens of men—military officers of varying rank, foot soldiers, prison guards, prisoners who had not managed to escape but had witnessed the operation, members of the administrative councils of Karak and Salt, and others. The deposition reports they produced recreate the interrogations word for word and show that the investigative team moved smoothly between Arabic and Ottoman Turkish as they questioned their subjects.[87]

Avi Rubin has argued persuasively that the office and functions of the public prosecutor were the main innovation of the nizamiye court system when compared to the sharia courts, which only ruled on issues brought to the judge by litigants themselves.[88] Rubin describes how in the various nizamiye courts, litigants found that public prosecutors often had more say than judges in the case proceedings. The investigation reviewed here, led by a special public prosecutor working for the administrative council in an investigation of a civil official, shows the aggressive nature of the public prosecutor and his subordinates and the way they methodically sifted through evidence, including both oral testimony and written records associated with the case.[89]

Despite the many attempts of the administrative council's investigative team, Cemal Bey refused to undergo any kind of formal interrogation in Damascus, arguing that the entire investigation process was colored by the bias of the governor of Syria, Şukri Paşa. Because of this controversy, the Council of State eventually reviewed the investigation in Istanbul on the heels of the 1908 revolution.[90] Many of Şükri Paşa's accusations against Cemal Bey were related to bribery. Cemal Bey was accused of taking bribes first and foremost from the Bedouin detained in relation to the Ayn Suwaylih attack in exchange for helping them get out of prison, apparently by having them moved to an insecure facility in Karak from which they could easily escape.[91]

The depositions of the soldiers who were interrogated about the bribery accusations illustrate both the militarized nature of rural taxation in the Hamidian period and the social relations the tax collection process created between local administrative officials, especially headmen, and the low-level military personnel assigned to rural taxation duty.[92] One sergeant's defense in denying his involvement in the bribery operation was simple: he said he could not have collected bribes from the prisoners in Salt because he was outside the town while they were in prison, busily collecting taxes from the cultivators and Bedouin of the district, some of whom camped far afield.[93] Their imprisonment, after all, happened at the height of both the harvest and tax seasons. His testimony gives the impression of a mobile tax-collecting operation involving not only Ottoman soldiers but the headmen of each community, who together went about the task of convincing the inhabitants of town, village, and encampment to pay the tithe, land taxes, and fees for their livestock.[94]

This picture gains further detail from the testimony of an officer, Abdullah Ilhas, who had met with Nahar al-Bakhit in prison in Karak and had allegedly taken money from him to pass on to the accused Cemal Bey.[95] Ilhas admitted to meeting with al-Bakhit in prison and buying a blanket for him at the market in Karak. Hearing this, the investigators were indignant: they asked Ilhas why he, as a military officer serving the state, would visit criminals in prison and run their errands. Ilhas explained that he had known al-Bakhit for a long time, al-Bakhit being the "shaykh of a tribe" (*shaykh 'ashīra*), and Ilhas had gone to the prison to see how al-Bakhit was doing. His testimony illustrates the way local administrative activities, including taxation, created social bonds between military men and Bedouin headmen. Low-level military officers needed Nahar al-Bakhit and his colleagues in order to enforce Ottoman policy, and the relationships between them created a mutual respect that Ilhas used to defend himself against accusations of corruption in his deposition.

Some of the most solvent inhabitants of the district of Salt, merchant capitalists, were also implicated in the investigation into the bribery of Cemal Bey. One of the bribery accusations involved Cemal Bey's alleged attempts to profit from an initiative to collect reparations from Bedouin communities for the attack on Ayn Suwaylih's Chechen community and the theft of their livestock and other movable property.[96] With so many prominent headmen in prison, merchant capitalists had stepped in both to help allocate and collect the reparations burden among Bedouin families and to defend against official attempts to collect property beyond what was ordered. Among the four main 'Abbadi communities accused of being involved in the attack, the prominent Salt merchants 'Alaa al-Din and Munib Tuqan accepted the unpaid duty to fairly distribute the reparations burden demanded from them among tent-dwelling families and coordinate collection.[97]

The investigative team was interested in the Tuqans' role in the reparations project because of accusations that Cemal Bey had requested that they collect twice what was demanded of the Bedouin so that he could pocket the difference. The team therefore summoned the Tuqans and asked them why, as merchants, they would have accepted the unpaid government duty to collect reparations from the Bedouin when, on the face of it, they had no interest in doing so. In his deposition, 'Alaa al-Din Effendi Tuqan described his interest in 'Abbadi fortunes: "I am involved with them. I have many outstanding loans with them and my interests (*maṣlaḥa*) are intertwined with theirs. I tried to help them because I was afraid they would be decimated. If they are decimated, all of my loans will default."[98] 'Alaa al-Din Effendi played the role of the headman for the Manasir and other 'Abbad groups in the reparations project: he made sure that the livestock already confiscated were auctioned and their value sent to the reparations fund toward the obligations of the Fuqaha and that only what was required of the other 'Abbad was taken in the form of more livestock confiscations. Other local merchants were also involved in the reparations; Salt merchant Nimr al-Haj collected the reparations from the Buqur 'Abbadi Bedouin.[99]

The role of Salt merchant capitalists in the collection of reparations for the Chechen refugee community illustrates the long-term relationships between tent-dwelling Bedouin and town-based merchants built on years of credit-based trade. These relationships were quite similar to those Beshara Doumani described between village-dwelling cultivators and city-dwelling merchants in eighteenth- and early nineteenth-century Nablus.[100] In the Salt district, these relationships revolved around producing grains and clarified butter and moving them from the encampments where Bedouin lived to the town of Salt to be transported to larger urban centers.

But the expansion of the Ottoman administration from the 1870s onward had rendered these ties more complex and multilayered. Nahar al-Bakhit was not only an agent of Manasir grains and clarified butter but also the Manasir's political representative to the district administrative council, their tax collector, and their advocate in court. Merchant capitalists like Tuqan played prominent roles in all these institutions. The headmen of these groups would stay at the merchants' houses when they visited the town for commercial, legal, and tax-related business at certain times of the year, and the Bedouin community could appeal to these well-connected men when they needed assistance in dealing with the town-based administration. As 'Alaa al-Din Tuqan's statement shows, this was not a one-way relationship, nor were the Bedouin simply providers of commodities; rather, their fortunes were closely intertwined. As with the relationship between the tent dwellers and the local military, headmen were crucial to the everyday maintenance of these commercial, political, and social ties.

In his written responses to the investigators' queries, Cemal Bey practiced his own tactics of redirection by projecting blame for rural conflict downstream in the imperial hierarchy. With regard to the Ayn Suwaylih attack, he blamed his immediate subordinate, the governor of Salt district Haşim Effendi, who he said had dragged his feet when presented with warnings from the immigrants that the Salti tent and village dwellers seemed to be planning an attack.[101] As for the prison escape, he launched an elaborate critique of the state of the rural police and military establishment in Syria, asking how the guards and soldiers posted to the Karak castle could have possibly missed the preparations for such a complex escape operation. Cemal Bey simply denied the accusations of bribery, saying there was no conclusive proof that he had taken extra money from anyone.[102] Indeed, the denial and redirection tactics employed by the prisoners, soldiers, merchant bureaucrats, and local officials alike underscore the legibility problems the investigative team faced in its attempts to examine Cemal Bey's case according to imperial regulations. These problems mirrored those faced by land administrators when they tried to compile information about "empty land" in the interior.

Headmen like Nahar al-Bakhit, the Ottoman administration's best hope for gaining the knowledge about the local population needed to monitor, survey, and tax effectively, were at the heart of these legibility problems. The personnel issues throughout the local administration were wider, however, and reflect the intertwined nature of modern administrative state functions during this period. The investigators from Damascus faced a district and county population of officials, as well as tent, village, and town dwellers connected not only by their commercial activities but by intrusive practices of governance. Taxation created ties between the military and headmen of both Bedouin and village groups, and the money allegedly required to grease the wheels of bureaucracy (and the palms of bureaucrats) cemented the connections between Bedouin, merchants, and even locally posted Ottoman officials who hailed from elsewhere. The web of connections between them and the shared knowledge those connections created made it easier for individuals to deflect blame onto others involved in networks of collection, surveillance, and law enforcement. The intrusive state policies of the late nineteenth century expanded bureaucratic processes to the extent that most of the county's population was involved in and knowledgeable about them.

The circumstantial evidence against Cemal Bey, especially with regard to bribery, was extensive: there were tens of claims that he had probably taken money illegally in relation to the Chechen reparations operation, the appointment of the treasurer, and the release of the Ayn Suwaylih prisoners. But whenever the investigators attempted to establish a confirmed trail for the money in question, denials ensued: the merchants and financial director denied providing cash for the bribes; the Bedouin presented themselves as pawns in a larger political game in the district; and the other Ottoman officials, while providing as much detail as they seemingly could, practiced strategies of redirection.[103] The investigators were left to insist that although they were faced with a wall of denial from the district's inhabitants, the circumstantial evidence was too much to ignore. Cemal Bey must have taken bribes, and his mismanagement of district affairs was obvious considering the level of crisis in Ayn Suwaylih, Salt, and the Karak castle in 1907.[104]

In the summer of 1908, as the Young Turk revolution turned the capital upside down, the Council of State reviewed the investigative team's extensive reports, summaries, and depositions, as well as Cemal Bey's responses to the accusations against him. While Şukri Paşa predictably secured the recommendation of the district administrative council to send Cemal Bey to criminal trial, the Council of State in Istanbul was ultimately unconvinced by the flood of circumstantial evidence its members reviewed, writing that the evidence presented against him was insufficient. In August 1908, the Council of State recommended that Cemal Bey be absolved of any wrongdoing and reinstated in the Ottoman civil service.[105]

In his memoirs written during the post-WWI Mandate period, Karaki notable 'Awda al-Qusus provided a view from the town of Karak on the Cemal Bey case. Al-Qusus was a member of the first ni-zamiye Court of First Instance in Karak in the 1890s and thus had a close relationship with the county's Ottoman officials who came from elsewhere. He included his description of Cemal Bey in a larger list of Ottoman governors of Karak county, whom he chronicled one by one in binary terms as either respectable public servants or bribe-collecting villains. According to al-Qusus, Cemal Bey was unquestionably on the respectable side, while his predecessor was interested only in bribery. He detailed Cemal Bey's attempts to build a road between Karak and Qatrana, claiming that he convinced the local people to help with the building project at no charge but was stymied by the machinations of the provincial government in Damascus.

Al-Qusus remembered going with Cemal Bey to the train station to see him off with other Karaki families and transmitting messages between Cemal Bey in Damascus and the shaykhs of Karak county while Cemal Bey was detained. He also recalled that Cemal Bey was eventually found innocent, and he argued that the Council of State's decision was based on a letter that the Karaki shaykhs wrote in his support.[106] While the Council of State's own record of its decision is much more complex, the letter from the Majali shaykhs of Karak pe-titioning for Cemal Bey's reinstatement remains in a file on the case preserved by the Ottoman Ministry of the Interior.[107] In his memoirs, al-Qusus rendered Karak the center of the Ottoman imperial world, with its shaykhs' endorsement of a governor the defining factor in his exoneration at the highest levels of the reformed justice system. His narrative recalls the stories Andrew Shryock heard from 'Adwani men in the 1980s about the reasons for the Ottoman incursion into Salt in the 1860s recounted in chapter 2. Both moments bring the simultaneity and intertwined nature of rationalized, generalized ad-ministration and local political intrigue into full relief. In the late nineteenth century, pleas from people like the Karak shaykhs took on new meaning precisely because they had become low-level Ottoman officials and members of councils whose activities were regulated by Ottoman law. Through the everyday work of these individuals, the social struggles of the Syrian interior entered the Ottoman bureaucracy.

While the Chechen refugees won reparations for the battle in Ayn Suwaylih, the Bedouin won the wider war over interior land. Ayn Suwaylih was the last refugee village established in the Balqa region in the late Ottoman period. Where Ottoman officials had dreamed of settling fifty thousand Muslim refugees, only about five thousand inhabited a handful of lasting villages in the 1910s.[108] This outcome was surely related to the ongoing high-level debates and confusion over lists of "empty land." But it was also related to Bedouin bureaucrats' ability to create a palpable threat of rural unrest that rendered their communities' further dispossession politically dangerous. In other words, they were able to take advantage of the Ottoman regime's precarious position on the interimperial stage of the late nineteenth century to maintain control over land.

Constant crises over land allocations were common to emergent spaces of state domain and land reallocation born of dispossession at the turn of the twentieth century.[109] These crises, however, carried more urgent imperial implications in the Ottoman context. In his initial complaints about Cemal Bey's conduct, Şukri Paşa had raised the specter of treason: so constant were the land conflicts in Karak county and Hawran before it, and so tenuous was the administration there, that Şukri Paşa was convinced Cemal Bey was purposefully making trouble in order to invite foreign attention to southern Syria.[110] The threat to Ottoman sovereignty was embodied not only in visions of the potential British military occupation that became reality a decade later but also in the figure of the insider spy in the ranks of the Ottoman civil service. Şukri Paşa seems to have been convinced that Cemal Bey had become such a spy. Considering British cultivation of such figures and the eventual advance of the Arab Revolt, his fears were grounded in a tangible context of territorial siege.[111]

Şukri Paşa's anxiety over violence in the Syrian interior was also related to wider frustrations over the process of administrative reform. The administrative grid established in the region after the 1870s in accordance with codified law was supposed to render processes of land allocation, tax assessment, and dispute resolution smooth, predictable, and, above all, legible to higher authorities external to the district communities they governed. The investigation into Cemal Bey's conduct demonstrates the system's rational, hierarchical design in its reliance on multiple types of evidence and how its appeals process functioned in accordance with codified law. Read from one perspective, the investigation represents the triumph of Ottoman reform, with its detailed interrogations, expert testimony, and precise measurements. From this angle, the investigation produced justice, perhaps correctly interpreting Cemal Bey's unfortunate summer in Karak county not as the machinations of a defecting governor but rather as the unlucky presence of a civil servant presiding over a local storm.

Read more closely, however, the investigation shows how masterful techniques of redirection, blame-deflection, and denial ultimately rendered prosecution impossible, not because the investigative team or the strict hierarchy of officials that read its reports were convinced that Cemal Bey was innocent but because the dense web of social ties the administrative grid created in the interior rendered it less, rather than more, legible to provincial-level officials like Şukri Paşa. Despite the expanded bureaucracy and its detailed regulations and reports, officials in Damascus and Istanbul were unable to control, or even to fully comprehend, the events in the interior district of Salt. Even as the district fit into a rationalized bureaucratic hierarchy with stated goals of producing predictable administration, its social landscape remained fundamentally unpredictable.[112]

This unpredictability also affected the judicial system: no matter how hard legislators attempted to create a mechanical process framed by meticulously detailed codified laws, social struggles continued to produce cases with elements beyond their reach. Cemal Bey's case, and especially the role of low-level Bedouin officials in it, embodies the deferred promise of predictable outcomes that continues to characterize the modern state form at its birth in the late nineteenth century.

For the Manasir and other 'Abbadi and 'Adwani communities in the Syrian interior, the active participation of Bedouin headmen in the web of political and social connections among military officials, court personnel, town dwellers, and councilmembers enabled their continuing control over interior land. This web, born of administrative expansion in the interior, deepened tent dwellers' existing ties with the merchant capitalists who bought their produce and gave them space to create relationships with local officials. Unlike Native Americans and Kazakhs, who were largely excluded from mechanisms of local representation, Bedouin entered the rural administration on similar footing as low-level headmen of villages and town quarters through the mechanism of the tribe. Over decades of iterative, repetitive performances of modern state power, including collecting taxes, signing land deeds, and witnessing in court, they had gained social positions not only within their own communities but also within the larger Ottoman bureaucracy. Like other members of that world, they brought social struggles into the bureaucracy, problematizing the provincial administration's ability to maintain an entity that was simultaneously external to social life and able to intervene in district-level social relations.

Beyond fitting into a global context of expansion, the debates among Ottoman lawmakers over the fate of the Syrian interior explain why the registration of land in the Balqa remained incomplete, unlike in Ajlun and other parts of Syria to the north; in the end, the Balqa region looked more like Iraq, where little state land was registered to individual owners.[113] This interior land remained in a highly contested state domain, theoretically available for state-engineered reallocation but suspended in a political limbo. In this context, local inhabitants strengthened their claims to land over time by engaging in an enduring "noncompliant" land market that continued to utilize shar'i *hujjas* throughout the twentieth century, severely compromising the central state's exclusive claim to land in the state domain and rendering projects like refugee camps and infrastructural development politically precarious.[114] As officials of the imperial land registry predicted at the beginning of the twentieth century, more and more men and women developed claims of prescription, further complicating imperial dreams of capital-infused prosperity.

5 TAXATION, PROPERTY, AND CITIZENSHIP

IN APRIL 1912, Fariʿ al-Husami, identified as a member of the ʿAbbadi Fuqaha tent dwellers who camped in the environs of the town of Salt, visited the district sharia court, where he registered a claim against the district tax collector, Mustafa Effendi.[1] Mustafa Effendi was in charge of collecting and recording the district's property taxes (*vergi*), which were assessed on immovable property (land and buildings) beginning in the 1860s and increased after the fiscal crises of the 1870s.[2] Fariʿ al-Husami accused Mustafa Effendi of illegally confiscating his yellow five-year-old workhorse and a small donkey. He explained that Mustafa Effendi had confiscated the animals, which belonged to him alone, in lieu of payment for collectively assessed tax debt that the entire Fuqaha tribe owed to the treasury. Fariʿ al-Husami continued, naming seven men as the headmen of the Fuqaha tribe (*ʿashīra*). He argued that the headmen were responsible for the tribe's tax, and since these headmen had no claim to his horse and donkey, the tax collector had no right to confiscate his individually owned animals for collectively assessed taxes. These taxes, he implied, were the burden of the headmen and the headmen alone. After he summoned two witnesses who corroborated his claim that his animals were his individual property, the judge ruled in Fari' al-Husami's favor, ordering Mustafa Effendi to return his livestock.

This chapter charts conflicts over taxation in the late Hamidian and post-1908 Syrian interior that hinged on the powers of headmen to represent administratively defined tribes to the Ottoman treasury. These conflicts referenced two interrelated tensions in late Ottoman tax and property law. The first was between individual property registration and collectively assessed and administered taxes. This tension centered on the figure of the rural headman and elder councils, elected for villages, tribes, and town quarters and the powers they had acquired to administer community-based apportionment (*tevzi*) of tax burdens during the Tanzimat and early Hamidian periods. The second was between the newly reconstituted categories of movable and immovable property—livestock and household goods, on the one hand; land and buildings, on the other—and the tax administration's prerogative and procedures for confiscating property for tax debt with the assistance of community headmen. Because administratively defined communities remained so crucial to processes of taxation, disputes over the powers of headmen to represent community wealth to the treasury centered on the boundaries of the tribe as a fiscal, administrative, and electoral category. In the early twentieth century, such categories constituted power fields within which Bedouin struggled to maintain control over resources and political influence.

In particular, cases like Fari' al-Husami's challenged the power of headmen to represent their administratively defined communities to the treasury. These disputes revolved around highly movable property identifiable and attachable to taxpaying human owners only within communities themselves: livestock. In the Balqa region, as elsewhere in the Syrian interior, livestock remained an important source of wealth well into the twentieth century. Especially in the case of horses, animals were the most valuable asset in the interior after land and buildings.[3] Because of their unique attributes, animals were a likely target for government confiscation: horses and donkeys were valuable, difficult to hide, and easy to move. Although familiar to members of administratively defined tribes, villages, and town quarters, however,

tax collectors from outside these communities were continually frustrated in their attempts to connect particular horses and donkeys to
individual taxpaying owners. Disputes around the wealth and representative powers of headmen were therefore closely related to imperial
attempts to connect people, land, and livestock.

On a broader level, cases like Fariʿ al-Husami's concerned the production of juridical property-owning individuals and the assignment of
those individuals and their taxable property to collectivities in relation
to the state. In this sense, cases like al-Husami's addressed the changing nature of Ottoman subjecthood and the dynamics of inclusion in
an emergent polity of property-owning, voting, semi-self-governing
citizens. In this analysis, I use *citizen* relationally to mark a line between two nested groups. The larger group were Ottoman subjects,
including all imperial nationals as stipulated by the 1869 Ottoman Nationality Law.[4] Continually reinforced in the identification of litigants
in local courts, this group included all the members of administratively defined Bedouin communities inhabiting the Syrian interior. In
contrast, those I am referring to as "citizens" were a much smaller
group of propertied men with the greatest extent of provincial-level
rights and privileges available to Ottoman subjects during the Hamidian period. Their registered immovable property gave them claims to
roles as headmen and on governing councils with wide-ranging local-
level powers related to the distribution of resources.[5]

Individual property registration and the establishment and everyday activities of local governing institutions in the 1870s and 1880s
introduced the category of the "man of property" (*sahib-i emlak/sāḥib
al-amlāk*) to the Syrian interior. According to late Ottoman codified
law, registering land and buildings ("immovable property") in one's
own name and paying required taxes entailed a set of rights beyond
control of the asset: the right to vote in elections for headmen and
district governing councils, the right to run for and serve in these positions and councils, and the right to bid on tax farms administered by
the same bodies.[6] Preceding chapters have demonstrated the crucial
work of local governing councils in the Syrian interior, especially in
determining rights to land. Local records also show that by the early

twentieth century, "man of property" had become a distinct marker of status, an elite group with unique claims to Ottoman citizenship.[7]

The phrase "men of property" recalls Sherene Seikaly's "men of capital" in Mandate Palestine in the interwar period, and there are important parallels between the dynamics she describes and the experience of Bedouin bureaucrats and other property owners I explore here. Both groups drew their wealth from a variety of assets not limited to land, and both navigated complex relationships with those excluded from their ranks. But while the men of capital in Seikaly's narrative labored under a Mandate administration designed to support a Zionist state-making project that excluded them, Ottoman state law placed men of property in the Syrian interior and elsewhere at the center of modern state formation.[8] The gender dynamics that Seikaly outlines are also important to clarify here: *sahib-i emlak* is not a gender-marked term in Ottoman Turkish, and women gained wider legal opportunities to become property owners under the Land Code and related legislation. Rather, the phrase "men of property" emphasizes the gendered nature of Ottoman legal connections between property ownership, taxation, and enfranchisement; women could own property and pay taxes, in other words, but they could not run for or serve on governing councils. I therefore use the phrase "men of property" to emphasize the exclusive political rights that property ownership conferred.

Existing historiography on late Ottoman taxation has focused largely on the state's revenue imperative, depicting oppression, resistance, and failed central attempts to shift the tax burden to urban areas.[9] As in other national-imperial polities at the turn of the twentieth century, however, Ottoman taxation was also a governing practice that constituted both the legal person of the individual taxpayer and connections between individual fiscal contributions and political representation at the provincial level.[10] Nineteenth-century Ottoman tax law aspired to individually assessed taxation proportionate to income. As in most rural imperial spaces of the late nineteenth century, the property registration that formed the actual basis of this type of taxation remained incomplete in the Syrian interior.[11] But partial registrations revealed interrelated potentials: direct links between

the treasury and individual owner/taxpayers and widening wealth inequalities that registration rendered visible and meaningful in new
ways. The aspiration to individual property registration and taxation
created space to imagine both a different distribution of assets and tax
burdens proportionate to that distribution. Because property ownership and taxation were legally connected to the right to vote for the
membership of local governing bodies, this promise also contained
the potential for a widened circle of political representation.

A few studies of late Ottoman citizenship have explored the links
between property ownership, taxation, and political participation, but
none have done so outside urban areas.[12] In this chapter, I argue that
court cases and investigations around taxation and the privileges of
headmen in the encampments of the Syrian interior were also debates
about the scope and parameters of Ottoman subjecthood and citizenship.[13] Although we know very little about the dynamics of elections
for headmen, we do know that their registered ownership of immovable property, their roles as credit providers, and their administrative
activities linked them closely to the largely town-based community
of men of property. By the turn of the twentieth century, headmen
embodied the accumulation of wealth, the visible inequality, and the
political privilege that the category "men of property," and with it an
exclusive and elite community of Ottoman citizens with full political
rights, entailed. Tax disputes like Fariʿ al-Husami's addressed this new
relationship between citizens and subjects that emerged in tandem
with the creation of state space. In that sense, they were also about
what it meant to be a member of a tribe in a national-imperial state.

Discussions of citizenship in the late Ottoman context have also
focused, understandably, on the politics of religious difference.[14]
Tanzimat-era law defined administrative communities not only in
terms of land use, productivity, and dwelling type, as with the category
of the tribe, but also in terms of religious affiliation. By stipulating
representation on governing councils for non-Muslim communities,
as Ussama Makdisi has argued, Tanzimat-era policies made religious
affiliation "the indispensable venue through which to demand specific
rights, tax relief, financial appropriation, and political representa-

tion."[15] As with the politics of "tribe," the literature's focus on religious difference has tended to elide contestations *within* administratively defined communities over political participation that centered in particular on wealth inequality. Here, I follow Will Hanley in suggesting a more rigorous distinction between Ottoman subjecthood, defined by the 1869 Nationality Law, which focused on the scope of sovereign jurisdiction over individual Ottoman subjects in relation to foreign powers, and Ottoman citizenship.[16] I examine citizenship in terms of the scope of individuals' political rights, in this case the right to participate in the practices of self-governance established across the empire in the mid-nineteenth century. Especially in rural provincial settings, the question of political rights went beyond and preceded constitutional politics to encompass the representative governing councils created by the Tanzimat, which became extremely powerful during the Hamidian period, especially in the realm of property relations.[17]

When Fariʿ al-Husami demanded just taxation by challenging the prerogative of his tribe's headmen to assist the treasury in confiscating his livestock, he was claiming a stake in the Ottoman polity and exercising an aspirational form of citizenship in the legal forum that was available to him.[18] Eliding the divide between subject and citizen obscures the stakes of al-Husami's claim, which specifically targeted the political and economic privileges that headmen enjoyed as men of property. The contestations around the role of the headmen also underline their power to connect their constituents to the possibilities of subjecthood and citizenship on a daily basis as street-level bureaucrats. The discussions around taxation and representation embedded in the court cases and investigations I present in this chapter elaborate the stakes of my argument in chapters 3 and 4: that Ottoman lawmakers expanding state space included the Syrian interior and its Bedouin inhabitants in the Ottoman polity of subjects and citizens and that tribes in this region were not juridically separated from other rural inhabitants of the empire.

Tent-dwelling Bedouin in Syria paid the same taxes and made claims about taxation alongside fellow village- and town-dwelling citizens in sharia and nizamiye courts. Tent dwellers in Syria were, in other words, taxpayers with a claim to citizenship in the final decades of Ottoman rule. But the process of making and peopling state space was as violently exclusionary in the Ottoman domains as elsewhere. The inclusion of Bedouin in the Syrian interior in particular responded to the political exigencies of a threatened imperial regime fighting to maintain its population in a contested borderland where lawmakers prioritized sovereignty concerns over the demands of capitalist expansion.

In the second half of the nineteenth century, and especially after the Russian-Ottoman war of 1877–78 and loss of territory to foreign-sponsored Balkan nationalist groups, these sovereignty concerns became increasingly linked to suspicion about the potential foreign connections and loyalty of Ottoman subjects. Long-standing legal privileges for foreign protégés and increasingly blatant Great Power sponsorship of separatist nationalist movements under the pretext of protecting coreligionists intensified these sovereignty concerns during the Hamidian period.[19] In this context, the Hamidian regime's paternalist and integrative attitude toward Bedouin that assumed they were loyal, potentially productive Muslims worked alongside the increasing exclusion of Ottomans suspected of having foreign connections, especially non-Muslims.[20] Bedouin in Syria were not marked as political others in the emergent discourse of "national economy" in the late Ottoman context, a discourse that was further articulated in widespread boycott movements against first foreign and then Ottoman Christians after 1908.[21]

This increasingly exclusionary national economy concept had antecedents in Hamidian policy, especially the exclusion of non-Muslims from property ownership in areas deemed "strategic," including the regions around the Hijaz Railway in the Syrian interior, as well as early iterations of collective violence against Armenians.[22] Making national state space entailed creating well-marked plots of land owned by juridically equal individuals, increasing the visibility of material inequality between those individuals and linking them to land that doubled as material wealth and sovereign territory. At the same time, Ottoman administrative policy sorted equal individuals into fixed collectivities marked as loyal or disloyal in the late Hamidian and post-1908 periods. While dispossession and property transfer, expulsion, and genocide were certainly contingent outcomes of the war, they would not have been thinkable in the same way without the processes of making territorial state space that unfolded over the preceding half-century.

This chapter begins with an overview of legislation undergirding the two main issues in court cases related to taxation and representation like Fariʿ al-Husami's: the relationship of the property-owning juridical individual to administratively defined collectives, like tribes and villages, and the limitation of political participation to "men of property"—that is, those who paid taxes on registered immovable property, which included buildings but excluded livestock. From this imperial-level overview, the chapter moves to the Syrian interior to explore the dynamics of the emergent group of men of property and the newly visible inequality their status entailed. Cases like Fariʿ al-Husami's contested their privilege through challenging the practice of confiscating movable property for tax debt. In a final section, I elaborate the political leverage the leaders of large, camel-herding communities with connections to the pilgrimage retained in the Ottoman administration through detailing disputes over their payment of the livestock tax.

HEADMEN, TAXATION, AND POLITICAL REPRESENTATION

As we have seen, midcentury imperial law codes granted community headmen extensive powers in the realm of taxation, especially with regard to apportionment of tax burdens. After the fiscal crises of the 1870s, imperial lawmakers began to consider the power headmen had acquired in everyday practices of tax apportionment and collection within their administrative communities as compromising the interests of the treasury. In this context, headmen came to embody a critical tension in late Ottoman law between individuated and collective property ownership and taxation practices.[23] At the same time, codified law stipulated a divide between movable and immovable property, limiting the right to participate in local political processes to those with immovable property registered in their names. Law codes limited the right to run and vote for the position of headman and membership on town-based governing councils to those who paid taxes on immovable property. These parallel dynamics provided the context for contestations of the position of the headman within administratively defined tribes and linked them closely to questions of the parameters of citizenship in the late Ottoman context.

In the early nineteenth century, lawmakers had imagined the office of the headman as an important element of a broader attempt to replace powerful regional leaders who had monopolized tax farming in the provinces with a more hierarchical and bureaucratic tax administration empowered to access individually held wealth. When attempts to create a salaried tax administration faltered, community-based headmen became the regime's "access points" to revenue in every community in the empire. To collect taxes in local communities as street-level bureaucrats, they relied on long-standing practices of lump-sum apportionment that had become ascendant in the eighteenth-century period of large-scale tax farming.

In the Syrian interior, headmen's roles in tax administration were particularly contentious with regard to the property tax instituted in the 1860s (vergi), which was a fixed tax on the value of land and buildings, and the livestock tax (ağnam resmi), which was assessed at a fixed rate on sheep and goats.[24] The property tax was theoretically based on a comprehensive survey of individual property ownership and value that was to follow, and was dependent on, the 1859 Title Regulation and the 1858 Land Code.[25] Although these taxes were meant to be administered in strict accordance with individual surveys, headmen's roles remained important for the assessment and collection of the property tax in the extensive regions of the empire that remained unsurveyed or only partially surveyed. In unsurveyed areas, imperial laws instructed headmen to follow long-standing community-level apportionment practices (tevzi), now codified in law.[26] Therefore, while the laws surrounding the administration of these new taxes explicitly anticipated individually assessed burdens, they were rooted in district-level institutions built around forms of community-based taxation that continued to privilege the roles of headmen.

After the fiscal crises of the 1870s, the central regime outlined a new tax administration with salaried tax collectors (*tahsildar*).[27] One law describing the requirements of these officials said they were to be "of the group who can read, write and calculate" (*okur ve yazar ve hesab bilir takımdan*).[28] Headmen retained important roles as the front-line receivers of cash (*kabzımal*) until 1902, when a new regulation placed the process of tax collection squarely in the purview of "collection commissions" (*tahsildar komisyonu*).[29] These were to be composed entirely of reading, writing, and calculating town-based officials.[30] Even so, headmen retained their roles in directing apportionment of tax burdens when surveys of property ownership were not complete. Furthermore, although property taxes were meant to be assessed on the registered value of land and buildings, Nadir Özbek asserts that administratively defined communities continued to pay predefined lump sums that were only *apportioned* according to property registers throughout the late Ottoman period.[31] Even when surveys were complete, therefore, headmen continued to have some role in haggling over the distribution of tax burdens. Throughout the late Ottoman period, community headmen stood at the center of the Ottoman regime's unfinished project to individualize the property tax. These frustrated efforts reflected the tensions between headmen's influence as men of local authority who could collect revenue even in spaces and communities illegible to the modern state's governing technologies and their roles as street-level bureaucrats tasked with bringing those technologies into every tent in the interior.

Özbek has demonstrated that the property tax's contribution to overall state tax revenue was inconsequential compared to the tithe on agricultural revenue.[32] But the property tax had other social meanings. The regulations governing the property tax came alongside the regulations outlining provincial administration to determine who could vote both for community headmen and for governing councils at the district, subprovincial, and provincial levels, setting minimum tax-payment requirements on registered immovable property both for voting and running. The Provincial Administration Regulation clearly stated that those who paid certain levels of the property tax were eligible to vote, and those who paid a higher level could run in elections. The limits rose as one moved through the provincial hierarchy, from village headmen to district, subprovincial, and provincial councils.[33]

Michelle Campos has shown that this limitation of voting rights to taxpayers with registered immovable property became particularly contentious in the context of parliamentary elections after the 1908 revolution, when people in Jerusalem had hoped that taxes beyond the property tax would be considered in assessments of eligibility for voting in parliamentary elections.[34] But the property requirements for voting preceded the empire's constitutional struggles. The combination of laws mandating property registration in the late 1850s and connecting tax payment on that registered property to voting eligibility created the category of the "man of property." This category denoted those Ottoman subjects with rights to participate in the fullest possible range of political activities in Ottoman villages, towns, districts, and provinces. In other words, these requirements created a foundation for a concept of Ottoman citizenship and set the dividing line between citizens and subjects at ownership of immovable property.

The status of "men of property" built on the reemergence of the legal category "immovable property." The immovable property category, which had a long history in Hanafi jurisprudence, had been somewhat diluted for much of the Ottoman period by the doctrine of state ownership of agricultural land. When the Land Code rendered usufruct rights over agricultural land alienable and the Title Regulation mandated registration of rights to agricultural land to individuals, the distinction between immovable and movable property regained legal traction.[35] Periodic "property surveys" of immovable property ownership determined the list of property owners and payers of the property tax. While these focused on fully owned property (*mülk*) still legally distinct from agricultural land held in tapu, the regulations governing them specifically included holdings in agricultural land (*arazi*).[36] While most existing research on property surveys has focused on urban areas, Susynne McElrone's research on property surveys in Palestine shows that they included agricultural land outside urban centers in their purview as stipulated in imperial law codes.[37]

These legal divisions contained another implication in regions like the Syrian interior: "men of property" with political privileges would include the owners of "immovable property" but not "movable property." Livestock, like nonperishable agricultural commodities that were subject to the tithe, were construed as movable property, and headmen retained important roles in administering livestock taxes in their communities. The attempts to make state space in the context of the Tanzimat entailed fundamental changes to the sheep tax (*ağnam resmi*), shifting it from a tax collected in kind to a fixed tax per animal. While there had been attempts since the 1860s to establish systematic registration of livestock owners, especially toward creating a revenue stream from sales and preventing animal theft, none of these attempts had been successful.[38] Accordingly, in the 1880s, collection of the livestock tax and the agricultural tithe was streamlined under a single agency.[39] Seasonally contracted town-based bureaucrats were to take on responsibilities of counting and collecting, but headmen were to prepare preliminary registers of livestock wealth in order to direct these collectors to points of livestock-counting and ensure that herders did not move their animals across borders before tax season.[40] All of this implied that headmen remained the figures with the most knowledge of the details of livestock wealth within their administratively defined communities.

This distinction between immovable and movable property and headmen's ongoing roles in the process of taxing livestock constitute the legal context for controversies surrounding headmen's other main role in taxation: designating particular individually owned movable property within their communities that could be confiscated and auctioned for tax debt. Based on information headmen provided, tax officials were to confiscate property for unpaid tax debt, beginning with household items, moving on to livestock and other movable property, and finally immovable property. Administrative councils would then auction enough of that property to cover the tax debt.[41] While imperial law granted the new tax administration this power beginning in the late 1870s, it would become particularly contentious in the Syrian interior after the turn of the century. In the version of the revenue collection law promulgated in 1909, in which most of the headman's duties had been handed over to revenue-collection commissions, they retained the duty of certifying whether indebted *individuals* had any confiscable property or cash wealth.[42] With many taxes still assessed on collectives, however, tax debt could easily become a collective affair. Especially in the absence of comprehensive property surveys, headmen remained the only bureaucratic officials in villages, town quarters, and tribes with enough knowledge of community wealth to connect movable property to individuals in *communities* that were indebted to the treasury.

In sum, the new tax laws of the early twentieth century preserved three important roles for headmen that would place them squarely at the center of the tension between collective tax burdens and individual property registration. Headmen retained roles as representatives of their communities in a financial capacity to the salaried bureaucracy; as distributors of the tax burden among their communities when surveys were absent; and as informants about community wealth in the service of resolving tax debt. This was the imperial legislative background to the scene in the Salt sharia court in 1912, when Fariʿ al-Husami protested the confiscation of his animals for the collective tax debt of the Fuqaha tribe, an administratively defined community, through the "access points" of its headmen. In regions like the Syrian interior, where property surveys were incomplete, the roles of headmen in both distributing the tax burden and ensuring that wealth reached the treasury remained indispensable. Headmen were the only local officials who could connect confiscable household goods, supplies, and especially valuable livestock to individuals and communities with tax debt.

Headmen's ongoing participation in increasingly intrusive and bureaucratic tax administration was a double-edged sword: their close involvement in taxation both contributed to their increasing wealth and brought them into a community of "men of property" closely aligned with setting and implementing Ottoman policy. In this sense, they became symbols of the increasing visibility of inequality within administratively defined communities and ensuing questions around the fairness of tax apportionment. These questions cut to the heart of the division between immovable-property-owning citizens, on the one hand, and subjects, on the other.

MEN OF PROPERTY: WEALTH ACCUMULATION
AND INEQUALITY IN THE INTERIOR

Codified imperial law demonstrates central lawmakers' concerns about the rising influence of community headmen that this book has documented. People within the communities headmen claimed to represent expressed their concerns in different venues, especially in court. Based on court cases in the Syrian interior, these concerns seem to have increased in the early twentieth century, especially around headmen's prerogatives in the realm of taxation. Cases like Fari' al-Husami's, in which he argued that headmen should shoulder more of the Fuqaha tax burden themselves, responded to the perception that headmen were the wealthiest members of their communities. While the quantitative validity of this perception is difficult to measure, individual property registration certainly increased the visibility of unequal wealth, not least by granting political rights to those with registered property. The new legal status of "men of property" served to sharpen the existing divide between those with registered property and those without.

Wealth accumulation and inequality were hardly new phenomena in the late nineteenth century. As reviewed in chapter 1, regional magnates like Zahir al-'Umar and Cezzar Ahmed Paşa accumulated spectacular wealth in the eighteenth century. While the doubtless myriad ways this accumulation was manifested in the interior remain somewhat unclear, lists of pilgrimage annuities from this period show a visible hierarchy of wealth and influence both between and within particular tent-dwelling communities. Furthermore, chronicles and poetry depict social and juridical hierarchies within Bedouin communities that hinged especially on widespread slave ownership. The poetry of and stories about Nimr bin ʿAdwan we encountered in chapter 2, for example, both highlight the roles of household slaves and clearly delineate tenthold-based hierarchies in the early nineteenth century.[43]

Three interlinked dynamics distinguished late nineteenth-century inequality in tent-dwelling communities from these earlier forms: widening and deepening credit relationships that were closely related both to the expansion of commercial agriculture in the interior and to cash-based taxation; the novel presence of a wage-earning community of agricultural laborers who worked on the farms of wealthy tent dwellers and whose status was difficult to fit into existing social categories; and the commodification of land and its registration with individuals, which both changed the nature of wealth and exposed gaps within administratively defined communities like town quarters, villages, and tribes. These shifts did not signal the transformation of the interior's political economy into a space of uniform plantation farms with standardized labor relations. They did, however, deepen and shift the dynamics of mid-nineteenth-century merchant capitalism.

Accumulation of wealth in the hands of individual leaders and their immediate households in the mid-nineteenth century is best expressed in the person of Dhiyab al-ʿAdwan, whose weapons, silk clothing, and plush tent furniture travelers noted in detail and whose grain stores were a prominent target of Ottoman military expeditions in the 1860s.[44] The first reference to the phrase "man of property" in the Balqa region of the interior was in Mehmed Yusuf's census of the Balqa district in the late 1870s discussed in chapter 3. Several ʿAdwani shaykhs, including Dhiyab al-Humud, his son ʿAli, and one of his main competitors within the ʿAdwan, Abu ʿUrabi, were listed in the census as "men of property and status" (sahib-i emlak ve haysiyyet). While many elites among the "Balqa tribes" (Balka aşayiri) were described as men of status (sahib-i haysiyyet), only four ʿAdwani men were elevated to "men of property."[45]

Dhiyab al-ʿAdwan and his son ʿAli amassed a fortune through selling surplus wheat and monopolizing the European travel business, and it was their wealth in particular that invited the expansive eye both of urban capitalists in Damascus, Nablus, and Jerusalem and of the Syrian provincial administration. It is important to distinguish between them and Bedouin bureaucrats like Minakid Dawjan and Nahar al-Bakhit. The latter made their fortunes through direct connections to the Ottoman administration and an expanded commercial landscape after the 1870s crises, especially though not exclusively as headmen.

Despite his checkered death in the Karak castle moat, Nahar al-Bakhit is a good example of wealth accumulation and the transformation of wealth into capital among tent-dwelling headmen at the turn of the twentieth century. In 1911, a Salt merchant provided a sketch of Nahar al-Bakhit's net worth at the time of his death in 1907 by making a claim against his three sons for two separate debts. The plaintiff said that he knew al-Bakhit's estate had been split between his three surviving wives and his three sons and that it included more than five hundred goats, fifty cows, five male camels, one female camel, and three horses.[46] The worth of these animals amounted to approximately sixty-two thousand piastres,[47] a significant fortune for the period under study. Although the merchant did not mention al-Bakhit's landholdings, property registers show that these were also extensive. Furthermore, court records indicate that al-Bakhit left his sons in a strong financial position after he died and that they continued the family's involvement in local commodity markets, becoming merchant capitalists. In November 1910, his son Naharayn registered a debt claim related to a forward purchase contract of wheat against another member of the Manasir.[48] This is one of the few cases in the Salt records in which someone described as tent-dwelling (or village-dwelling, for that matter) acted as investor in a forward purchase contract; it shows the ways in which Bedouin bureaucrats created both lasting wealth within their families and internal credit relationships within their communities. In line with imperial law codes, headmen of tent-dwelling communities were invariably men of property.

Eugene Rogan and Raouf Abujaber have analyzed how new plantation farms exporting wheat to Palestine transformed labor patterns and the social meaning of property ownership in the Syrian interior. These labor patterns included both migration and the expansion of a

population owning little but their own labor.⁴⁹ One court case from October 1897 provides a vivid example of the tensions over labor arrangements, land, and social status in late nineteenth-century tentholds.
This case involved a prominent ʿAdwani tent dweller accusing a town-
based merchant of possessing his missing ox, but its most revealing
aspect was a dispute around the validity of witness testimony. The
plaintiff, ʿId bin ʿAmr, called two witnesses from among the men who
worked for him to prove that the ox was his. The record described the
first witness, Hamid bin Salim al-Marsa, as a Muslim from the town of
Salt, and the second, Ahmad bin Maraʿi, as "from Jabal al-Quds (the Jerusalem district), currently living with the ʿArab al-ʿId," presumably in
ʿId bin ʿAmr's own encampment. After these witnesses testified, the defendant, Muhammad bin Khalil Effendi, protested that the witnesses
were not qualified to provide objective information because they were
the plaintiff's "servants and wage workers" who "always eat and drink
from his house."

In his response to these claims, ʿId bin ʿAmr insisted on important
distinctions between these last two terms, *partner* vs. *servant*: "Ahmad
bin Maraʿi is my ploughman (*ḥārith*), and he has been eating and drinking from my house for three or four years. However, Hamad is my partner in agricultural work only." When the judge asked the defendant,
Muhammad Effendi, to prove his claim that Hamad was ʿId bin ʿAmr's
servant, that he "stayed in his house in order to serve him," Muhammad Effendi called two witnesses who corroborated his claim. They
said that Hamad was ʿId bin ʿAmr's servant, that he "always eats and
drinks from his house, serves his guests and his horses, and does any
work he (ʿId) needs." The first witness also asserted that Hamad could
not be ʿId's partner in agriculture because he "does not own anything,
because of his intense poverty."⁵⁰

The contestation in this case over the relationship between ʿId
bin ʿAmr, Ahmad bin Maraʿi, and Hamad al-Marsa highlights the dynamics of inequality around labor, agricultural practice, and property ownership in the late nineteenth-century interior and how they
were manifested in the households of wealthy tent dwellers, especially
those involved in commercial agriculture. ʿId bin ʿAmr, in his expla-

nation of Ahmad al-Mara'i's presence in his household and his hiring of Hamad, posited a labor dynamic detailed by Raouf Abujaber in his discussion of nineteenth-century sharecropping arrangements in the interior. On the one hand, 'Id claimed that Ahmad bin Mara'i, a poor man from outside 'Adwan country, was a sharecropping ploughman: he was fed and clothed by 'Id, and in a typical relationship he would receive one-fourth of the harvest of the area he ploughed. 'Id claimed that Hamad, on the other hand, was a "partner farmer," distinguished from a ploughman by the fact that he owned something, probably either land or tools, which entitled him to a greater share of both risk and revenue.[51] In contrast, Muhammad Effendi's description of the absolute loyalty he claimed both Hamad and Ahmad owed 'Id bin 'Amr recalls Ihsan Nimr's discussion of a group of people in eighteenth- and nineteenth-century Nablus called "tāb'īn," who, while they were not legally owned slaves, exchanged clothing, food, and shelter from upper-class individuals such as effendis, shaykhs, and wealthy merchants for ongoing work of a nature that sharecroppers or partner farmers would not have performed. Nimr adds that tāb'īn were expected to "provide their masters (asyāduhum) with the utmost loyalty,"[52] implying that this type of relationship would indeed render testimony from a "tāb'" on behalf of his "master" questionable.

The tasks that Ahmad and Hamad allegedly performed for 'Id bin 'Amr imply that 'Id possessed a prominent household and engaged in diverse forms of exploitation; they fed 'Id's horses, tended to his guests, and "did anything else he needed." This case helps us imagine how inequalities related to widening commercial agriculture, increasingly stratified and codified property relations, and an expanding pool of wage labor from Egypt, Palestine, and northern Syria took shape in certain tentholds in the late nineteenth century. Although there is no indication that 'Id bin 'Amr served as headman of the Kayid al-'Adwan, we can imagine that the variegated forms of labor in his household and his fields were similar to those in the households and agricultural properties of wealthy tent-dwelling headmen like Nahar al-Bakhit and Minakid Dawjan al-Wiraykat. The conflicting descriptions of the witnesses' status and, by implication, their level of independence from 'Id bin 'Amr support Eugene Rogan's point that a clear distinction existed between those "who were masters of their own labor and those who sold their labor" in the late nineteenth-century Syrian interior. The dividing line between masters and sellers of labor was often control of land.[53]

Beyond the social and material influence inherent in landholding, the establishment, far-ranging responsibilities, and increasing political dominance of town-based governing councils with elected members further marked the status of "men of property" in the Syrian interior and elsewhere in the Ottoman countryside. Petitions from the district of Salt show that eligibility and elections for these councils were highly contentious affairs. While no complete archive of their practices exists, fragmentary archival evidence shows that the Salt administrative council had far-reaching powers, especially in settling disputes over land.[54] The property-ownership requirements for participation in the politics of councils, combined with their central roles in local property administration, created a powerful club of town-based men of property.

Depositions from the investigation into Cemal Bey's conduct imply that town-based men self-consciously used the label "man of property" to assert their status in times of conflict. In his deposition to the investigative team in 1907, a prominent town-based merchant of the Abu Jabir family, Farah Abu Jabir, used the phrase to assert that Cemal Bey had mistreated him and his colleagues when he summoned them to Karak for questioning around the survey process in the town of Salt.[55] Abu Jabir was scandalized by his treatment at the hands of Cemal Bey's soldiers: they had come to his house asking for money, demanding that he go with them to Karak, and threatening him with exile if he tried to leave Salt without Cemal Bey's permission. Abu Jabir said he told them, "I am not just anyone, I am a man of property and wealth (*sāḥib al-amlāk wa al-tharwa*), I am well known."

The property requirements for the franchise for town-based council members extended theoretically to community-based headmen as well, although there is little evidence of whether or how such elections actually occurred. We do not have records of men like Nahar al-Bakhit,

Minakid Dawjan, or the headmen in Fariʿ al-Husami's case describing themselves explicitly as men of property. Based on the legislation reviewed above, community headmen occupied the edges of communities of men of property, just as the tribe occupied the edges of state space. Bedouin headmen were registered property owners who spent most of their time outside town-based centers of power. Still, they operated within a circle of Ottoman citizenship that became more visible as it became more exclusive and status-based. In the twentieth century, the inequality that fueled the status of "men of property" came under increasing scrutiny from within the communities of Bedouin headmen. Internal contestations centered on the politics of taxation and the tax administration's struggles to assign confiscable movable property to individual members of bounded categorical communities like tribes.

CONNECTING PEOPLE, ANIMALS, AND THINGS

In the late Hamidian and post-1908 periods, the growing visibility of inequality within tent-dwelling communities and the rise of a group of "men of property," many of them headmen, created new tensions within administratively defined communities that centered on increasingly aggressive tax-collection practices. These tensions responded to a contradiction in late Ottoman tax law between a vision of proportionate taxation of individual property holdings and an ongoing practice of apportionment of tax burdens within communities. Proportioned property and livestock taxes charged individuals a percentage of the value of their holdings. This required detailed and updated property registers and threatened disruption to the tax base. Ottoman officials' compromise, especially in partially surveyed regions like the Syrian interior, was to charge lump-sum amounts to communities that headmen would apportion according to relative wealth.[56] This compromise conflicted with the practice of confiscating the movable property of individuals for unpaid tax debt, because the tax debt remained essentially collective. These processes of apportionment and confiscation placed headmen front and center. In court, tent dwellers challenged headmen's right to simultaneously distribute tax burdens within their administratively defined tribes and identify movable property for confiscation for tax debt. These men and women questioned headmen's ability to perform state functions disassociated from local networks, demanding a more uniform and just basis for quotidian taxation. In doing so, they problematized not only the category of the tribe as the basis for political representation but also its boundaries, devising novel ways to avoid the treasury's multifaceted strategies of accessing their most valuable movable property: livestock.

Beginning in 1879, tax collection regulations granted government officials the right to confiscate the movable property of those indebted to the treasury and auction it to cover tax debts, including those incurred from the property tax.[57] Although there are indications that this practice existed in the interior during the Hamidian period, court cases suggest that it became widespread and routine in the district of Salt after the revolution of 1908, which brought a Committee of Union and Progress (CUP)-dominated government into power. Contestations over this unpopular practice centered on the local government's ability to connect movable objects like household commodities and grains, as well as livestock, to individual taxpayers and to connect those taxpayers to particular communities whose taxes were collectively assessed. Like the case of Fari' al-Husami, tent dwellers' claims targeted the headmen of their administratively defined tribes, contesting their authority to collect movable property in lieu of unpaid tax debts assessed collectively on the tribe and implying that wealthy headmen should shoulder these burdens themselves. Because livestock was the most valuable movable property in the interior, these cases often revolved around confiscations of oxen, goats, and the ultimate prize, horses.[58]

The phenomenon of headmen confiscating animals from Bedouin in their communities lives on in vernacular memory in the Balqa region and seems to date at least to the 1880s. When Andrew Shryock did ethnographic research among oral historians from the 'Abbad and 'Adwan tribes in the 1980s, 'Adwani narrators told him stories about Abu 'Urabi, their ancestor who allied with the Ottoman administration against his distant relative and rival, Dhiyab al-'Adwan, in the 1860s.[59]

They explained how Abu ʿUrabi, flanked by "Turkish" soldiers, would come to ʿAdwani households and confiscate goats for the head tax on livestock, sometimes precipitating violence when other ʿAdwani men tried to stop them. In one story, a rival ʿAdwani leader, Abu l-ʿAmash, came to blows with Abu ʿUrabi after defending the rights of a poverty-stricken widow under his protection to keep her goats.[60] In ʿAdwani oral history, the "tax ledger" that Abu ʿUrabi carried, in direct accordance with Ottoman codified law, became an object of contestation in itself, with Abu l-ʿAmash threatening to burn Abu ʿUrabi's ledger and "break the state."

After the 1908 revolution, the rising number of individuals attempting to reclaim their confiscated property in court indicates that the tax administration under the CUP government may have been more aggressive in confiscating movable property for tax debt than its Hamidian predecessor. Confiscations of movable property for tax debt during the second constitutional period were controversial all over the region. Ahmed Şerif, a journalist who toured Anatolia and Syria in 1909 and 1910, recorded complaints of officials selling household items down to "pots and bedding" for tax debt.[61] In the Syrian interior, the fact that individuals' movable property was being confiscated for collectively assessed tax burdens compounded frustrations around this practice. These confiscations gave headmen, who were the "access points" in this process because of their intimate knowledge of community holdings of movable property, quite visible power.

The history of the career of ʿAbd al-Muhsin al-Bakhit, one of the headmen mentioned by Fariʿ al-Husami in the lawsuit that opened this chapter, illustrates both the centrality of livestock property for wealth-building in the Syrian interior and the way this valuable, movable, and confiscable property became a flashpoint for the conflicts over headmen's power after 1908. Like other ʿAbbadi and ʿAdwani headmen, ʿAbd al-Muhsin al-Bakhit built his wealth through involvement in commodity markets in the interior. He established himself as a supplier of agricultural and animal products to merchants in the expanding markets of the town of Salt in the 1880s and 1890s. He first appears in the court records in 1902, when one of Salt's wealthiest men of property, Fayyad al-Nabulsi, registered a claim against him for a debt of wheat, barley, clarified butter made from goats' milk, and cash.[62] In that claim alone, al-Nabulsi referred to eleven previous contracts he had concluded with al-Bakhit beginning in 1899. Al-Bakhit also had a long-standing relationship with the Mihyar family, the prominent commercial capitalists who migrated to Salt from Nablus in the 1880s, served on governing councils in Salt, and traded in both Fuqaha and Wiraykat wheat.[63]

Al-Bakhit was not involved in the earliest land surveys in Salt among 'Abbadi communities in 1879, probably because he was too young at the time. In 1904, however, al-Bakhit consolidated his growing wealth by registering land in his name at the property registration office in Salt. He registered seven plots in seven different locations controlled by the Fuqaha community.[64] He registered these lands with prescriptive right after the district administrative office and the Fuqaha headmen issued a decision attesting to his long-standing and uncontested control and cultivation of the land. With a successful claim of prescriptive right, al-Bakhit paid fees for only the paper title deeds to the land, which the property registration office estimated as valuing more than twenty thousand piastres. Al-Bakhit's trajectory shows how Bedouin bureaucrats managed to retain control over land amid the threats of dispossession described in chapter 4. By the first decade of the twentieth century, al-Bakhit had become a man of property, registering rights to land with the full privileges of house-dwelling local inhabitants. These registrations contrasted sharply with the initial registration of 1879, when tent dwellers' rights were subject to imperial decree rather than standardized law.

A string of five court cases recorded during a single week in August 1903 illustrates al-Bakhit's deep involvement with the dynamics of livestock property, his familiarity with the Ottoman court system, and his involvement in tax collection within the Fuqaha community. Three of the five cases involved livestock directly, and one involved debt for animal products. In one case, al-Bakhit accused another man from the Fuqaha of giving him a cow as a gift and then illegally taking the cow back after al-Bakhit had taught it to plow, thereby increasing its value.[65]

In another, a woman from the town of Salt accused him of lending a workhorse he had borrowed from her two years earlier to another man to carry a heavy tent to the faraway encampment of Naur. On the return trip, she explained, the exhausted animal fell and died. In his defense, al-Bakhit explained that he had been forced to find a trusted friend to transport the tent because he had been busy collecting agricultural taxes from other members of the Fuqaha.[66] Although this case shows his involvement in tax collection as early as 1903, al-Bakhit is first identified as headman of the Fuqaha in court cases like Fari' al-Husami's after the 1908 revolution, in 1910. He continued to be a mainstay in the sharia court until World War I, providing witness testimony and verifying the testimony of other witnesses, and the records show his continuing involvement in tax collection.

Court cases also show that men like 'Abd al-Muhsin al-Bakhit worked closely with salaried, town-based tax collectors (*tahsildar*), who entered the district administration in Salt in the 1880s.[67] District-level tax collectors were usually hired from local towns and often on a seasonal basis. Fari' al-Husami's claim was not against the Fuqaha headmen directly but the district tax collector, Mustafa Effendi. Fari' al-Husami questioned Mustafa Effendi's decision to confiscate his animals for the collective tax debt of the Fuqaha when, he argued, the tax was the responsibility of the six presumably wealthier headmen, "men of property," including 'Abd al-Muhsin al-Bakhit. In effect, he construed the headmen's privilege of representing the Fuqaha as entailing the responsibility to pay their property taxes.

Fari' al-Husami's case was not the only one of its kind. A month after the litigation of his case, a woman named 'Ashtiyya of the Khusaylat Bedouin,[68] also administratively attached to the Salt district, registered a similar claim regarding goats that the same tax collector, Mustafa Effendi, had confiscated in lieu of the Khusaylat agricultural tithes. Like Fari', 'Ashtiyya claimed that the Khusaylat headmen had no right to her goats, which she owned privately as part of her dowry. In that claim, Mustafa Effendi mounted a defense, saying he had found the goats in question with the headman of the Khusaylat himself.[69] He implied that either the headmen had already taken 'Ashtiyya's goats for tax debt or that the goats had never belonged to her in the first place.

The backstories of these cases remain somewhat obscure; it is entirely possible that headmen encouraged people in their communities
to initiate sharia court claims with the argument that the animals belonged to them and not to the headmen from whom they were confiscated in order to shield the community from taxation. It is equally
possible, however, that the tent dwellers like ʿAshtiyya and Fariʿ al-
Husami noted the increasing estates of headmen like ʿAbd al-Muhsin
al-Bakhit and concluded that they should shoulder the tax burdens
themselves, since they were the ones materially benefiting from their
connections with Ottoman state officials.

The Salt cases also show how confiscation of movable property for
tax debt politicized the boundaries of the administratively defined
tribe as a tax category, with representatives elected to manage apportionment and collection. In 1910, Mustafa Effendi's predecessor as
tax official in Salt, Farid Effendi, was brought to court to defend his
confiscation of livestock for tax debt. Hamad bin ʿAwad al-Sulayman,
identified as a member of the Bani Hassan tribe, registered a claim
against both Farid Effendi (the tax collector) and Fawwaz Effendi, a
leader of the Bani Sakhr tribe whose tent was captured by a German
photographer in 1906 (fig. 5.1).[70] Fawwaz Effendi was among the Bani
Sakhr leaders who attained bureaucratic positions in the Ottoman administration above the level of headman when they became directors
of a new subdistrict (nahiye) composed of interior land in their control
in the 1890s.[71] Hamad bin ʿAwad accused Farid Effendi of taking his
valuable horse in lieu of taxes that Fawwaz Effendi owed to the treasury for the tax on Bani Sakhr agricultural property.

Farid Effendi's defense was similar to that of Mustafa Effendi in 1912
but with more detail and more serious counteraccusations. He said
that contrary to the plaintiff's claim, the horse in question, which was
tied to the court door for identification purposes, actually belonged to
Fawwaz Effendi of the Bani Sakhr and that Fawwaz Effendi had already
tried to retrieve it from the tax office. Farid Effendi claimed that even
though the plaintiff, Hamad, was not a member of the Bani Sakhr, he
had colluded with Fawwaz Effendi to mount a case in the sharia court

FIGURE 5.1. Lager der Beni Sachr-Beduinen Zelt des Scheich Fauâz, 1906 (Camp of the Bani Sakhr Bedouins Tent of Shaykh Fawwaz, 1906). Photograph by Bernhard Moritz. Published in Berlin by Deitrich Reimer in 1916 and accessed through the Library of Congress. www.loc.gov/item/2014648734.

in which he would say the horse was his, produce bribed witnesses to corroborate his claim, and obtain a ruling from the sharia court judge to force the tax office to return the confiscated horse. In effect, he accused Fawwaz Effendi of moving animals over "tribal lines" in order to avoid losing them to confiscation for collectively assessed tax debt. Had Hamad bin ʿAwad been an administrative member of Fawwaz Effendi's tribe, the Bani Sakhr, Farid Effendi could have argued that the horse was part of the same tax burden, but because he was not, Farid Effendi had little claim to the horse. Farid Effendi accused the Bedouin of "fabricating" sharia court claims to subvert his efforts at revenue collection. When Fawwaz Effendi got to court, he claimed that he had no right to the horse in question. Furthermore, he argued, since Hamad bin ʿAwad was not even a member of the Bani Sakhr, why would he collude with him? Despite Farid Effendi's pleas, the judge ruled for Hamad bin ʿAwad, ordering Farid Effendi to return the horse after two witnesses corroborated his claims.

Farid and Mustafa Effendis' cases emphasize the challenges tax officials faced identifying both human and equine individuals and connecting them to collectively assessed tax burdens. In the late 1860s, central lawmakers had attempted to address the widespread issue of animal theft by instituting a title-deed scheme for livestock that would both connect individual animals to individual human owners and create a source of revenue for district-level market officials, who would oversee and tax official sales. By the early twentieth century, this scheme had been abandoned owing to the realization that confining livestock sales to official markets was potentially detrimental to far-flung rural communities.[72] In a related move in 1901, the central regime attempted to institute a tax on livestock beyond the sheep tax, covering various types of horses, mules, donkeys, water buffalo, and camels and requiring individual owners to pay fixed fees per head.[73] By 1907, this tax was also cancelled because of complaints that it was squeezing an already-squeezed population of poor farmers and that the administrative apparatus to keep all of these animals within district borders in order to count them and connect them to individual taxpaying owners did not exist.[74]

Salt court cases involving the confiscation of livestock show that while the identity of particular animals and their owners was well-known within particular communities, both tent- and house-dwelling, it was difficult for appointed district officials like Mustafa Effendi and Farid Effendi to discern. The sharia court had time-honored methods for identifying particular animals, including requiring litigants to specify their age, size, color, and specific features like a white nose or a particular type of tail.[75] But particular animals could not be definitively connected to individual human owners or sometimes even to particular communities for tax purposes without a more intrusive system. Individuals who wished to retain animals seized for unpaid tax debt could argue that they really belonged to a relative, that they had sold the animal, or that it belonged to another tribe altogether.[76]

Fawwaz Effendi also took advantage of sharia court procedure in this case. In the sharia court, no matter the protests of tax collectors about paid witnesses, two verifiable witnesses were enough to obtain a favorable ruling. Unlike in the nizamiye courts, where a public prosecutor would have followed up on the case facts with the interest of the treasury in mind, the sharia court judge made his ruling based on litigant and witness statements alone. It is also striking that the sharia court continued to rule on these and other cases of "livestock theft" throughout the Ottoman period, troubling the claim that its purview was limited to "personal status." The court's willingness to hear such cases, even as it rejected cases involving agricultural land during the same period, suggests that the divide between movable and immovable property was important to jurisdictional practice alongside emergent understandings of personal status.[77]

Because we do not have a full record of the Salt Court of First Instance, it is difficult to know if tax collectors like Farid and Mustafa Effendi took these cases to the nizamiye system to attempt to carry out auctions of confiscated livestock property after failing to produce favorable sharia court rulings. In the absence of a comprehensive property survey, however, connecting taxpaying humans to particular confiscable animals would remain elusive even for a more formal investigation. The role of headmen, especially in seasonally mobile tent-dwelling communities, remained crucial to uneven processes of building a bureaucratic state in the Syrian interior.

What do these court cases from the Syrian interior have to do with debates over subjecthood and citizenship? Headmen like ʿAbd al-Muhsin al-Bakhit gained powerful claims to entry into the status group of men of property through their work as headmen in the final decades of the nineteenth century. They owned registered land, they invested in their constituents' agricultural production, and they were closely involved in governing practices with taxation at their center. While we know little about how headmen became headmen or con-testations over the office itself, imperial law stipulated the same re-quirements for the position as membership in town-based governing councils: ownership of registered immovable property and election by a community of property-owning citizens. Whether or not these elections occurred in practice, Bedouin bureaucrats were closely as-sociated with the men of property in Salt who were the main local interpreters and enforcers of imperial tax policy. When this policy entailed confiscating the privately owned livestock of Ottoman sub-jects without any type of franchise for tax debts that retained collec-tive elements, the privileges of men of property, including headmen, became egregious. Interior court cases suggest that this confiscation practice intensified after 1908, leading people to take their protests to court. These protests challenged the prerogatives of men of property and the administrative boundaries of "tribe" as a political community. As such, they addressed the conditions of subjecthood and citizenship in the rural reaches of a state space populated, theoretically, by equal individuals.

SUBVERTING THE SHEEP TAX

The cases presented above addressed taxes on landownership and ag-ricultural commodities. People from communities like the Fuqaha, the Manasir, and the Wiraykat were important participants in the administration of these taxes in the Syrian interior because of their close involvement in both agricultural commodity markets and land registration. While members of the Bani Sakhr and other large camel-herding communities also registered land, they were more directly embroiled in disputes over the sheep tax. Alongside many familiar tensions between individual ownership and collective taxation, the sheep tax introduced the problematic of counting and monitoring mobile property. Furthermore, in the Syrian interior, leaders of communities like the Bani Sakhr with large numbers of taxable animals had high-ranking roles in the provincial administration because of their long-standing connections to the pilgrimage. These men proved adept at minimizing the tax burdens of their communities by leveraging their political connections and power. In particular, they used the British occupation of Egypt to their advantage by threatening to move their communities to enemy territory, and they employed threats of violence to villages inhabiting land they regarded as theirs to force tax reductions.

As with land taxes, attempts to transform the sheep tax involved recruiting town-based tax collectors to take over many of the responsibilities of rural elites who lived much closer to sites of herding, breeding, and manufacture and were often directly involved in these activities themselves. The investigation into the conduct of the subprovincial governor Cemal Bey recounted in chapter 4 provides some insight into these politics in the interior district of Karak, south of Salt. Beginning in the 1880s, central lawmakers began mandating the employment of temporarily appointed town-based men "of the group who can read, write and calculate" to collect the sheep tax, limiting headmen's roles to conducting preliminary animal counts.[78] In August 1907, a conflict around the taxes assessed on the livestock of the Bani 'Atiya community,[79] which inhabited the arid regions around Karak and Ma'an during the summer months, illustrates the continuing political influence of high-level Bedouin leaders in processes of tax assessment and collection.

The investigative team's interest in the Bani 'Atiya animal count centered on a telegram-style petition a Bani 'Atiya leader, Shaykh Harb, wrote to the provincial government after Cemal Bey was dismissed from his post and detained in Damascus. Shaykh Harb held the position of "preeminent shaykh" of the Bani ʿAtiya and had become involved in the pilgrimage administration sometime in the nineteenth century. Judging from the deposition he later provided to investigators, Shaykh Harb played many of the roles legally granted to headmen like Nahar al-Bakhit for the Bani ʿAtiya, but he probably represented a larger number of people. Furthermore, without land registers for Karak, it is difficult to know if Shaykh Harb had acquired legal claims to land in the town's vicinity.[80]

Shaykh Harb's complaint highlights both the frustration some rural leaders experienced when dealing with the newly established bureaucracy and how those affiliated with the pilgrimage administration could use their political leverage to influence tax disputes. Shaykh Harb explained that he had initiated the tax collection process when the Bani ʿAtiya began camping in the environs of the town of Karak in early summer, requesting that tax collectors (tahsildar) be sent to complete the Bani ʿAtiya's animal count and assess taxes in accordance with imperial law. Two seasonally hired professional tax collectors visited the Bani ʿAtiya encampment in May 1907, and, following the protocol laid out in imperial law for collecting the livestock tax, they met with Shaykh Harb initially in his capacity as a headman with knowledge of the community's livestock holdings. When they told him the total they wished to collect, however, Shaykh Harb balked; the amount was twice as much as the Bani ʿAtiya had paid in previous years. The tax collectors insisted that they were acting on county governor Cemal Bey's orders, and Shaykh Harb testified that they had agreed to return to Karak together to meet with Cemal Bey and sort out the confusion. When Shaykh Harb arrived at the designated meeting place with his men, however, he found that the tax collectors had already "mounted their horses and ridden off to Karak" without him, having collected the tax they demanded from individual livestock holders in his encampment the day before.[81]

Shaykh Harb described more scenes of exclusion and disrespect at the government offices in Karak, where he quickly went to appeal to Cemal Bey himself. A colleague had found a ripped form written by one of the tax collectors that they believed proved the correct tax assessment for the Bani 'Atiya, and Shaykh Harb painstakingly repaired the form as evidence to take to Cemal Bey. When he finally met Cemal Bey in the government building in Karak, however, he barely glanced at the carefully pieced-together form and dismissed Shaykh Harb's claims, saying he should file his appeal with the county accountant. Shaykh Harb did this, but he said there was no use. Feeling exposed in a government office full of people he did not know, he decided to leave.

Here it might seem that Shaykh Harb's options were similar to those of Nahar al-Bakhit: he could comply with the tax order, or he could attempt to organize his community in opposition. But Shaykh Harb had another pathway to the provincial government that men like Nahar al-Bakhit and Minakid al-Dawjan did not enjoy. He wrote a telegram directly to Damascus and threatened to lead the Bani 'Atiya across the border into Egypt if the tax issue was not resolved.[82] He emphasized the Bani 'Atiya's long-standing loyalty to and cooperation with the Ottoman administration. Besides working closely with tax collectors to count livestock and collect the usual amount assessed on each head, they were also the official protectors of the pilgrimage route between Mudawwara, south of Ma'an, and al-Muazzam, south of Tabuk, in northern Hijaz. In his deposition, Shaykh Harb played on the same perceptions of a hierarchy of bureaucratic knowledge he felt threatened to exclude him: "My people are desert people; they don't understand anything." It was his duty to protect them from Cemal Bey's corruption and from the poverty he claimed double taxation would entail.

Shaykh Harb's deposition and telegram reflect the tensions around belonging in a new Ottoman bureaucratic administration that was dominated by town dwellers, but they also speak to the influence he ultimately maintained even as this town-based administration gained traction. While Shaykh Harb accused Cemal Bey and the tax collectors of excluding him from their deliberations, his claim to represent the Bani 'Atiya and especially his threat to lead them to Egypt produced a swift provincial-level response. By the early twentieth century, provincial and district-level bureaucrats knew they could not afford to alienate figures like Shaykh Harb. With the exception of the Hijaz Railway, the capital-intensive projects and tens of thousands of immigrants that lawmakers and officials had imagined in the 1870s had not materialized. Furthermore, on the consolidation of the British occupation of Egypt, Karak had become a borderland outpost. Both Karak and the neighboring district of Ma'an were sparsely populated, and tent-dwelling groups were both a revenue source and a claim to a loyal local population.[83] Shaykh Harb's threat to defect to Egypt if his tax issue was not resolved garnered the governor's attention in Damascus and led him to add the mismanagement of the Bani 'Atiya livestock count to a long list of accusations against Cemal Bey.

Beyond the political leverage Shaykh Harb wielded when communications with Ottoman tax officials broke down, the investigation also showed the complex arrangements Shaykh Harb had crafted with the provincial administration with regard to the Bani 'Atiya livestock tax. One of the district tax collectors described the livestock taxation process to the investigators in detail. Contrary to codified law, the count of Bani 'Atiya animals did not take place on the same date each year; rather, it was timed to coincide with the Bani 'Atiya's seasonal presence in the district during the summer harvest so they could also buy supplies while they were near town.[84] The accountant in the Karak government office explained that the Bani 'Atiya tax rate was doubled in 1907 because they had a special arrangement to pay taxes to the two different fiscal districts they inhabited, Karak and neighboring Ma'an. That year, he and Cemal Bey claimed, the Bani 'Atiya had evaded payment in Ma'an, so the Karak district had charged them for both districts.[85]

This arrangement reflected the complex tax structures that the combination of mobile populations and district, county, and provincial borders engendered, borders that were first and foremost established to erect a fiscal grid on the semiarid landscape. Like other modern bureaucratic tax regimes, especially those targeting movable property like livestock, the Ottoman system recognized the importance of both a fixed annual tax date and fixed jurisdictional boundaries. The Bani 'Atiya's arrangement was a form of accommodation, but it problematizes the oft-made claim that modern forms of governance are incompatible with mobile populations. Shaykh Harb recognized the lengths to which the provincial administration had gone in order to keep the Bani ʿAtiya within the transformed sphere of submission: he emphasized that his problem was not with the Ottoman government (*al-ḥakūma*) writ large but with the "harshness" (*qasāwa*) of Cemal Bey in particular. Shaykh Harb's situation shows that despite the Hamidian-era attempts to bureaucratize rural taxation and reduce the influence of rural community elites, leaders of large camel-herding communities were able to consolidate their positions during this period, taking advantage of the incomplete nature of property registration and survey, their sustained demographic leverage, and their ongoing mobility.

While Shaykh Harb of the Bani ʿAtiya used the threat of decamping from Ottoman territory to avoid excessive taxation, Talal Paşa of the Bani Sakhr used his political leverage in the pilgrimage administration to avoid paying the Bani Sakhr livestock tax altogether. Beyond the Bani Sakhr's ongoing weight in the pilgrimage administration, Talal Paşa's political leverage stemmed from his long-standing claims against the Ottoman administration for allocating land in his family's control to Christian settlers relocating from Karak in the early 1880s. This complex political situation, which spiraled out of control while the Salt Bedouin were in prison in Karak, became another element of the wider crisis of Ottoman administration in the summer of 1907.

After Midhat Paşa's decision, under French consular pressure, to allocate land near the village of Madaba, sixty kilometers south of Salt, to Christian settlers in 1880, Bani Sakhr herders continued to attempt to regain control of this fertile land, just as the tent-dwelling groups around the town of Salt refused to back down from what they considered their historical right to land settled by refugees in Ayn Suwaylih. Between 1880 and 1907, numerous skirmishes sprang up between the Bani Sakhr and Madaban settlers, and Bani Sakhr leaders repeatedly attempted to register their claims to the fertile lands near the village.[86] These struggles were seasonal, occurring in the summer months when Bani Sakhr families moved their animals across the line of the pilgrimage route and into the gridded, cultivated spaces of the Balqa for pasture.

Meanwhile, shaykhs from the al-Fayiz Bani Sakhr community obtained important positions in the expanding rural bureaucracy: in
1907, Talal Paşa, the great grandson of 'Awad al-Fayiz, was the director
of the subdistrict of Jiza to the south of Salt and, as his title of *paşa* implies, a decorated Ottoman citizen. The rise of the al-Fayiz community,
dating from their prominence in the eighteenth-century pilgrimage
administration, culminated in the careers of men like Talal Paşa and
would continue in the form of close contacts with the Hashemite successors to Ottoman rule.[87] Although the Bani Sakhr never managed to
reclaim the land they had lost to the Christian settlers in Madaba, Talal
Paşa was able to use the land dispute to make other claims, especially
on the Ottoman treasury.

In the summer of 1907, Cemal Bey received numerous pleas to travel
to Madaba in person and conclude a settlement among the Bani Sakhr,
the Christian settlers in Madaba, and another tent-dwelling group
that claimed control over land in the region, the Abu al-Ghanam. The
provincial governor, alongside leaders from all three parties to the
conflict, pleaded with Cemal Bey to defuse the situation in Madaba,
presumably through convincing the Bani Sakhr to retreat by granting them tax breaks.[88] Salim Abu al-Ghanam said that he wrote to
Cemal Bey, complaining of Bani Sakhr aggressions including theft
and murder, but received no response, later opting to appeal to higher
authorities.[89] Talal Paşa, in his capacity as leader of the Bani Sakhr,
described how the Abu al-Ghanam had prevented the Bani Sakhr from
watering their animals or even drinking from the well of Hisban near
Madaba, detailing the cries of thirsty women and children.[90] Cemal
Bey, however, declined to go to Madaba, arguing that he was tied up in
Karak with the Bani 'Atiya animal count.[91]

Cemal Bey elaborated on his reasons for staying out of Madaba in
his written defense to the investigation. He explained that the conflicts
over land between these three parties occurred every summer, that
he had been aware of them when he was governor of Hawran county,
and that he had asked the provincial government to take steps to avoid
them in 1907—all to no avail. He saw the conflicts as the direct result
of the protections the Bani Sakhr enjoyed because of their privileged

position with the administration of the Hajj route. While the governor of Syria and the investigators explained the Madaba conflicts as arguments over resources without assigning blame, Cemal Bey argued that the violence in Madaba was largely due to Bani Sakhr aggression but that whenever local authorities tried to "discipline" them, they encountered opposition from the chief protector of the Hajj route based in Damascus.[92] The Bani Sakhr's status was certainly bolstered by Talal Paşa's position both as an Ottoman bureaucrat and as a man capable of gathering other Bani Sakhr leaders. As the fighting in Madaba escalated, the district governor in Salt heard that Talal Paşa had gathered the Bani Sakhr leaders at his house in Jiza to discuss what to do about the conflict. They reportedly decided that after the ongoing survey of Bani Sakhr animals was finished, they would attack the village of Madaba in what was rendered in both Ottoman Turkish and Arabic as "general killing."[93]

When news of this meeting reached Damascus, Şukri Paşa began sending Cemal Bey direct and increasingly frantic orders to go to Madaba and conclude a settlement between the conflicting parties in order to avoid a "bloodbath."[94] Cemal Bey still refused to travel to Madaba. The governor of Syria finally sent two officials from neighboring districts to make a deal with Talal Paşa, who had said that the attack would wait until the Bani Sakhr animal survey was concluded. In the end, Talal Paşa managed to obtain an exemption from the Bani Sakhr animal tax, more than one hundred thousand piastres, in exchange for the safety of the villagers in Madaba.[95] This type of settlement had been crucial to maintaining "peace and security" in the interior in previous years.

Talal Paşa's ability to use the situation in Madaba to the financial advantage of the Bani Sakhr, as well as Cemal Bey's complaints about the Hajj administration's granting the Bani Sakhr virtual political immunity, is important to understanding how the historical ties between particular large and regionally powerful tent-dwelling groups and the Ottoman administration both maintained their salience and operated in novel ways in the context of modern bureaucratic governance. The continuing importance of the overland pilgrimage route between Damascus and Mecca is largely overshadowed in existing literature by the opening of the Suez Canal in 1869 and the British-regulated steamship route between Suez and Jeddah, which many pilgrims coming from points west chose for its speed over the historical caravan from Damascus.[96] But William Ochsenwald's estimates of the distribution of pilgrims among the different routes show that the overland route remained quite important.[97] In short, the pilgrimage route remained an important avenue to political influence for Bedouin elites, especially from camel-herding communities like the Bani Harb and Bani 'Atiya with historical connections to pilgrimage administration, into the early twentieth century.

The struggles of Talal Paşa and Shaykh Harb illuminate the dynamics of a different sort of Ottoman political participation and citizenship in the early twentieth century. Talal Paşa and, probably, Shaykh Harb were "men of property." Talal Paşa registered significant tracts of land in and around the town of Jiza, where he held his government posts in the early twentieth century. But the influence of both men was concentrated in circles of power beyond the political sphere of the district or even the subprovince that regional men of property dominated. Their political influence transcended, both spatially and temporally, the still relatively new apparatuses of Ottoman state space, causing immense frustration to the keepers of that space like Cemal Bey. This kind of lasting influence, and these circles of power beyond those mandated in codified law, would continue to frustrate men of property throughout the Ottoman period. Although we know little about the internal politics of the Bani Sakhr and Bani 'Atiya, the ongoing weight of men like Talal Paşa and Shaykh Harb in the Ottoman administration meant both continued access to land and reduced tax burdens for both communities.

Shaykh Harb, Talal Paşa, 'Abd al-Muhsin al-Bakhit, Minakid al-Wiraykat, and Nahar al-Bakhit exercised Ottoman citizenship in different ways. Bedouin headmen worked through an increasingly entrenched Ottoman bureaucratic system that privileged their property ownership, as well as their knowledge of and ability to access wealth within their administratively defined communities. Shaykh Harb and Talal Paşa capitalized on their reputations and those of their fathers and grandfathers in the Ottoman regime. Both groups asserted their membership in an exclusive circle of Ottoman citizens with rights to govern themselves and their communities of subjects.

To illuminate the stakes of the inclusion of these men in that contested community of citizens, I return to the story of Farah Abu Jabir, who protested his mistreatment at the hands of imperial soldiers by asserting that he was a well-known man of property. After initially evading soldiers' attempts to escort him under arms to Karak, Abu Jabir was finally detained at the newly built train station in the village of Amman, waiting for a train to Damascus with ten tins of olive oil he planned to present to the governor of Syria while insisting on his loyalty to the Ottoman regime. With these actions, Abu Jabir asserted both types of Ottoman citizenship: from within the system as a man of property and from above it as a man of political influence with direct connections to governors and high-ranking officials. The Abu Jabir family has played crucial roles in various moments of this book's narrative: as "pioneer" merchant capitalists from Palestine making early deals with the Bani Sakhr to start a plantation in the North, as builders of Ottoman state space on administrative and judicial councils in the Balqa district, and as prominent merchant landowners creating some of the first sites of daily wage labor in the interior. Their positions on governing councils followed, in some part, from their claims to represent their small Latin Christian community in Salt. In a broader sense, however, they represented a group of men of property that transcended administrative divisions of tribe and sect to dominate and exploit the interior's labor and commodity production through landholding, credit provision, and commerce.

In the summer of 1907, however, Farah Abu Jabir had multiple reasons to evade Cemal Bey's soldiers and attempt to contact the governor of Syria directly. Archival records show that his family's landholdings in Salt district had come under the direct scrutiny of the Ministry of the Interior. In particular, Ministry officials were concerned that these landholdings, some of them dating to the 1850s, circumvented a recent ban on Christians holding land in the vicinity of the newly laid Hijaz Railway. The correspondence explicitly refers to this ban

as responding to security concerns.[98] Questions about the Abu Jabirs'
loyalty to the Ottoman imperial cause would continue during World
War I.[99] They demonstrate the increasingly precarious nature of non-
Muslim citizenship in regions deemed "strategic" in the late Ottoman
context.[100] As we saw in chapter 4, Ottoman officials who placed their
anxieties about territorial sovereignty over capitalist prerogatives to
develop the interior won out.

In certain ways, Bedouin bureaucrats were also precarious members of the community of men of property. As members of tribes, they
were marked as in need of improvement and as potentially unready for
self-government. This designation led to impoverishment and violence
at the hands of modernizing state officials backed by military forces
in other communities placed in the same administrative categories in
both Adana and Iraq.[101] Cemal Bey, committed as he was to a vision of
a settled, productive interior, advocated "disciplining" the Bani Sakhr
into a vision of capitalist state space. But the fact that Bedouin communities in Syria fell on the right side of Ottoman security concerns,
increasingly defined by assumptions about foreign influence that were
tied to religious affiliation, was ultimately decisive. In the eyes of Şukri
Paşa, the governor of Syria, they were potentially productive and loyal
subjects and citizens who represented the regime's best hope for maintaining sovereignty in the southern interior.

The inclusion of Bedouin in the polity of Ottoman citizens and
subjects meant that when Fari' al-Husami, 'Ashtiyya al-Khusaylat, and
Hamad bin 'Awad challenged the practices of tax collectors and headmen in court, their arguments reverberated beyond the circumstances
of their particular cases. Their claims spoke to and within a universe
of codified administrative law that created a web of reference points
for an increasingly standardized vision of Ottoman population and
economy. Their claims challenged the structure of that web: the prerogatives of headmen to represent them both as (movable) property
owners and as members of administratively defined tribes to the treasury. In the case of Hamad bin 'Awad's claim, this challenge cut to the
heart of the illegibility of the human boundaries of the tribe to those
outside the local community.

There is no indication that these actors were men of property, meaning they had no legal claim to choose either their community's headmen or the membership of district governing councils with wide-ranging powers to determine landownership in the interior. This jurid-ical status-based exclusion adds texture to a literature largely focused on questions of ethnic and religious status in the late Ottoman period. Excluded from the fullest expression of Ottoman citizenship that men of property enjoyed, Fari', Hamad, and 'Ashtiyya did inhabit an Ot-toman polity as subjects, a status that enabled them to make claims both to justice and to potential citizenship. They could protest what they saw as the unjust actions of their community representatives that were part of an ongoing process of defining imperial population, territory, and markets through fiscal regulations. The foundational institutions framing these processes were a universalized network of districts, councils, and headmen across a defined territory, one that included the Syrian interior but excluded, to an extent, regions like Hijaz and Yemen, where the full range of new administrative and judicial entities were not established.[102] Hamad, 'Ashtiyya, and Fari' were taxpayers without representation in an emergent and exclusive Ottoman polity whose shape and membership were redefined after the devastating losses of the 1870s.

The tax laws and conflicts around their implementation cemented the tribe as an administrative category in the modern imperial and postimperial states of the Eastern Mediterranean. While the Ottoman administration did not juridically isolate tribes, it did embed a sepa-rate, community-based category of administration within an increas-ingly geographically organized system of villages, towns, and districts. As we have seen, the historical distinction between community-based and geographically based categories was hardly clear-cut. Centuries of community-based taxation hardened the human boundaries of Ot-toman villages, and tribes were explicitly attached to particular geo-graphically based districts for administrative purposes.

The foundational importance of the tribe in everyday contests over tax administration ensured its centrality to processes of rural gover-nance in the late Ottoman period and beyond. This category would endure as a defining factor in resource distribution and governance in the Mandate and national periods in both Jordan and Syria and in informal and vernacular remnants of these processes until today. Both Mandate administrations would juridically isolate Bedouin in ways that the Ottoman government did not.[103] This policy would not have been possible without late Ottoman administration's linkage of the tribe to everyday processes of modern state administration, resource allocation, and taxation beginning in the Hamidian period.[104] These legal and administrative categories became reference points for organizing people, land, and commodities across a particular, bordered territory, as well as for human claims for a more just distribution of resources.

CONCLUSION

IN THE YEARS after the 1948 establishment of the State of Israel and the 1967 Israeli occupation of the West Bank and Gaza Strip, hundreds of thousands of Palestinian refugees entered the Syrian interior. The town of Amman swelled in size, and both refugees and investors began attempting to build on and buy land at the new city's edges that Bedouin communities continued to control. This land was largely outside the boundaries of the successive land registration efforts of the Ottoman, British, and Jordanian regimes, all of which had focused on arability and agricultural production as the main determinant of ownership.[1] When Bedouin elites attempted to register their landholdings in the suburbs of Amman, however, they found that the Jordanian state authorities no longer considered the land marginal, asserting state domain and demanding legal title deeds for the land before they would sanction sales.[2] In the absence of a legal settlement or state-sanctioned documentation, Bedouin sold unregistered land to refugees and investors using documents called *hujja*s. In recent decades, the sale of unregistered land with *hujja*s has been documented across the post-Ottoman interior, from the suburbs of Amman to the Azraq oasis on the road to Iraq to the Euphrates Valley in Syria.[3]

Just as in the late nineteenth century, the rising value of land precipitated by influxes of refugees and investor interest changed central
lawmakers' opinion about the marginality of unregistered land that
Bedouin communities used and controlled. This shift led to limited
state land agency attempts to outlaw the use of *hujjas*, to reach settlements and conduct registration among rival claimants, and to under-
take protracted demolition campaigns targeting "illegal" structures
on unregistered lands in the Amman suburbs.[4] It also led to trenchant
conflict between Bedouin claimants and state agencies.

For some observers, the persistence of *hujja*-based rural land markets signals the persistence of the political power of "tribes" in modern
Jordan, as organizations that problematize the central state's claim to
monopolize power.[5] But as the preceding chapters have shown, the
construction of the "tribe" and other rural categories of governance
for organizing land and people were crucial and inseparable elements
of the construction of the modern state in the late Ottoman period. The
tribe and the modern state were born simultaneously in a process that
also transformed, in an unfinished and contested manner, the interior
landscape into exclusive spheres of private and state domain. The persistence of a "noncompliant" practice of employing legal documentary
forms, *hujjas*, that provided the conditions for a "semiautonomous"
land market speaks to the unfinished nature and contingent outcomes
of the modern state project. This project aimed to categorize the landscape and its inhabitants and monopolize the distribution of resources
within a bounded territory.

This book has argued that in the Syrian interior, this project of theoretically comprehensive categorization and distribution began in the
late nineteenth century Ottoman context, in the wake of the global
financial crises of the 1870s. In the ideal Ottoman iteration of categories of land and people, administrative hierarchies spread into the
countryside in the form of bureaucratic expansion, providing direct
legal channels that connected the Balqa interior directly to Damascus
and ultimately to Istanbul. Although their aim was to create a centralized chain of command, these channels also reflected the deep and
long-standing commercial, political and legal connections among

inhabitants of towns, villages, and encampments in the Syrian interior. They built on two centuries of close Ottoman engagement with camel-herding tent dwellers and their participation in imperial fiscal and administrative transformation, especially in the context of the pilgrimage.

With this administrative and legal edifice, Ottoman lawmakers named and aimed to improve—that is, settle—communities they designated as "tribal." As competition over land increased in the 1890s, officials and investors also used this designation to attempt, often unsuccessfully, to deny tent-dwelling people their historic land rights. Just as their successors did in the late twentieth century in the wake of waves of Palestinian, Iraqi, and finally Syrian dispossession and displacement, Ottoman lawmakers declared land Bedouin used for part-time farming and grazing "empty" state domain and tried to reallocate it to refugees and capitalists. Late Ottoman attempts to claim "empty land" occurred alongside similar efforts in other contiguous empires competing for sovereignty in the British-centered global economic order of the late nineteenth century. A global perspective reveals striking similarities in both the chronology and substance of Ottoman, American, and Russian policies toward landscapes formerly deemed peripheral and marginal, especially because of the perceived mobility and underproductivity of their inhabitants. Amid the increased inter-imperial competition of the final quarter of the nineteenth century, efforts to claim such landscapes as state domain, reallocate them to settlers and investors toward increasing productivity, and ensure the loyalty of their inhabitants to new imperial nation-building projects intensified.

But while locating Ottoman lawmakers' visions of developed, loyal rural landscapes alongside those of their counterparts, a global framework of contiguous empires also reveals the historically contingent outcomes of the process of implementing Ottoman policy. In particular, the integration of the tribe alongside the village into a contiguous juridical and administrative space that stretched across the empire meant that Bedouin were able to carve space for themselves in the expanding and transforming imperial bureaucracy.[6] The United States' imperial regime in North America confined Native American communities to reservations in the northern plains, and the Russian regime kept Kazakhs under military rule in Central Asia. Both communities occupied juridically isolated spaces. In contrast, Bedouin and the landscapes they inhabited existed under the same legal framework governing Anatolia and what remained of the Ottoman Balkans. Ottoman officials' precarious position on the interimperial Eurasian stage, especially the threats of British and Russian encroachment and the imperative to retain a loyal population in contested regions, gave Bedouin bureaucrats political leverage as they worked both within and without the imperial system to maintain rights over land in a context of refugee resettlement and capitalist expansion.[7]

The argument that an emergent Ottoman national-imperial governing politics included the Syrian interior as an integral space and its Bedouin inhabitants as loyal subjects does not deny the violent and exclusionary nature of those politics in the intensely competitive environment of post-1870s Eurasia. The Armenian Genocide underlined the fact that the Ottoman version of nation-making was potentially exterminatory in many of the same ways as the Russian and American. Rather, unlike their imperial counterparts' images of Native Americans in the northern plains or Kazakhs in the Central Asian steppe, late Ottoman lawmakers imagined Bedouin as potentially productive and loyal. In the categorical political climate of the late nineteenth century, this vision had much to do with the assumptions both that most Bedouin were loyal Muslims and that, like peasants, they were downtrodden subjects who needed to be rescued from the rapacious elites in their own communities.[8]

In contrast to this late Ottoman inclusion of the Syrian interior in an integrated administrative landscape, the late twentieth- and twenty-first-century scholarly tendency to regard tribal spaces as essentially different from urban/settled ones more closely reflects the administrative policies of British and French lawmakers toward Bedouin in the interwar mandate administrations. Both the French and British mandate administrations juridically separated "the desert" from "the sown"[9] within their territorial boundaries (see map 6.1). They employed

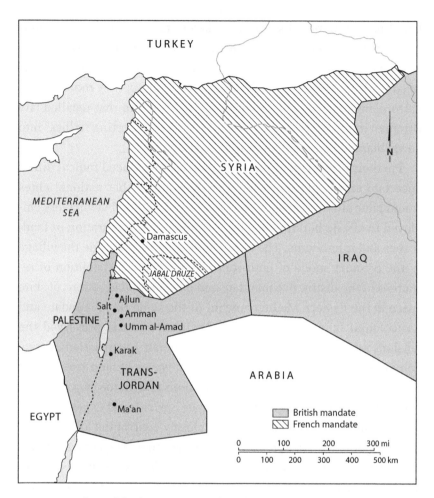

MAP 6.1. Borders of the interwar French and British Mandates.

not only separate categories of land but separate categories of people, with those designated as "nomadic Bedouin" answering to a wholly distinct legal and administrative apparatus. Whereas Ottoman officials like Midhat Paşa dreamed of closing the coastal-interior divisions he perceived by eventually eliminating the category of "tribe," colonial regimes aimed to entrench those divisions to preclude the kinds of rural-urban connections and the possibility of rural resistance that anticolonial revolts of the 1920s and 1930s embodied. In the postcolonial period, nationalist elites worked to transcend these divisions with developmentalist attempts to reintegrate interior landscapes into a standardized administrative order, now on a geographic scale defined by the postwar national borders. In doing so, they returned to a patronizing discourse of inclusion toward Bedouin that recalled late Ottoman imperial nation-making efforts while inserting "tribes" into newly bounded national territorial geographies.[10]

Furthermore, even as mandate policies introduced radical difference into an integrationist late Ottoman policy that national elites would later aim to revive, both colonial and national lawmakers employed the basic building blocks of Ottoman administration of landscapes and inhabitants. The tribe would endure alongside the village as the primary mode of both social identity and distribution of resources in the distinctive mandate and postcolonial iterations of state space in the Eastern Mediterranean. At the same time, mandate and postcolonial land policies in both Jordan and Syria preserved the tensions and contestations of the late Ottoman construction of state domain outside regions deemed arable in waves of land registration between the 1870s and 1970s. These tensions rest on the contradiction between lawmakers' desire to encourage agricultural expansion and investment, on the one hand, and to closely control the allocation of land and preempt rural resistance, on the other. The contradictions of the Ottoman legacy of state domain have left large swaths of arid and semiarid land under continuing forms of Bedouin administrative sovereignty in the form of *hujja*-based local land markets, sometimes until the present. These markets that Bedouin elites continue to administer are the historical outcome of contestations over state domain. In their reliance on *hujjas*, these markets retain the traces of a robust Ottoman-Islamic shared legal framework that preceded the expansion of state space in the Syrian interior. These markets insist, in the face of doctrines of state domain, that the notion of "empty" landscapes is never more than a legitimizing discourse for the expansive and interrelated projects of capital and the modern state.

THE SYRIAN INTERIOR IN GLOBAL PERSPECTIVE

This book has chronicled transformations in the Ottoman regime's policies toward the Syrian interior and its tent-dwelling inhabitants from the eighteenth century through the twentieth. Like the Kazakh steppe in Central Asia and the North American plains, the Syrian interior was a marginal, but also familiar, imperial space from the perspective of Ottoman lawmakers prior to the mid-nineteenth century. These spaces of familiar marginality were common to early modern contiguous empires. The complex historical relationships central imperial regimes maintained with the inhabitants of these spaces were crucial to efforts to integrate them into modern state frameworks in the second half of the nineteenth century. This type of multicentury relationship differed fundamentally from the experience of European colonizers encountering societies for the first time in the late imperial push to fill in, settle, and commodify global landscapes. It is also markedly different from the multicentury colonial experiences of British India or French Algeria, because when the nineteenth-century process of making state space occurred, it aimed for an integrated national-imperial territory rather than an intensified metropole-colony relationship.

A broad framework of contiguous nationalizing empires is also useful for the internal nuances it reveals. In the Ottoman context, the centuries of administrative involvement in a multilayered system of imperial sovereignty that some Bedouin communities experienced was an important precedent for the Bedouin bureaucrats who took part in the process of modern state-building in the nineteenth century. Their roles had long-term effects on the shape of the modern state in the post-Ottoman era, including the importance of local administration, a politically active and legally integrated population outside of cities, and a tribal population with deep investment in modern state structures.

Between the sixteenth and eighteenth centuries, the Ottoman regime focused direct administration on "nodes and corridors," including the pilgrimage route, in variegated geographical regions, including mountains, marshes, and deserts beyond zones of intensive agriculture in Syria and elsewhere in the empire.[11] Russian officials claimed Kazakhs inhabiting the Central Asian steppe as their subjects in the early eighteenth century. Until then, however, these officials were mainly concerned with Kazakh lands for their commercial through-routes to Central Asia and Persia. The imperial regime built a line of fortifications and small towns on the northern edge of the steppe in the mid-eighteenth century, a "corridor" of direct administration that precipitated struggles over land between Cossacks, Russian settlers, and Kazakhs who used the land surrounding the forts for pasture.[12] Beyond that corridor, Russian officials engaged in imperial expansion by alliance building, which was attractive to Kazakh leaders for internal political purposes. This process of alliance building was similar to the Ottoman forms of eighteenth-century layered sovereignty described in chapter 1 that delegated household-based administration to Bedouin elites like Qaʿdan al-Fayiz.[13] Like the Ottoman regime in the Syrian interior, the Russian government would not move to closely administer the Central Asian steppe's population, and later its land, until the nineteenth century.[14]

The political situation in the North American plains was more complex in the eighteenth century, as expanding Native American communities like the Lakota gained ground in a region of interimperial competition.[15] Representatives of French, British, Spanish, and eventually American imperial enterprises exerted power through forts and trading posts, lobbying for spheres of influence through trade.[16] None of these imperial entities attempted to intensively regulate the relationship between people and the landscape beyond the Mississippi River. North American and Ottoman experiences began to converge later in the eighteenth century, when the new United States developed a system of subsidies and gifts in its territories that brought the central government into a wide swathe of interior households despite a thin official presence on the ground.[17] Similarly, the increasingly complex Ottoman system of subsidies to particular Bedouin groups who provided security and provisions along the pilgrimage route incorporated them into fiscal arrangements salient throughout the empire. Alongside this administrative integration, Bedouin groups in the Syrian interior participated in a legal and commercial environment that stretched across the Arabian Peninsula, Palestine, and the Syrian interior. This commercial environment revolved around competitive tax farming and expanding trade in lucrative commodities that reflected an increasingly global market, especially in wheat and weapons.[18]

The sharp interstate competition and aggressive colonial tactics of the late eighteenth century, especially between the British and French empires, hardened political boundaries across Eurasia and the Americas and heralded a long period of Ottoman defensiveness against European expansion. This competition took different forms within the Ottoman Empire; in the Syrian interior, the rise of the Saudi state, followed by Mehmed 'Ali's insurgent regime, initiated a profound crisis in the existing Ottoman system of layered sovereignty that left much of the daily business of direct administration to local groups. The competition among these entities eventually precipitated a newly territorial relationship between the Ottoman state, the tent-dwelling inhabitants of the Syrian interior, and its semiarid landscape. Even so, the human alliances and administrative forms built during the preceding period of layered sovereignty would leave their mark on the process of making state space in the nineteenth century.

Imperial nation-building projects in the nineteenth century involved interrelated goals of tightening sovereign control over physical landscapes and their inhabitants, on the one hand, and increasing their productivity, on the other. In both the United States and the Ottoman Empire, processes of imperial nation-making responded to secession crises during the first half of the nineteenth century.[19] The Russian and Ottoman regimes shared the experience of intense inter-imperial competition—Russian expansionism into Ottoman territories was a crucial motivator for military reform—and a coinciding focus on sovereignty over borderland regions across nineteenth-century Eurasia. Alongside this competition, in the mid-nineteenth century the Ottoman, Russian, and new American regimes faced the challenges and opportunities of a wheat boom in an increasingly integrated global market and unprecedented levels of migration, especially of cultivating settlers.

Nationalizing imperial entities responded to these challenges and opportunities with legal reforms that privileged settled cultivation and sidelined the historic land rights of people using the land for grazing and part-time farming, implementing a growing consensus around the parameters of "improvement" in a competitive national-imperial global context. Imperial lawmakers saw efficient administration of land and people as integral to encouraging the settlement, prosperity, and civilizational development of populations full of potential, on the one hand, and asserting the imperial state's prerogative to allocate arable land, on the other.[20]

The Russian imperial regime formally annexed the Kazakh steppe in the 1820s, building fortresses, setting up court systems, and attempting to tax the population. The Great Reforms that began with the 1861 emancipation of serfs ultimately aimed to transform the empire's agrarian landscape. An 1868 Provisional Statute reorganized the administration of the steppe, increased the number of Russian and Kazakh bureaucrats, and restricted Kazakh movement between newly defined administrative districts.[21]

This process of dismantling and recreating the administrative sovereignty of Kazakh elites had parallels in the reconstructed United States. After the Civil War, the United States federal regime abolished its existing treaty system, ceasing to acknowledge Native American nations as sovereign entities. The restrictions Kazakhs faced in the steppe were a lesser version of the experience of Native Americans inhabiting reservations on the northern plains in the 1870s, reservations that came with federally appointed agents of the Indian Office, new roles for chiefs in resource allocation and security provision, strict curtailment of mobility, and dependence of Native communities on the American government for food and shelter.[22]

In parallel, the Ottoman regime extended increasingly standardized imperial administrative practice into the Syrian interior between the 1840s and 1870s. The central government's construction of tribes as uniform categories of rural administration, and the simultaneous plan for their assimilation into district and village administration, was also a move to undermine regional forms of administrative sov-

ereignty. During the same period, the Russian imperial regime organized Kazakh communities into legible administrative districts with
a hierarchy of elite intermediaries.[23] In the United States, the complex
relationship between federal agents and Sioux "head chiefs," whom
agents simultaneously depended on and aimed to eventually obviate,
directly recalls the status of the Ottoman tribe as an administrative
tool that lawmakers saw as marking a human evolutionary phase that
would be transcended at an undefined future point. In the meantime,
hierarchies of chiefs and headmen created tangible shifts in power and
wealth within their own communities.[24]

In all three empires, attempts to integrate, transform, and ultimately usurp existing forms of administrative sovereignty were closely
related to imperial moves to reallocate land to cultivating settlers and
refugees perceived as more industrious and productive than the existing inhabitants. This phenomenon was most dramatic in the case of
the United States, where historians have treated the increasing flow of
white settlers, their violent conflicts with Native Americans, and capitalist interest in the plains as a main impetus for the establishment
of reservations and the eventual extension of federal sovereignty in
the 1870s.[25] Beginning in the late 1830s, the Russian regime allowed
Russian peasants in regions "exceptionally short of land" to migrate
and resettle in Siberia and the Kazakh Steppe, conducting surveys to
identify those regions most suitable for Russian colonization.[26] The
Ottoman regime's privileging of the rights of cultivators and open
policies toward refugees and settlers in the late 1850s provided the
administrative basis for granting land to immigrants constructed as
productive. In all three cases, midcentury imperial laws demonstrate
a willingness to deny the historic land rights of existing populations
constructed as unproductive.

Despite these broad similarities, attempts to transform and standardize agrarian property relations as a foundational element of imperial nation-making responded to multilayered and complex existing
property regimes within each empire.[27] In the mid-nineteenth century, the Kazakh steppe, the North American plains, and the Syrian
interior shared layered legal frameworks for determining land rights,

on the one hand, and regulating growing settler interest, on the other. But the legal and commercial space shared among Bedouin leaders, merchant capitalists, and wage laborers who settled in the Syrian interior rested on a foundation of mutually recognizable forms of contract and legal norms that stretched across the Arabian Peninsula to the Indian Ocean world.[28] This was also the shared legal foundation for Ottoman officials' attempts to transform the interior landscape into state space by implementing a private property regime. The Syrian interior was not a "middle ground" between two distinct legal traditions as in the Kazakh steppe or the North American plains.[29] Rather, Ottoman officials, capitalist entrepreneurs, and Bedouin elites worked from shared, if highly contested, Islamic legal traditions for governing property relations. This legal landscape was a coterminous lived experience that Ottoman officials' modernizing claims of underdevelopment and the need for improvement denied.

This shared legal and commercial world helps explain the contingent ways administrative sovereignty shifted in the nineteenth-century Syrian interior, especially with regard to property relations, mobility, and land rights. In contrast to their American and Russian imperial counterparts, Ottoman officials did not systematically limit Bedouin mobility. The ʿAdwan continued to move between the wadi and the shifa seasonally, and the Bani Sakhr continued their longer migrations across the pilgrimage route that sustained camel-herding livelihoods even as their leadership became more involved in directing lucrative agricultural projects. Furthermore, the administrative status of the Syrian interior differed from that of the North American plains or the Central Asian steppe. Native American reservations were exceptional spaces in the administrative law of the United States.[30] While chiefs and headmen certainly participated in American politics and performed daily administrative duties vis-à-vis their communities, they did not enter a wider hierarchy of administration governing an increasingly cohesive imperial state space. Rather, Jeffrey Ostler described their work as an attempt to "transform the prison of the reservation into a homeland."[31] Similarly, when the Russian imperial state moved to directly administer the Kazakh steppe in the late 1860s, mechanisms of self-government that were instituted elsewhere in Russia as part of the Great Reforms were not extended to Central Asia.[32] The Kazakh steppe remained under a form of military rule until 1917, a point crucial to its construction as a "colony" in the Russian imperial imagination.[33] In both of these cases, the local population was deemed unready for the limited forms of self-government that full imperial inclusion entailed.

In the Syrian interior, even as they focused on improving what they saw as a backward and stubbornly mobile population, lawmakers attempted to implement an administrative hierarchy that applied to the entire empire. To be sure, lawmakers and local officials saw the province as bifurcated between an advanced coast and an underdeveloped interior, but they did not place the interior under an exceptional form of rule. Rather, prominent lawmakers like Midhat Paşa believed that integration into existing administrative structures would lead to assimilation. In practice, this meant that even though they presided over tribes rather than villages, headmen like Minakid and Rufayf al-Wiraykat became part of the same community of bureaucrats that village- and town-based headmen entered. They dealt directly with an administrative hierarchy that began with salaried tax collectors and local governing councils and moved quickly to district, subprovincial, and provincial governors. The status of Bedouin headmen and the social and political power they acquired in this period of making state space would prove crucial in the following decades, as competition over interior land increased.

Ottoman lawmakers' compromise on settlement initiatives and decision to integrate the Syrian interior into standardized forms of imperial administration responded both to the existing legal environment on the ground and to the imperative to maintain regional communities' loyalty and reduce the possibility of rural unrest and rebellion. This meant that Bedouin did not experience the wide-scale rupture to their livelihoods and means of sustenance that native communities in both the Central Asian steppe and North American plains underwent in the 1870s and 1880s. American and Russian lawmakers were hardly immune to interimperial competition, with a broader challenge to British hegemony inspiring imperial state-space-making projects in multiple locations across Eurasia and the Americas.[34] But they did not face the same daily threats to administrative sovereignty that shaped Ottoman officials' experience in the post-1870s Syrian interior.

On a discursive level, Ottoman lawmakers certainly fit Bedouin and other communities they defined as nomadic into an evolutionary narrative of human development that resembled the civilizational understandings of their Western European, Russian, and American counterparts.[35] But descriptions of "Ottoman Orientalism" too easily obscure the political roles Bedouin bureaucrats began to acquire in a wider framework of administrative inclusion in the 1870s and 1880s in the Syrian interior. Ottoman modernizers were hardly beyond excluding particular populations from administrative reforms on the basis of civilizational metrics: Thomas Kuehn's work on Yemen shows that the civil court system was not implemented there because of the local population's "customs and dispositions."[36] But even in Yemen, Ottoman lawmakers articulated an ultimate goal of administrative integration. For reasons of geopolitical and fiscal exigency, as well as the long history of Bedouin connections to Ottoman governance, the imperial regime integrated the tent-dwelling population of the Syrian interior into an increasingly standardized imperial administrative framework through the mechanism of the tribe, which mirrored the village in all the power it conferred but marked its members as not producing sufficiently.[37]

Despite this administrative integration, conflicts over property between state-backed refugees and tent-dwelling Bedouin became sharper and more violent in the Ottoman context as elsewhere in the aftermath of the global crises of the 1870s. The official optimism around potential agricultural prosperity that had driven expansive policies on immigration, internal migration, and land grants for settlers in the 1850s and 1860s gave way to anxiety over identifying land in the state domain and resolving escalating disputes between settlers and existing inhabitants in the 1880s and 1890s. These crises not only undermined confidence in the value of grain but also initiated a more intense period of global interimperial competition. The combination of imperial competition, human migration, and economic anxiety in the final decades of the nineteenth century led to new modes of imagining imperial space as bounded, delimited territory.[38]

In the Russian and especially the American cases, escalating disputes over land were closely related to a massive influx of settlers in the northern plains and a more measured but steady flow of emancipated peasants from central Russia into the Kazakh steppe. Subjecting the North American plains and the Kazakh steppe to more intrusive forms of administration and survey that aggressively asserted state domain over purportedly unused land laid the groundwork for allotting land to individuals and households and parceling the "extra" to settlers.[39] In the Ottoman context, the territorial losses in the Balkans after the 1877–78 war signaled an influx of Muslim refugees on a scale unimagined when regulations granting land to immigrants were issued in 1857.[40] While the numbers of refugees remained relatively limited in the Syrian interior in the 1870s and 1880s, plans for refugee resettlement were a major impetus for developing a birds-eye view of available agricultural land on the imperial level.

In this broad sense, the Ottoman, Russian, and American empires shared a context of imperial anxiety over administering land and people in the aftermath of global crisis. The official Ottoman position toward the Syrian interior shifted toward legal exclusion of existing Bedouin forms of land use in the 1890s. Ottoman debates over refugee resettlement, capitalist expansion, and the land around the prospective Hijaz Railway route employed an emergent concept of exclusive state domain that resonated across contiguous empires in the late nineteenth century. A concept of the American West as public domain available for reallocation as private property to white settlers animated the Republican "free soil" arguments of midcentury.[41] While the federal government had limited this process with Native American reservations, the 1887 Dawes Act mandated the individualization of Native American title and opened "excess" reservation land to white settlement. By 1900, Native Americans held half the land they had held in 1881, reduced further in the early twentieth century.[42] In the 1890s, Ottoman land administrators envisioned a similar future, one in which newly registerable and alienable "routes of Bedouin" would be made available on an open market so that they could become objects of capitalist investment, increasing both treasury revenue and a purportedly shared experience of rural prosperity.

At the same time, in the Russian imperial context, a group of technocrats in the Resettlement Administration formed in 1896 conceived of a state fund of empty land on the empire's steppe borderlands, some of which were inhabited by mobile populations they saw as insufficiently productive. They aimed to populate these borderlands with loyal and industrious Russian peasants from the interior, simultaneously solving land and peasant questions, increasing agricultural productivity in the steppe, and securing its "Russian" character.[43] The Stolypin land reforms after the 1905 revolution targeted colonial regions, including the Kazakh steppe, for resettlement, surveying, and registering the holdings of settled individuals and taking the surplus for the state domain. The Russian case differed from the American in that the goal of individualization was to extend the state's birds-eye view beyond the commune to the individual, who would not have the right to alienate land or use it as collateral except with state-run credit agencies.[44] In the Ottoman context, Interior Ministry officials shared both the Russian government's desire for an empty land fund that the state could intimately know and technocratically engineer, on the one hand, and their anxieties about the potential outcomes of an open land market, on the other. Both regimes were deeply concerned with the demographic makeup of borderland regions and saw careful matching of population to plots of land as the best way to secure territory with loyal, productive subjects.

Anxieties over the capacity and potential corruption of the agents of land administrations, seen as in league with local capitalists, were also a shared feature of processes of registration and reallocation across the American, Russian, and Ottoman contexts.[45] As land allocations and settlement progressed, litigation and violence also became common across these spaces. Sioux communities protesting the allotment of their reservation, often peacefully, faced violent repression at the hands of the US military.[46] In Central Asia, land disputes were widespread, and historians count frustration over resettlement policies and extensive land loss among Kazakh communities as the main long-term cause of their participation in the Central Asian revolt during World War I.[47] Constant crises over land allocations were common to emergent spaces of state domain born of dispossession in the American West, the Kazakh steppe, and the Syrian interior at the turn of the twentieth century.

It was in these processes of litigation and administrative haggling over tax burdens and bureaucratic offices that the administrative integration of the Syrian interior became most important. Litigation focused on the interrelated pillars of property registration and taxation. Indirectly, and in combination with ongoing contestations over elected and appointed offices, this litigation referenced the privileges that registered property owners had come to enjoy, especially in terms of political representation. Like in rural regions of imperial Russia, property registrations that formed the basis of theoretically individualized and proportionate taxation remained incomplete in the Syrian interior.[48] But partial registrations revealed interrelated potentials: direct links between the treasury and individual owners/taxpayers and widening wealth inequalities that registration rendered visible and meaningful in new ways. The promise of individual property registration and taxation created space to imagine both a different distribution of assets and tax burdens proportionate to that distribution. Because property ownership and taxation were legally connected to the right to vote for the membership of local governing bodies, this promise also contained the potential for a widened circle of political representation.

The active participation of a population legally and administratively marked as in need of improvement—that is, Bedouin—in these contests over property, taxation, and representation in the Syrian interior was somewhat unique from a global imperial perspective. In the United States, property taxation was an important element of local constitution-making processes in newly forming western states, part of the intensive redefinition of the American political economy post-Reconstruction.[49] New western states shared numerous challenges with the subprovinces and districts of the Syrian interior: comparatively sparse human population, conflicts over the status of Native

American and settler land titles, and the perception that the property tax burden fell unfairly on rural populations.[50] As Noam Maggor has argued, the presence of nonpropertied white men in constitutional struggles in the new states of the post-Reconstruction American West was a key determinant of the nature of those debates.[51] But this expansion of political participation did not extend to Native Americans, whose juridical and spatial isolation on reservations increased markedly during this period.[52] Native Americans' legal acquisition of citizenship was explicitly linked both to individual landownership and to documented claims of disengagement from administratively defined tribes.[53]

In this sense, Native Americans' exceptional political status as "wards of the state" was similar to that of Central Asian inhabitants of the steppe, who were excluded from institutions of self-government under military rule and whose freedom of movement was severely curtailed as Russian immigration to the region increased, especially under an aggressive doctrine of state ownership and right to redistribute land to settlers.[54] This geographically designated exclusion from certain potentialities of imperial political participation occurred in the shadow of an increasingly unified and standardized notion of subjects' rights and obligations in the rest of the empire.[55]

In the Ottoman Syrian interior, Bedouin headmen's struggles over territory and property, whether with tax collectors or within their own communities, were similar to the struggles of other rural community leaders in the Syrian interior and across the Anatolian peninsula, and they referenced the same body of imperial law. Shaykh Harb, ʿAbd al-Muhsin al-Bakhit, and other rising tent dwellers experienced the same dynamics of bureaucratic inclusion and exclusion as town- and village-dwelling men of property. They also faced the same challenges to their power, wealth, and influence as possibilities for widened forms of wealth accumulation and political participation became more imaginable. In the American context, the "tribe" remained sovereign over a juridically isolated and materially dispossessed polity and shrinking territory—a sovereignty that was mainly a tool of social and juridical exclusion in a context of restricted mobility. In contrast, in the Ottoman context, the tribe became an administrative category in an integrated hierarchy of rural domination alongside the privileged agrarian category of the village.

If the contours of Ottoman imperial inclusion became most stark in debates over property registration, taxation, and representation, imperial exclusion also came to be experienced through these vectors. As Ottoman lawmakers felt increasingly encircled by European powers claiming roles as protectors of different religious groups within the empire, and in concert with hardening linkages between notions of territoriality and exclusive property ownership, the specter of land "falling into the wrong hands" became difficult to ignore. From the 1890s onward, exclusionary landownership policies in particular, "sensitive" regions targeted non-Muslims, both explicitly and implicitly, alongside increasing incidents of state-sponsored violence, especially against Armenians.[56] This exclusionary approach to the allocation of land rights would reach the Syrian interior, especially in the context of the construction of the Hijaz Railway, which further increased the potential economic and strategic value of the interior landscape.[57]

The administrative inclusion of Bedouin as *potential* Muslim property-owning citizens in the context of an imperial nation-building project through the precarious and marked category "tribe" stands in contrast to the exclusion of Native Americans and Khazakhs on both racial and religious grounds from the emergent American and Russian polities. To be sure, the Ottoman official desire to integrate the tribal Bedouin population into an emergent national polity on the same terms as village-dwelling Muslim communities responded to the precarity of the Ottoman imperial position in the early twentieth century. But it also heralded active roles for tent-dwelling actors in politics alongside their village-dwelling counterparts and commercial relationships between town and countryside that increased in strength in the first decades of the twentieth century. In the context of aggressive global imperial expansion in the late nineteenth century, the unique integration of the Syrian interior in an emergent Ottoman state space created the conditions for Bedouin bureaucrats' performance of imperial power across villages and tent-dwelling communities. One of the distinct legacies of Ottoman rule, therefore, was rural communities primed for political action with long-standing commercial and political ties to cities when European colonial regimes attempted to exclude and divide them after World War I.

MANDATES, REVOLTS, STATE-BUILDING

The importance of the political connections forged across town-, village-, and encampment-dwelling communities in the process of building late Ottoman state space is especially apparent in the post–World War I Eastern Mediterranean. After the fall of Ottoman armies, British, French, and Hashemite leaders haggled over the terms of League of Nations Mandates in Paris and London. During this uncertain period, between 1918 and 1920, district governments formed under the jurisdiction of the Arab Kingdom that King Faysal al-Hussein, of the sharifian Hashemite family in Mecca, ruled in Damascus after leading the anti-Ottoman, British-backed Arab Revolt.[58] In Jabal Druze in Hawran, in Balqa encampments, in the Kura region of Ajlun, and in the southern town of Karak, these district governments increasingly saw themselves as administrative reference points. Their leaders, however, also asserted their stake in wider regional political debates, especially around questions of anticipated European rule and the desire for a unified Greater Syria.[59] They had, after all, been closely involved in regional political and economic networks for half a century, both through their involvement in grain and other commodity trades and their participation in the administration of land and revenue. When the British-Hashemite and French regimes consolidated sovereignty over the interior, these district governments became loci for anticolonial resistance movements.

The British and French Mandates over Palestine, Syria, Iraq, and the newly conceived political entity of Transjordan were the legal culmination of long-standing Western European claims that the Ottoman Eastern Mediterranean was a space of ineffective sovereignty. In the aftermath of the First World War, the League of Nations classified former Ottoman and German territories as "not-yet peoples," justifying the spatial and temporal extension of European colonial rule and dividing the non-European world into various classes of advancement as nations in need of tutelage for self-rule.[60] As the Mandate regimes and various forms of resistance to colonial rule coalesced, separating political activity into a town-based "nationalist" realm and an interior "tribal" realm became one of the hallmarks of European colonial governance in the Eastern Mediterranean. In contrast to the Ottoman order, the British and French regimes created separate jurisdictions, law codes, and policing regimes for communities they defined as Bedouin, sometimes specifically delineating separate jurisdictions on maps.[61] In certain ways, these regimes of separation codified the vestiges of early modern forms of layered sovereignty that Ottoman modernizers had worked to erase. Elite, town-based nationalists would continue to attempt to transcend this separation, in paternalist and developmentalist terms that recalled late Ottoman modernization efforts, throughout the Mandate period and beyond. The standardized administrative category "tribe" was one of the enduring legacies of late Ottoman attempts to make state space: both the colonial and the postcolonial states rested firmly on this category to understand Bedouin communities and distribute resources among them.

After the 1920 French military defeat of a hastily procured and largely rural defense force at Maysalun, the fall of Amir Faysal's regime, and the consolidation of the French occupation over Syria, a group of city-based, educated Syrian nationalists left Damascus for the southern interior. Amir Faysal's brothers and father still held Hijaz, and the regional political organizations around Karak, Salt, and Ajlun that had reported to Amir Faysal's regime in Damascus were haggling with British authorities in Palestine over the political future of the interior lands east of the Jordan River. One of these exiled nationalists was Khayr al-Din al-Zirikli, who traveled first to Mecca and then to Amman ahead of Amir Faysal's brother, Amir Abdullah, in early 1921 and wrote a detailed account of his two-year stay.

Zirikli's account is one of the more colorful depictions of the dynamics of interior politics in the aftermath of World War I, and it captures the perspective of a group of Damascene nationalists who were warily supportive of the Hashemite project to build a British-backed Arab Kingdom in the post-Ottoman Eastern Mediterranean. Recounting his earliest days in Amman before Amir Abdullah arrived from Mecca, Zirikli recalled hearing about the "ministry (wizāra) of Umm al-Amad" from one of his colleagues, Kamil al-Budayri. Umm al-Amad was and is a village south of Amman where Qaʿdan al-Fayiz's descendant Mithqal made his base in the years after the war, about five miles from the Abu Jabir estate at Yaduda. Al-Budayri told al-Zirikli about a land dispute between the al-Fayiz elite and the Abu Jabir family that ended up in court in Salt, a court that was part of the regional governing apparatus that reported to Amir Faysal's then-exiled government in Damascus. When the court summoned Mithqal al-Fayiz, he refused to appear. The British officer Frederick Peake headed toward Umm al-Amad to convince him to go to court. Mithqal al-Fayiz had Peake detained in the warehouse used for fodder in the village while men Zirikli described as al-Fayiz's slaves tried out Peake's horse, and Umm al-Amad "declared its independence" from the regional government in Salt. This arrangement lasted for only about twenty-four hours, after which the Salt government made a deal with Mithqal al-Fayiz, who released the humiliated Peake.[62]

For Zirikli, the idea that a remote location like Umm al-Amad could serve as a self-governing, independent entity, or the center of any kind of Bedouin-led administrative power, was ludicrous. Rhetorically, he used this episode as an ominous sign of the fragmentation and localization of political action in the Eastern Mediterranean at a time when elite nationalists were arguing for unification and independence across Greater Syria. The dangers of fragmentation seemed to legitimize his tepid support for and participation in building a British-backed Hashemite state under Amir Faysal's brother Abdullah in the new entity of Transjordan, even as he subjected Amir Abdullah's governing tactics to unrelenting and caustic sarcasm. Like other elite, highly educated and town- and city-based politicians who had thrown in their lots with the Hashemite regime, Zirikli saw the southern interior as a second- or third-rate space of refuge that became a domain of nationalist politics only when he and his colleagues arrived in the aftermath of their exile at the hands of the French occupation of the center of their projected Arab Kingdom, Damascus.[63]

But Zirikli also captured a liminal moment of political haggling over the future of governance in the district of Salt and the Balqa region that would continue long after Amir Abdullah reached Amman and concluded deals with the British Mandate authorities. When Mithqal al-Fayiz refused to appear in court, he was not only continuing what had become a four-decade fight between the Abu Jabir family and al-Fayiz elites over land rights; he was also openly resisting the authority of the British-backed government in Salt. Peake himself claimed that Mithqal resisted his attempts at negotiation because nationalists, probably al-Budayri's colleagues, told Mithqal he was a Zionist agent.[64] Zirikli and other Damascene nationalists chose to ignore the extent to which the tent dwellers and village dwellers of the interior had become stakeholders in processes of state-building over the previous half-century, especially registering land rights, resolving disputes over land and other property, and administering taxation. For Balqa-based Bedouin bureaucrats, the idea of a regional government headed by a Bani Sakhr al-Fayiz or ʿAdwan leader was no more fantastical than the idea of a Hashemite sharif from Mecca ruling the North.[65]

The resistance movements of the 1920s, from the 1921 Kura Revolt in Ajlun and the 1923 Balqa Revolt against Hashemite-British rule to the most extended and successful anti-French Great Revolt in Jabal Druze and across Syria in 1925–26 were armed rejections of the disenfranchisement that came with the Mandate regimes. The connections between these movements were both ideological and tangible. In 1923, Dhiyab al-ʿAdwan's grandson Sultan mounted an armed revolt against the aggressive taxation policies and lack of political representation for local tent and town-based elites in the nascent Hashemite-British regime.[66] After the failure of the revolt at the hands of the British Royal Air Force, Sultan al-ʿAdwan headed north, finding shelter in Jabal Druze with Sultan al-Atrash, who was already mobilizing against French rule and would go on to lead the 1925 Great Revolt.[67] Many scholars have recognized the connections forged between nonelite interwar revolutionaries in late Ottoman military academies, relationships that converged in Palestine in 1936.[68] These connections stretched further, however, to the administrative and political practices of the late Ottoman period.[69] In the southern Syrian interior, the revolts were directed not only toward the British, but toward the Hashemite and Damascene elites who had claimed authority in matters of daily administration: property relations, taxation, and public spending. Farther north, intrusive French corvee labor policies in Hawran were the immediate impetus for revolutionary organizing. In all these settings, rural activists demanded political representation commensurate with their extensive commercial influence as producers and taxpayers.

These patterns of interior resistance extended and deepened the debates and contestations of the 1890s and 1900s, when late Ottoman administrative practice created space for the emergence of Bedouin bureaucrats and other newly coalesced communities of political actors, but also left them politically marginalized or insufficiently represented. In this sense, revolts like the 1907 Suwaylih attack on Chechen refugees and the 1910 events in Karak were the precursors for the encampment-and-village-based anticolonial resistance of the 1920s. The men behind these events articulated demands for changes in policy and a bigger piece of the decision-making pie for the inhabitants of villages and encampments most directly affected by tax and land regulations. As Michael Provence and Abdullah Assaf have argued, these issues of taxation and political representation were hardly disassociated from matters of sovereignty or the "national"; in fact, they were questions at the heart of the quotidian process of building sovereign national states, a process the rural elites who initiated the 1920s revolts had been part of as headmen and appointed officials.[70] The resistance of the 1920s was a fight over who would build the post-Ottoman state and who would receive its benefits.

Despite this continuity in the forms and aims of armed resistance, the Mandate regimes' governing strategies in the interior were markedly different from those of their Ottoman predecessors. In particular, Mandate officials consciously constructed regimes of separation based on their perception of "mode of life" in the Syrian interior, creating separate jurisdictions for Bedouin communities deemed nomadic with new institutions like the 1924 Tribal Courts Law and 1929 Bedouin Control Laws in Transjordan and the Contrôle Bédouin in Syria.[71] In Transjordan, while extending the Ottoman "tribe," these laws introduced the category of the "nomadic tribe" and placed those they listed by name as nomadic under a separate jurisdiction.[72] In the 1930s, this system evolved into direct British military and administrative control of the regions deemed to have "nomadic populations" under Glubb Paşa and through the Bedouin Control Board. Throughout, a list of tribes named "nomadic," including the Bani Sakhr but excluding the ʿAdwan and ʿAbbad, were subject to an entirely separate legal apparatus run by elite members of their own communities with increasingly intrusive British supervision.[73]

The institution of the Contrôle Bédouin in Syria rested on similar assumptions, most notably the belief that "Bedouin tribes constituted a distinct, autonomous culture within predominantly Arab states."[74] Without an intermediary figure like Amir Abdullah, French officials cultivated relationships with particular Bedouin elites who cooperated with the Contrôle Bédouin and granted them extensive administrative autonomy, hoping they would reward French authorities in the legislature in exchange.[75] While maintaining the tribe as a vehicle for political representation and the distribution of subsidies, this framework also entailed an assumption that politics in the Syrian countryside was entirely the work of local strongmen, rendering it impossible for French officials to see rural resistance as anything but banditry instigated by feudal elites in danger of losing their privileges.[76]

As Robert Fletcher has argued, the effect of these assumptions-turned-policy was to "give institutional expression to old tropes about 'the desert and the sown.'"[77] While Ottoman yearbooks and reports had often drawn distinctions between "nomadic" and "settled" tribes, they did not place either under an administratively elaborated and largely separate jurisdiction. In fact, as we saw in chapters 4 and 5, when Ottoman lawmakers tried to deny "tribes" the historic land rights afforded to village and town dwellers, they met powerful resistance. Ottoman lawmakers responded to this resistance because tribes operated in the same legal and administrative space as the rest of the local inhabitants in a contiguous imperial polity. In contrast, French and British policies of separation amounted to powerful divide-and-rule tactics of administration that frustrated the kinds of regional social connections that debates and litigation over land distribution, taxation, and trade had engendered in the late Ottoman period.

Mandate-era measures institutionalized the British and French belief in a Bedouin legal system with distinct customs, precedents, and procedures. Beyond separate judicial systems, they also taxed and policed communities defined as Bedouin and nomadic according to different rules and employing different authorities. While creating distinct experiences of Mandate rule, these measures also solidified connections, especially monetary ones, between European officials and Bedouin elites who retained extensive administrative sovereignty under the Bedouin Control Laws.[78]

In an important sense, British and French policies of urban-tribal separation codified a regime of exceptions for certain powerful tent-dwelling elites that had irked Ottoman modernizers like Cemal Bey, especially as he tried to implement standardized taxation and policing in the Balqa in the 1900s. As detailed in chapter 4, the Bani Sakhr won extensive tax breaks from the Ottoman regime both through utilizing their historical leverage in the pilgrimage administration and in exchange for peaceful relationships with communities who used land around Madaba that they regarded as their own. In the Ottoman case, however, these elite exceptions were not the result of a legally articulated and separate system for "nomadic Bedouin." Rather, annually contested tax breaks for communities like the Bani Sakhr and the Bani ʿAtiya in the late nineteenth and early twentieth centuries were remnants of the history of the Damascus pilgrimage route. They extended the long-standing ties between Ottoman and Meccan officials, on the one hand, and *particular* Bedouin elites, and by extension the communities among whom they distributed subsidies, on the other.

While most Bani Sakhr elites remained loyal to the Ottoman cause to the bitter end of World War I, they were also some of the first to demonstrate their allegiance to Amir Abdullah in contradistinction to the British-backed local governments in the interior.[79] The literature on the close relationship between Bani Sakhr al-Fayiz leaders and the sharifian Hashemite regime in twentieth-century Transjordan generally misses the fact that Bani Sakhr leaders had been collecting and redistributing Ottoman subsidies based on agreements with Meccan sharifs since at least the seventeenth century and that the Bani Sakhr had been an important linchpin of the four-century Ottoman-Hashemite relationship prior to its souring in the Arab Revolt. British officials like Frederick Peake read Amir Abdullah's close relationship with Bani Sakhr elites as rooted in his apparent preference for "nomads" over "sedentary" tribes like the 'Adwan,[80] but it followed a much more specific history of engagement with particular communities that Ottoman modernizers like Cemal Bey had tried, and failed, to transcend.

In Syria, the discursive bifurcation of the "desert" from the "sown" roughly corresponds to a bifurcation between the coastal littoral and the interior region. As this book has shown, the idea of a bifurcated landscape was produced in the nineteenth century through Ottoman reform discourses legitimized by a denial and willful amnesia of the long history of connections between tent- and town-dwelling communities and the role of institutions like the pilgrimage administration in state formation. While Ottoman modernizers pledged to bridge this gap, the dynamics of which they articulated in order to justify intrusive reform programs, Mandate officials reified it in a separate legal regime for communities defined as Bedouin tribes. This reification has been entrenched in recent scholarship that locates modernity in the coastal cities of the Eastern Mediterranean, eliding the rural interior claims to state formation that the anticolonial nationalist movements of the interwar period made.[81] This book has revealed these discourses of bifurcation as historically produced effects of modern state formation that erased a long history of interregional connections between the Arabian Peninsula, the Syrian interior, and the coastal regions.[82] Likewise, the history of anticolonial nationalism has reflected both these coastal-interior divisions and the boundaries of the mandates themselves, even when historical actors consistently crossed them.[83]

OTTOMAN LEGACIES: TRIBES, PROPERTY, AND CONTESTED STATE DOMAIN

The colonial regime of categorical separation between the desert and the sown represented a break with late Ottoman policy, which had outlined a single, contiguous administrative space reaching as far as possible into the Syrian steppe. But British and French policy did build on late Ottoman administration in important ways that would continue to shape both identity formation and resource distribution in the postcolonial period. In particular, in both "nomadic Bedouin" regions and elsewhere, the tribe remained a basic unit of administration in Mandate-era law. In Transjordan, in "sown" regions outside the scope of the Bedouin Control Laws, the lists of tribes and villages with headmen were remarkably similar to the administrative divisions created by the 1864 and 1871 Provincial Administration Regulations.[84] Throughout the Mandate period, the tribe remained a foundational category for organizing social life, from resource distribution to taxation to dispute resolution, in the modern state environments of British and French rule in the Eastern Mediterranean. What distinguished this tribe from its historical predecessors was its form and iterative function within a modern state—as the basis for the distribution of resources among all the human inhabitants of a particular landscape according to codified laws. This was a form and function the tribe acquired in the post-1870s process of building Ottoman state space in the Syrian interior.

In the wake of World War II, postcolonial elites in the Syrian interior would renew late Ottoman attempts to transcend a much more institutionalized and entrenched regime of juridical isolation within then-distinct national boundaries. Postcolonial nation-builders saw Bedouin in particular as an untapped human resource for new state-building projects and embarked on new forms of knowledge production that nationalized Bedouin communities while continuing to privilege the tribe as a foundational unit of analysis. Many of the compilations of tribal histories on which this book has relied were written in the early postcolonial period, in neat and largely nationally distinct volumes. Following their late Ottoman predecessors, authors from Damascus to Baghdad to Amman listed communities as comparable tribes in lists, with many communities appearing in multiple volumes with titles like "tribes of Syria" and "tribes of Transjordan."[85] For some authors, these compilations were a way to assert the agency of these communities in a narrative of nation-building.[86] For others, it was a way to incorporate them as potential, but still not quite formed, productive members of that nation.[87]

National governments also renewed what they referred to as sedentarization programs, which usually involved grants of "state land" to Bedouin communities.[88] The contested and contradictory designation of massive uncultivated semiarid and arid landscapes as "state land" available for top-down reallocation is the most enduring feature of the legal administration of late Ottoman landscapes. In both Jordan and Syria, colonial land registration efforts followed the work of their Ottoman predecessors closely, limiting their efforts to cultivated regions and leaving large swathes of "state land" under the everyday administrative sovereignty of Bedouin communities.[89] A similar trajectory occurred in Palestine, where British mandate registration efforts remained geographically limited and Israeli authorities refused to recognize many Bedouin claims in waves of registration in the 1970s.[90] As in the late Ottoman and Mandate periods, the obstacle to claiming unregistered land as absolute state domain through a comprehensive survey has been the expense and political risk required to adjudicate and settle existing claims and dispossess and evict existing inhabitants. In contemporary Israel, extremely aggressive state attempts to claim land under historic Bedouin control have rested on a simplistic reading of the categories of the 1858 Ottoman Land Code and a persistent denial of both long-standing Bedouin land claims and a regional land market that has existed for decades. In the southern Naqab region, these aggressive attempts have paved the way for hundreds of house demolitions and evictions.[91]

In Jordan, as in the late nineteenth century, the persistence of Bedouin administrative sovereignty over unregistered state domain has been particularly contentious in moments of regional crisis when refugee resettlement projects, often followed by and in competition with capitalist investors, display new interest in a landscape heretofore deemed marginal by city-dwelling lawmakers. In this context, when the state has been unwilling to register land it claims as state domain to Bedouin holders, a "noncompliant" market conducted with non-court-issued *hujjas* has endured. Like the out-of-court land market of the late nineteenth century, this market shifts constantly and adapts in response to state-sanctioned practice. In some cases, Bedouin owners affix government stamps and seals to the *hujjas* they sell, increasing their market value and asserting a kind of liminal state recognition. As in the nineteenth century, state courts recognize *hujjas* as valid claims to possession and use of land, even if they are not sufficient to counter claims of state domain or state-issued land deeds.[92] The enduring practice of administrative sovereignty that *hujjas* assert references forms of contract relevant across the Eastern Mediterranean prior to the extension of standardized Ottoman state space. Rather than vestiges of tribal law, these records represent the enduring status of Bedouin bureaucrats in a deeply uneven process of modern state formation.

ACKNOWLEDGMENTS

This book began and ended in California with long detours in Amman, Istanbul, Doha, and Abu Dhabi. I am grateful to mentors, friends, and students in each of these places. The support of many institutions made research and writing possible: the National Endowment for the Humanities, the Stanford Humanities Center, the Stanford History Department, the NYU Abu Dhabi Arab Crossroads Studies Program, the Global Asia Initiative at NYU Abu Dhabi funded by the Luce Foundation, the Fulbright Institute of International Education, Fulbright-Hays, the Council on Library and Information Resources, the Mellon Foundation, the Council of American Overseas Research Centers, the American Center for Oriental Research, the University of California at Berkeley Center for Middle East Studies, the University of California at Berkeley History Department, and the US Department of Education Foreign Language and Area Studies program.

Beginning in Berkeley, Beshara Doumani introduced me to historiography and court records and has been a source of profound support since. James Vernon started my thinking about empire. Huri İslamoğlu welcomed my growing family into her homes in Berkeley, Istanbul, and Büyükada and continues to be an exacting, fierce, and generous source of strength and inspiration. I thank my Berkeley siblings: Faiz Ahmed, Chris Church, Murat Dağlı, Heather Ferguson, Zoe

Griffith, Osamah Khalil, Alan Mikhail, Carrie Ritter, Beatrice Schraa, and Melanie Tanielian. At the University of Jordan in Amman, I am indebted to Dr. Muhammad Khuraysat, Dr. Adnan al-Bakhit, the late Dr. Nawfan al-Humud, Dr. Abdullah al-Assaf, Dr. Ibrahim Saif, Dr. Muhammad al-Masri, Manal Haddad, and Ahmad Khuraysat. At the Amman Department of Lands and Surveys, many thanks to Mahmud Qaryuti, Ismail Allawi, and Ishaq Khalil. Thanks to the patient staff and scholars at the American Center for Oriental Research, especially Barbara Porter, Nisreen Abu al-Shaikh, Humi Ayyoubi, Samya Kafafi, and Julie Peteet, and to an extremely supportive group of friends: Tamara al-Maaita, Allison Monroe, Natasha Quraib, Israa Thiab, and Sarah Tobin. Thanks to Duha Thiab for her assistance with final research stages. In Istanbul, I am grateful to the staff and archivists at the Prime Ministry Ottoman Archives, the Center for Islamic Studies, and the Millet Kütüphanesi.

At Qatar University in Doha, thanks to Ola Abu Rajoh, Reem Meshal, Ghada Moussa, Issam Nassar, and Farid al-Salim for their generosity and for teaching me about Gulf history. I found an unparalleled community of mentors, colleagues, and students during four deeply generative years at NYU Abu Dhabi: Robert Allen, Swethaa Ballakrishnen, Andrew Bush, Nelida Fuccaro, Huma Gupta, Sophia Kalantzakos, Maya Kesrouany, Fiona Kidd, Martin Klimke, Taneli Kukkonen, Monica Marks, Erin Pettigrew, Nathalie Peutz, Maurice Pomerantz, Matthew Silverstein, Justin Stearns, and Mahnaz Yousefzade. I am particularly indebted to Masha Kirasirova, who read large sections of the manuscript, and Mark Swislocki, who cowrote and read chapters over many morning writing sessions. I also thank Willard Sunderland, Michael Chen, and Huri İslamoğlu for participating in a joint manuscript workshop at NYUAD.

At Stanford, I thank ʿAli Yaycıoğlu, for his deep support and solidarity in deciphering fiscal details, and Aron Rodrigue and Priya Satia, for reading the manuscript and providing transformational comments. Special thanks to Parth Shil for his support in the final stages of revision. I also thank Gregory Ablavsky, Samer Al-Saber, Evan Alterman, Farah Bazzi, Marina Bergenstock, Lisa Blaydes, Patricia Blessing,

Joel Cabrita, Giovanna Cesarani, BuYun Chen, Emre Can Dağlıoğlu, Jacob Daniels, Özgür Dikmen, Rowan Dorin, Farah el-Sharif, Sebastian Felten, Brenda Finkel, Jonathan Gienapp, Denise Gill, Fiona Griffiths, Colin Hamill, Burçak Keskin Kozat, Alexander Key, Nancy Kollmann, Kathryn Olivarius, Matthew Sommer, Salim Tamari, Merve Tekgürler, Maria van Buiten, Caroline Winterer, Mikael Wolfe, and Serkan Yolaçan. Thanks to Reşat Kasaba and Pekka Hämäläinen for their review of the manuscript with the Stanford Humanities Center and invaluable comments.

Many other colleagues have contributed to my thinking over the years: Fahad Bishara, Johann Büssow, Rosie Bsheer, Sam Dolbee, Ella Fratantuono, Rashid Khalidi, Tyler Kynn, Adam Mestyan, James Reilly, Eugene Rogan, Safa Saraçoğlu, Baki Tezcan, and Tariq Tell. The final stages of writing this book owe much to Peter Hill and the members of the Ottoman Political Economies working group, particularly Herman Adney, Önder Akgül, Nader Atassi, Murat Bozluolcay, Lâle Can, Tolga Cora, Matthew Ghazarian, Zoe Griffith, Antonis Hadjikryiacou, Vladimir Hamed-Troyansky, Joanna Innes, Yanni Kotsonis, Ceyda Karamürsel, Anaïs Massot, Nada Moumtaz, Ellen Nye, Daniel Stoltz, and Stefan Winter. Special thanks to Camille Cole, Naz Yücel, and Aviv Derri, who read the manuscript in its entirety. I am also deeply indebted to the students and colleagues associated with the OpenGulf research network at NYU Abu Dhabi and Stanford, especially Munther al-Sabbagh, Nada Ammagui, Camille Cole, Rhea Kale, Suphan Kırmızıaltın, Mohammad Khalil, and Everett Pruett. David Joseph Wrisley has inspired this book in more ways than he knows, changing the way I think about space, data, scholarship, mentorship, and pedagogy and sticking with me even when I moved across the world. I thank Kate Wahl, both for what she has created with Stanford University Press's Middle East list and for supporting my project, the press's anonymous reviewers who strengthened the manuscript in the final stages, and Bill Nelson for creating the book's maps.

I would never publish anything without the aid of Hilary Falb Kalisman, who is a constant source of emotional and intellectual support, from teaching to navigating academia to parenting, not to mention a formidable and deeply sympathetic editor and procurer-of-titles. Elizabeth Williams has been thinking with me since our chance meeting in Madaba many years ago, and I am humbled and honored to have gone through the publishing process by her virtual side.

Writing and small children create conflicting demands, and the first depends on support for the second. I owe an indescribable debt to Annifer Diana for taking care of our youngest children in the first three years of their lives in Abu Dhabi. Back in California, we were immensely lucky to find the Del Cambre Neighborhood Association. Special thanks to Catalina Godoy and Olga Laurenty for their companionship and for producing a tireless group of playmates for our children.

I thank my late father-in-law, Silmey Barakat, and my mother-in-law, Yusra Alayyan, for their love and support and for welcoming me into their family. I am grateful for the sisterhood of Huda Mustafa, Aisha al-Shaikh Qasim, and Hedaya Mattar, who inspire me with their faith, their humor, and their patience. I dedicate this book to my parents, Edward and Diana Cundy, who have been a constant source of intellectual and emotional affirmation. I thank them for weathering my mobility, which keeps them far from half of their grandchildren, and my mother in particular for dedicating immense time and energy to learning Arabic. My sister, Julia O'Donnell, showed me how to be a parent and continues to show up through many years of distance. Nearly two decades on, Ahmad Barakat keeps reminding me to look at the twenty-first-century world around me. Omar, Ibrahim, Abdullah, and Rayyan keep my feet on the ground and create hope for a brighter future. I am profoundly grateful to them.

NOTES

ABBREVIATIONS
A.MKT.MHM: Sedaret Mektubi Mühimme Evrakı
ASCR: Amman Sharia Court Records
BEO: Bab-ı ʿAli Evrak Odası
BOA: Başbakanlık Osmanlı Arşivi (Prime Ministry Ottoman Archives)
CUP: Committee of Union and Progress
DH.EUM: Dahiliye Nezareti Emniyet-i Umumiye
DH.MKT: Dahiliye Nezareti Mektubi Kalemi
DLS: Department of Lands and Surveys
EV.HMK.SR: Evkaf-ı Harameyn Sürre Defterleri
FO: Foreign Office
İ.DH: Irade Dahiliye
İ.HUS: İrade Hususi
İ.MMS: İrade Meclis-i Mahsus
İ.MSM: Mesail-i Mühimme İradeleri
İ.MVL: İrade Meclis-i Vala
MAD: Maliyeden Müdevver
ML: Maliye
ML.CRD: Maliye Ceride Defterleri
MVL: Meclis-i Vala
ŞD: Şura-yı Devlet
SSCR: Salt Sharia Court Records

TNA: The National Archives, Kew
Y.PRK.UM: Yıldız Perakende Evrak-ı Umumi

INTRODUCTION
1. This sketch of what the October 1879 land registration in Salt may have entailed is based on DLS Register 1, *yoklama*, Teşrinievvel 1295/Oct. 1879. I would like to thank Eugene Rogan for providing me with a copy of this register, which was not in the DLS archives in Jabal Luwaybda, Amman, when I worked there in 2012.
2. The Wiraykat registrations are in DLS Register 1, *yoklama*, Teşrinisani 1295/Oct. 1879, p. 7, entries 170-80.
3. According to Martha Mundy and Richard Saumarez Smith, residents of villages in the regions north of the Wiraykat lands identified the British use of steel boundary markers in 1930s Transjordan as a rupture in community land relations. See Mundy and Smith, *Governing Property*, 103, 235.
4. DLS Register 1, Teşrinievvel 1295/Oct. 1879, p. 1, entry 7.
5. Khuraysāt and Dāwūd, *Sijill Maḥkamat Al-Salṭ al-Sharʿiyah*, 204.
6. DLS Register 1, Teşrinievvel 1295/Oct. 1879, p. 7, entries 170-76. These entries include a marginal note confirming the subsequent mortgage of the property to the Agricultural Bank in 1932.
7. The LawPedia Project published two Hashemite Kingdom of Jordan Cassation Court civil rulings related to this case: 2008/1639 and 2010/1616. www.lawpedia.jo.
8. Rogan, *Frontiers of the State*, 1-2; Bunton, *Colonial Land Policies in Palestine*, 5-6; Fischbach, *State, Society and Land*, chaps. 3 and 4; Mark LeVine, *Overthrowing Geography*, 184-85.
9. For the integration of the global wheat market, see Findlay and O'Rourke, *Power and Plenty*, 404-5. For other examples of agrarian visions of "empty land," see Belich, *Replenishing the Earth*, chap. 3; and Weaver, *The Great Land Rush*, 135-36, 147-48.
10. Arrighi, *The Long Twentieth Century*, chap. 4.
11. Holquist, "In Accord with State Interests," 163; Otis, *Dawes Act*; Banner, *How the Indians Lost Their Land*, chap. 8.
12. See Brenner et al., *State/Space: A Reader*, especially the contributions of Nicos Poulantzas ("The Nation," 65-83) and Henri Lefebvre ("Space and the State," 84-100). I rely in particular on Manu Goswami's use of the concept of state space to describe modern state formation in British India after 1858. Goswami, *Producing India*, 9.
13. "Neo-Europes" is Alfred Crosby's phrase, adopted in a number of works on imperial frontiers. See, e.g., Crosby, *Ecological Imperialism*, 4; Weaver, *The Great Land Rush*, 4-5; and Hopkins, *Ruling the Savage Periphery*, chaps. 5 and 6.

For a similar narrative focusing on the "Anglo-world," see Belich, *Replenishing the Earth*, 49–51.

14. Burbank and Cooper, *Empires in World History*, chap. 9. See also Weaver, *The Great Land Rush*, 41–43; Osterhammel, *Transformation of the World*, 362–68; and Sabol, *The Touch of Civilization*.

15. Maier, *Once within Borders*, 145.

16. Minawi, *The Ottoman Scramble*, 2–4.

17. Hahn, "Slave Emancipation," 309.

18. İslamoğlu, "Towards a Political Economy," 11–12.

19. Sunderland, *Taming the Wild Field*, chap. 5; Martin, *Law and Custom*, chaps. 2 and 3; Richard White, *It's Your Misfortune*, chaps. 6 and 15; Bensel, *Political Economy*, 15, chap. 5.

20. Banner, *How the Indians Lost Their Land*, 151–53; Pravilova, "The Property of Empire," 374–76. On discourses of productivity in late Ottoman society more broadly, see Hafez, *Inventing Laziness*.

21. In some regions of the Ottoman Empire, these notions of progress produced violent forced-settlement campaigns and dispossession of populations deemed "nomadic" in the 1860s and 1870s. See Gratien, *The Unsettled Plain*, chap. 2; and Toksöz, *Nomads, Migrants and Cotton*, 65–73.

22. On extraterritoriality, see Can, *Spiritual Subjects*, chap. 3; and Low, *Imperial Mecca*, chap. 2. On the effects of the climate of interimperial competition of the late nineteenth century on immigration policies, see Fratantuono, "Producing Ottomans," 5–6; and Kale, "Transforming an Empire," 259–60.

23. Can and Low rightly caution against the tendency to view questions of territoriality and nationality primarily through the prism of religious identity, although European consuls' practice of appointing coreligionist protégés and supporting separatist movements associated with non-Muslims did increase the politicization of religious identity, especially when it came to landholding. See Can and Low, "'Subjects' of Ottoman International Law," 224–25.

24. Klein, *The Margins of Empire*, chap. 4; Astourian, "Silence of the Land," 77–78; Rafeq, "Ownership of Real Property," 223–24; Derri, "Imperial Creditors," 10; Fitzmaurice, *Sovereignty, Property and Empire*, 6–9.

25. Satia, *Spies in Arabia*, 4.

26. With "politics of administration," I refer to Huri İslamoğlu's framework for understanding administrative regulations and rules as "power fields where multiple actors, including administrative ones, confront each other to negotiate the terms of their existence." İslamoğlu, "Politics of Administering Property," 277.

27. For conceptualizations of quotidian modern state practices as performances, see Saha, *Law, Disorder and the Colonial State*, 10–14; and Martinez,

States of Subsistence, 8–14. Both draw on Judith Butler's theory of performance in Butler, "Performative Acts."

28. İslamoğlu, "Politics of Administering Property," 276–81.

29. Razzaz, "Contestation and Mutual Adjustment," 12–14; Al Naber and Molle, "Politics of Accessing Desert Land," 500–501.

30. Scott, *Seeing like a State*, 1; see also Scott, *Against the Grain*, chap. 9.

31. The literature that views Bedouin in this way is voluminous. A foundational example is Gibb, *Islamic Society and the West*, 266–67.

32. Deringil, "'They Live'"; Makdisi, "Ottoman Orientalism." For scholars of the Mandates, this victimization occurred only after the disappearance of the Ottoman Empire, which they regarded as premodern. See Massad, *Colonial Effects*, 11; Dodge, *Inventing Iraq*, chaps. 4 and 5; Neep, *Occupying Syria*; and Hopkins, *Ruling the Savage Periphery*, 70–73.

33. Bhandar, *Colonial Lives of Property*, 37–39.

34. Fitzmaurice, *Sovereignty, Property and Empire*, 3, 19; Meek, *Social Science*, 20–22, 119–21. Assi, *History and Politics*, 8–9.

35. Twentieth-century Marxian historians and anthropologists, while adhering to evolutionist theories, focused extensively on the relationship between tribes and property. See Caton, "Anthropological Theories," 75–85; see also David Sneath's analysis of Soviet scholars' debates over "nomadic feudalism" in Central Asia. Sneath, *The Headless State*, chap. 3. Hanna Batatu's work on Iraq is a good example of this literature. Batatu argued that in Iraq, tribal shaykhs retained their power in the modern period, which he saw as distorting the natural course of history, because the British supported them. Batatu, *Old Social Classes*, 78; see also Haj, "The Problems of Tribalism."

36. Much of this literature is discussed in Khoury and Kostiner, *Tribes and State Formation*, introduction.

37. Abu-Lughod, "Zones of Theory," 285–87.

38. This continuum follows the discourse of elite members of camel-herding communities themselves. See Ibn Sbayyil, *Arabian Romantic*, 106n16. For a recent employment of this framework, see Çiçek, *Negotiating Empire*, 14–15.

39. Sam White, *Climate of Rebellion*, 229–43. For a critique of the historical role of Bedouin in White's narration of the seventeenth-century crisis, see Meier and Tell, "World the Bedouin Lived In," 24–25. For a sustained discussion of the overlaps between literary and historiographical representations of locusts, nomads, and other human communities conceived as mobile (e.g., refugees), see Dolbee, *Locusts of Power*.

40. Asad, "Beduin as a Military Force," 71; Asad, "Equality in Nomadic Social Systems?" 423–24; Sneath, *The Headless State*, 16–21.

41. Doumani, *Rediscovering Palestine*, 201–5; Khoury, *State and Provincial Society*, 31–32; Shields, *Mosul before Iraq*, chap. 5; Lancaster, *People, Land and Water*, 62–63.

42. Belich, *Replenishing the Earth*; Weaver, *The Great Land Rush*, 17–30; Fields, *Enclosure*, x–xiv; Hopkins, *Ruling the Savage Periphery*, chap. 1.

43. Its salience in French imperial contexts has also been demonstrated. See, e.g., Davis, *Resurrecting the Granary of Rome*, chap. 3; Duffy, *Nomad's Land*, 108–26; Roberts, "Almost as It Is Formulated."

44. Mundy and Smith show that in some villages, certain shareholding practices endured even in the context of individuated registration. See Mundy and Smith, *Governing Property*, 234, chaps. 10 and 12. A reading, however, of tax and land law together, especially amendments to the Land Code after the 1870s, clearly points toward Ottoman lawmakers' commitment to fully individuated and alienable title in agricultural land. See Kaya and Terzibaşoğlu, "Tahrir'den Kadastro'ya," 38–39; Cin, *Osmanlı Toprak Düzeni ve Bu Düzenin Bozulması*, 310–30; and İslamoğlu, "Politics of Administering Property," 279–80.

45. Mundy and Smith, *Governing Property*, 5.

46. Muslu, "'Nomadic' Borders"; Lindner, *Nomads and Ottomans*, 30–31; Avcı, "Tanzimat in the Desert," 970.

47. See, e.g., Fleischer, "Royal Authority"; Topal, "Order as a Chronotope"; Gratien, *The Unsettled Plain*, 76–77; Schaebler, "Civilizing Others," 16–20; and Adamiak, "To the Edge," 28–29, 47–50.

48. On anthropologists' employment of Khaldunian theory in functionalist notions of tribes, especially through the work of Ernest Gellner, see Caton, "Anthropological Theories," 94.

49. Fleischer, "Royal Authority," 215–16.

50. See, e.g., the discussion of uninhabited farms (*mezraas*) in İslamoğlu-İnan, *State and Peasant*, 40, 45–46, 147–48. Especially in the later sixteenth century, Ottoman administrators clearly privileged settled cultivation. My point here is simply that these earlier laws anticipated and sanctioned more diverse land-use patterns than their later iterations. See also Hütteroth and Abdulfattah, *Historical Geography*, 29.

51. Kasaba, *A Moveable Empire*, chap. 3; Winter, "Alep et l'émirat du désert," 46.

52. Topal, "Order as a Chronotope," 29–30.

53. Kılınçoğlu, *Economics and Capitalism*, 19–25. See in particular Kılınçoğlu's discussion (24–25) of the debates over agriculture vs. industry among Ottoman intellectuals and officials in the nineteenth century.

54. Johansen, *Islamic Law*; Mundy and Smith, *Governing Property*, chaps. 1–4.

55. Barakat, "Making 'Tribes,'" 484.

56. Gary Fields's analysis of the way discourses of landscape improvement entered law and became "facts on the ground" through architectural changes is particularly helpful here. See Fields, *Enclosure*, 9–10. For private property as a globally constructed institution of the nineteenth century, see İslamoğlu, "Towards a Political Economy," 12–13.

57. For examples of dispossession that followed the legal channels of the Land Code, see Gratien, *The Unsettled Plain*, 98–99; Williams, *States of Cultivation*; and Ben-Bassat, "Bedouin Petitions," 143–44.

58. Kedar, Yiftchatel, and Amara, *Emptied Lands*, chap. 2; Nasasra, *Naqab Bedouins*, chaps. 10–11.

59. İslamoğlu, "Property as a Contested Domain," 7.

60. Pamuk, "Ottoman Empire in the 'Great Depression'"; Schilcher, "The Great Depression."

61. Goswami locates the "rise of nationally regulated capitalism" in contradistinction to Britain's global hegemony in Germany, France, the United States, and Japan. Ottoman lawmakers did not have the financial sovereignty to resist British hegemony in all of the same ways, but Ottoman internal administration in particular responded to this larger context of resistance. See Goswami, *Producing India*, 11.

62. Osterhammel, *Transformation of the World*, 54; Pamuk, *The Ottoman Empire*, 13–15; Findlay and O'Rourke, *Power and Plenty*, 426–27.

63. Hobsbawm, *The Age of Capital*, chap. 7.

64. Beshara Doumani uses the phrase "periphery's periphery" in reference to Nablus; see Doumani, *Rediscovering Palestine*, 3. The dismissal of late Ottoman sovereignty dovetails with a tendency among historians of the twentieth-century Middle East to locate the foundations of the modern state in the British and French Mandate administrations. See Neep, *Occupying Syria*; and Massad, *Colonial Effects*, 11.

65. Birdal, *Political Economy*, 7.

66. Minawi, *The Ottoman Scramble*; Derri, "Imperial Creditors," 2.

67. Barakat, "Underwriting the Empire," 391.

68. Lewis, *Nomads and Settlers*, 59–63, 126–31.

69. Abujaber, *Pioneers over Jordan*, 137–40.

70. Levine and Foner, *Half Slave*, 209.

71. Belich, *Replenishing the Earth*, 84.

72. Especially the latter remain largely undocumented, and it is unclear how many of them remained. See, e.g., BOA.MVL 755/12, 14 S 1276/12 Sept. 1859, which documents the migration of eight thousand cultivators from the hinterlands of Nablus over the Jordan River to Ajlun in the late 1850s. Norman Lewis also discussed the phenomenon of cultivators working for Bedouin elites

on plantation-style farms in the northern interior from the 1850s. See Lewis, *Nomads and Settlers*, 69–72, 126–31; and Abujaber, *Pioneers over Jordan*, 187–90.

73. Roberts, "Almost as It Is Formulated," 610.

74. Clark, "Agrarian Context," 33; Weaver, *The Great Land Rush*, 321; Foner, *Free Soil*, 27–29.

75. Chatty, *Displacement and Dispossession*, 97–98; Fratantuono, "Producing Ottomans," 2–4.

76. İnalcık and Quataert, *Economic and Social History*, 2:856–57; Vladimir Hamed-Troyansky has also recognized the confluence between these laws, as well as the resettlement of peasants in the Russian context. See Hamed-Troyansky, "Imperial Refuge," 16–17.

77. For the ways these global debates played out in French Algeria, see Roberts, "Almost as It Is Formulated."

78. Genetin-Pilawa, *Crooked Paths to Allotment*, chap. 7. Jason Moore's concept of "commodity frontiers" as "cheap" landscapes that gain value through commodification after profit-threatening crises is useful for linking the experiences of the Syrian interior and the American West here. See Moore, *Capitalism in the Web*, 15–17.

79. Derri, "Imperial Creditors," 4; Zandi-Sayek, *Ottoman Izmir*, chap. 1; Cole, "Empire on Edge," chap. 4.

80. Blumi, *Ottoman Refugees*, chap. 1; Hamed-Troyansky, "Imperial Refuge," 15–16.

81. Kiyotaki, *Ottoman Land Reform*, 20–21, 162, 200–202; Çetinsaya, "Politics of Reform in Iraq."

82. On the Stolypin land reforms, see Yaney, *The Urge to Mobilize*, chaps. 5–6; and Pallot, "The Stolypin Land Reforms."

83. Holquist, "In Accord with State Interests," 157; Pravilova, "The Property of Empire"; Masoero, "Territorial Colonization," 85.

84. As we will see, in both contexts there was also extensive official anxiety about peasants both meeting their productive potential and claiming more land than they deserved. See Masoero, "Territorial Colonization," 76.

85. Polatel and Üngör, *Confiscation and Destruction*, chap. 4; Morack, *The Dowry of the State?*; Kürt, *The Armenians of Aintab*, chap. 4.

86. Astourian, "Silence of the Land," 76–80; Klein, *The Margins of Empire*, chap. 4.

87. Kuehn, *Empire, Islam, and Politics of Difference*; Low, *Imperial Mecca*, 33; Morrison, "Metropole, Colony, and Imperial Citizenship," 329–30.

88. "Vasite-i tevsil." See the "Financial Affairs Regulation" of 1867, Article 6, in *Düstur*, 2:4.

89. Weber, *Economy and Society*, 2:956–58; Swedberg and Agevall, *The Max Weber Dictionary*, 20.

90. Felten and von Oertzen, "Bureaucracy as Knowledge," 3.

91. I owe this point to conversations about nineteenth-century adminis-tration with Camille Cole. See also Cole, "Empire on Edge," 142; Yaycıoğlu, *Partners of the Empire*, 47; and Yaycıoğlu, "Karlofça Ânı," 19.

92. Lipsky, *Street-Level Bureaucracy*, 4. Ilana Feldman's observations about the importance of repetitive, daily practice in extending bureaucratic power are relevant here; see Feldman, *Governing Gaza*, 10–17.

93. İslamoğlu, "Politics of Administering Property," 277.

94. I use "practice" here in the sense of Bourdieu, as a structured process referring to certain rules, in this case rules expressed in codified law, with contingent and unpredictable outcomes. See Bourdieu, *Outline of a Theory*. On the unpredictable outcomes of modern bureaucracy, see also Gupta, *Red Tape*; and İslamoğlu, "Politics of Administering Property," 311n3.

95. Saraçoğlu, *Nineteenth-Century Local Governance*, 51.

96. This argument takes into account the productive recent scholarship on the distinctions between subjecthood, nationality, and citizenship in the late Ottoman context and connects citizenship to political participation con-ditioned by taxation in particular. See Can, *Spiritual Subjects*, 24, 157; and Hanley, "What Ottoman Nationality Was," 278.

97. Sneath, *The Headless State*, chap. 3; Hämäläinen, *The Comanche Empire*; Hämäläinen, *Lakota America*, chap. 4.

98. Hämäläinen, "What's in a Concept?," 87–88.

99. On the transformations of the pilgrimage administration in the eigh-teenth century, see Barbir, *Ottoman Rule in Damascus*, chap. 3; Rafeq, "Qāfilat al-Ḥajj al-Shāmī"; and Petersen, *Medieval and Ottoman Hajj Route*, 27.

100. Hull, *Government of Paper*; Cole, "Empire on Edge," 14–20.

101. For an account of how local communities have reacted to capital and state expansion resting on some of the same approaches as this book, see Tutino, *The Mexican Heartland*.

102. Razzaz, "Contestation and Mutual Adjustment," 12.

103. Hanley, "What Ottoman Nationality Was," 278.

104. Özbek, "Osmanlı İmparatorluğunda Gelir Vergisi."

105. Razzaz, "Contestation and Mutual Adjustment," 14–15.

106. Al Naber and Molle, "Politics of Accessing Desert Land," 501.

CHAPTER 1

1. "Adem deryası." Dankoff, Kahraman, and Dağlı, *Evliya Çelebi Seyahat-namesi*, 9:514.

2. This somewhat imaginative sketch of the scene at Muzayrib draws on Evliya Çelebi's account, as well as other rich descriptions, especially of the distribution of subsidies to Bedouin at Muzayrib in the late eighteenth and

early nineteenth centuries. See Miknāsī, *Riḥlat al-Miknāsī*, 485; Seetzen, "Mémoire," 284; Burckhardt, *Travels in Syria*, 241–46.

3. These subsidies were spread across four Bani Sakhr families. See BOA. EV.HMK.SR 825 (1718), 30–46.

4. Findlay and O'Rourke, *Power and Plenty*, chap. 5; İnalcık and Quataert, *Economic and Social History*, 2:637–738.

5. Barbir, *Ottoman Rule in Damascus*, chap. 3; Taylor, "Fragrant Gardens," chap. 5.

6. Rogan, *Frontiers of the State*, 6–9; Alon, *The Making of Jordan*, 3; Low, *Imperial Mecca*, 37; Rogan, "Aşiret Mektebi."

7. As Mostafa Minawi and Cem Emrence have pointed out, discussions of the coloniality of the late Ottoman regime have mapped onto discussions of the decentralization of the early modern empire that follow a center-periphery model. See Minawi, "Beyond Rhetoric," 79–81; and Emrence, "Imperial Paths, Big Comparisons," 297–98.

8. Elden, *The Birth of Territory*; Rankin, *After the Map*; Benton, *A Search for Sovereignty*.

9. Benton, *A Search for Sovereignty*, 2.

10. Benton, "Empires of Exception," 55.

11. İnalcık et al., *Economic and Social History*, 1:108–18.

12. Forms of this phrase appear in a variety of sources; see, e.g., Ṣabbāgh, *Al-Rawḍ al-Zāhir fī Tārīkh Ḍāhir*, 70. See also the Nablus Advisory Council record that opens chap. 2.

13. Ferguson, *Proper Order of Things*, chap. 5. See also Barkey, *Bandits and Bureaucrats*; and İnalcık, "Centralization and Decentralization."

14. Fattah, *Politics of Regional Trade*, chap. 1.

15. Elden, "Land, Terrain, Territory."

16. Fattah, *Politics of Regional Trade*, 22; Dolbee, *Locusts of Power*.

17. Findlay and O'Rourke, *Power and Plenty*, chap. 5.

18. See the extensive discussion of landscape and water sources in Lancaster, *People, Land and Water*, chap. 3.

19. See, e.g., the map of rainfall distribution in Jordan reproduced in Mustafa and Rahman, "Assessing the Spatio-temporal Variability," 252.

20. These ties seem to have become quite weak in the fifteenth century; see Walker, "Mamluk Investment," 248–49.

21. Bakhīt, *Ottoman Province of Damascus*, chap. 1; Conermann and Şen, *The Mamluk-Ottoman Transition*.

22. Imber, *Ebu's-Suʿud*, 41; Akgündüz, *Osmanlı Kanunnameleri ve Hukuki Tahlilleri*; Ferguson, *Proper Order of Things*, 86.

23. Singer, *Palestinian Peasants*.

24. Bakhīt, *Ottoman Province of Damascus*, chap. 2; Bakhīt and Ḥamūd, *Deft-*

er-i Mufassal Liva 'Ajlun; Bakhīt and Ḥamūd, *Daftar Mufaṣṣal Nāḥiyat Marj Banī 'Āmir.*

25. Akgündüz, *Osmanlı Kanunnameleri ve Hukuki Tahlilleri*, 4:313. On the general lawbook I refer to here, see Ferguson, *Proper Order of Things*, 90. On changing clauses on nomads in early lawbooks, see Lindner, *Nomads and Ottomans.*

26. İslamoğlu-İnan, *State and Peasant*, 45. For an explanation of the meaning of this term in Bilad al-Sham and its connection to the local term *khirba*, see Walker, "Early Ottoman/Late Islamic I/Post-Mamluk," 362n40.

27. Refik, *Anadolu'da Türk Âşiretleri*, vi.

28. References to the presence of other Bani Sakhr groups around the southern Karak citadel date to the late Mamluk period. See al-Qalqashandī, *Qalā'id al-Jumān fī Ta'rīf bi-Qabā'il al-Zamān.* For al-Qalqashandi's work and writing, see Abdelhamid and El-Toudy, *Selections from "Subh al-A'sha*," 8–10; and Walker, "Mamluk Investment," 241–42.

29. Bakhīt and Ḥamūd, *Defter-i Mufassal Liva 'Ajlun*, 136.

30. Bakhīt and Ḥamūd, 22.

31. *'Arab* is the singular form of *'urban*. For an exploration of usages of this term in the Arabic literature of the medieval period, see Leder, "Nomadische Lebensformen"; and Leder, "Towards a Historical Semantic."

32. Bakhīt and Ḥamūd, *Defter-ı Mufassal Liva 'Ajlun*, 99.

33. Bakhīt and Ḥamūd, *Daftar Mufaṣṣal Nāḥiyat Marj Banī 'Āmir*, 36.

34. Hütteroth and Abdulfattah's efforts to map the boundaries of sixteenth-century revenue-grant regions based on the fiscal registers illustrate the spatial dynamics of villages added to the register; see Hütteroth and Abdulfattah, *Historical Geography.* Charles Wilkins describes the phrase "haric" referring to tax exemptions in seventeenth-century Aleppo; see Wilkins, *Forging Urban Solidarities*, 30.

35. Akgündüz, *Osmanlı Kanunnameleri ve Hukuki Tahlilleri*, 4:393.

36. "Wild land" is my translation of *berriye*. See Hütteroth and Abdulfattah, *Historical Geography*, 24.

37. Muslu, "'Nomadic' Borders."

38. Bakhīt, *Ottoman Province of Damascus*, 207.

39. Barbir, *Ottoman Rule in Damascus*, 135–36; Petersen, *Medieval and Ottoman Hajj Route*, 24.

40. Jeddah was an exception, however, which was administered directly from Egypt. See 'Abd al-Mu'ṭī, *Al-'Alāqāt al-Miṣrīyah al-Ḥijāzīyah*, 25–26.

41. Barbir, *Ottoman Rule in Damascus*, 105; Hiyari, "Origins and Development"; Winter, "Alep et l'émirat du désert," 93–98; see also Dolbee, *Locusts of Power.*

42. Faroqhi, *Pilgrims and Sultans*, 32–33.

43. See Faroqhi's discussion of the Mufarija, a Sardiyya community, in her study of the seventeenth-century Hajj administration. Faroqhi, 65–66; see also al-Fawwaz, *'Umarā' Ḥawrān*, 65–70; and Bakhīt, *Ottoman Province of Damascus*, 217.

44. Zakarīyā, *'Ashā'ir al-Shām*, 362.

45. Al-Fawwaz, *'Umarā' Ḥawrān*, 56–59, 66. The Jughayman fort was renamed Mudawwara after Ottoman renovations in the eighteenth century. Petersen, *Medieval and Ottoman Hajj Route*, 121–27; Bakhīt, *Ottoman Province of Damascus*, 217–21.

46. The earliest reference to the office of "Shaykh al-Sham" seems to be from 1642. See Rogan, "Incorporating the Periphery," 90–91. It appears in lists of allocations to Bedouin for the protection and provisioning of the Damascus Hajj route in 1674. See BOA.MAD 4901 (1674/75), 3.

47. The creation of the shaykh al-Sham office seems to roughly coincide with the office of the "çöl beyliği" in northern Syria around Aleppo and Raqqa, which Winter also describes as growing out of the earlier office of the Arab Emirate. See Winter, "Alep et l'émirat du désert," 93–98.

48. Zakarīyā, *'Ashā'ir al-Shām*, 363; Peake, *Tārīkh Sharqī al-Urdun*, 234.

49. Lancaster, *People, Land and Water*, 69–70.

50. Bakhīt, *Ottoman Province of Damascus*, 109, 213–17; Rogan, "Incorporating the Periphery," 31–32; Ze'evi, *An Ottoman Century*, chap. 2; Bakhīt, "Al-Usra al-Ḥārithīyah"; Abu-Husayn, *Provincial Leaderships in Syria*.

51. A number of authors address the issue of the transition from Mamluk to Ottoman rule in Syria in Conermann and Şen, *The Mamluk-Ottoman Transition*.

52. Bakhīt and Ḥamūd, *Defter-ı Mufassal Liva 'Ajlun*, 136. For more on the Bani Mahdi (Mahdawiyya), see chap. 2.

53. Benton, *A Search for Sovereignty*, 10.

54. Ṭayyib, *Mawsūʿat al-Qabā'il al-'Arabīyah*, vol. 2, part 1, 43–44. On the northern migrations of the Shammar, see also Dolbee, *Locusts of Power*.

55. Parker, *Global Crisis*; Faroqhi, "Crisis and Change, 1590–1699"; Hathaway, *The Arab Lands*, 62–64.

56. İnalcık, "Military and Fiscal Transformation"; Ze'evi, *An Ottoman Century*. Fixed-term tax farms had been a feature of Ottoman fiscal administration in Syria since the early sixteenth century, although the practice increased in the late seventeenth. See Abu-Husayn, *Provincial Leaderships in Syria*; and Rafeq, "Qāfilat al-Ḥajj al-Shāmī," 7–10.

57. Barbir, *Ottoman Rule in Damascus*, 109; Taylor, "Fragrant Gardens," 197–202.

58. Hathaway, *The Arab Lands*, 76–78; Rafeq, "Qāfilat al-Ḥajj al-Shāmī," 11–12.

59. The sharifate held a share of customs revenues from Jeddah, which had increased along with the rise of the Red Sea coffee trade in the seventeenth century. ʿAbd al-Muʿṭī, *Al-ʿAlāqāt al-Miṣrīyah al-Ḥijāzīyah*, 45; Kynn, "Encounters of Islam and Empire," 195.

60. Kynn, "Encounters of Islam and Empire," 200. On the connections between the grain and coffee trades in the Hijaz and Egypt during this period, see Tuchscherer, "Coffee in the Red Sea Area," 54; Hathaway, *Politics of Households*, 35–37; and Wick, *The Red Sea*, 71.

61. Kynn, "Encounters of Islam and Empire," 214–15. On the complex relationship between the Harb and the sharifs of Mecca, as well as their connections to the Egyptian pilgrimage, see Ṭayyib, *Mawsūʿat al-Qabāʾil al-ʿArabīyah*, vol. 2, part 1, 763–66. For the Bani Sakhr's possible genealogical connection to the Harb, see Peake, *Tārīkh Sharqī al-Urdun*, 215.

62. Peake, *Tārīkh Sharqī al-Urdun*, 215–16; Rawābidah, *Muʿjam al-ʿAshāʾir al-Urdunīyah*, 115.

63. Recent histories of the Bani Sakhr published in Jordan have obscured the community's historical connections in Hijaz, arguing based on the Ottoman fiscal registers cited above that the community resided around Karak throughout the period treated in this chapter. See, e.g., Al-Fayiz, *ʿAshāʾir Bani Ṣakhr*. But Qaʿdan al-Fayiz's influence in al-Ula and Madayin Salih is clear in the 1718 register of pilgrimage subsidies, in which he collects portions of the money expended for provisions at both forts. See BOA.EV.HMK.SR 825 (1718), 5.

64. This story was related to the British officer Frederick Peake in the 1920s. See Peake, *Tārīkh Sharqī al-Urdun*, 215.

65. Sowayan, *Al-Ṣaḥrāʾ al-ʿArabīyah*; Meier and Tell, "World the Bedouin Lived In."

66. Ṭayyib, *Mawsūʿat al-Qabāʾil al-ʿArabīyah*, vol. 2, part 1, 45.

67. Ṭayyib, 43; Dolbee, "The Desert at the End of Empire," 208.

68. Peake, *Tārīkh Sharqī al-Urdun*, 216.

69. Peake, 217.

70. Al-Fawwaz, *ʿUmarāʾ Ḥawrān*, 150.

71. Al-Fawwaz, 161–62.

72. Meier and Tell, "World the Bedouin Lived In," 38–39.

73. Kasaba, *A Moveable Empire*, chap. 3; Winter, "The Province of Raqqa"; Winter, "Alep et l'émirat du désert"; Orhonlu, *Osmanlı İmparatorluğu'nda Aşiretlerin İskanı*.

74. Kasaba, *A Moveable Empire*, 57–59.

75. Halaçoğlu, 18, 51; Refik, *Anadolu'da Türk Âşiretleri*.

76. Malissa Taylor argues that the extensive use of the term *ahali-i karye* (the people of the village), in contrast to the earlier use of *reaya*, to refer

to the entire corps of nonruling-class Ottoman subjects began in the mid-seventeenth century. See Taylor, "Fragrant Gardens," chap. 1; see also Taylor, "Forcing the Wealthy to Pay." On the corporate "ahl al-qarya" in seventeenth-century fatwas, see Mundy and Smith, *Governing Property*, 26.

77. Mundy and Smith, *Governing Property*, 37.

78. Lindner, *Nomads and Ottomans*.

79. Faroqhi, *Pilgrims and Sultans*, 57–58.

80. See BOA.EV.HMK.SR 192, which is a compiled register including information on pilgrimage route subsidies from the late seventeenth century through the mid-eighteenth. The 1672 defter is on pp. 20–23 and includes a total of 1,275.5 piastres in twenty-six separate allocations to Bani Sakhr individuals. See also BOA.MAD 4901 (1674/75), 4, which lists eleven allocations for a total of 1,131 piastres. In both registers, the total listed for the office of Shaykh al-Sham is 13,500 piastres.

81. Kynn, "Encounters of Islam and Empire," 209–10.

82. BOA.EV.HMK.SR 825 (1718) is divided into sections based on when allocations were agreed on.

83. Barbir, *Ottoman Rule in Damascus*, 157.

84. BOA.EV.HMK.SR 825 (1718), 31.

85. Rafeq, "Qāfilat al-Ḥajj al-Shāmī," 8–10.

86. Barbir, *Ottoman Rule in Damascus*, 137.

87. Barbir, 141; Petersen, *Medieval and Ottoman Hajj Route*, 27; Petersen, "Ottoman Conquest of Arabia."

88. The most detailed registers of subsidies to Bedouin groups are held in the Evkaf-ı Hümayun collection. They do not cover all years; I have compared the five *urban sürreleri* registers available. The numbers presented here can be compared with tables compiled by Faroqhi and Barbir from Maliyeden Mudevver registers, which present similar numbers but much less detail. See BOA.EV.HMK.SR 192 (1672); BOA.EV.HMK.SR 825 (1718); BOA.EV.HMK.SR 2221 (1772); BOA.EV.HMK.SR 2422 (1779); BOA.EV.HMK.SR 3207 (1803).

89. The 1772 register specifies that some of this money was for the provision of camels and sheep. This corresponds to what Barbir found in 1740s receipts in the Cevdet Dahiliye collection. See Barbir, *Ottoman Rule in Damascus*, appendix 4; and BOA.EV.HMK.SR 2221 (1772), 4.

90. BOA.MAD 4901 (1674/75), 4.

91. BOA.EV.HMK.SR 3207 (1803), 26.

92. These were the collectors of the highest allocations in each group according to BOA.EV.HMK.SR 825 (1718).

93. For the Bani Sakhr subsidies, see BOA.EV.HMK.SR 825 (1718), 30–66; BOA.EV.HMK.SR 2221 (1772), 62–92; BOA.EV.HMK.SR 2422 (1779), 23–33; BOA.EV.HMK.SR 3207 (1803), 18–23.

94. See, e.g., BOA.EV.HMK.SR 2221 (1772), 59.

95. Veinstein, "İnalcık's Views," 5; Darling, *Revenue-Raising and Legitimacy*, 175; Taylor, "Forcing the Wealthy to Pay," 53.

96. For an explanation of this system in the Balkans, see Bruce McGowan, *Economic Life in Ottoman Europe*, 151–68; Wilkins, *Forging Urban Solidarities*, 24; and 'Ali Yaycıoğlu, *Partners of the Empire*, 122–24.

97. BOA.EV.HMK.SR 2422 (1779), 22.

98. Burckhardt, *Notes on the Bedouins*, 1:73, 119.

99. BOA.EV.HMK.SR 825 (1718).

100. This data points to the stability but long-term inflation of the Ottoman piastre, grain prices that fluctuated with events but rose steadily, and relatively stable prices for luxuries like tobacco. See Grehan, *Everyday Life*, chap. 2 and conclusion; and Establet and Pascual, "Damascene Probate Inventories," 381–83.

101. Burckhardt, *Notes on the Bedouins*, 1:70–71.

102. Seetzen, "Mémoire," 283–85. Seetzen focuses on particular 'Anaza shaykhs in his account: Samir al-Dukhi and Mahannah al-Fadl.

103. Cohen, *Palestine in the 18th Century*, 15.

104. Findlay and O'Rourke, *Power and Plenty*, 247–75.

105. Barbir, *Ottoman Rule in Damascus*, 174–77.

106. This point does not diminish historians' recent critiques of nationalist Saudi historical narratives that draw linear connections between the eighteenth-century Saudi enterprise and the twentieth-century British-supported Saudi state. See Bsheer, *Archive Wars*; and Vitalis, *America's Kingdom*.

107. Pamuk, *Monetary History*, 161.

108. Philipp, *Acre*, 15; Tuchscherer, "Coffee in the Red Sea Area," 56; Pamuk, *Monetary History*.

109. Pamuk, *Monetary History*, 165–67; Establet and Pascual, "Damascene Probate Inventories," 376–77.

110. BOA.EV.HMK.SR 825 (1718); BOA.EV.HMK.SR 2221 (1772).

111. Tuchscherer, "Coffee in the Red Sea Area"; Tuchscherer, "La flotte impériale de Suez."

112. Cohen, *Palestine in the 18th Century*, 122, 191.

113. Alon, *The Making of Jordan*, 127; Alon, *The Shaykh of Shaykhs*, 112–13.

114. Satia, *Empire of Guns*, 3–4.

115. Şevket Pamuk charts the consolidation of the silver *kuruş* in Syria and elsewhere in the eighteenth century; see Pamuk, *Monetary History*, 165–66. For more on the currencies used to pay Bedouin on the pilgrimage route in the seventeenth century, see Faroqhi, *Pilgrims and Sultans*, 54–65; and Tuchscherer, "Coffee in the Red Sea Area."

116. Heyd, *Ottoman Documents on Palestine*; Petersen, *Medieval and Ottoman Hajj Route*, 24.

117. Burckhardt, *Notes on the Bedouins*, 2:1–49.

118. Cohen, *Palestine in the 18th Century*, 123.

119. Philipp, *Acre*, 3, 98–99, 106–7; Ṣabbāgh, *Al-Rawḍ al-Zāhir fī Tārīkh Ḍāhir*, 26; Cohen, *Palestine in the 18th Century*, 12–15, 22.

120. Cohen, *Palestine in the 18th Century*, 22.

121. Cohen, 15.

122. Peake, *Tārīkh Sharqī al-Urdun*, 169–70, chap. 2.

123. Cohen, *Palestine in the 18th Century*, 46.

124. Cohen's meticulous work in tax registers from the eighteenth century shows that advance monies (muʿacele) paid for the tax farm of Ajlun, north of Salt in the interior, rose precipitously in the late eighteenth century, with members of the sultan's immediate retinue taking over the contracts. Cohen, 187.

125. On the conflicts between both Zahir al-ʿUmar and Cezzar Ahmed Paşa and the al-ʿAzm governors, see Cohen, 52–53, 65.

126. Rafeq, *The Province of Damascus*, 52–53; Barbir, *Ottoman Rule in Damascus*, 122–25.

127. This assertion is also evidenced in Ulrich Seetzen's interlocutor's description of haggling over the contents of the register at Muzayrib. See Seetzen, "Mémoire." For examples of the governors of Sidon and Damascus making specific additional allocations to the register, see BOA.EV.HMK. SR.3207 (1803), 13.

128. Rafeq, *The Province of Damascus*, 215–16.

129. See Hathaway's discussion of al-Budayri's colorful description of the attack, in Hathaway, *The Arab Lands*, 89–90.

130. Rafeq, *The Province of Damascus*, 216.

131. BOA.EV.HMK.SR 2221 (1772).

132. Burckhardt, *Notes on the Bedouins*, 1:3.

133. Vassiliev, *History of Saudi Arabia*, 226–32.

134. Fattah, *Politics of Regional Trade*, 46–47.

135. Vassiliev, *History of Saudi Arabia*, 206–7.

136. Grehan, *Everyday Life*, 53.

137. ʿAwrah, *Tārīkh Wilāyat Sulaymān Bāshā al-ʿĀdil*, 109–10.

138. Burckhardt, *Travels in Syria*, 264–65, 352–57, 367–69.

139. Doğan, "18 ve 19 Yüzyıllarda Şam-Medine Hac Yolu."

140. Tanūkhī, *Al-Riḥlah al-Tanūkhīyah*, 22–23.

141. Fahmy, *All the Pasha's Men*.

142. Benton, *A Search for Sovereignty*, 34–35.

143. Sneath, *The Headless State*, 44–45; Asad, "Equality in Nomadic Social Systems?," 423–24.

144. Beshara Doumani's detailed overview of politics in Nablus before and after the Egyptian period shows the way certain families charted political gains during the Egyptian period, emerging much more powerful in the 1840s. See Doumani, *Rediscovering Palestine*, 52–53.

CHAPTER 2

1. Beshara Doumani explains the soap-making process of the period and the role of Balqa Bedouin in it; see Doumani, *Rediscovering Palestine*, 193, 203. See also Abujaber, *Pioneers over Jordan*, 135; and Burckhardt, *Travels in Syria*, 354. On the ʿAbd al-Hadis, see also Abubakr, "Properties of Aal Abdul-Hadi."

2. The date of the petition is 21 R 1269/30 April 1853, no. 264. I thank Beshara Doumani for providing me with access to his collection of the minutes of the Nablus Advisory Council.

3. Levy, *Ages of American Capitalism*, xx.

4. On the creation of an integrated global grain market in the mid-nineteenth century, see Findlay and O'Rourke, *Power and Plenty*, 384–85. On the wheat boom in the Eastern Mediterranean and globally, see Owen, *Middle East in the World Economy*; Goodwin and Grennes, "Tsarist Russia"; and Hobsbawm, *The Age of Capital*, 173–74. I use the term *merchant capitalist* to refer to the practice of investing in assets like land with the expectation of future wealth accumulation, in the sense of Banaji. See Banaji, *Brief History of Commercial Capitalism*.

5. For an example of such an out-of-court property contract, see Doumani, *Family Life*, 262.

6. Bhattacharya, *The Great Agrarian Conquest*.

7. Hopkins, *Ruling the Savage Periphery*, 5–8.

8. Maggor, "To Coddle and Caress," 79; Goodwin and Grennes, "Tsarist Russia."

9. Teitelman, "The Properties of Capitalism"; Pravilova, "The Property of Empire."

10. Peake, *Tārīkh Sharqī al-Urdun*, 166; al-ʿUzayzī, *Nimr al-ʿAdwān*, 25–27; Rawābidah, *Muʿjam al-ʿashāʾir al-Urdunīyah*.

11. Al-ʿUzayzī, *Nimr al-ʿAdwān*, 25–26; Shryock, *Nationalism and the Genealogical Imagination*, 202–3; Palva, "Arabic Texts." This story recalls the widely circulated reports of the deadly banquet Mehmed ʿAli Paşa threw for the heads of the Mamluk households in Cairo in 1811. See Fahmy, *All the Pasha's Men*, 84–85.

12. C. R. Conder created a map of ʿAdwan country in collaboration with his ʿAdwani interlocutors after surveying the region in the late 1870s. The map is accompanied by short descriptions of 703 locations in ʿAdwan country, many

of which refer to the holdings of the ʿAdwan, Bani Sakhr, and other Bedouin communities. See Conder, *Survey of Eastern Palestine*; on Conder, see Assi, *History and Politics*, 28–32.

13. Shryock, *Nationalism and the Genealogical Imagination*, 199; Peake, *Tārīkh Sharqī al-Urdun*, 169–70.

14. Conder, *Survey of Eastern Palestine*, 217, 227–28; Finn, *Byeways in Palestine*, 15.

15. Cohen, *Palestine in the 18th Century*, 22, 187.

16. Burckhardt, *Travels in Syria*, 368–70.

17. Al-ʿUzayzī, *Nimr al-ʿAdwān*, 28.

18. Ibn Sbayyil, *Arabian Romantic*, liv, nn29, 31.

19. Rukus al-ʿUzayzi's accounting of the social tensions surrounding Nimr and Wadha's relationship recalls the tensions around the relationship between the Ottoman sultan Sulayman I and Hürrem Sultan. See Peirce, *Empress of the East*; and al-ʿUzayzī, *Nimr al-ʿAdwān*, 41.

20. Sowayan, *Al-Ṣaḥrāʾ al-ʿArabīyah*, 311.

21. Al-ʿUzayzī, *Nimr al-ʿAdwān*.

22. BOA.EV.HMK.SR 3207 (1803), 19.

23. Al-ʿUzayzī, *Nimr al-ʿAdwān*, 79.

24. Al-ʿUzayzī, 48–50.

25. A number of anthropologists have discussed similar social stratification in the twentieth century; see, e.g., Abu-Lughod, *Veiled Sentiments*, 79–81.

26. On Musa Tuqan, see Nimr, *Tārīkh Jabal Nāblus*, 1:289–92; and Doumani, *Rediscovering Palestine*, 190.

27. Burckhardt, *Travels in Syria*, 355.

28. Peake, *Tārīkh Sharqī al-Urdun*, 170–71; Burckhardt, *Travels in Syria*, 368; Buckingham, *Travels among the Arab Tribes*, 14–15.

29. Peake, *Tārīkh Sharqī al-Urdun*, 170.

30. Shryock, *Nationalism and the Genealogical Imagination*, 80–81.

31. Ṣāfī, *Al-Ḥukm al-Miṣrī fī Filasṭīn*, 129–30; Rogan, "Incorporating the Periphery," 59.

32. Rustum, *Al-Maḥfuẓāt al-Malakīyah al-Miṣriyah*, 1:300, no. 923.

33. Abū Ṣīnī, "Muḥammad ʿAlī Bāshā wa al-Qabāʾil al-Badūwīyah"; Rustum, *Al-Maḥfuẓāt al-Malakīyah al-Miṣriyah*, 1:302, no. 931; Rustum, *Al-Maḥfuẓāt al-Malakīyah al-Miṣriyah*, 4:225, no. 255.

34. Peake, *Tārīkh Sharqī al-Urdun*, 170.

35. Ṣāfī, *Al-Ḥukm al-Miṣrī fī Filasṭīn*, 8–12.

36. See, e.g., Rustum, *Al-Maḥfuẓāt al-Malakīyah al-Miṣriyah*, 4:222–25.

37. Doumani, *Rediscovering Palestine*, 234–35; Makdisi, *The Culture of Sectarianism*.

38. Ṣāfī, *Al-Ḥukm al-Miṣrī fī Filasṭīn*, 106–10.

39. Spyridon, "Annals of Palestine, 1821–1841," 90–91; Hill, "How Global Was the Age of Revolutions?"

40. Spyridon, "Annals of Palestine, 1821–1841," 100–110.

41. Abū Ṣīnī, "Muḥammad ʿAlī Bāshā wa al-Qabāʾil al-Badūwīyah."

42. Tell, *Social and Economic Origins*, 43; Mundy, "Village Authority," 67; Issawi, *The Fertile Crescent, 1800–1914*, 271; Owen, *Middle East in the World Economy*, 167; Schölch, *Palestine in Transformation*, 91.

43. Findlay and O'Rourke, *Power and Plenty*, 383–87.

44. Historians of the American West in particular have narrated the fundamental technological and social changes of the mid-nineteenth-century grain boom. See Cronon, *Nature's Metropolis*; and Owen, *Middle East in the World Economy*, 167.

45. Doumani, *Rediscovering Palestine*, 135–40; Burckhardt, *Travels in Syria*, 355.

46. Abubakr, "Properties of Aal Abdul-Hadi."

47. Nimr, *Tārīkh Jabal Nāblus*, 1:372–75; Schölch, *Palestine in Transformation*, 210–12; Finn and Finn, *Stirring Times*, 239.

48. BOA.MVL 1062/13, 7 S 1283/21 June 1866.

49. Nimr, *Tārīkh Jabal Nāblus*, 1:374–75.

50. Doumani, *Rediscovering Palestine*, 159–60; Abubakr, "Properties of Aal Abdul-Hadi."

51. Reilly, "Shariʿa Court Registers."

52. On the "bundle of rights" involved in land administration during this period, see İslamoğlu, "Property as a Contested Domain," 18. On the administrative and investment prerogatives of tax farmers in the Nablus region in the 1850s, see Doumani, *Rediscovering Palestine*, 47.

53. BOA.I.MVL 238/8436, 5 B 1268/25 April 1852.

54. Cuno, "Was the Land of Ottoman Syria *Miri* or *Milk*?"; Johansen, *Islamic Law*; Mundy and Smith, *Governing Property*, chap. 3.

55. Cuno, "Was the Land of Ottoman Syria *Miri* or *Milk*?"; Doumani, *Family Life*, 228–30.

56. BOA.I.MVL 238/8436, 5 B 1268/25 April 1852.

57. Mundy and Smith, *Governing Property*, 48–49. See chapter 3 herein for further discussion of these debates and their long-term implications.

58. Abubakr, "Properties of Aal Abdul-Hadi"; Alff, "Levantine Joint-Stock Companies."

59. Wåhlin, "How Long?"; Tristram, *The Land of Israel*, 557; Hamarneh, "Amman in British Travel Accounts," 67; Abujaber, *Pioneers over Jordan*, 70–71; Finn, *Byeways in Palestine*, 18–20.

60. Tristram, *The Land of Israel*, 552.

61. Finn, *Byeways in Palestine*, 19; Conder, *Survey of Eastern Palestine*; Tristram, *The Land of Israel*. The importance of slave labor to the burgeoning agricultural production of the mid-nineteenth century in the Eastern Mediterranean is a crucial subject for further study; my sources say relatively little about it. Benjamin Reilly fits slavery on 'Adwan farms in the Jordan Valley into a general pattern of Bedouin leaders enslaving Africans, usually purchased in Mecca, in valleys with high rates of malaria in the nineteenth century. See Reilly, *Slavery, Agriculture, and Malaria*, 70.

62. Warren, "Expedition to East of Jordan," 287.

63. TNA/FO 78/139, 176, 30 Sept. 1850.

64. Finn, *Byeways in Palestine*, 20.

65. Finn, 2; Tristram, *The Land of Israel*, 516–17; Luynes, *Voyage d'exploration, Extrait des notes*, 16.

66. See Rogan, *Frontiers of the State*, 21; Shryock, *Nationalism and the Genealogical Imagination*, 37; Alon, *The Shaykh of Shaykhs*, 14.

67. There is a distinct parallel here with contemporaneous British frustration at their inability to replace, or even insert themselves into, long-standing rural credit networks around Damascus. See Derri, "Bonds of Obligation," chap. 1.

68. Abujaber, *Pioneers over Jordan*.

69. Rogan, "Moneylending and Capital Flows."

70. Abujaber, *Pioneers over Jordan*, 135.

71. Abujaber, 138–40.

72. Doumani, *Family Life*, 259–60.

73. Al-Juhany, *Najd before the Salafi*, 53, 141–45.

74. Al-Juhany documents similar agreements in Najd, based mainly on Najdi chronicles, in the sixteenth and seventeenth centuries. See al-Juhany, 101–2.

75. BOA.I.MVL 755/12, 14 S 1276/12 Sept. 1859. This voluminous Meclis-i Vala file includes great detail on the migration and the Ottoman attempt to return cultivators to their villages.

76. In later decades, the Yaduda operation did develop highly stratified plantation-style methods of organizing farm labor. Abujaber describes how work teams were organized at al-Yaduda, probably around the turn of the twentieth century, in detail in Abujaber, *Pioneers over Jordan*, chap. 3. For an appraisal of the interior economy as precapitalist, see Lewis, *Nomads and Settlers*, 52.

77. Alff, "Landed Property"; Jakes and Shokr, "Capitalism in Egypt."

78. Abujaber, *Pioneers over Jordan*, 146.

79. Abujaber, 159. The Bisharat, Qaʿwar, Nabulsi, and Sharabi families were among the early investors who came from Damascus and Nablus during this period. Doumani relates the movement of Nabulsi families to the East Bank

of the Jordan River to the rise of Jerusalem as an economic center over Nablus in the 1860s. See Doumani, *Rediscovering Palestine*, 47.

80. Tell, *Social and Economic Origins*.

81. Finn, *Byeways in Palestine*, 35.

82. Bishara, *A Sea of Debt*, 20.

83. I borrow the idea of an "agrarian imaginary" from Neeladri Bhattacharya's work on British Punjab, to emphasize the privileging of the village as the foundational category of administration in nineteenth-century official Ottoman ideals about the countryside and agrarian law. See Bhattacharya, *The Great Agrarian Conquest*, 64–70.

84. See Kasaba, *A Moveable Empire*, chap. 4.

85. A number of these decrees discuss "settlement of tribes" (*iskan-i aşair*). See, e.g., BOA.I.MSM 68/2000, 24 Ra 1259/24 April 1843; and BOA.I.MSM 69/2003, 8 S 1259/10 March 1843.

86. The order refers specifically to "aşair," the Arabic plural of *aşiret*, as a population category (*taife-i aşair*).

87. Barakat, "Making 'Tribes,'" 482.

88. BOA.I.MSM 69/2005, 8 Z 1260/19 Dec. 1844, p. 2.

89. See BOA.ML.CRD.d 1377, 13 C 1267/15 April 1851. For more on this collection of registers, see Kasaba, *A Moveable Empire*, 160n105; Dolbee, *Locusts of Power*; and Lewis, *Nomads and Settlers*, 9.

90. Reşat Kasaba describes these projects as a major turning point in Ottoman administration of nomadic groups, but I have not found any evidence that this project extended south of Aleppo. See BOA.ML.CRD; and Kasaba, *A Moveable Empire*, 106–8.

91. Rogan, *Frontiers of the State*, 46–48. This attempt included an initiative to settle Algerian refugees in Ajlun, but archival records show that the resettlement plan was more closely related to a desire to isolate the refugees from foreign, especially French, interests than a commitment to develop the interior region. See BOA.MVL 32/31 Z 24 1269/28 Sept. 1853.

92. Doumani, *Rediscovering Palestine*, 233–35; Nimr, *Tārīkh Jabal Nāblus*, 1:379–83.

93. BOA.MVL 755/12, 14 S 1276/12 Sept. 1859; BOA.MVL 754/89, 14 S 1276/12 Sept. 1859.

94. Taylor, "Fragrant Gardens," 36–39; Mundy and Smith, *Governing Property*, 26.

95. İslamoğlu, "Property as a Contested Domain," 26–34; Terzibaşoğlu, "Landlords, Nomads and Refugees." For amendments to the Land Code that moved the definition of tapu right closer to fee simple title in succeeding decades, see Cin, *Osmanlı Toprak Düzeni*.

96. Mundy and Smith, *Governing Property*, 73.

97. See Kasaba, *A Moveable Empire*, chap. 4; Gratien, *The Unsettled Plain*, chap. 2; and Gratien, "The Ottoman Quagmire," 590; see also Köksal, "Coercion and Mediation."

98. Akiba, "Local Councils"; Yaycıoğlu, *Partners of the Empire*, chap. 3; Taylor, "Fragrant Gardens," chap. 1.

99. Saraçoğlu, *Nineteenth-Century Local Governance*; Gerber, *Ottoman Rule in Jerusalem*.

100. On the election of headmen and their administration, see Büssow, *Hamidian Palestine*, 74; Gerber, *Ottoman Rule in Jerusalem*; Çadırcı, "Türkiye'de Muhtarlık"; and Güneş, *Osmanlı Döneminde Muhtarlık*.

101. Çadırcı, *Tanzimat döneminde*, 38.

102. Çadırcı, "Türkiye'de Muhtarlık," 413-414. .

103. Cohen, *Palestine in the 18th Century*; Cuno, *The Pasha's Peasants*; Yaycıoğlu, *Partners of the Empire*.

104. Güneş, *Osmanlı Döneminde Muhtarlık*, 11. Nadir Özbek makes the important point that these attempts to transform tax farming did not aim to eliminate provincial notables who had been local subcontractors of pre-Tanzimat tax-farming arrangements. See Özbek, "Tax Farming."

105. Çadırcı, "Türkiye'de Muhtarlık," 416-20.

106. On the design and dismantling of the muhassilik institution, see Şener, *Tanzimat Dönemi Osmanlı Vergi Sistemi*; see also İslamoğlu, "Politics of Administering Property," 301-4.

107. Çadırcı, "Türkiye'de Muhtarlık," 414.

108. See the Land Title Regulation (Tapu Nizamnamesi) of 1859. For the role of the *mukhtar*, see Article 3, *Düstur*, 1:300.

109. *Düstur*, 1:618-20.

110. Lewis, *Nomads and Settlers*, 29-30; Gross, "Ottoman Rule," 128-29.

111. BOA.I.DH 570/39711, 14 Teşrinisani 1283/26 Nov. 1867, p. 1.

112. Gross, "Ottoman Rule," 148; Schilcher, "Hauran Conflicts," 173-75. On simultaneous expansion of Aleppo landowners' holdings in Dayr al-Zor, see Çiçek, *Negotiating Empire*, 110.

113. Schilcher, "Hauran Conflicts," 174.

114. As'ad Manşūr, *Tārīkh al-Nāṣirah*, 73-81; Schölch, *Palestine in Transformation*, 199-209.

115. BOA.MVL 1062/35, 29 Safar 1283/13 July 1866, p. 2. See also Abujaber, *Pioneers over Jordan*; and Rogan, "Incorporating the Periphery," 78.

116. After his campaign, Mehmed Raşid petitioned Istanbul to have six men who helped him with his Muzayrib mission decorated, both in his work in Hawran and in his attempts to apprehend Dhiyab al-Humud, including Kayid Abu 'Urabi, Kayid al-Khitalayn, and Husayn al-Sabah; see BOA.I.DH 568/39569, 29 Eylül 1283/11 Oct. 1867.

117. Shryock, *Nationalism and the Genealogical Imagination*, 84–85.

118. On 'Anaza cooperation with Ottoman military campaigns in the interior during this period, see Çiçek, *Negotiating Empire*, 149–53.

119. Mehmed Raşid Paşa's detailed report on the 1867 campaign is in the file BOA.I.DH 568/39592, 5 C 1284/21 Eylül 1283/4 Oct. 1867, p. 1.

120. BOA.I.DH 568/39592, 13 B 1284/10 Nov. 1867, p. 1.

121. For a description of these grain storage sites, see Warren, "Expedition to East of Jordan," 287.

122. Abujaber, *Pioneers over Jordan*.

123. Çiçek, *Negotiating Empire*, 149.

124. Gross, "Ottoman Rule," 147–48.

125. BOA.Y.PRK.UM 2/7, 2 N 1296/20 August 1879, pp. 5–7.

126. BOA.BEO 317/23720, 16 Ca 1311/25 Nov. 1893.

127. Al-'Assāf, *Thawrat al-Balqā'*; Alon, "The Balqā' Revolt."

128. Bsheer, *Archive Wars*, 34.

129. Hämäläinen, *Lakota America*, chap. 8. The idea that agriculture was "completely alien" to Bedouin, who acted according to a "tribal insistence on their lifestyle," has impeded analysis of this type of "shape-shifting" in the context of the Ottoman Empire and Middle East more broadly and has also become a catchall explanation for Bedouin resistance to capitalist expansion. See, e.g., Çiçek, *Negotiating Empire*, 51–52.

130. Fratantuono, "Producing Ottomans," 2; Chatty, *Displacement and Dispossession*.

131. Richard White, *The Middle Ground*; Moon, "Agriculture and Environment."

132. Ho, "Afterword"; Bishara, *A Sea of Debt*.

CHAPTER 3

1. DLS Salt *yoklama*, vol. 1, Teşrinievvel 1295/Oct. 1879. The first page of the register, which mentions the Wasiya region, is partly torn and difficult to read; entry 4 has a son of Muhammad al-Lawzi registering one hundred donums there.

2. This settlement also included an agreement that Habib Effendi would act as guarantor for Raja and Fadl al-Wiraykat. See SSCR, vol. 5, 15 S 1315/16 July 1897, p. 119, record 122.

3. Çiçek notes the important function of sharia courts as providers of notary services among Shammar and 'Anaza Bedouin; see Çiçek, *Negotiating Empire*, 243.

4. Gratien, *The Unsettled Plain*, 75–83; Toksöz, *Nomads, Migrants and Cotton*, 64–73.

5. Barakat, "Making 'Tribes,'" 482–83.

6. Cole, "Empire on Edge," 90–91, 95–96.

7. As we will see in chapter 4, however, they also had the power to disrupt this line. See Saha, *Law, Disorder and the Colonial State*, chap. 1.

8. Kale, "Transforming an Empire," 260.

9. For a similar dynamic in Dayr al-Zor, see Çiçek, *Negotiating Empire*, 130.

10. Findley, *Bureaucratic Reform*; Wishnitzer, *Reading Clocks, Alla Turca*.

11. Salname-i Vilayet-i Suriye, vol. 1, 1285 (1868–69), 59.

12. On the rise of this group of merchants in the Balqa, first in Salt and later in Amman, see Rogan, *Frontiers of the State*, chap. 4; and Hamed-Troyansky, "Circassian Refugees," 610–13.

13. Salname-i Vilayet-i Suriye, vol. 8, 1293 (1876/77), 122–23.

14. Gross, "Ottoman Rule," 208–10.

15. Doumani also argued that these merchant families looked to the East Bank of the Jordan River as a new frontier after Nablus was eclipsed by Jerusalem and coastal cities in the 1870s. See Doumani, *Rediscovering Palestine*, 47; see also Rogan, "Moneylending and Capital Flows," 239–40; and Schilcher, "Hauran Conflicts," 174.

16. For an analysis of mentions and activities of Bedouin in earlier court cases across the Eastern Mediterranean, see Meier, "Bedouins in the Ottoman Juridical Field."

17. Doumani, *Family Life*, 238; Reilly, "Shariʿa Court Registers," 158–59; Reilly, "Status Groups and Propertyholding," 518.

18. This practice was widespread in Egyptian villages much earlier; see Cuno, *The Pasha's Peasants*. In general, the Salt sharia court procedures reflect the same kinds of influences from the developing nizamiye system that Iris Agmon found for the Jaffa court; see Agmon, *Family and Court*, 102. On the nizamiye court system, see Rubin, *Ottoman Nizamiye Courts*; and Rafeq, "Ownership of Real Property," 175.

19. Reilly, "Shariʿa Court Registers."

20. For further analysis based on these three registers of transactions, see Rogan, "Moneylending and Capital Flows."

21. On the importance of witnesses in the procedure of qadi courts, see Fahmy, *In Quest of Justice*, 104; and Peirce, *Morality Tales*.

22. Barakat, "Regulating Land Rights," 110–11.

23. See chap. 2.

24. Wåhlin, "How Long?"

25. SSCR, vol. 1, 5 Za 1883/7 Sept. 1883, records 8 and 9.

26. SSCR, vol. 1, 25 Ş 1300/29 August 1883, record 5.

27. The record refers to the Abu al-Ghanam as an *ʿashīra* of the environs of Salt, but as a *jamāʿa* when describing Rashid Abu al-Ghanam's wikala to represent its members in the land sale.

28. Rogan, "Moneylending and Capital Flows."

29. Rogan, *Frontiers of the State*, 100–101; Rafeq, "Ownership of Real Property," 176–77.

30. Rafeq found that these detailed identifications entered the Damascus court records in the mid-1860s. He relates them specifically to concerns about identifying individual owners in order to regulate non-Muslim foreign protégés' landownership. See Rafeq, "Ownership of Real Property," 177–78.

31. Masud, Peters, and Powers, "Qadis and Their Courts," 25–26.

32. The differences between identification requirements in sharia and nizamiye courts during this period follow Fahmy's findings on these differences between qadi courts and siyasa courts in Egypt. See Fahmy, *In Quest of Justice*, 102–3.

33. The text of this letter appears in Dāwūd, *Al-Salṭ Wa-Jiwāruhā*, 47.

34. İslamoğlu, "Property as a Contested Domain," 17–19.

35. Davison, *Reform in the Ottoman Empire*.

36. Gedikli, "Midhat Paşa'nın Suriye Layihası"; Shamir, "The Modernization of Syria," 353–56; Gross, "Ottoman Rule," 265. Gross argues that Midhat Paşa was proposing for Syria what he saw as appropriate for the entire empire.

37. Gedikli, "Midhat Paşa'nın Suriye Layihası," 184.

38. Shamir, "The Modernization of Syria," 363–67.

39. Dolbee, *Locusts of Power*; Çiçek, *Negotiating Empire*, 48–49.

40. Avcı, "Tanzimat in the Desert"; Amara, "Civilizational Exceptions."

41. BOA.ŞD 2272/27, 31 Mart 1295/12 April 1879.

42. Schilcher, "Hauran Conflicts," 173.

43. Halil Sahilioğlu reproduced this document in Sahilioğlu, *Studies on Ottoman Economic and Social History*, 181–83.

44. Kamil Paşa's dismissal of the strategic value of camels is somewhat puzzling considering both the Egyptian regime's sustained struggle to procure them and the Russian and American regimes' preoccupation with camels for military purposes. See Morrison, *Russian Conquest*, chap. 2; and Nelson, "Death in the Distance," 36.

45. Gross, "Ottoman Rule in the Province of Damascus."

46. BOA.Y.PRK.UM 2/7, 2 N 1296/20 August 1879.

47. BOA.Y.PRK.UM 2/7, 2 N 1296/20 August 1879, p. 3 (my translation).

48. Davis, *Resurrecting the Granary of Rome*; Duffy, *Nomad's Land*.

49. Mundy and Smith, *Governing Property*, 66–67.

50. On the *yoklama* process, see Mundy and Smith, 51, 70–73. For a more detailed account of these initial registers, see Rogan, "Incorporating the Periphery," 110–11.

51. DLS Salt *yoklama*, vol. 1, Teşrinievvel 1295/Oct. 1879, p. 7, entries 170–76.

52. BOA.BEO 317/23720, 16 Ca 1311/25 Nov. 1893, p. 2.

53. These plots were in Ard Suwaylih and Ard al-Batiha. No specific division of shares is mentioned. See DLS Salt *yoklama*, vol. 1, Teşrinievvel 1295/ Oct. 1879, p. 11, entries 269–84.

54. Mundy and Smith, *Governing Property*, 71.

55. A similar politics of administration seems to have attended registrations of Bani Hassan land rights in the Ajlun district in the 1880s. See Mundy and Smith, 99, 236.

56. BOA.Y.PRK.UM 2/7, 2 N 1296/20 August 1879, p. 1; BOA.ŞD. 2272/27, Ca 22 1304/16 Feb. 1887.

57. Maoz, *Ottoman Reform*. Susynne McElrone subjects this argument to comprehensive historiographical deconstruction in her dissertation, "From the Pages of the Defter," 5–25. The most recent iteration of this argument, to describe the exceptionalism (or premodernity) of the Ottoman land regime, is Fields, *Enclosure*, 193–94; see also Williams, *States of Cultivation*.

58. These transactions follow the same format outlined in detail by Reilly and used tapu deeds and rulings issued by the sharia court as evidence for prior use rights interchangeably as Reilly described. See Reilly, "Shari'a Court Registers," 157–61.

59. Khuraysāt and Dāwūd, *Sijill Maḥkamat Al-Salṭ al-Sharʿīyah*, 204. The date of this case is 25 Ca 1304/19 Feb. 1887.

60. DLS Salt *yoklama*, vol. 1, Teşrinievvel 1295/Oct. 1879, p. 7, entry 170.

61. SSCR, vol. 3, 13 Ca 1305/27 Jan. 1888, pp. 5–6, record 7. This contract followed the terms of the bey' bil-vefa as stipulated in the 1858 Land Code, which legalized mortgaging miri land, although not in sharia courts.

62. Doumani, *Rediscovering Palestine*, chap. 4.

63. Moumtaz, *God's Property*, 129–32; Mundy and Smith, *Governing Property*, 235; Rogan, "Moneylending and Capital Flows"; Derri, "Bonds of Obligation," 174.

64. BOA.Y.PRK.UM 2/7, 2 N 1296/20 August 1879. On the production of an Ottoman discourse of usury aimed at provincial creditors in the mid-nineteenth century, see Derri, "Bonds of Obligation," 133–38.

65. Rogan, *Frontiers of the State*, 110.

66. SSCR, vol. 9, 20 C 1320/24 Sept. 1902, p. 53, record 84.

67. SSCR, vol. 11, 3 B 1322/13 Sept. 1304, pp. 201–3, records 170–72.

68. DLS Salt *Defter-i Hakani*, vol. 30/1/2, Nisan 1318/April 1902, p. 76, entry 10; vol. 31/1/2, Teşrinisani 1320/Nov. 1904 *yoklama*, p. 77, entry 39; vol. 32/1/2, Kanunuevvel 1328/Dec. 1912, p. 346, entries 6–7.

69. DLS Salt *Defter-i Hakani*, vol. 30/1/2, Eylül 1317/Sept. 1901 *yoklama*, p. 49, entries 8–9; vol. 31/1/2, Teşrinievvel 1321/Oct. 1905, p. 115, entry 24; vol. 32/1/2, Kanunuevvel 1328/Dec. 1912, p. 350, entries 22–23.

70. SSCR, vol. 8, sec. 2, 9 Za 1330/20 Oct. 1912, p. 14, record 12; SSCR, vol. 8, sec. 2, 19 Z 1330/29 Nov. 1912, p. 23, record 21.

71. This is similar to property transactions in the Damascus and Aleppo courts Rafeq described prior to the 1870s. See Rafeq, "Ownership of Real Property," 175.

72. Khuraysāt and Dāwūd, *Sijill Maḥkamat al-Salṭ al-Sharʿiyah*; Rafeq, "Ownership of Real Property," 180.

73. See Article 3 of the Tapu Nizamnamesi (Tapu Regulation), *Düstur*, 1:200.

74. DLS Salt *Defter-i Hakani*, vol. 30/1/2, Nisan 1318/April 1902, p. 76, entry 10; vol. 31/1/2, Teşrinisani 1320/Nov. 1904 *yoklama*, p. 77, entry 39; vol. 32/1/2, Kanunuevvel 1328/Dec. 1912, p. 346, entries 6–7.

75. SSCR, vol. 5, n.d., p. 122, record 124. Based on the records around this one, which is missing a date because the ruling is missing, it was recorded sometime in mid-1899.

76. Like many cases in this particular volume of proceedings, this one was left hanging, without a ruling. The volume includes notes taken during court proceedings that do not always include rulings. Possibly, the case was resolved in a later session, the record of which failed to enter the bound volume of court cases available to researchers today. See Agmon, *Family and Court,* 100–105.

77. It is likely that they played similar roles in the new judicial council, which became an official Court of First Instance beginning in the 1890s, although the lack of surviving records from that body leave this point open to question.

78. Tell, *Social and Economic Origins,* 45.

79. This conceptualization is also particularly prominent in the historiography of Iraq. See Batatu, *Old Social Classes.* For a critique, see Haj, "The Problems of Tribalism."

80. Meeker, *A Nation of Empire.*

81. For a narrative of the life and work of Sattam al-Fayiz and his sons, see Abujaber, *Pioneers over Jordan,* chap. 10.

82. Shryock, *Nationalism and the Genealogical Imagination,* 133.

83. Lipsky, *Street-Level Bureaucracy,* introduction. On bureaucratic modern state practice as performance, see Saha, *Law, Disorder and the Colonial State,* 12.

84. Rogan, *Frontiers of the State,* 189–90.

85. The original telegram, in Arabic, states that the Bani Hamida owned the villages and the land (*tamlak thamānya khirba bi-arḍiha al-fasīḥa*). The translation into Ottoman, however, describes them as "owners and usufruct holders" (*malik ve mutasarrif*). While the Bani Hamida may have owned buildings and perhaps trees in villages, their rights over wide swaths of agricultural land were conceived, in Istanbul, as ultimately usufructuary. This discrepancy speaks, once again, to the gaps in understandings of the legal basis for local property right between the Syrian interior and the imperial center. See BOA. HR.TO 392/99, 14 Sept. 1889, p. 2.

86. BOA.HR.TO 392/99, 14 Sept. 1889, p. 2.

87. The signatories include the headmen of the following communities: al-ʿAbbad (three); al-Nimr (two); al-Salih, al-ʿAdwan, al-ʿAjarma, al-Shawabka, al-ʿAwamla, al-Akrad (two); and al-Kayid, Masihiyin al-Salt, al-Marashda, al-Azayda (two).

88. Yuval Ben-Bassat has also shown the important roles of *muhtars* in Palestine who led initiatives to petition authorities, especially with regard to land lost to absentee landowners and Jewish colonists. See Ben-Bassat, "Bedouin Petitions," 142n22.

89. Rogan, *Frontiers of the State*, 85–86.

90. Based on Midhat Paşa's final ruling on this case, Rogan portrayed him as attempting to send a message to the Bani Sakhr with a strong ruling encouraging land registration. While this may have been part of his aim, his earlier correspondence with regard to this case shows that he felt extremely pressured by the British and French consuls and supported the Karaki Christians largely to avoid the threat of foreign intervention. See BOA.ŞD 2272/68, 19 Ca 1297/29 April 1880; and Rogan, *Frontiers of the State*, 79.

91. Terzibaşoğlu, "Land Disputes and Ethno-politics"; Fratantuono, "Producing Ottomans," 21.

92. Conder, *Survey of Eastern Palestine*, 291.

93. DLS Salt *Defter-i Hakani*, vol. 30/1/2, Şubat 1328/Feb. 1913, p. 414, entry 115.

94. Saha, *Law, Disorder and the Colonial State*, 13–14; Mitchell, "Society, Economy, and the State Effect," 82–85.

95. Goswami, *Producing India*, 2.

96. Findlay and O'Rourke, *Power and Plenty*, chap. 7; Arrighi, *The Long Twentieth Century*, 176–77.

97. Rafeq, "Ownership of Real Property," 224–26; Zandi-Sayek, *Ottoman Izmir*; Derri, "Imperial Creditors," 4.

CHAPTER 4

1. Ayn Suwaylih was the fourth village settled by Chechens in the Balqa region and was established in 1906. See Rogan, "Incorporating the Periphery," 121; see also Dāwūd, *Al-Salṭ Wa Jiwāruhā*, chap. 4; and Lewis, *Nomads and Settlers*, 96–123.

2. These weapons were described simply as "Martin tüfengi" by the local investigation into the events described here and were assumed to have been smuggled from Egypt. See Grant, "Sword of the Sultan," 15.

3. This sketch is based on Cemal Bey's description of events, and his claim that the attack was caused by a quarrel over land that left a Bedouin man wounded. BOA.A.MKT.MHM 530/32, 7 Mayis 1323/20 May 1907, p. 2.

4. Based on late twentieth-century interviews, Mohammed Haghandoqa estimated Ayn Suwaylih to consist of forty-one Chechen families in the late nineteenth century. See Haghandoqa, *The Circassians*, 137.

5. Moumtaz, *God's Property*, 132; Derri, "Bonds of Obligation," 174.

6. Mundy and Smith, *Governing Property*, 234.

7. Gary Fields's description of the cartographic, legal, and architectural phases of enclosure is useful here. See Fields, *Enclosure*, 10; and Nichols, *Theft Is Property!*

8. This change in the perception of territory and concern with who owned what land has been well-documented in the Balkans; see, e.g., Hamed-Troyansky, "Imperial Refuge," 277–78. On the expansion of territorial thinking into formerly lightly governed regions in a context of border-making, see Blumi, "Contesting the Edges."

9. See Low, *Imperial Mecca*, 253–77.

10. C. B. Macpherson's description of state property as "a corporate right to exclude" is relevant here. See Macpherson, *Property*, 5.

11. Reşat Kasaba has noted the structural similarities of the positions of "nomads" and refugees in late Ottoman society. See Kasaba, *A Moveable Empire*, chap. 4.

12. Toksöz, *Nomads, Migrants and Cotton*; Kasaba, *A Moveable Empire*, 99–108; Gratien, *The Unsettled Plain*, chaps. 2–3.

13. Ben-Bassat, "Bedouin Petitions," 142–44; Fishman, *Jews and Palestinians*, 42–43.

14. Razzaz, "Contestation and Mutual Adjustment," 12–13; Ababsa, "Fifty Years," 54; Al Naber and Molle, "Politics of Accessing Desert Land," 497.

15. Elsewhere, I have described the use of *hujjas* to trade in land outside of courts as an "extra-state land market," but this is imprecise because this market relied heavily on state-sanctioned forms. Razzaz's concept of "non-compliance" is much more precise. See Barakat, "Regulating Land Rights," 103.

16. Richard White, *The Republic*; Yaney, *The Urge to Mobilize*.

17. Das and Poole, "State and Its Margins," 14.

18. Mitchell, "Society, Economy and the State Effect," 89–91.

19. Das, "Signature of the State"; Saha, *Law, Disorder and the Colonial State*, 7–8.

20. Rogan, *Frontiers of the State*, 55.

21. Hamed-Troyansky, "Circassian Refugees," 608.

22. Kale, "Transforming an Empire," 259–61.

23. Fratantuono, "Producing Ottomans," 15, 17; Terzibaşoğlu, "Land Disputes and Ethno-politics."

24. BOA.DH.MKT 217/23, 7 Ş 1311/13 Feb. 1894.

25. Oliphant, *The Land of Gilead*, 286.

26. Fishman, *Jews and Palestinians*, 44. See also BOA.I.MMS 66/3114, 29 Ca 1297/9 May 1880, p. 1.

27. On slightly earlier iterations of this conundrum in Damascus, see Derri, "Bonds of Obligation," 146.

28. See Birdal, *Political Economy*.

29. For reports on some of these attempts from British observers, see Rogan, "Incorporating the Periphery," 111–12. For wider context on Baron Rothschild's work in Palestine, see Penslar, *Zionism and Technocracy*; Shafir, *Land, Labor and the Origins*; Aaronsohn, *Rothschild and Early Jewish Colonization*; and Schama, *Two Rothschilds*.

30. BOA.BEO 238/17824, 3 Temmuz 1909/15 July 1893.

31. Mundy and Smith, *Governing Property*, 44; Khoury, *State and Provincial Society*, 105.

32. Gratien, "The Ottoman Quagmire," 593; Toksöz, *Nomads, Migrants and Cotton*.

33. There have been reports that the investment requirement was waived, or extended, in the 1860s. See Masters, "Political Economy of Aleppo," 309.

34. Gratien, "The Ottoman Quagmire"; see also Gratien, *The Unsettled Plain*, 98–99.

35. A copy of the letter from the Grand Vezirate communicating this order to the Ministry of the Interior is in BOA.BEO 1023/76607, 1 M 1311/3 Temmuz 1309/15 July 1893, p. 9.

36. The ban was similar to a ban on the sale of state land in Iraq beginning in 1880. See Çetinsaya, "Politics of Reform in Iraq."

37. BOA.BEO 238/17824, 3 Temmuz 1909/15 July 1893.

38. BOA.BEO 1023/76697, 11 Teşrinievvel 1310/23 Oct. 1894, p. 8.

39. BOA.DH.MKT 785/23, 18 Ş 1321/25 Kanunuevvel 1319/7 Jan. 1904, p. 12.

40. BOA.DH.MKT 785/23, 2 Ca 1323/22 Haziran 1321/5 July 1905, p. 14.

41. Sluglett, "Economy and Society in the Syrian Provinces."

42. Oliphant, *The Land of Gilead*, 291.

43. The Saltis had first petitioned the governor of Damascus; see Rogan, "Incorporating the Periphery," 116n38; and Barakat, "Regulating Land Rights," 116–18.

44. Fratantuono, "Producing Ottomans," 17–18.

45. BOA.BEO 1023/76697, 5 Ca 1315/20 Eylül 1313/2 Oct. 1897, p. 2; BOA.BEO 1063/79680, 4 Ş 1315/16 Kanunuevvel 1313/29 Dec. 1897; BOA.BEO 1159/86922, 25 S 1316/3 Temmuz 1314/15 July 1898.

46. BOA.BEO 1327/99496, 12 M 1317/11 Mayis 1315/22 May 1899, p. 6.

47. The closest equivalent to *mevki* might be "neighborhood," although in rural areas this would not be relevant. One example is Siyah Diyab, which is now a village in Jordan's Zarqa governorate.

48. The points positively identified on the base map show that these lands surround the contemporary Zaatari refugee camp in northern Jordan.

49. BOA.DH.MKT 75/23, 12 B 1321/21 Eylül 1319/4 Oct. 1903, p. 10.

50. BOA.DH.MKT 75/23, 7 B 1322/4 Eylül 1320/17 Sept. 1304, p. 11.

51. See Barakat, "Regulating Land Rights," 115.

52. Rubin, "Civil Disputes."

53. In Homs, the merchant capitalists vying for control of state land were often former tax farmers, a theme not as prevalent, at least from the available records, in the Balqa. See Guéno, "La bureaucratie ottomane locale."

54. Khuraysāt and Dāwūd, *Sijill Maḥkamat al-Salṭ al-Sharʿīyah*, 14–15. The date of the case is 14 Ca 1302/25 August 1885.

55. Shryock, *Nationalism and the Genealogical Imagination*.

56. See, e.g., BOA.MVL 302/98, 23 S 1273/23, 11 Teşrinievvel 1272/Oct. 1856.

57. For details of the election process as it was outlined in codified law, see Büssow, *Hamidian Palestine*, 73–74. There are very few details about the elections of Bedouin mukhtars in the documentary record, but see chap. 5 for further discussion.

58. See BOA.DH.EUM.4Şb.3/72, 27 Za 1333/6 Oct. 1915. See also BOA.ŞD 2304/6, 26 Teşrinievvel 1323/8 Nov. 1907, p. 92.

59. For the breakdown of how many properties were registered by each group in the region, see Rogan, *Frontiers of the State*, 86.

60. Khuraysāt and Dāwūd, *Sijill Maḥkamat al-Salṭ al-Sharʿīyah*, 14–15. The date on the case is 14 Ca 1302/25 August 1885.

61. Khuraysāt and Dāwūd, 99. The date of the case is 4 S 1303/12 Nov. 1885.

62. DLS Salt *Defter-i Hakani*, vol. 30/1/2, Haziran 1318/June 1902, p. 182, entry 1, *daimi*, and p. 184, entry 1, *yoklama*.

63. SSCR, vol. 6, 8 Ş 1319/20 Nov. 1901, p. 58, record 46; vol. 6, 9 S 1320/18 May 1902, p. 186, record 161; vol. 6, 9 S 1320/18 May 1902, p. 187, record 162; vol. 6, 9 S 1320/18 May 1902, p. 188, record 163.

64. DLS Salt *Defter-i Hakani*, vol. 18, *yoklama*, Ağustos 1311/August 1895, p. 136, entry 9.

65. SSCR, vol. 5, n.d., record 20. The records around this case are from 1897.

66. Admittedly, sharia court records tell us little about the enforcement of their rulings or if the same case may have been taken into the nizamiye system.

67. Many of Bakhit's fellow prisoners, as well as the prison officials, described this operation in depositions after the fact. See BOA.ŞD 2304/6, 12 Teşrinievvel 1323/25 Oct. 1907, p. 92.

68. BOA.ŞD 2304/6, 12 Teşrinievvel 1323/25 Oct. 1907, p. 92.

69. BOA.ŞD 2304/6, 6 Haziran 1323/19 June 1907, p. 202.

70. BOA.ŞD 2304/6, 29 Mayis 1323/11 June 1907, p. 208.

71. BOA.ŞD 2304/6, 8 Teşrinievvel 1323/21 Oct. 1907, p. 92; BOA.ŞD 2304/6, 7 Teşrinievvel 1323/20 Oct. 1907, p. 127. See also BOA.ŞD 2304/6, 10 Teşrinievvel 1323/23 Oct. 1907, p. 128. For prison conditions in the late Ottoman context more generally, see Schull, *Prisons in the Late Ottoman Empire*, 113-18.

72. BOA.ŞD 2304/6, 13 Teşrinievvel 1323/26 Oct. 1907, p. 92.

73. BOA.ŞD 2304/6, 13 Teşrinievvel 1323/26 Oct. 1907, p. 92; see also 28 Teşrinievvel 1323/10 Nov. 1907.

74. BOA.ŞD 2304/6, 9 Teşrinievvel 1323/22 Oct. 1907, p. 92.

75. BOA.ŞD 2304/6, 12 Teşrinievvel 1323/25 Oct. 1907, p. 92.

76. BOA.ŞD 2304/6, 23 Temmuz 1323/5 August 1907, p. 183.

77. BOA.ŞD 2304/6, 8 Teşrinievvel 1323/21 Oct. 1907, p. 92. The death of Nahar al-Bakhit is also described in BOA.ŞD 2304/6, 26 Teşrinisani 1323/9 Dec. 1907, p. 17.

78. Shryock, *Nationalism and the Genealogical Imagination*, 128-29; BOA.ŞD 2304/6, 12 Teşrinievvel 1323/25 Oct. 1907, p. 92.

79. Sowayan, *Al-Ṣaḥrāʾ al-ʿArabīyah*, 312.

80. Mitchell, "Limits of the State," 90.

81. See Feldman, *Governing Gaza*, 13.

82. Hull, *Government of Paper*; Cole, "Empire on Edge," 95-96.

83. Barakat, "Underwriting the Empire," 377-78; Fahmy, *In Quest of Justice*, 130-31; Mitchell, "Society, Economy and the State Effect," 77-8.

84. Veena Das has explored this entanglement of modern bureaucracies with forces seemingly opposed to the state in the Indian context. See Das, "Signature of the State," 227-30.

85. Rubin, *Ottoman Nizamiye Courts*.

86. BOA.ŞD 2304/6, 23 Temmuz 1323/5 August 1907, p. 183. See also Gratien, "The Ottoman Quagmire"; and Gratien, *The Unsettled Plain*, 98-99.

87. For the depositions, see especially BOA.ŞD 2304/6, 27 Teşrinievvel 1323/9 Nov. 1907, p. 92; and BOA.ŞD 2304/6, 9 Teşrinievvel 1323/22 Oct. 1907, p. 127.

88. This prosecutorial capacity was very similar to the powers of siyasa courts that Fahmy describes in khedival Egypt. See Fahmy, *In Quest of Justice*, chap. 2.

89. Rubin, *Ottoman Nizamiye Courts*, chap. 5.

90. The final results of this review are in BOA.ŞD 2304/6, with the chair of the Council of State issuing a final decision on 6 B 1326/21 Temmuz 1324/3 August 1908, p. 1.

91. A summary of the detailed accusations related to the prisoner escape can be found in BOA.ŞD 2304/6, 27 Kanunusani 1323/9 Feb. 1908, p. 17.

92. Özbek, "The Politics of Taxation."

93. BOA.ŞD 2304/6, 22 Teşrinievvel 1323/4 Nov. 1907, p. 92.

94. For more on the role of the local military force in tax collection, see Rogan, "Incorporating the Periphery," 119.

95. BOA.ŞD 2304/6, 22 Teşrinievvel 1323/4 Nov. 1907, p. 92.

96. BOA.ŞD 2304/6, 7 Mayis 1323/20 May 1907, p. 98.

97. BOA.ŞD 2304/6, 7 Mayis 1323/20 May 1907, p. 98; BOA.ŞD 2304/6, 25 Teşrinievvel 1323/7 Nov. 1907, p. 92.

98. BOA.ŞD 2304/6, 25 Teşrinievvel 1323/7 Nov. 1907, p. 92.

99. BOA.ŞD 2304/6, 27 Kanunuevvel 1323/9 Jan. 1908, p. 36.

100. Doumani, *Rediscovering Palestine*, chap. 2. See also Derri, "Bonds of Obligation," 132-33.

101. BOA.ŞD 2304/6, 27 Kanunusani 1323/9 Feb. 1908, p. 17.

102. BOA.ŞD 2304/6, 27 Kanunusani 1323/9 Feb. 1908, p. 27.

103. Çiçek also found that the "partisanship of imperial officials for their tribal comrades" complicated the judicial process in northern Syria during this period. See Çiçek, *Negotiating Empire*, 190.

104. BOA.ŞD 2304/6, 24 Kanunusani 1323/6 Feb. 1908, p. 29.

105. BOA.ŞD 2304/6, 21 Temmuz 1324/3 August 1908, p. 1.

106. Qusūs, *Mudhakkirāt*, 1:44.

107. BOA.DH.MKT 1156/72, 16 Teşrinisani 1323/29 Nov. 1907, p. 25.

108. Troyansky, "Circassian Refugees," 607.

109. Martin, *Law and Custom*, chap. 5; Chokobaeva, Drieu, and Morrison, "Editors' Introduction," 9.

110. BOA.I.HUS 158/86, 4 Eylül 1323/17 Sept. 1907, p. 1.

111. See Satia, *Spies in Arabia*, chap. 1; Low, *Imperial Mecca*, 283-87.

112. Gupta, *Red Tape*.

113. Kiyotaki, *Ottoman Land Reform*.

114. Razzaz, "Contestation and Mutual Adjustment"; Al Naber and Molle, "Politics of Accessing Desert Land"; Ababsa, "Fifty Years."

CHAPTER 5

1. SSCR, vol. 18, 25 R 1330/13 April 1912, p. 159.

2. On the property tax, see Özbek, *İmparatorluğun Bedeli*, 29-38; Shaw, "Nineteenth-Century Ottoman Tax Reforms," 428; Kaya and Terzibaşoğlu, "Tahrir'den Kadastro'ya," 35.

3. Barakat, "Marginal Actors?," 125.

4. See Hanley, "What Ottoman Nationality Was," 278.

5. On the complex relationship between nationality, subjecthood, and citizenship in the late Ottoman context, see Can, *Spiritual Subjects*, 15-16, 157; see also Can and Low, "'Subjects' of Ottoman International Law" and the articles in the Volume 3.2 (2016) special issue of the *Journal of the Ottoman and Turkish*

Studies Association. On the important roles of provincial councils in processes of resource distribution, see Saraçoğlu, *Nineteenth-Century Local Governance.*

6. The connection between the right to vote in local elections and payment of the tax on immovable property was established in the Provincial Administration Regulations (Vilayet Nizamnamesi), chap. 5, *Düstur,* 1:625. For connections between owning registered property and the right to bid on tax farms, see Barakat, "Underwriting the Empire," 389; and Büssow, *Hamidian Palestine,* 72–80.

7. See, e.g., the depositions related to the investigation of Cemal Bey detailed in chap. 4, in which certain witnesses define themselves as "men of property" (*ṣāḥib al-amlāk*) in their initial self-identifications. BOA.ŞD. 2304/6, 7 Teşrinievvel 1323/20 Oct. 1907, p. 127.

8. See Seikaly, *Men of Capital,* 5, 21.

9. This is largely the position of Nadir Özbek, who has written on late Ottoman tax policy in the most detail; see Özbek, *İmparatorluğun Bedeli,* 43–44; Özbek, "The Politics of Taxation," 775–76; and Özbek, "Osmanlı İmparatorluğunda Gelir Vergisi," 56. See also Aytekin, "Tax Revolts," 319–20. İslamoğlu, Kaya and Terzibaşoğlu, and Mundy and Smith focus more on taxation as a technique of governance; see İslamoğlu, "Politics of Administering Property," 286–87; Kaya and Terzibaşoğlu, "Tahrir'den Kadastro'ya," 7–8; and Mundy and Smith, *Governing Property,* 42–43.

10. Kotsonis, *States of Obligation,* 27–28.

11. Kotsonis, 27–28; Fisher, *The Worst Tax?,* chap. 7.

12. See, e.g., Campos, *Ottoman Brothers,* 114; Büssow, *Hamidian Palestine,* 72–73; Gerber, *Ottoman Rule in Jerusalem,* chap. 5; and Sharif, *Imperial Norms.*

13. Khoury and Glebov note the close relationship between Ottoman citizenship and property ownership. See Khoury and Glebov, "Citizenship, Subjecthood, and Difference," 49.

14. Campos, *Ottoman Brothers*; Cohen, *Becoming Ottomans*; Makdisi, *Age of Coexistence,* 12.

15. Makdisi, *Age of Coexistence,* 63; see also Clements, "Documenting Community."

16. Hanley, "What Ottoman Nationality Was."

17. See Saraçoğlu, *Nineteenth-Century Local Governance,* chap. 3; Akiba, "Local Councils"; and Petrov, "Everyday Forms of Compliance," 754–56.

18. Khoury and Glebov, "Citizenship, Subjecthood, and Difference," 55–56; Benton, "Colonial Law."

19. Bloxham, *Great Game of Genocide,* 12–16.

20. Makdisi makes the same point about the inclusion of Kurds as Muslims in the late Ottoman polity. See Makdisi, *Age of Coexistence,* 83.

21. Çetinkaya, *Young Turks*; Polatel and Üngör, *Confiscation and Destruction*, 27–36, 61–63.

22. Klein, *The Margins of Empire*, chap. 2; Astourian, "Silence of the Land," 65–69; Gratien, *The Unsettled Plain*, 124–35.

23. Kaya and Terzibaşoğlu, "Tahrir'den Kadastro'ya," 12–15, 41–45; Özbek, "Osmanlı İmparatorluğunda Gelir Vergisi," 53. The discussion in existing literature has focused mainly on the success or failure of individualization, as well as the extent of Ottoman lawmakers' intention or commitment to individualization as a goal. Here, I am more interested in how the clear tension in the law codes between individually and collectively based taxation played out in practices of taxation in the Syrian interior. See İslamoğlu, "Politics of Administering Property," 291; and Mundy and Smith, *Governing Property*, 127.

24. For useful overviews of these taxes see Şener, *Tanzimat Dönemi Osmanlı Vergi Sistemi*, 140–44; and Özbek, *İmparatorluğun Bedeli*.

25. Kaya and Terzibaşoğlu connect the method of surveying property directly to the temmettuat surveys of the 1840s. Kaya and Terzibaşoğlu, "Tahrir'den Kadastro'ya," 13–14.

26. Özbek, "Osmanlı İmparatorluğunda Gelir Vergisi," 54–55.

27. "Regulation on Tax Collection" (1875), *Düstur*, 3:269–71; Özbek, *İmparatorluğun Bedeli*, 235–36.

28. See "Financial Affairs Regulation" (1867), Article 6, *Düstur*, 2:4.

29. "Revenue Collection Regulation" (1879), *Düstur*, 4:382–92.

30. "Revenue Collection Regulation" (1902), *Düstur*, 7:831.

31. Özbek, "Osmanlı İmparatorluğunda Gelir Vergisi," 57–58.

32. See Özbek, *İmparatorluğun Bedeli*.

33. "Provincial Administration Regulation" (1871), *Düstur*, 1:619–22.

34. Campos portrays the laws as connecting the franchise specifically to urban property (i.e., houses and buildings), but the laws specifically include land in the scope of the vergi tax. See Campos, *Ottoman Brothers*, 111.

35. Mundy and Smith, *Governing Property*, 51.

36. "Revenue Collection Regulation" (1879), *Düstur*, 4:382–92.

37. McElrone, "From the Pages of the Defter," chaps. 3 and 4.

38. Barakat, "Marginal Actors?," 113–16.

39. "Instructions for employees of the tithe and sheep tax collection agency" (1880), *Düstur*, 4:755; Özbek, "Tax Farming," 240.

40. Young, *Corps de droit ottoman*, 5:294–95.

41. See Articles 16–19 and 39 of the Revenue Collection Regulation (1879), in *Düstur*, 4:382–92.

42. "Revenue Collection Regulation," Article 17, *Düstur: Ikinci Tertip*, 1:624.

43. Al-ʿUzayzī, *Nimr al-ʿAdwān*, 48–53.

44. See chap. 2.

45. BOA.Y.PRK.UM 2/7, 28 N 1297/20 August 1879, p. 5.

46. SSCR, vol. 16, 23 M 1329/24 Jan. 1911, pp. 147–48.

47. I calculated Nahar al-Bakhit's net worth using the average values of livestock provided in Barakat, "Marginal Actors?," 125.

48. SSCR, vol. 16, 27 Z 1328/30 Nov. 1910, p. 97.

49. Rogan, *Frontiers of the State*, 167–70; Abujaber, *Pioneers over Jordan*, chap. 5; Lewis, *Nomads and Settlers*, 130.

50. SSCR, vol. 5, n.d., pp. 13–14. This court session recording does not include a date, but at one point the judge postpones proceedings to October 31, 1897, meaning the claim was probably initiated in early October 1897. All translations in discussion of this case are mine.

51. For a more detailed explanation of such arrangements, see Abujaber, *Pioneers over Jordan*, 88–92.

52. Nimr, *Tārīkh Jabal Nāblus*, 2:311–12.

53. Rogan, *Frontiers of the State*, 169.

54. Barakat, "Regulating Land Rights," 116–18.

55. BOA.ŞD 2304/6, 23 Teşrinievvel 1323/5 Nov. 1907, p. 92.

56. Özbek, "Osmanlı İmparatorluğunda Gelir Vergisi," 46, 54–55.

57. "Revenue Collection Regulation" (1879), *Düstur*, 4:382–92.

58. Barakat, "Marginal Actors?," 125. For dynamics of livestock taxes among the Shammar and ʿAnaza communities, see Çiçek, *Negotiating Empire*, chap. 6.

59. See chap. 2.

60. Shryock, *Nationalism and the Genealogical Imagination*, 86–87.

61. Ahmad, "Agrarian Policy of the Young Turks," 176. These frustrations recall the anger around wartime requisitions of property, but the legal connections have yet to be examined. See Akın, *When the War Came Home*, 115–16.

62. SSCR, vol. 6, 19 Ş 1319/29 Jan. 1902, p. 84, record 63.

63. For the commercial relationship between ʿAbd al-Muhsin al-Bakhit and various Mihyar merchants, see SSCR, vol. 9, 10 C 1320/14 Sept. 1902, p. 43; and SSCR, vol. 9, 22 C 1320/26 Sept. 1902, p. 55. For the career of especially Dawud Mihyar on Salt's governing councils, see Salname-i Vilayet-i Suriye, vols. 17–30 (1885–98). Dawud al-Mihyar's commercial relationship with the Wiraykat ʿAdwan family of Bedouin is also documented in chap. 2.

64. DLS *Defter-i Hakani*, vol. 31/1/2, Teşrinisani 1320/Nov. 1904, p. 77, entries 43–49. The date listed for the decision of the administrative council approving the registration of the land with prescriptive right is 8 Teşrinisani 1320/21 Nov. 1904.

65. SSCR, vol. 11, 4 C 1321/28 August 1903, p. 14, record 18.

66. SSCR, vol. 11, 6 C 1321/30 August 1903, pp. 11, 14, record 15.

67. See Salname-i Vilayet-i Suriye, vol. 12, 1297 (1880).

68. The records identify the Khusaylat as a Daʿja community.

69. SSCR, vol. 18, 2 Ca 1330/19 April 1912, p. 167.

70. SSCR, vol. 16, 1 Z 1328/4 Dec. 1910, pp. 115–16.

71. Alon, *The Shaykh of Shaykhs*, 19–20, 29–30.

72. Barakat, "Marginal Actors?," 113.

73. *Düstur*, 7:1060; see also the instructions for collecting fees on domestic animals, *Düstur*, 8:115.

74. *Düstur*, 8:657.

75. Barakat, "Marginal Actors?," 125–26.

76. For more examples of these tactics, see SSCR, vol. 16, p. 92; and SSCR, vol. 19, p. 65.

77. For a discussion of sharia vs. siyasa court procedure similar to the distinction I draw here, see Fahmy, "The Anatomy of Justice," 263–66. For the claim that the sharia courts were relegated to personal status cases as of the late nineteenth century, see Hallaq, *Sharī'a: Theory, Practice, Transformations*, 428–29. For an exploration of jurisdiction and legal pluralism, especially with regard to land disputes, see Barakat, "Regulating Land Rights."

78. Young, *Corps de droit ottoman*, 5:293–96.

79. Peake, *Tārīkh Sharqī al-Urdun*, 225; Kaḥḥāla, *Muʿjam Qabāʾil al-ʿArab*, 791.

80. While land registration was conducted in Karak and its environs beginning in the 1890s, the registers have not been uncovered, and it is generally believed that they were destroyed during the 1910 Karak Revolt.

81. BOA.ŞD 2304/6, 8 Teşrinievvel 1323/21 Oct. 1907, p. 111.

82. BOA.ŞD 2304/6, 8 Teşrinievvel 1323/21 Oct. 1907, p. 111.

83. On the importance of maintaining a subject/citizen population to claims of sovereignty in interimperial disputes, see Minawi, *The Ottoman Scramble*, 48–50.

84. BOA.ŞD 2304/6, 8 Teşrinievvel 1323/21 Oct. 1907, p. 111.

85. BOA.ŞD 2304/6, 9 Teşrinievvel 1323/22 Oct. 1907, p. 131.

86. Rogan notes that Bani Sakhr leaders registered a claim to the lands of Jalul in the sharia court in 1904, but there is no corresponding registration in the land records. It is possible that such a registration was lost, but, more likely, the Bani Sakhr were unable to obtain formal title to the land, so they registered their claim in the sharia court as a possible defense against others' claims later. See Rogan, "Incorporating the Periphery," 137.

87. See Alon, *The Shaykh of Shaykhs*, chaps. 2 and 3.

88. BOA.ŞD 2304/6, 27 Kanunuevvel 1323/9 Jan. 1908, p. 36.

89. BOA.ŞD 2304/6, 18 Temmuz 1323/31 July 1907, p. 188.

90. BOA.ŞD 2304/6, 21 Temmuz 1323/3 August 1907, p. 186.

91. BOA.ŞD 2304/6, 19 Temmuz 1323/1 August 1907, p. 189.

92. BOA.ŞD 2304/6, 27 Kanunusani 1323/9 Feb. 1908, p. 28.

93. BOA.ŞD 2304/6, 27 Kanunuevvel 1323/9 Jan. 1908, p. 36.

94. BOA.ŞD 2304/6, 27 Temmuz 1323/9 August 1907, p. 180.

95. BOA.ŞD 2304/6, 27 Kanunuevvel 1323/9 Jan. 1908, p. 36.

96. Özyüksel, *Hicaz Demiryolu*; Low, "Empire and the Hajj."

97. Ochsenwald, *Religion, Society, and the State*. Lâle Can's exploration of the experiences of Central Asian pilgrims emphasizes the particular disease-ridden dangers and hardships faced by those who traveled via steamships. See Can, *Spiritual Subjects*, 35–36.

98. BOA.DH.MKT 1174/26, R 20 1325/8 June 1907, p. 2.

99. BOA.DH.EUM.4Şb C.12.1333/28 March 1915.

100. The changing status of the Abu Jabirs over the long trajectory of Otto-man reforms recalls Richard Antaramian's account of the changing political trajectories of Armenian elites and clergy. See Antaramian, *Brokers of Faith*.

101. See Gratien, *The Unsettled Plain*, chap. 2; and Ceylan, *Ottoman Origins*.

102. Kuehn, *Empire, Islam, and Politics of Difference*; Ochsenwald, *Religion, Society, and the State*.

103. Massad, *Colonial Effects*, chap. 2; Neep, *Occupying Syria*; Fletcher, *British Imperialism*, chap. 2.

104. Henry Clements has explored the connections between claims-making and community politics in the Tanzimat period. See Clements, "Documenting Community."

CONCLUSION

1. Fischbach, *State, Society and Land*; Al Naber and Molle, "Politics of Ac-cessing Desert Land," 493.

2. Razzaz, "Contestation and Mutual Adjustment," 16–17.

3. Al Naber and Molle, "Politics of Accessing Desert Land," 498; Ababsa, "Fifty Years," 54n13. See also Alnajada, "'This Camp Is Full of Hujjaj!'".

4. Razzaz, "Contestation and Mutual Adjustment," 28–30.

5. Al Naber and Molle, "Politics of Accessing Desert Land," 501–2.

6. Findley, *Bureaucratic Reform*, 227–28; Wishnitzer, *Reading Clocks, Alla Turca*, 57–62; Derri, "Bonds of Obligation," 270–71.

7. Çiçek found a similar dynamic to the north in Dayr al-Zor in the late nineteenth century, when Shammar and 'Anaza Bedouin were able to main-tain control over land because the Ottoman regime did not want to provoke resistance or opposition. See Çiçek, *Negotiating Empire*, 130.

8. Williams, *States of Cultivation*; Derri, "Bonds of Obligation," 138.

9. Fletcher, *British Imperialism*; Thomas, "Bedouin Tribes"; Massad, *Colo-nial Effects*, 58–64.

10. Zakariyā, *'Ashā'ir al-Shām*, 6; see my discussion of this literature in Barakat, "Making 'Tribes,'" 486–87.

11. Benton, *A Search for Sovereignty*, 10–12.

12. Khodarkovsky, *Russia's Steppe Frontier*, 216.

13. Morrison, *Russian Conquest*, 75; Sabol, *The Touch of Civilization*, 90.

14. Morrison, *Russian Conquest*, 76. David Moon argues for characterizing the Central Asian steppe as a "middle ground" in reference to Richard White's description of the North American context, which shifted decisively in the early nineteenth century. See Moon, "Peasant Migration," 862.

15. Hämäläinen, *Lakota America*, chaps. 3 and 4; Richard White, "Winning of the West," 321–22; Hämäläinen, *The Comanche Empire*; Witgen, *An Infinity of Nations*.

16. Richard White, *The Middle Ground*.

17. Ablavsky, *Federal Ground*, 171.

18. Satia, *Empire of Guns*, chap. 3; Findlay and O'Rourke, *Power and Plenty*, 404–5.

19. Hahn, "Slave Emancipation"; West, *The Last Indian War*, 319.

20. Fratantuono, "Producing Ottomans"; Richard White, *It's Your Misfortune*, 137–45; Holquist, "In Accord with State Interests," 159. See also Fitzmaurice on the connections between doctrines of improvement and claims of territorial sovereignty in the nineteenth century. Fitzmaurice, *Sovereignty, Property and Empire*, 6–7.

21. Martin, *Law and Custom*, 48–51. For a comparison of Russian and American mobility restrictions, see Sabol, *The Touch of Civilization*, 185–86.

22. Biolsi, *Organizing the Lakota*, 7–19; Ostler, *Plains Sioux*, 109–25. Hämäläinen emphasizes the Lakota expansion in the early 1870s, taking advantage of the Great Sioux Reservation's lack of a northern border. See Hämäläinen, *Lakota America*, chap. 8.

23. Martin, *Law and Custom*, 48–54; Morrison, *Russian Conquest*, 78–79.

24. Ostler, *Plains Sioux*, 195–96; Sabol, *The Touch of Civilization*, 185–86.

25. Richard White, *It's Your Misfortune*, 91–99; Clark, "Agrarian Context"; Hahn, *A Nation without Borders*; Banner, *How the Indians Lost Their Land*, chap. 7.

26. Sabol, *The Touch of Civilization*, 178.

27. Teitelman, "The Properties of Capitalism"; Pravilova, "The Property of Empire."

28. Bishara, *A Sea of Debt*.

29. Richard White, *The Middle Ground*; Moon, "Peasant Migration," 862. Osterhammel disagrees with the "middle ground" description of Central Asia because of the legacies of centuries of what he terms "multiethnic symbiosis" that preceded the imperial expansion of the nineteenth century. Osterhammel, *Transformation of the World*, 361.

30. Biolsi, *Organizing the Lakota*, 7–13.

31. Ostler, *Plains Sioux*, 109.

32. Petrov, "Crowning the Edifice"; Emmons and Vucinich, *The Zemstvo in Russia*.

33. Morrison, "Metropole, Colony, and Imperial Citizenship," 347. On the changing status of people defined as "aliens" in the Russian administrative structure, see Sunderland, *Taming the Wild Field*; and Martin, *Law and Custom*, 38.

34. Goswami, *Producing India*.

35. Makdisi, "Ottoman Orientalism"; Deringil, "'They Live.'"

36. Kuehn, *Empire, Islam, and Politics of Difference*, 3.

37. In the case of Yemen, Kuehn also argues that the Ottoman imperial position differed fundamentally from the European colonial mode because of the goal of bridging, rather than entrenching, these perceived gaps. Kuehn, *Empire, Islam, and Politics of Difference*. For a similar dynamic in southern Palestine, see Amara, "Civilizational Exceptions," 930.

38. Hannah, "Space and Social Control"; Sabol, *The Touch of Civilization*; Fratantuono, "Producing Ottomans," 6.

39. Genetin-Pilawa, *Crooked Paths to Allotment*; Gates, *History of Public Land Law Development*.

40. Kale, "Transforming an Empire," 263.

41. Ablavsky, *Federal Ground*; Foner, *Free Soil, Free Labor*.

42. Genetin-Pilawa, *Crooked Paths to Allotment*, 134–43; Richard White, *The Republic*, 606.

43. Holquist, "In Accord with State Interests"; Masoero, "Territorial Colonization"; Pravilova, "The Property of Empire"; Sahadeo, "Progress or Peril."

44. Kotsonis, "Problem of the Individual."

45. Richard White, *The Republic*; Yaney, *The Urge to Mobilize*, chaps. 3 and 4.

46. Ostler, *Plains Sioux*; Richard White, *It's Your Misfortune*, 95–99; Hämäläinen, *Lakota America*, 371–73.

47. Campbell, *Knowledge and the Ends of Empire*; Martin, *Law and Custom*, chap. 5; Chokobaeva, Drieu, and Morrison, "Editors' Introduction," 9–10.

48. Kotsonis, *States of Obligation*.

49. Bensel, *Political Economy*.

50. Fisher, *The Worst Tax?*, 12–13.

51. Maggor, "To Coddle and Caress," 60–61.

52. Banner, *How the Indians Lost Their Land*, 247–53; Biolsi, *Organizing the Lakota*, chap. 1.

53. Kantrowitz, "'Not Quite Constitutionalized.'"

54. Holquist, "In Accord with State Interests"; Masoero, "Territorial Colonization"; Pravilova, "The Property of Empire"; Morrison, "Metropole, Colony, and Imperial Citizenship," 350.

55. Lohr, *Russian Citizenship*.

56. Klein, *The Margins of Empire*, 138–43; Kürt, *The Armenians of Aintab*, 45–49.

57. Özyüksel, *The Hejaz Railway*; Ochsenwald, *The Hijaz Railroad*.

58. Rogan, *Frontiers of the State*, 242–45.

59. Rogan, 243–44; Provence, *The Great Syrian Revolt*, 45–47, 149; Gelvin, *Divided Loyalties*, 104.

60. Seikaly, *Men of Capital*, 4.

61. Neep, *Occupying Syria*; Fletcher, *British Imperialism*, 127–28; Massad, *Colonial Effects*, 51–58.

62. Ziriklī, "'Āmān fī 'Ammān," 7–8.

63. Gelvin, *Divided Loyalties*, 22–23.

64. Alon, *The Shaykh of Shaykhs*, 48; Jarvis, *Arab Command*, 73–74.

65. A number of Bedouin communities that had been prominent in regional politics in the late Ottoman period supported Mithqal al-Fayiz at the time of his conflict with the British-backed government of Mathhar Raslan in Salt. Assaf lists the 'Ajarma, the 'Abbad, and the Lawzi 'Adwani community. See 'Assāf, *Thawrat al-Balqā*', 72.

66. 'Assāf, *Thawrat al-Balqā*'; Schwedler, *Protesting Jordan*, 47–49; Alon, "The Balqā' Revolt."

67. 'Assāf, *Thawrat al-Balqā*', 201–3.

68. See, e.g., Parsons, "Rebels without Borders"; and Provence, *The Great Syrian Revolt*, 115, 153. Charles Anderson's scholarship on rural Palestinian rebels' state formation projects is another example of the state-building aspirations of these regional movements. See Anderson, "State Formation from Below."

69. On the complex effects of these regional affiliations that became "transnational" in the interwar period on processes of state and nation-building under the Mandates, see Falb Kalisman, *Teachers as State-Builders*.

70. 'Assāf, *Thawrat al-Balqā*', 120–22; Provence, *The Great Syrian Revolt*, 53.

71. Massad, *Colonial Effects, 52*; Thomas, "Bedouin Tribes"; Neep, *Occupying Syria*.

72. The texts of the Tribal Courts Law and the Bedouin Control Laws and their amendments can be found in Arabic in Abū Ḥassān, *Turāth al-Badū al-Qaḍā'ī*, 599–619.

73. Fletcher, *British Imperialism*, chap. 2.

74. Thomas, "Bedouin Tribes," 561.

75. Khoury, "The Tribal Shaykh."

76. Provence, *The Great Syrian Revolt*, 27–29.

77. Fletcher, *British Imperialism*, 127.

78. Fletcher, 127; see also Khoury, "The Tribal Shaykh"; Massad, *Colonial Effects*, 58.

79. Alon, *The Shaykh of Shaykhs*, 18; ʿAssāf, *Thawrat al-Balqāʾ*, 80.

80. Fletcher, *British Imperialism*, 115–16.

81. Schayegh, *The Middle East*. Tariq Tell has also emphasized the importance of rural, nonelite political actors to the dynamics of this period; see Tell, "Guns, Gold and Grain."

82. Related is the proposal of a regional, rather than imperial, framework for understanding historical change that potentially reifies the bifurcation between the coastal and interior landscapes. See Emrence, *Remapping the Ottoman Middle East*.

83. Hilary Falb Kalisman insists on the importance of a transnational framework that takes mobility into account for the study of what nationalism meant to actors in the interwar mandates. See Falb Kalisman, *Teachers as State-Builders*, 14–15.

84. The Tribal Courts Law gave a new layer of institutional specificity to the "tribe," defining its human boundaries by linking collective monetary responsibility for crimes to relatives "of the fifth degree." Abū Ḥassān, *Turāth al-badw al-qaḍāʾī*, 600.

85. See Zakarīyā, *ʿAshāʾir al-Shām*; Peake, *Tārīkh Sharqī al-Urdun*; ʿAzzāwī, *ʿAshāʾir al-ʿIrāq*; Barakat, "Making 'Tribes,'" 487.

86. See, e.g., ʿAbbādī, *Muqaddimah li-Dirāsat al-ʿAshāʾir al-Urdunīyah*.

87. Zakarīyā, *ʿAshāʾir al-Shām*, 6. See also Assi, *History and Politics*, chap. 4.

88. ʿAwad, "Settlement of Nomadic and Semi-nomadic Tribal Groups"; Bocco, "Settlement of Pastoral Nomads."

89. Fischbach, *State, Society and Land*; Al Naber and Molle, "Politics of Accessing Desert Land," 493; Ababsa, "Fifty Years," 38–39.

90. Kedar, Yiftchatel, and Amara, *Emptied Lands*, 13.

91. Kedar, Yiftchatel, and Amara, chap. 9; Nasasra, *Naqab Bedouins*, 231–32.

92. Al Naber and Molle, "Politics of Accessing Desert Land," 501–2.

BIBLIOGRAPHY

ARCHIVES

Jordan

Center for Documents and Manuscripts, University of Jordan
    Amman Sharia Court Records
    Salt Sharia Court Records
Department of Lands and Surveys
    Salt Property Registers
    Salt Tax Registers
National Library
    Mirza Wasfi Collection
    Private Papers Collection

Turkey

Center for Islamic Studies (İSAM)
    Awamir Sultaniyya
    Homs Court of First Instance Records
    Salname-i Vilayet-i Suriye
National Library (Milli Kütüphanesi)
    Suriye Gazetesi
Presidential Ottoman Archives (BOA)

United Kingdom

The National Archives, Kew
    Foreign Office Records

PUBLISHED SOURCES

Aaronsohn, Ran. *Rothschild and Early Jewish Colonization in Palestine*. Lanham, MD: Rowman and Littlefield, 2000.

Ababsa, Myriam. "Fifty Years of State Land Distribution in the Syrian Jazira: Agrarian Reform, Agrarian Counter-Reform, and the Arab Belt Policy (1958–2008)." In *Agrarian Transformation in the Arab World: Persistent and Emerging Challenges*, edited by Habib Ayeb and Reem Saad, 33–63. Cairo: American University in Cairo Press, 2013.

ʿAbbādī, Aḥmad ʿUwaydī. *Muqaddimah li-Dirāsāt al-ʿAshāʾir al-Urdunīyah*. ʿAmmān: al-Dār al-ʿArabīyah, 1985.

ʿAbd al-Muʿṭī, Ḥusām. *Al-ʿAlāqāt al-Miṣrīyah al-Ḥijāzīyah fī al-Qarn al-Thāmin ʿAshar*. Cairo: Al-Hayʾah al-Miṣrīyah al-ʿĀmmah lil-Kitāb, 2008.

Abdelhamid, Tarek Galal, and Heba El-Toudy, eds. *Selections from "Subh al-Aʿsha" by al-Qalqashandi, Clerk of the Mamluk Court*. London: Routledge, 2017.

Ablavsky, Gregory. *Federal Ground: Governing Property and Violence in the First U.S. Territories*. Oxford: Oxford University Press, 2021.

Abubakr, Amin. "Properties of Aal Abdul-Hadi in Palestine, 1804–1967." *Majallat Jāmiʿat al-Najāḥ lil-Abḥāth* 20, no. 2 (2006): 451–94.

Abū Ḥassān, Muḥammad. *Turāth al-Badw al-Qaḍāʾī: Naẓarīyan wa-ʿAmalīyan*. ʿAmmān: Dāʾirat al-Thaqāfah wa al-Funūn, 1987.

Abu-Husayn, Abdul-Rahim. *Provincial Leaderships in Syria, 1575–1650*. Beirut: American University of Beirut, 1985.

Abujaber, Raouf Saʿd. *Pioneers over Jordan: The Frontiers of Settlement in Transjordan, 1850–1914*. London: I.B. Tauris, 1993.

Abu-Lughod, Lila. *Veiled Sentiments: Honor and Poetry in a Bedouin Society*. Berkeley: University of California Press, 1986.

———. "Zones of Theory in the Anthropology of the Arab World." *Annual Review of Anthropology* 18 (1989): 267–306.

Abū Ṣīnī, ʿAbd al-Ḥamīd Muḥammad Aḥmad. "Muḥammad ʿAlī Bāshā wa al-Qabāʾil al-Badūwīyah fī Junūb Bilād al-Shām." *Al-Majallah al-Urdunīyah lil-Tārīkh wa-al-Athār* 12, no. 1 (2018): 67–90.

Adamiak, Patrick. "To the Edge of the Desert: Caucasian Refugees, Civilization, and Settlement on the Ottoman Frontier, 1866–1918. PhD diss., University of California, San Diego, 2018.

Agmon, Iris. *Family and Court: Legal Culture and Modernity in Late Ottoman Palestine*. Syracuse, NY: Syracuse University Press, 2006.

Ahmad, Feroz. "The Agrarian Policy of the Young Turks, 1908–1918." In *Économie et sociétés dans l'Empire ottoman*, edited by Irène Mélikoff and Robert Mantran, 275–88. Paris: Centre national de la recherche scientifique, 1983.

Akgündüz, Ahmed. *Osmanlı Kanunnameleri ve Hukuki Tahlilleri*. Vol. 4. Istanbul: Osmanlı Araştırmaları Vakfı, 1992.

Akiba, Jun. "The Local Councils as the Origin of Parliamentary Government in the Ottoman Empire." In *Development of Parliamentarism in the Modern Islamic World*, edited by Tsugitaka Sato, 176–204. Tokyo: Toyo Bunko, 2009.

Akın, Yiğit. *When the War Came Home: The Ottomans' Great War and the Devastation of an Empire*. Stanford, CA: Stanford University Press, 2018.

Al-ʿAssāf, ʿAbd Allāh Muṭlaq. *Thawrat al-Balqāʾ wa Mashrūʿ al-Dawlah al-Mājidīyah, Muḥarram 1342 H/Aylūl 1923 M*. Amman: n.p., 2015.

Al-Fawwāz, Klayb Sāʿud. *ʿUmarāʾ Ḥawrān: Āl al-Fawwāz Mashayikh al-Sardiyyah*. Beirut: Al-Muʾassasah al-ʿArabīyyah li-l-Dirāsāt wa al-Nashr, 2017.

Al-Fayiz, Mifliḥal-Nimr. *ʿAshāʾir Bani Ṣakhr: Tārīkh wa Mawāqif hata Sanat 1950*. ʾAmmān: Maṭābiʿ al-Qūwwāt al-Muṣallaḥah, 1995.

Alff, Kristen. "Landed Property, Capital Accumulation, and Polymorphous Capitalism." In *A Critical Political Economy of the Middle East and North Africa*, edited by Joel Beinin, Bassam Haddad, and Sherene Seikaly, 25–45. Stanford, CA: Stanford University Press, 2021.

———. "Levantine Joint-Stock Companies, Trans-Mediterranean Partnerships, and Nineteenth-Century Capitalist Development." *Comparative Studies in Society and History* 60, no. 1 (2018): 150–77.

Al-Juhany, Uwidah Metaireek. *Najd before the Salafi Reform Movement*. Reading, UK: Ithaca Press, 2002.

Al Naber, Majd, and Francois Molle. "The Politics of Accessing Desert Land in Jordan." *Land Use Policy* 59 (2016): 492–503.

Alnajada, Heba. "'This Camp Is Full of Hujjaj!': Claims to Land and the Built Environment in a Contested Palestinian Refugee Camp in Amman." *Comparative Studies of South Asia, Africa and the Middle East*, forthcoming.

Alon, Yoav. "The Balqāʾ Revolt: Tribes and Early State-Building in Transjordan." *Die Welt des Islams* 46, no. 1 (2006): 7–42.

———. *The Making of Jordan: Tribes, Colonialism and the Modern State*. London: I.B. Tauris, 2009.

———. *The Shaykh of Shaykhs: Mithqal al-Fayiz and Tribal Leadership in Modern Jordan*. Stanford, CA: Stanford University Press, 2016.

Al-Qalqashandī, Aḥmad ibn ʿAlī. *Qalāʾid al-Jumān fī Taʿrīf bi-Qabāʾil al-Zamān*. Cairo: Dār al-Kutub al-Ḥadīthah, 1963.

Al-ʿUzayzī, Rūkus ibn Zāʾid. *Nimr Al-ʿAdwān: Shāʿir al-Ḥubb wa-al-Wafāʾ*. Kuwait: Sharikat al-Rabīʿān lil-Nashr wa-al-Tawzīʿ, 1997.

Amara, Ahmad. "Civilizational Exceptions: Ottoman Law and Governance in Late Ottoman Palestine." *Law and History Review* 36, no. 4 (2018): 915–41.

Anderson, Charles W. "State Formation from Below and the Great Revolt in Palestine." *Journal of Palestine Studies* 47, no. 1 (2017): 39–55.

Antaramian, Richard E. *Brokers of Faith, Brokers of Empire: Armenians and the*

Politics of Reform in the Ottoman Empire. Stanford, CA: Stanford University Press, 2020.

Arrighi, Giovanni. *The Long Twentieth Century: Money, Power, and the Origins of Our Times*. London: Verso, 2010.

Asad, Talal. "The Beduin as a Military Force: Notes on Some Aspects of Power Relations between Nomads and Sedentaries in Historical Perspective." In *The Desert and the Sown: Nomads in the Wider Society*, edited by Cynthia Owen, 61–74. Berkeley: University of California Press, 1973.

———. "Equality in Nomadic Social Systems? Notes towards the Dissolution of an Anthropological Category." *Critique of Anthropology* 3, no. 11 (1978): 57–65.

Assi, Seraj. *The History and Politics of the Bedouin: Reimagining Nomadism in Modern Palestine*. London: Routledge, 2018.

Astourian, Stephan. "The Silence of the Land: Agrarian Relations, Ethnicity and Power." In *A Question of Genocide: Armenians and Turks at the End of the Ottoman Empire*, edited by Ronald Grigor Suny, Fatma Müge Göçek, and Norman N. Naimark, 55–81. Oxford: Oxford University Press, 2011.

Avcı, Yasemin. "Tanzimat in the Desert: The Bedouins and the Creation of a New Town in Southern Palestine (1860–1914)." *Middle Eastern Studies* 45, no. 6 (2009): 969–83.

ʿAwad, Mohamed. "Settlement of Nomadic and Semi-nomadic Tribal Groups in the Middle East." *International Labor Review* 25 (1959): 25–56.

ʿAwrah, Ibrāhīm bin Ḥannā. *Tārīkh Wilayat Sulaymān Bāshā al-ʿĀdil, 1804–1819*. Bayrūt: Dār Laḥd Khāṭir, 1989.

Aytekin, E. Attila. "Tax Revolts during the Tanzimat Period (1839–1876) and before the Young Turk Revolution (1904–1908): Popular Protest and State Formation in the Late Ottoman Empire." *Journal of Policy History* 25, no. 3 (2013): 308–33.

ʿAzzāwī, ʿAbbās. *Ashāʾir al-ʿIrāq*. Baghdād: Maṭbaʿat Baghdād, 1937.

Bakhīt, Muḥammad ʿAdnān. "Al-Usrah al-Ḥārithīyyah fī Marj Banī ʿAmr." *Al-Abhath: Journal of the Faculty of Arts and Sciences of the American University of Beirut* 27 (1980): 55–78.

———. *The Ottoman Province of Damascus in the Sixteenth Century*. Beirut: Librairie du Liban, 1982.

Bakhīt, Muḥammad ʿAdnān, and Nūfān Rajā Ḥamūd, eds. *Daftar mufaṣṣal nāḥiyat Marj Banī ʿĀmr wa Tawābiʿihā wa Lawāḥiqihā allatī Kānat fī Taṣarruf al-Amīr Ṭarah Bāy Sanat 945 H/1538 M = Defter-i mufassal-ı nahiye-ye Merc Bu Amir*. ʿAmmān: University of Jordan, 1989.

———. *Defter-ı Mufassal Liva ʿAjlun = Kanûn Nâme Liva ʿAjlun:Tapū Defteri Rakam-i 970*. ʿAmmān: University of Jordan, 1989.

Banaji, Jairus. *A Brief History of Commercial Capitalism*. Chicago: Haymarket, 2020.

Banner, Stuart. *How the Indians Lost Their Land: Law and Power on the Frontier.* Cambridge, MA: Harvard University Press, 2009.

Barakat, Nora. "Marginal Actors? The Role of Bedouin in the Ottoman Administration of Animals as Property in the District of Salt, 1870–1912." *Journal of the Economic and Social History of the Orient* 58, no. 1/2 (2015): 105–34.

———. "Regulating Land Rights in Late Nineteenth-Century Salt: The Limits of Legal Pluralism in Ottoman Property Law." *Journal of the Ottoman and Turkish Studies Association* 2, no. 1 (2015): 101.

———. "Underwriting the Empire: Nizamiye Courts, Tax Farming and the Public Debt Administration in Late Ottoman Syria." *Islamic Law and Society* 26 (2019): 374–404.

Barakat, Nora Elizabeth. "Making 'Tribes' in the Late Ottoman Empire." *International Journal of Middle East Studies* 53, no. 3 (2021): 482–87.

Barbir, Karl. *Ottoman Rule in Damascus, 1708–1758.* Princeton, NJ: Princeton University Press, 1980.

Barkey, Karen. *Bandits and Bureaucrats: The Ottoman Route to State Centralization.* Ithaca, NY: Cornell University Press, 1996.

Batatu, Hanna. *The Old Social Classes & the Revolutionary Movement in Iraq.* London: Saqi Books, 2004.

Belich, James. *Replenishing the Earth: The Settler Revolution and the Rise of the Anglo-World, 1783–1939.* Oxford: Oxford University Press, 2009.

Ben-Bassat, Yuval. "Bedouin Petitions from Late Ottoman Palestine: Evaluating the Effects of Sedentarization." *Journal of the Economic and Social History of the Orient* 58 (2015): 135–62.

Bensel, Richard Franklin. *The Political Economy of American Industrialization, 1877–1900.* Cambridge: Cambridge University Press, 2000.

Benton, Lauren A. "Colonial Law and Colonial Difference: Jurisdictional Politics and the Formation of the Colonial State." *Comparative Studies in Society and History* 41, no. 3 (1999): 563–88.

———. "Empires of Exception: History, Law, and the Problem of Imperial Sovereignty." *Quaderni di Relazioni Internazionali* 6 (2007): 54–67.

———. *A Search for Sovereignty: Law and Geography in European Empires, 1400–1900.* Cambridge: Cambridge University Press, 2010.

Bhandar, Brenna. *Colonial Lives of Property: Law, Land, and Racial Regimes of Ownership.* Durham, NC: Duke University Press, 2018.

Bhattacharya, Neeladri. *The Great Agrarian Conquest: The Colonial Reshaping of a Rural World.* Albany: State University of New York Press, 2018.

Biolsi, Thomas. *Organizing the Lakota: The Political Economy of the New Deal on the Pine Ridge and Rosebud Reservations.* Tucson: University of Arizona Press, 1992.

Birdal, Murat. *The Political Economy of Ottoman Public Debt: Insolvency and Eu-*

ropean Financial Control in the Late Nineteenth Century. London: I.B. Tauris, 2010.

Bishara, Fahad Ahmad. *A Sea of Debt: Law and Economic Life in the Western Indian Ocean, 1780–1950.* Cambridge: Cambridge University Press, 2017.

Bloxham, Donald. *The Great Game of Genocide: Imperialism, Nationalism, and the Destruction of the Ottoman Armenians.* Oxford: Oxford University Press, 2005.

Blumi, Isa. "Contesting the Edges of the Ottoman Empire: Rethinking Ethnic and Sectarian Boundaries in the Malesöre, 1878–1912. *International Journal of Middle East Studies* 35, no. 2 (2003): 237–56.

———. *Ottoman Refugees, 1878–1939: Migration in a Post-Imperial World.* London: Bloomsbury, 2013.

Bocco, Ricardo. "The Settlement of Pastoral Nomads in the Arab Middle East: International Organizations and Trends in Development Policies, 1950–1990s." In *Nomadic Societies in the Middle East and North Africa: Entering the 21st Century,* edited by Dawn Chatty, 302–32. Leiden: Brill, 2006.

Bourdieu, Pierre. *Outline of a Theory of Practice.* Translated by Richard Nice. Cambridge: Cambridge University Press, 1977.

Brenner, Neil, Bob Jessop, Martin Jones, and Gordon Macleod, eds. *State/ Space: A Reader.* Malden, MA: Blackwell, 2003.

Bsheer, Rosie. *Archive Wars: The Politics of History in Saudi Arabia.* Stanford, CA: Stanford University Press, 2020.

Buckingham, James Silk. *Travels among the Arab Tribes Inhabiting the Countries East of Syria and Palestine.* London: Longman, 1825.

Bunton, Martin P. *Colonial Land Policies in Palestine, 1917–1936.* Oxford: Oxford University Press, 2007.

Burbank, Jane, and Frederick Cooper. *Empires in World History: Power and the Politics of Difference.* Princeton, NJ: Princeton University Press, 2011.

Burckhardt, John Lewis. *Notes on the Bedouins and Wahabys, Collected during His Travels in the East.* Vols. 1 and 2. London: H. Colburn and R. Bentley, 1831.

———. *Travels in Syria and the Holy Land.* London: John Murray, 1822.

Büssow, Johann. *Hamidian Palestine: Politics and Society in the District of Jerusalem, 1872–1908.* Leiden: Brill, 2011.

Butler, Judith. "Performative Acts and Gender Constitution: An Essay in Phenomenology and Feminist Theory." *Theatre Journal* 40, no. 4 (1988): 519–31.

Çadırcı, Musa. *Tanzimat Döneminde Anadolu Kentleri'nin Sosyal ve Ekonomik Yapıları.* Ankara: Türk Tarih Kurumu Basımevi, 1991.

———. "Türkiye'de Muhtarlık Teşkilatının Kurulması Üzerine Bir İnceleme." *Belleten* 34, no. 135 (1970): 409–20.

Campbell, Ian W. *Knowledge and the Ends of Empire: Kazak Intermediaries and*

Russian Rule on the Steppe, 1731–1917. Ithaca, NY: Cornell University Press, 2017.

Campos, Michelle U. *Ottoman Brothers: Muslims, Christians, and Jews in Early Twentieth-Century Palestine*. Stanford, CA: Stanford University Press, 2011.

Can, Lâle. *Spiritual Subjects: Central Asian Pilgrims and the Ottoman Hajj at the End of Empire*. Stanford, CA: Stanford University Press, 2020.

Can, Lâle, and Michael Christopher Low. "The 'Subjects' of Ottoman International Law." *Journal of the Ottoman and Turkish Studies Association* 3, no. 2 (2016): 223–34.

Caton, Stephen. "Anthropological Theories of Tribe and State Formation in the Middle East: Ideology and the Semiotics of Power." In *Tribes and State Formation in the Middle East*, edited by Philip Khoury and Joseph Kostiner, 74–108. Berkeley: University of California Press, 1990.

Çetinkaya, Y. Doğan. *The Young Turks and the Boycott Movement: Nationalism, Protest, and the Working Classes in the Formation of Modern Turkey*. Cambridge: Cambridge University Press, 2016.

Çetinsaya, Gökhan. "The Politics of Reform in Iraq under Abdülhamid II, 1878–1908." *Turkish Journal of Islamic Studies* 3 (1999): 41–72.

Ceylan, Ebubekir. *The Ottoman Origins of Modern Iraq: Political Reform, Modernization and Development in the Nineteenth Century Middle East*. London: I.B. Tauris, 2011.

Chatty, Dawn. *Displacement and Dispossession in the Modern Middle East*. New York: Cambridge University Press, 2010.

Chokobaeva, Aminat, Chloé Drieu, and Alexander Morrison. "Editors' Introduction." In *The Central Asian Revolt of 1916: A Collapsing Empire in the Age of War and Revolution*, edited by Aminat Chokobaeva, Chloé Drieu, and Alexander Morrison, 1–26. Manchester: Manchester University Press, 2019.

Çiçek, M. Talha. *Negotiating Empire in the Middle East: Ottomans and Arab Nomads in the Modern Era, 1840–1914*. Cambridge: Cambridge University Press, 2021.

Cin, Halil. *Osmanlı Toprak Düzeni ve Bu Düzenin Bozulması*. 5th ed. Ankara: Berikan Yayınevi, 2019.

Clark, Christopher. "The Agrarian Context of American Capitalist Development." In *Capitalism Takes Command: The Social Transformation of Nineteenth-Century America*, edited by Michael Zakim and Gary J. Kornblith, 13–38. Chicago: University of Chicago Press, 2012.

Clements, Henry. "Documenting Community in the Late Ottoman Empire." *International Journal of Middle East Studies* 51, no. 3 (2019): 423–43.

Cohen, Amnon. *Palestine in the 18th Century: Patterns of Government and Administration*. Jerusalem: Hebrew University Press, 1973.

Cohen, Julia Philips. *Becoming Ottomans: Sephardi Jews and Imperial Citizenship.* Oxford: Oxford University Press, 2014.

Cole, Camille Lyans. "Empire on Edge: Land, Law and Capital in Gilded Age Basra." PhD diss., Yale University, 2020.

Conder, C. R. *The Survey of Eastern Palestine: Memoirs of the Topography, Orography, Hydrography, Archaeology, Etc. v.1—The 'Adwân Country.* London: Committee of the Palestine Exploration Fund, 1889.

Conermann, Stephen, and Gül Şen, eds. *The Mamluk-Ottoman Transition: Continuity and Change in Egypt and Bilad al-Sham in the Sixteenth Century.* Göttingen: Bonn University Press, 2017.

Cronon, William. *Nature's Metropolis: Chicago and the Great West.* New York: Norton, 1992.

Crosby, Alfred. *Ecological Imperialism: The Biological Expansion of Europe, 900–1900.* Cambridge: Cambridge University Press, 1986.

Cuno, Kenneth M. *The Pasha's Peasants: Land, Society, and Economy in Lower Egypt, 1740–1858.* Cambridge: Cambridge University Press, 1992.

———. "Was the Land of Ottoman Syria *Miri* or *Milk*? An Examination of Juridical Differences within the Hanafi School." *Studia Islamica,* no. 81 (1995): 121–52.

Dankoff, Robert, Seyit 'Ali Kahraman, and Yücel Dağlı, trans. *Evliya Çelebi Seyahatnamesi.* Vol. 9. Istanbul: Yapı Kredi Yayınları, 1996.

Darling, Linda. *Revenue-Raising and Legitimacy: Tax Collection and Finance Administration in the Ottoman Empire, 1560–1660.* Leiden: Brill, 1996.

Das, Veena. "The Signature of the State: The Paradox of Illegibility." In *Anthropology in the Margins of the State,* edited by Veena Das and Deborah Poole, 225–52. Oxford: James Currey, 2004.

Das, Veena, and Deborah Poole. "State and Its Margins: Comparative Ethnographies." In *Anthropology in the Margins of the State,* edited by Veena Das and Deborah Poole, 3–33. Oxford: James Currey, 2004.

Davis, Diana K. *Resurrecting the Granary of Rome: Environmental History and French Colonial Expansion in North Africa.* Athens: Ohio University Press, 2007.

Davison, Roderic. *Reform in the Ottoman Empire, 1856–1876.* Princeton, NJ: Princeton University Press, 2015.

Dāwūd, Jūrj Farīd Ṭarīf. *Al-Salṭ wa Jiwāruhā.* Amman: Jordan Press, 1994.

Deringil, Selim. "'They Live in a State of Nomadism and Savagery': The Late Ottoman Empire and the Postcolonial Debate." *Comparative Studies in Society and History* 45 (2003): 311–42.

Derri, Aviv. "Bonds of Obligation, Precarious Fortunes: Empire, Non-Muslim Bankers, and Peasants in Late Ottoman Damascus, 1820s-1890s." PhD diss., New York University, 2021.

———. "Imperial Creditors, 'Doubtful' Nationalities and Financial Obligations in Late Ottoman Syria: Rethinking Ottoman Subjecthood and Consular Protection." *International History Review* 43, no. 5 (2020): 1–20.

Dodge, Toby. *Inventing Iraq: The Failure of Nation Building and a History Denied.* New York: Columbia University Press, 2003.

Doğan, Faruk. "18 ve 19 Yüzyıllarda Şam-Medine Hac Yolu ve Güvenliği: Cerde Başbuğluğu." *Tarih Okulu Dergisi* 6, no. 15 (2013): 127–57.

Dolbee, Samuel. "The Desert at the End of Empire: An Environmental History of the Armenian Genocide." *Past and Present* 247, no. 1 (2020): 197–233.

———. "The Locust and the Starling: People, Insects and Disease in the Ottoman Jazira and After, 1860–1940." PhD diss., New York University, 2017.

———. *Locusts of Power: Borders, Empire, and Environment in the Modern Middle East, 1858–1939.* Cambridge: Cambridge University Press, forthcoming.

Doumani, Beshara. *Family Life in the Ottoman Mediterranean: A Social History.* Cambridge: Cambridge University Press, 2017.

———. *Rediscovering Palestine: Merchants and Peasants in Jabal Nablus, 1700–1900.* Berkeley: University of California Press, 1995.

Duffy, Andrea. *Nomad's Land: Pastoralism and French Environmental Policy in the Nineteenth-Century Eastern Mediterranean World.* Lincoln: University of Nebraska Press, 2019.

Dupeyron, De Ségur. "La Syrie et les Bédouins sous l'administration Turque." *Revue des deux mondes* 10 (1855): 339–59.

Düstur: I. Tertib. Vol. 1. Istanbul: Matbaa-yi Amire, 1289.

Düstur: I. Tertib. Vol. 2. Istanbul: Matbaa-yi Amire, 1289.

Düstur: I. Tertib. Vol. 3. İstanbul: Matbaa-yi Amire, 1289.

Düstur: I. Tertib. Vol. 4. Istanbul: Mahmud Bey'in Matbaası, 1299.

Düstur: I. Tertib. Vol. 7. Ankara: Devlet Matbaası, 1939.

Düstur: I. Tertib. Vol. 8. Ankara: Devlet Matbaası, 1943.

Düstur: Ikinci Tertip. Vol. 1. Istanbul: Matbaa-yi Osmaniye, 1329.

Elden, Stuart. *The Birth of Territory.* Chicago: University of Chicago Press, 2013.

———. "Land, Terrain, Territory." *Progress in Human Geography* 34, no. 6 (2010): 799–817.

Emmons, Terence, and Wayne S. Vucinich, eds. *The Zemstvo in Russia: An Experiment in Local Self-Government.* Cambridge: Cambridge University Press, 1982.

Emrence, Cem. "Imperial Paths, Big Comparisons: The Late Ottoman Empire." *Journal of Global History* 3, no. 3 (Nov. 2008): 289–311.

———. *Remapping the Ottoman Middle East: Modernity, Imperial Bureaucracy, and the Islamic State.* London: I.B. Tauris, 2011.

Establet, Colette, and Jean-Paul Pascual. "Damascene Probate Inventories of the 17th and 18th Centuries: Some Preliminary Approaches and Results."

International Journal of Middle East Studies 24, no. 3 (1992): 373–93.

Fahmy, Khaled. *All the Pasha's Men: Mehmed 'Ali, His Army and the Making of Modern Egypt*. Cambridge: Cambridge University Press, 1997.

——. "The Anatomy of Justice: Forensic Medicine and Criminal Law in Nineteenth-Century Egypt." *Islamic Law and Society* 6, no. 2 (1999): 224–71.

——. *In Quest of Justice: Law and Forensic Medicine in Modern Egypt*. Berkeley: University of California Press, 2018.

Falb Kalisman, Hilary. *Teachers as State-Builders: Education and the Making of the Modern Middle East*. Princeton, NJ: Princeton University Press, 2022.

Faroqhi, Suraiya. "Crisis and Change, 1590–1699." In *An Economic and Social History of the Ottoman Empire*, edited by Suraiya Faroqhi, Bruce McGowan, Donald Quataert, and Şevket Pamuk, 2:411–623. Cambridge: Cambridge University Press, 1994.

——. *Pilgrims and Sultans: The Hajj under the Ottomans, 1517–1683*. London: I.B. Tauris, 1994.

Fattah, Hala. *The Politics of Regional Trade in Iraq, Arabia, and the Gulf, 1745–1900*. Albany, NY: State University of New York Press, 1997.

Felten, Sebastian, and Christine von Oertzen. "Bureaucracy as Knowledge." *Journal for the History of Knowledge* 1, no. 1 (2020): 1–16.

Ferguson, Heather. *The Proper Order of Things: Language, Power, and Law in Ottoman Administrative Discourses*. Stanford, CA: Stanford University Press, 2018.

Fields, Gary. *Enclosure: Palestinian Landscapes in a Historical Mirror*. Berkeley: University of California Press, 2017.

Findlay, Ronald, and Kevin H. O'Rourke. *Power and Plenty: Trade, War, and the World Economy in the Second Millennium*. Princeton, NJ: Princeton University Press, 2009.

Findley, Carter V. *Bureaucratic Reform in the Ottoman Empire: The Sublime Porte, 1789–1922*. Princeton, NJ: Princeton University Press, 1980.

Finn, James. *Byeways in Palestine*. London: James Nisbet, 1877.

Finn, James, and Elizabeth Anne McCaul Finn. *Stirring Times: Or, Records from Jerusalem Consular Chronicles of 1853 to 1856*. London: C. K. Paul, 1878.

Fischbach, Michael. *State, Society and Land in Jordan*. London: Brill, 2000.

Fisher, Glenn. *The Worst Tax? A History of the Property Tax in America*. Lawrence: University Press of Kansas, 1996.

Fishman, Louis A. *Jews and Palestinians in the Late Ottoman Era, 1908–1914: Claiming the Homeland*. Edinburgh: Edinburgh University Press, 2020.

Fitzmaurice, Andrew. *Sovereignty, Property and Empire, 1500–2000*. Cambridge: Cambridge University Press, 2014.

Fleischer, Cornell. "Royal Authority, Dynastic Cyclism, and 'Ibn Khaldûnism' in Sixteenth-Century Ottoman Letters." *Journal of Asian and African Studies*

18, no. 3–4 (1983): 198–220.

Fletcher, Robert. *British Imperialism and the "Tribal Question": Desert Administration and Nomadic Societies in the Middle East, 1919–1936.* Oxford: Oxford University Press, 2015.

Foner, Eric. *Free Soil, Free Labor, Free Men: The Ideology of the Republican Party before the Civil War.* Oxford: Oxford University Press, 1970.

Fratantuono, Ella. "Producing Ottomans: Internal Colonization and Social Engineering in Ottoman Immigrant Settlement." *Journal of Genocide Research* 21, no. 1 (2019): 1–24.

Gates, Paul W. *History of Public Land Law Development.* Washington, DC: Public Land Law Review Commission, 1968.

Gedikli, Fethi. "Midhat Paşa'nın Suriye Layihası." *Divan*, no. 2 (1999): 169–89.

Gelvin, James L. *Divided Loyalties: Nationalism and Mass Politics in Syria at the Close of Empire.* Berkeley: University of California Press, 1999.

Genetin-Pilawa, Joseph. *Crooked Paths to Allotment: The Fight over Federal Indian Policy after the Civil War.* Chapel Hill: University of North Carolina Press, 2012.

Gerber, Haim. *Ottoman Rule in Jerusalem, 1890–1914.* Berlin: Klaus Schwarz, 1985.

Gibb, H. A. R. *Islamic Society and the West; a Study of the Impact of Western Civilization on Moslem Culture in the Near East.* London: Oxford University Press, 1960.

Goodwin, Barry, and Thomas J. Grennes. "Tsarist Russia and the World Wheat Market." *Explorations in Economic History* 35 (1998): 405–30.

Goswami, Manu. *Producing India: From Colonial Economy to National Space.* Chicago: University of Chicago Press, 2004.

Grant, Jonathan. "The Sword of the Sultan: Ottoman Arms Imports, 1854–1914." *Journal of Military History* 66, no. 1 (Jan. 2002): 9–36.

Gratien, Chris. "The Ottoman Quagmire: Malaria, Swamps, and Settlement in the Late Ottoman Mediterranean." *International Journal of Middle East Studies* 49, no. 4 (Nov. 2017): 583–604.

———. *The Unsettled Plain: An Environmental History of the Ottoman Frontier.* Stanford, CA: Stanford University Press, 2022.

Grehan, James. *Everyday Life and Consumer Culture in 18th-Century Damascus.* Seattle: University of Washington Press, 2016.

Gross, Max. "Ottoman Rule in the Province of Damascus, 1860–1909." PhD diss., Georgetown University, 1979.

Guéno, Vanessa. "La bureaucratie ottomane locale et ses usagers: Exemples de conflits ruraux dans le qaḍā' Homs en Syrie Moyenne à la fin du XIXe siècle." In *Lire et écrire l'histoire ottomane*, edited by Vanessa Guéno and

Stefan Knost, 147–72. Beirut: Orient-Institut Beirut, 2015.

Güneş, Mehmet. *Osmanlı Döneminde Muhtarlık ve Ihtiyar Meclisi.* İstanbul: Kitabevi, 2012.

Gupta, Akhil. *Red Tape: Bureaucracy, Structural Violence, and Poverty in India.* Durham, NC: Duke University Press, 2012.

Hafez, Melis. *Inventing Laziness: The Culture of Productivity in Late Ottoman Society.* Cambridge: Cambridge University Press, 2021.

Haghandoqa, Mohammad Khayr. *The Circassians: Origin, History, Customs, Traditions, Immigration to Jordan.* Amman: Rafidi Press, 1985.

Hahn, Steven. *A Nation without Borders: The United States and Its World in an Age of Civil Wars, 1830–1910.* New York: Penguin, 2016.

———. "Slave Emancipation, Indian Peoples, and the Projects of a New American Nation-State." *Journal of the Civil War Era* 3, no. 3 (2013): 307–30.

Haj, Samira. "The Problems of Tribalism: The Case of Nineteenth-Century Iraqi History." *Social History* 16, no. 1 (Jan. 1, 1991): 45–58.

Halaçoğlu, Yusuf. *18. Yüzyılda Osmanlı İmparatorluğu'nun İskan Siyaseti ve Aşiretlerin Yerleştirilmesi.* Ankara: Türk Tarih Kurumu Basımevi, 1991.

Hallaq, Wael B. *Sharī'a: Theory, Practice, Transformations.* Cambridge,: Cambridge University Press, 2009.

Hämäläinen, Pekka. *The Comanche Empire.* New Haven, CT: Yale University Press, 2008.

———. *Lakota America: A New History of Indigenous Power.* New Haven, CT: Yale University Press, 2019.

———. "What's in a Concept? The Kinetic Empire of the Comanches." *History and Theory* 52 (2013): 81–90.

Hamarneh, Mustafa B. "Amman in British Travel Accounts of the 19th Century." In *Amman: Ville et société,* edited by Jean Hannoyer and Seteney Shami, 57–85. Beirut: Cermoc, 1996.

Hamed-Troyansky, Vladimir. "Circassian Refugees and the Making of Amman, 1878–1914." *International Journal of Middle East Studies* 49, no. 4 (Nov. 2017): 605–23.

———. "Imperial Refuge: Resettlement of Muslims from Russia in the Ottoman Empire, 1860–1914." PhD diss., Stanford University, 2018.

Hanley, Will. "What Ottoman Nationality Was and Was Not." *Journal of the Ottoman and Turkish Studies Association* 3, no. 2 (2016): 277–98.

Hannah, Matthew G. "Space and Social Control in the Administration of the Oglala Lakota ('Sioux'), 1871–1879." *Journal of Historical Geography* 19, no. 4 (1993): 412–32.

Hathaway, Jane. *The Arab Lands under Ottoman Rule, 1516–1800.* New York: Routledge, 2008.

———. *The Politics of Households in Ottoman Egypt: The Rise of the Qazdağlis*. Cambridge: Cambridge University Press, 1997.

Heyd, Uriel. *Ottoman Documents on Palestine, 1552–1615*. Oxford: Clarendon Press, 1960.

Hill, Peter. "How Global Was the Age of Revolutions? The Case of Mount Lebanon, 1821." *Journal of Global History* 16, no. 1 (June 2020): 65–84.

Hiyari, M. A. "The Origins and Development of the Amīrate of the Arabs during the Seventh/Thirteenth and Eighth/Fourteenth Centuries." *Bulletin of the School of Oriental and African Studies* 38, no. 3 (Oct. 1975): 509–24.

Ho, Engseng. "Afterword: Mobile Law and Thick Transregionalism." *Law and History Review* 32, no. 4 (2014): 883–89.

Hobsbawm, Eric. *The Age of Capital, 1848–1875*. New York: Vintage, 1996.

Holquist, Peter. "'In Accord with State Interests and the People's Wishes': The Technocratic Ideology of Imperial Russia's Resettlement Administration." *Slavic Review* 69, no. 1 (2010): 151–79.

Hopkins, Benjamin D. *Ruling the Savage Periphery: Frontier Governance and the Making of the Modern State*. Cambridge, MA: Harvard University Press, 2020.

Hull, Matthew. *Government of Paper: The Materiality of Bureaucracy in Urban Pakistan*. Berkeley: University of California Press, 2012.

Hütteroth, Wolf Dieter, and Kamal Abdulfattah. *Historical Geography of Palestine, Transjordan and Southern Syria in the Late 16th Century*. Erlangen: Fränkische Geographische Ges., 1977.

Ibn Sbayyil, ʿAbdallāh. *Arabian Romantic: Poems on Bedouin Life and Love*. Translated by Marcel Kurpershoek. New York: New York University Press, 2020.

Ilana Feldman. *Governing Gaza: Bureaucracy, Authority, and the Work of Rule, 1917–1967*. Durham, NC: Duke University Press, 2008.

Imber, Colin. *Ebu's-Suʿud: The Islamic Legal Tradition*. Stanford, CA: Stanford University Press, 2009.

İnalcık, Halil. "Centralization and Decentralization in Ottoman Administration." In *Studies in Eighteenth Century Islamic History*, edited by Thomas Naff and Roger Owen, 27–52. Carbondale: Southern Illinois University Press, 1977.

———. "Military and Fiscal Transformation in the Ottoman Empire." *Archivum Ottomanicum* 6 (1980): 283–337.

İnalcık, Halil, Suraiya Faroqhi, Bruce McGowan, Donald Quataert, and Şevket Pamuk, eds. *An Economic and Social History of the Ottoman Empire, 1300–1914*. Vol. 1. Cambridge: Cambridge University Press, 1995.

İnalcık, Halil, and Donald Quataert. *An Economic and Social History of the Ottoman Empire*. Vol. 2. Cambridge: Cambridge University Press, 1994.

İslamoğlu, Huri. "Politics of Administering Property: Law and Statistics in the Nineteenth-Century Ottoman Empire." In *Constituting Modernity: Private Property in the East and West,* edited by Huri İslamoğlu, 276–319. London: I.B. Tauris, 2004.

———. "Property as a Contested Domain: A Reevaluation of the Ottoman Land Code of 1858." In Owen, *New Perspectives on Property and Land,* 3–62.

———. "Towards a Political Economy of Legal and Administrative Constitutions of Individual Property." In *Constituting Modernity: Private Property in the East and West,* edited by Huri İslamoğlu, 3–34. London: I.B. Tauris, 2004.

İslamoğlu-İnan, Huri. *State and Peasant in the Ottoman Empire.* Leiden: Brill, 1994.

Issawi, Charles. *The Fertile Crescent, 1800–1914: A Documentary Economic History.* Oxford: Oxford University Press, 1988.

Jakes, Aaron, and Ahmad Shokr. "Capitalism in Egypt, Not Egyptian Capitalism." In *A Critical Political Economy of the Middle East and North Africa,* edited by Joel Beinin, Bassam Haddad, and Sherene Seikaly, 123–42. Stanford, CA: Stanford University Press, 2021.

Jarvis, C. S. *Arab Command: The Biography of Lieutenant-Colonel F. G. Peake Pasha.* London: Hutchinson, 1946.

Johansen, Baber. *The Islamic Law on Land Tax and Rent.* London: Croom Helm, 1988.

Kaḥḥāla, ʿUmar Riḍā. *Muʿjam Qabāʾil al-ʿArab al-Qadīmah wa al-Ḥadīthah.* 5 vols. Bayrūt: Muʾassasat al-Risāla, 1982.

Kale, Başak. "Transforming an Empire: The Ottoman Empire's Immigration and Settlement Policies in the Nineteenth and Early Twentieth Centuries." *Middle Eastern Studies* 50, no. 2 (2014): 252–71.

Kantrowitz, Stephen. "'Not Quite Constitutionalized': The Meanings of 'Civilization' and the Limits of North American Citizenship." In *The World the Civil War Made,* edited by Gregory P. Downs and Kate Masur, 75–105. Chapel Hill: University of North Carolina Press, 2015.

Kasaba, Reşat. *A Moveable Empire: Ottoman Nomads, Migrants, and Refugees.* Seattle: University of Washington Press, 2009.

Kaya, Alp Yücel, and Yücel Terzibaşoğlu. "Tahrir'den Kadastro'ya: 1874 İstanbul Emlak Tahriri ve Vergisi 'Kadastro Tabir Olunur Tahrir-i Emlak.'" *Tarih ve Toplum Yeni Yaklaşımlar* 9 (2009): 7–56.

Kedar, Alexandre, Oren Yiftchatel, and Ahmad Amara. *Emptied Lands: A Legal Geography of Bedouin Rights in the Negev.* Stanford, CA: Stanford University Press, 2018.

Khodarkovsky, Michael. *Russia's Steppe Frontier: The Making of a Colonial Empire, 1500–1800.* Bloomington: Indiana University Press, 2002.

Khoury, Dina. *State and Provincial Society in the Ottoman Empire: Mosul, 1540–1834*. Cambridge: Cambridge University Press, 1997.

Khoury, Dina Rizk, and Sergey Glebov. "Citizenship, Subjecthood, and Difference in the Late Ottoman and Russian Empires." *Ab Imperio*, no. 1 (2017): 45–58.

Khoury, Philip S. "The Tribal Shaykh, French Tribal Policy, and the Nationalist Movement in Syria between Two World Wars." *Middle Eastern Studies* 18, no. 2 (1982): 180–93.

Khoury, Philip S., and Joseph Kostiner, eds. *Tribes and State Formation in the Middle East*. Berkeley: University of California Press, 1990.

Khuraysāt, Muḥammad ʿAbd al-Qādir, and Jūrj Farīd Ṭarīf Dāwūd. *Sijill Maḥkamat al-Salṭ al-Sharʿiyah: 5 Dhī al-Qaʿdah 1302 H-Ghurrat Rabīʿ al-Thānī 1305 H, 1885–1888 M*. Amman: Ministry of Culture, 2007.

Kılınçoğlu, Deniz. *Economics and Capitalism in the Ottoman Empire*. New York: Routledge, 2015.

Kiyotaki, Keiko. *Ottoman Land Reform in the Province of Baghdad*. Leiden: Brill, 2019.

Klein, Janet. *The Margins of Empire: Kurdish Militias in the Ottoman Tribal Zone*. Stanford, CA: Stanford University Press, 2011.

Köksal, Yonca. "Coercion and Mediation: Centralization and Sedentarization of Tribes in the Ottoman Empire." *Middle Eastern Studies* 42, no. 3 (2006): 469–91.

Kotsonis, Yanni. "The Problem of the Individual in the Stolypin Reforms." *Explorations in Russian and Eurasian History* 12, no. 1 (2011): 25–52.

———. *States of Obligation: Taxes and Citizenship in the Russian Empire and Early Soviet Republic*. Toronto: University of Toronto Press, 2014.

Kuehn, Thomas. *Empire, Islam, and Politics of Difference: Ottoman Rule in Yemen, 1849–1919*. Leiden: Brill, 2011.

Kürt, Ümit. *The Armenians of Aintab: The Economics of Genocide in an Ottoman Province*. Cambridge, MA: Harvard University Press, 2021.

Kynn, Tyler. "Encounters of Islam and Empire: The Hajj in the Early Modern World." PhD diss., Yale University, 2020.

Lancaster, William and Fidelity Lancaster. *People, Land and Water in the Arab Middle East: Environments and Landscapes in the Bilâd Ash-Shâm*. Abingdon: Routledge, 2012.

Leder, Stefan. "Nomadische Lebensformen und ihre Wahrnehmung im Spiegel der arabischen Terminologie." *Die Welt des Orients* 34 (2004): 72–104.

———. "Towards a Historical Semantic of the Bedouin, Seventh to Fifteenth Centuries: A Survey." *Der Islam* 92, no. 1 (2015): 85–123.

Levine, Bruce, and Eric Foner. *Half Slave and Half Free: The Roots of Civil War*. New York: Hill and Wang/Noonday Press, 1992.

LeVine, Mark. *Overthrowing Geography: Jaffa, Tel Aviv, and the Struggle for Palestine, 1880–1948*. Berkeley: University of California Press, 2005.

Levy, Jonathan. *Ages of American Capitalism: A History of the United States*. New York: Random House, 2021.

Lewis, Norman. *Nomads and Settlers in Syria and Jordan, 1800–1980*. Cambridge: Cambridge University Press, 1987.

Lindner, Rudi Paul. *Nomads and Ottomans in Medieval Anatolia*. Bloomington: Research Institute for Inner Asian Studies, Indiana University, 1983.

Lipsky, Michael. *Street-Level Bureaucracy: Dilemmas of the Individual in Public Services*. 2nd ed. New York: Russel Sage, 2010.

Lohr, Eric. *Russian Citizenship: From Empire to Soviet Union*. Cambridge, MA: Harvard University Press, 2012.

Low, Michael Christopher. "Empire and the Hajj: Pilgrims, Plagues, and Pan-Islam under British Surveillance, 1865–1908." *International Journal of Middle East Studies* 40, no. 2 (May 1, 2008): 269–90.

———. *Imperial Mecca: Ottoman Arabia and the Indian Ocean Hajj*. New York: Columbia University Press, 2020.

Luynes, Duc de. *Voyage d'exploration à la Mer Morte, à Petra, et sur la rive gauche du Jourdain*. Edited by Arthur Bertrand. Paris: Librairie de la Société de Géographie, 1874.

Macpherson, C. B. *Property: Mainstream and Critical Perspectives*. Toronto: University of Toronto Press, 1978.

Maggor, Noam. "To Coddle and Caress These Great Capitalists: Eastern Money, Frontier Populism, and the Politics of Market-Making in the American West." *American Historical Review*, no. 1 (2017): 55–84.

Maier, Charles S. *Once within Borders: Territories of Power, Wealth, and Belonging since 1500*. Cambridge, MA: Harvard University Press, 2016.

Makdisi, Ussama. *Age of Coexistence: The Ecumenical Frame and the Making of the Modern Arab World*. Oakland: University of California Press, 2019.

———. *The Culture of Sectarianism: Community, History, and Violence in Nineteenth-Century Ottoman Lebanon*. Berkeley: University of California Press, 2000.

———. "Ottoman Orientalism." *American Historical Review* 102, no. 3 (1997): 768–96.

Manṣūr, Asʿad. *Tārīkh al-Nāṣirah min Aqdam ʿAzmānihā ila Ayyāminā al-Ḥāḍirah*. Miṣr: Maṭbaʾat al-Hilāl, 1924.

Maoz, Moshe. *Ottoman Reform in Syria and Palestine*. Oxford: Oxford University Press, 1968.

Martin, Virginia. *Law and Custom in the Steppe: The Kazakhs of the Middle Horde and Russian Colonialism in the Nineteenth Century*. Richmond, Surrey: Curzon, 2001.

Martinez, José Ciro. *States of Subsistence: The Politics of Bread in Contemporary Jordan*. Stanford, CA: Stanford University Press, 2022.

Masoero, Alberto. "Territorial Colonization in Late Imperial Russia." *Kritika: Explorations in Russian and Eurasian History* 14, no. 1 (2013): 59–91.

Massad, Joseph. *Colonial Effects: The Making of National Identity in Jordan.* New York: Columbia University Press, 2001.

Masters, Bruce. "The Political Economy of Aleppo in an Age of Ottoman Reform." *Journal of the Economic and Social History of the Orient* 53, no. 1/2 (2010): 290–316.

Masud, Muhammad Khalid, Rudolph Peters, and David S. Powers, eds. *Dispensing Justice in Islam: Qadis and Their Judgments.* Leiden: Brill, 2006.

McElrone, Susynne. "From the Pages of the Defter: A Social History of Rural Property Tenure and the Implementation of the Tanzimat Land Reform in Hebron, Palestine (1858–1900)." PhD diss., New York University, 2016.

McGowan, Bruce. *Economic Life in Ottoman Europe: Taxation, Trade, and the Struggle for Land, 1600–1800.* Cambridge: Cambridge University Press, 1981.

Mecmua-ı Kavanin (Düstur). Istanbul: Takvimhane-i Amire, 1851.

Meek, Ronald. *Social Science and the Ignoble Savage.* Cambridge: Cambridge University Press, 1976.

Meeker, Michael. *A Nation of Empire: The Ottoman Legacy of Turkish Modernity.* Berkeley: University of California Press, 2002.

Meier, Astrid. "Bedouins in the Ottoman Juridical Field: Select Cases from Syrian Court Records, Seventeenth to Nineteenth Centuries." *Eurasian Studies* 9, no. 1–2 (2011): 187–211.

Meier, Astrid, and Tariq Tell. "The World the Bedouin Lived In: Climate, Migration and Politics in the Early Modern Arab East." *Journal of the Economic and Social History of the Orient* 58, no. 1/2 (2015): 21–55.

Miknāsī, Muḥammad ibn ʿUthmān. *Riḥlat al-Miknāsī: Iḥrāz al-Muʿalla wa al-Raqīb fī Ḥajj Bayt Allāh al-Ḥarām wa Ziyārat al-Quds al-Sharīf wa al-Khalīl wa al-Tabarruk bi-Qabr al-Ḥabīb 1785.* Beirut: Al-Muʾassasah al-ʿArabīyah lil-Dirāsāt wa al-Nashr, 2003.

Milli Tetebbular Mecmuası. Istanbul: Matbaa-i Amire, 1903.

Minawi, Mostafa. "Beyond Rhetoric: Reassessing Bedouin-Ottoman Relations along the Route of the Hijaz Telegraph Line at the End of the Nineteenth Century." *Journal of the Economic and Social History of the Orient* 58, no. 1/2 (March 2015): 75–104.

———. *The Ottoman Scramble for Africa: Empire and Diplomacy in the Sahara and the Hijaz.* Stanford, CA: Stanford University Press, 2016.

Mitchell, Timothy. "The Limits of the State: Beyond Statist Approaches and Their Critics." *American Political Science Review* 85, no. 1 (1991): 77–96.

———. "Society, Economy, and the State Effect." In *State/Culture: State-Formation after the Cultural Turn*, edited by George Steinmetz, 76–97. Ithaca, NY: Cornell University Press, 1999.

Moon, David. "Agriculture and Environment on the Steppes in the Nineteenth Century." In *Peopling the Russian Periphery: Borderland Colonization in Eurasian History*, edited by Nicholas B. Breyfogle, Abby Schrader, and Willard Sunderland, 81–105. London: Routledge, 2007.

———. "Peasant Migration and the Settlement of Russia's Frontiers, 1550–1897." *Historical Journal* 40, no. 4 (1997): 859–93.

Moore, Jason W. *Capitalism in the Web of Life: Ecology and the Accumulation of Capital*. London: Verso, 2015.

Morack, Ellinor. *The Dowry of the State? The Politics of Abandoned Property and the Population Exchange in Turkey, 1921–45*. Bamberg: University of Bamberg Press, 2017.

Morrison, Alexander. "Metropole, Colony, and Imperial Citizenship in the Russian Empire." *Kritika: Explorations in Russian and Eurasian History* 13, no. 2 (2012): 327–64.

———. *The Russian Conquest of Central Asia: A Study in Imperial Expansion, 1814–1914*. Cambridge: Cambridge University Press, 2020.

Moumtaz, Nada. *God's Property: Islam, Charity, and the Modern State*. Oakland: University of California Press, 2021.

Mundy, Martha. "Village Authority and the Legal Order of Property (the Southern Hawran, 1876–1922)." In Owen, *New Perspectives on Property and Land*, 63–92.

Mundy, Martha, and Richard Saumarez Smith. *Governing Property, Making the Modern State: Law, Administration and Production in Ottoman Syria*. London: I.B. Tauris, 2007.

Muslu, Cihan Yüksel. "'Nomadic' Borders of Ottoman Provinces during the Mamluk-Ottoman Imperial Transition." In Conermann and Şen, *The Mamluk-Ottoman Transition*, 295–326.

Mustafa, Ahmed, and Ghani Rahman. "Assessing the Spatio-temporal Variability of Meteorological Drought in Jordan." *Earth Systems and Environment* 2 (2018): 247–64.

Nasasra, Mansour. *The Naqab Bedouins: A Century of Politics and Resistance*. New York: Columbia University Press, 2017.

Neep, Daniel. *Occupying Syria under the French Mandate: Insurgency, Space and State Formation*. New York: Cambridge University Press, 2012.

Nelson, Megan Kate. "Death in the Distance: Confederate Manifest Destiny and the Campaign for New Mexico, 1861–1862." In *Civil War Wests: Testing the Limits of the United States*, edited by Adam Arenson and Andrew R. Graybill, 33–52. Oakland: University of California Press, 2015.

Nimr, Iḥsān. *Tārīkh Jabal Nāblus wa al-Balqaʾ*. 4 vols. Nablus: Maṭbaʿat Jamʿīyat ʿUmmāl al-Maṭābiʿ al-Taʿāwunīyah bi-Nābulus, 1936.

Ochsenwald, William. *The Hijaz Railroad.* Charlottesville: University Press of Virginia, 1980.

———. *Religion, Society, and the State in Arabia: The Hijaz under Ottoman Control, 1840–1908.* Columbus: Ohio State University Press, 1984.

Oliphant, Laurence. *The Land of Gilead, with Excursions in the Lebanon.* Edinburgh: W. Blackwood and Sons, 1880.

Orhonlu, Cengiz. *Osmanlı İmparatorluğu'nda Aşiretlerin İskanı.* Istanbul: Eren, 1987.

Osterhammel, Jürgen. *The Transformation of the World: A Global History of the Nineteenth Century.* Translated by Patrick Camiller. Princeton, NJ: Princeton University Press, 2014.

Ostler, Jeffrey. *The Plains Sioux and U.S. Colonialism from Lewis and Clark to Wounded Knee.* Cambridge: Cambridge University Press, 2004.

Otis, D. S. *The Dawes Act and the Allotment of Indian Lands.* Edited by Francis Paul Prucha. Norman: University of Oklahoma Press, 1973.

Owen, Roger, ed. *New Perspectives on Property and Land in the Middle East.* Cambridge, MA: Harvard University Press, 2000.

———. *The Middle East in the World Economy, 1800–1914.* London: Methuen, 1981.

Özbek, Nadir. *İmparatorluğun Bedeli: Osmanlı'da Vergi, Siyaset ve Toplumsal Adalet (1839–1908).* Istanbul: Boğaziçi University Press, 2015.

———. "Osmanlı İmparatorluğunda Gelir Vergisi: 1903–1907 Tarihli Vergi-i Şahsi Uygulaması." *Tarih ve Toplum Yeni Yaklaşımlar* 10 (2010): 43–80.

———. "The Politics of Taxation and the 'Armenian Question' during the Late Ottoman Empire, 1876–1908." *Comparative Studies in Society and History,* no. 4 (2012): 770–97.

———. "Tax Farming in the Nineteenth Century Ottoman Empire: Institutional Backwardness or the Emergence of Modern Public Finance?" *Journal of Interdisciplinary History* 49, no. 2 (2018): 219–45.

Özyüksel, Murat. *Hicaz Demiryolu.* İstanbul: Türkiye Ekonomik ve Toplumsal Tarih Vakfı, 2000.

———. *The Hejaz Railway and the Ottoman Empire: Modernity, Industrialisation and Ottoman Decline.* New York: I.B. Tauris, 2014.

Pallot, Judith. "The Stolypin Land Reforms as 'Administrative Utopia': Images of Peasantry in Nineteenth Century Russia." In *Social Identities in Revolutionary Russia,* edited by Madhavan K. Palat, 113–33. London: Palgrave Macmillan, 2001.

Palva, Heikki. "Arabic Texts in the District of Es-Salt, Jordan." *Acta Orientalia* 68 (2007): 161–205.

Pamuk, Şevket. *A Monetary History of the Ottoman Empire.* Cambridge: Cambridge University Press, 2003.

———. *The Ottoman Empire and European Capitalism, 1820–1913*. Cambridge: Cambridge University Press, 1987.

———. "The Ottoman Empire in the 'Great Depression' of 1873–1896." *Journal of Economic History* 44, no. 1 (1984): 107–18.

Parker, Geoffrey. *Global Crisis: War, Climate Change and Catastrophe in the Seventeenth Century*. New Haven, CT: Yale University Press, 2013.

Parsons, Laila. "Rebels without Borders: Southern Syria and Palestine, 1919–1936." In *The Routledge Handbook of the History of the Middle East Mandates*, edited by Cyrus Schayegh and Andrew Arsan, 395–407. Oxford: Routledge, 2015.

Peake, Frederick Gerard. *Tārīkh Sharqī al-Urdun wa Qabā'iluhā*. ʿAmmān: Al-Dār al-ʿArabīyah, 1935.

Peirce, Leslie. *Empress of the East: How a European Slave Girl Became Queen of the Ottoman Empire*. New York: Basic Books, 2017.

———. *Morality Tales: Law and Gender in the Ottoman Court of Aintab*. Berkeley: University of California Press, 2003.

Penslar, Derek. *Zionism and Technocracy: The Engineering of Jewish Settlement in Palestine, 1870–1918*. Bloomington: Indiana University Press, 1991.

Petersen, Andrew. *The Medieval and Ottoman Hajj Route in Jordan: An Archaeological and Historical Study*. Oxford: Oxbow, 2012.

———. "The Ottoman Conquest of Arabia and the Syrian Hajj Route." In *The Frontiers of the Ottoman World*, edited by A. C. S. Peacock, 81–94. Oxford: Oxford University Press, 2009.

Petrov, Fedor A. "Crowning the Edifice: The Zemstvo, Local Self-Government, and the Constitutional Movement, 1864–1881." In *Russia's Great Reforms, 1855–1881*, edited by Ben Eklof, John Bushnell, and Larissa Zakharova, translated by Robin Bisha, 197–213. Bloomington: Indiana University Press, 1994.

Petrov, Milen V. "Everyday Forms of Compliance: Subaltern Commentaries on Ottoman Reform, 1864–1868." *Comparative Studies in Society and History* 46, no. 4 (2004): 730–59.

Philipp, Thomas. *Acre: The Rise and Fall of a Palestinian City, 1730–1831*. New York: Columbia University Press, 2002.

Polatel, Mehmet, and Uğur Ümit Üngör. *Confiscation and Destruction: The Young Turk Seizure of Armenian Property*. London: Bloomsbury, 2011.

Pravilova, Ekaterina. "The Property of Empire: Islamic Law and Russian Agrarian Policy in Transcaucasia and Turkestan." *Kritika: Explorations in Russian and Eurasian History* 12, no. 2 (2011): 353–86.

Provence, Michael. *The Great Syrian Revolt and the Rise of Arab Nationalism*. Austin: University of Texas Press, 2005.

Qusūs, ʿAwdah. *Mudhakkirāt ʿAwdah Salmān al-Qusūs al-Halasā, 1877–1943.* ʿAmmān: Nāyif Jūrj al-Qusūs al-Halasā, 2006.

Rafeq, Abdul-Karim. "Ownership of Real Property by Foreigners in Syria, 1869 to 1873." In Owen, *New Perspectives on Property and Land,* 175–239.

———. *The Province of Damascus, 1723–1783.* Beirut: Khayats, 1966.

———. "Qāfilat al-Ḥajj al-Shāmī wa-ʾAhammīyatuhā fi al-ʿAhd al-ʿUthmānī." *Dirāsāt Tārīkhīyah* 6 (1981): 5–28.

Rankin, William. *After the Map: Cartography, Navigation, and the Transformation of Territory in the Twentieth Century.* Chicago: University of Chicago Press, 2018.

Rawābidah, ʿAbd al-Raʾūf. *Muʿjam al-ʿAshāʾir al-Urdunīyah.* ʿAmmān: Dār al-Shurūq lil-Nashr wa-al-Tawzīʿ, 2010.

Razzaz, Omar M. "Contestation and Mutual Adjustment: The Process of Controlling Land in Yajouz, Jordan." *Law and Society Review* 28, no. 1 (1994): 7–40.

Redhouse, Sir James W. *A Turkish and English Lexicon.* 3rd ed. Istanbul: Çağrı Yayınları, 2006. First printed for the American Mission by A. H. Boyajian, Constantinople, 1890.

Refik, Ahmet. *Anadolu'da Türk Âşiretleri, 966–1200: Anadolu'da Yaşayan Türk Aşiretleri Hakkında Divani Hümayun Mühhime Defterlerinde Mukayyet Hükümleri Havidir.* İstanbul: Devlet Matbaası, 1930.

Reilly, Benjamin. *Slavery, Agriculture, and Malaria in the Arabian Peninsula.* Athens: Ohio University Press, 2015.

Reilly, James A. "Shariʿa Court Registers and Land Tenure around Nineteenth-Century Damascus." *Middle East Studies Association Bulletin* 21, no. 2 (1987): 155–69.

———. "Status Groups and Propertyholding in the Damascus Hinterland, 1828–1880." *International Journal of Middle East Studies* 21, no. 4 (1989): 517–39.

Richter, Daniel K. *Facing East from Indian Country: A Native History of Early America.* Cambridge, MA: Harvard University Press, 2001.

Roberts, Timothy. "Almost as It Is Formulated in the So-Called 'Homestead Act': Images of the American West in French Settlement of French Algeria." *Journal of World History* 32, no. 4 (2021): 601–29.

Rogan, Eugene. "Aşiret Mektebi: Abdülhamid II's School for Tribes (1892–1907)." *International Journal of Middle East Studies* 28, no. 1 (Feb. 1, 1996): 83–107.

———. *Frontiers of the State in the Late Ottoman Empire: Transjordan, 1850–1921.* Cambridge: Cambridge University Press, 2000.

———. "Incorporating the Periphery: The Ottoman Extension of Direct Rule over Southeastern Syria (Transjordan), 1867–1914." PhD diss., Harvard University, 1991.

——. "Moneylending and Capital Flows from Nablus, Damascus and Jerusalem to Qada' al-Salt in the Last Decades of Ottoman Rule." In *The Syrian Land in the 18th and 19th Century: The Common and the Specific in the Historical Experience*, edited by Thomas Philipp, 239–60. Berlin: Franz Steiner, 1992.

Rubin, Avi. *Ottoman Nizamiye Courts: Law and Modernity.* New York: Palgrave Macmillan, 2011.

Rustum, Asad. *Al-Maḥfuẓāt al-Malakīyah al-Miṣriyah.* 4 vols. Cairo: Dār al-Maʿārif bi-Miṣr, 1952.

Ṣabbāgh, ʿAbbūd. *Al-Rawḍ al-Zāhir fī Tārīkh Ḍāhir.* ʿAmmān: Dār al-Shurūq lil-Nashr wa-al-Tawzīʿ, 2017.

Sabol, Steven. *The Touch of Civilization: Comparing American and Russian Internal Colonization.* Boulder: University Press of Colorado, 2016.

Ṣāfī, Khālid Muḥammad. *Al-Ḥukm al-Miṣrī fī Filasṭīn, 1831–1840.* Beirut: Muʾassasat al-Dirāsāt al-Filasṭīnīyya, 2010.

Saha, Jonathan. *Law, Disorder and the Colonial State: Corruption in Burma, c. 1900.* New York: Palgrave Macmillan, 2013.

Sahadeo, Jeff. "Progress or Peril: Migrants and Locals in Russian Tashkent, 1906–14." In *Peopling the Russian Periphery: Borderland Colonization in Eurasian History,* edited by Nicholas B. Breyfogle, Abby Schrader, and Willard Sunderland, 148–65. New York: Routledge, 2007.

Sahilioğlu, Halil. *Studies on Ottoman Economic and Social History.* Istanbul: IRCICA, 1999.

Saraçoğlu, M. Safa. *Nineteenth-Century Local Governance in Ottoman Bulgaria: Politics in Provincial Councils.* Edinburgh: Edinburgh University Press, 2018.

Satia, Priya. *Empire of Guns: The Violent Making of the Industrial Revolution.* Stanford, CA: Stanford University Press, 2018.

——. *Spies in Arabia: The Great War and the Cultural Foundations of Britain's Covert Empire in the Middle East.* Oxford: Oxford University Press, 2008.

Schaebler, Birgit. "Civilizing Others: Global Modernity and the Local Boundaries (French/German, Ottoman and Arab) of Savagery." In *Globalization and the Muslim World: Culture, Religion, and Modernity,* edited by Birgit Schaebler and Leif Stenberg, 3–29. Syracuse, NY: Syracuse University Press, 2004.

Schama, Simon. *Two Rothschilds and the Land of Israel.* London: Collins, 1978.

Schayegh, Cyrus. *The Middle East and the Making of the Modern World.* Cambridge, MA: Harvard University Press, 2017.

Schilcher, Linda Schatkowski. "The Great Depression (1873–1896) and the Rise of Syrian Arab Nationalism." *New Perspectives on Turkey* 5–6 (1991): 167–89.

——. "The Hauran Conflicts of the 1860s: A Chapter in the Rural History of Modern Syria." *International Journal of Middle East Studies* 13, no. 2 (1981): 159–79.

Schölch, Alexander. *Palestine in Transformation, 1856–1882: Studies in Social, Economic, and Political Development*. Washington, DC: Institute for Palestine Studies, 1993.

Schull, Kent. *Prisons in the Late Ottoman Era: Microcosms of Modernity*. Edinburgh: Edinburgh University Press, 2014.

Schwedler, Jillian. *Protesting Jordan: Geographies of Power and Dissent*. Stanford, CA: Stanford University Press, 2022.

Scott, James C. *Against the Grain: A Deep History of the Earliest States*. New Haven, CT: Yale University Press, 2017.

——. *Seeing like a State: How Certain Schemes to Improve the Human Condition Have Failed*. New Haven, CT: Yale University Press, 1999.

Seetzen, Ulrich. "Mémoire pour servir à la connaissance des tribus arabes en Syrie et dans l'Arabie déserte et Pétrée." *Annales des voyages, de la géographie et de l'histoire*, no. 8 (1809): 281–324.

Seikaly, Sherene. *Men of Capital: Scarcity and Economy in Mandate Palestine*. Stanford, CA: Stanford University Press, 2016.

Şener, Abdüllatif. *Tanzimat Dönemi Osmanlı Vergi Sistemi*. İstanbul: İşaret, 1990.

Shafir, Gershon. *Land, Labor and the Origins of the Israeli-Palestinian Conflict, 1882–1914*. Berkeley: University of California Press, 1996.

Shamir, Shimon. "The Modernization of Syria: Problems and Solutions in the Early Period of Abdülhamid." In *Beginnings of Modernization in the Middle East*, edited by William R. Polk and Richard L. Chambers, 351–82. Chicago: University of Chicago Press, 1968.

Sharif, Malek. *Imperial Norms and Local Realities: The Ottoman Municipal Laws and the Municipality of Beirut, 1860–1908*. Beirut: Orient-Institut, 2014.

Shaw, Stanford J. "The Nineteenth-Century Ottoman Tax Reforms and Revenue System." *International Journal of Middle East Studies* 6, no. 4 (1975): 421–59.

Shields, Sarah D. *Mosul before Iraq: Like Bees Making Five-Sided Cells*. Albany: State University of New York Press, 2000.

Shryock, Andrew. *Nationalism and the Genealogical Imagination: Oral History and Textual Authority in Tribal Jordan*. Berkeley: University of California Press, 1997.

Singer, Amy. *Palestinian Peasants and Ottoman Officials: Rural Administration around Sixteenth-Century Jerusalem*. New York: Cambridge University Press, 1994.

Sluglett, Peter. "Economy and Society in the Syrian Provinces." In *Modernity and Culture from the Mediterranean to the Indian Ocean*, edited by Laila Tarazi Fawaz and C. A. Bayly. New York: Columbia University Press, 2002.

Sneath, David. *The Headless State: Aristocratic Orders, Kinship Society, and Misrepresentations of Nomadic Inner Asia*. New York: Columbia University Press, 2007.

Sowayan, Saad Abdullah. *Al-Ṣaḥrā' al-ʿArabīyah: Thaqāfatuhā wa Shiʿruhā ʿabra al-ʿUṣūr, Qirāʾah Anthrūbūlūjīyah*. Bayrūt: Al-Shabakah al-ʿArabīyah lil-Abḥāth wa-al-Nashr, 2010.

Spyridon, J. N. "Annals of Palestine, 1821–1841." *Journal of the Palestine Oriental Society* 18 (1938): 63–132.

Sunderland, Willard. *Taming the Wild Field: Colonization and Empire on the Russian Steppe*. Ithaca, NY: Cornell University Press, 2004.

Swedberg, Richard, and Ola Agevall. *The Max Weber Dictionary: Key Words and Central Concepts*. 2nd ed. Stanford, CA: Stanford University Press, 2016.

Tanūkhī, ʿIzz al-Dīn. *Al-Riḥlah al-Tanūkhīyah min Ḥalab ila al-Jawf, 1332 H. / 1914 M*. Edited by Fāyiz Ruwaylī. Bayrūt: Al-Dār al-ʿArabīyah lil-Mawsūʿāt, 2015.

Taylor, Malissa. "Forcing the Wealthy to Pay Their Fair Share? The Politics of Rural Taxes in 17th-Century Ottoman Damascus." *Journal of the Economic and Social History of the Orient* 62 (2019): 35–66.

Taylor, Malissa Anne. "Fragrant Gardens and Converging Waters: Ottoman Governance in Seventeenth-Century Damascus." PhD diss., University of California, Berkeley, 2012.

Ṭayyib, Muḥammad Sulaymān. *Mawsūʿat al-Qabāʾil al-ʿArabīyah: Buḥūth Maydānīyah wa-Tārīkhīyah*. Vol. 2, part 1. Cairo: Dār al-Fikr al-ʿArabī, 1997.

Teitelman, Emma. "The Properties of Capitalism: Industrial Enclosures in the South and the West after the American Civil War." *Journal of American History* 106, no. 4 (2020): 874–900.

Tell, Tariq. "Guns, Gold, and Grain: War and Food Supply in the Making of Transjordan." In *War, Institutions, and Social Change in the Middle East*, edited by Steven Heydemann, 33–58. Berkeley: University of California Press, 2000.

Tell, Tariq Moraiwed. *The Social and Economic Origins of Monarchy in Jordan*. New York: Palgrave Macmillan, 2013.

Terzibaşoğlu, Yücel. "Land Disputes and Ethno-politics: Northwestern Anatolia, 1877–1912." In *Land Rights, Ethno-nationality, and Sovereignty in History*, edited by Stanley Engerman and Jacob Metzer, 153–80. London: Routledge, 2004.

———. "Landlords, Nomads and Refugees: Struggles over Land and Population Movements in North-Western Anatolia, 1877–1914." PhD diss., Birkbeck College, University of London, 2003.

Thomas, Martin. "Bedouin Tribes and the Imperial Intelligence Services in Syria, Iraq and Transjordan in the 1920s." *Journal of Contemporary History* 38, no. 4 (2003): 539–61.

Toksöz, Meltem. *Nomads, Migrants and Cotton in the Eastern Mediterranean: The Making of the Adana-Mersin Region, 1850–1908*. Leiden: Brill, 2010.

Topal, Alp Eren. "Order as a Chronotope of Ottoman Political Writing." *Contemporary Levant* 5, no. 1 (2020): 24–32.

Tristram, H. B. *The Land of Israel; a Journal of Travels in Palestine, Undertaken with Special Reference to Its Physical Character*. 4th ed., Rev. Piscataway, NJ: Gorgias, 2002.

Tuchscherer, Michel. "Coffee in the Red Sea Area from the Sixteenth to the Nineteenth Century." In *The Global Coffee Economy in Africa, Asia and Latin America*, edited by William Gervase Clarence-Smith and Steven Topik, 50–66. Cambridge: Cambridge University Press, 2003.

———. "La flotte impériale de Suez de 1694 à 1719." *Turcica* 29 (1997): 47–69.

Tutino, John. *The Mexican Heartland: How Communities Shaped Capitalism, a Nation, and World History, 1500–2000*. Princeton, NJ: Princeton University Press, 2017.

Vassiliev, Alexei. *The History of Saudi Arabia*. London: Saqi Books, 1998.

Veinstein, Gilles. "İnalcık's Views on the Ottoman Eighteenth Century and the Fiscal Problem." *Oriente Moderno* 18, no. 1 (1999): 1–10.

Vitalis, Robert. *America's Kingdom: Mythmaking on the Saudi Oil Frontier*. Stanford, CA: Stanford University Press, 2006.

Wåhlin, Lars. "How Long Has Land Been Privately Held in Northern Al-Balqa', Jordan?" *Geografiska Annaler. Series B, Human Geography* 76, no. 1 (1994): 33–49.

Walker, Bethany. "Early Ottoman/Late Islamic I/Post-Mamluk: What Are the Archaeological Traces of the 16th Century in Syria?" In Conermann and Şen, *The Mamluk-Ottoman Transition*, 343–66.

———. "Mamluk Investment in Southern Bilād Al-Shām in the Eighth/Fourteenth Century: The Case of Hisban." *International Journal of Near Eastern Studies* 62, no. 4 (2003): 241–61.

Warren, Charles. "Expedition to East of Jordan, July and August, 1867." *Palestine Exploration Fund Quarterly* 6 (1869): 284–306.

Weaver, John C. *The Great Land Rush and the Making of the Modern World, 1650–1900*. Montreal: McGill-Queen's University Press, 2003.

Weber, Max. *Economy and Society: An Outline of Interpretive Sociology*. Edited by Guenther Roth and Claus Wittich. Vol. 2. Berkeley: University of California Press, 1978.

West, Elliott. *The Last Indian War: The Nez Perce Story*. Oxford: Oxford University Press, 2009.

White, Richard. *"It's Your Misfortune and None of My Own": A History of the American West*. Norman: University of Oklahoma Press, 1991.

———. *The Middle Ground: Indians, Empires, and Republics in the Great Lakes Region, 1650–1815*. Cambridge: Cambridge University Press, 1991.

——. *The Republic for Which It Stands: The United States during Reconstruction and the Gilded Age, 1865–1896.* Oxford: Oxford University Press, 2017.

——. "The Winning of the West: The Expansion of the Western Sioux in the Eighteenth and Nineteenth Centuries." *Journal of American History* 65, no. 2 (1978): 319–43.

White, Sam. *The Climate of Rebellion in the Early Modern Ottoman Empire.* Cambridge: Cambridge University Press, 2011.

Wick, Alexis. *The Red Sea: In Search of Lost Space.* Oakland: University of California Press, 2016.

Wilkins, Charles L. *Forging Urban Solidarities: Ottoman Aleppo, 1640–1700.* Leiden: Brill, 2010.

Williams, Elizabeth. *States of Cultivation: Imperial Transition and Scientific Agriculture in the Eastern Mediterranean.* Stanford, CA: Stanford University Press, forthcoming.

Winter, Stefan. "Alep et l'émirat du désert (çöl beyliği) au XVIIe–XVIIIe siècle." In *Aleppo and Its Hinterland in the Ottoman Period/Alep et sa province à l'époque ottomane,* edited by Stefan Winter and Mafalda Ade, 86–108. Leiden: Brill, 2019.

——. "The Province of Raqqa under Ottoman Rule, 1535–1800: A Preliminary Study." *Journal of Near Eastern Studies* 68, no. 4 (2009): 253–68.

Wishnitzer, Avner. *Reading Clocks, Alla Turca: Time and Society in the Late Ottoman Empire.* Chicago: University of Chicago Press, 2015.

Witgen, Michael. *An Infinity of Nations: How the Native New World Shaped Early North America.* Philadelphia: University of Pennsylvania Press, 2011.

Yaney, George. *The Urge to Mobilize: Agrarian Reform in Russia, 1861–1930.* Urbana: University of Illinois Press, 1982.

Yaycıoğlu, ʿAli. "Karlofça ânı: Osmanlı İmparatorluğu 18. Yüzyıla Nasıl Başladı?" *Tarih ve Toplum Yeni Yaklaşımlar* 18 (2021): 8–56.

——. *Partners of the Empire: The Crisis of the Ottoman Order in the Age of Revolutions.* Stanford, CA: Stanford University Press, 2016.

Young, George. *Corps de droit ottoman.* 7 vols. Oxford: Clarendon, 1905–6.

Zakariyā, Waṣfī. *ʿAshāʾir al-Shām.* Damascus: Dār al-Fikr, 1983.

Zakim, Michael. *Capitalism Takes Command: The Social Transformation of Nineteenth-Century America.* Chicago: University of Chicago Press, 2011.

Zandi-Sayek, Sibel. *Ottoman Izmir: The Rise of a Cosmopolitan Port, 1840–1880.* Minneapolis: University of Minnesota Press, 2011.

Ze'evi, Dror. *An Ottoman Century: The District of Jerusalem in the 1600s.* Albany: State University of New York Press, 1996.

Ziriklī, Khayr al-Dīn. *ʿĀmān fī ʿAmmān: Mudhakkirāt ʿāmayn fī ʿāṣimat Sharq al-Urdun.* Cairo: Al-Maṭbaʿah al-ʿArabīyah bi-Miṣr, 1925.

INDEX

Page numbers in italics refer to maps, figures, and tables. Numbers following the letter n *refer to notes.*

'Anaza: annual expenses of, 62–63; attacks on pilgrimage by, 68–69; control of land, 313n7; during Egyptian occupation, 88; immigration from Najd, 50, 52–53, 54; between Ottoman and Saudi spheres of influence, 69–70; and politics of administration, 37–38; regional autonomy of elites, 73; subsidies to, 34, 55, 56, 57, 59–60, 62; use of sharia courts by, 298n3. *See also* Hassana ('Anaza); Wuld 'Ali ('Anaza); Ya'ish (Hassana)
anticolonial resistance, 262–69
'Aqil Agha, 109
Arab Emirate (*imārat al-'arab*), 46–47, 287n47
'Arab al-'Id, 218
Armenian Genocide, 21–22, 246
Armenians, 208, 261, 313n100
Assaf, Abdullah, 266
al-Atrash, Sultan, 265
'Awazim (Abu al-Ghanam), 96, 129
Ayn Suwaylih attack, 158–59; aftermath, 185–91, 193–94; causes of, 159–65; investigation of Cemal Bey, 191–201; village description, 303n1, 304n4. *See also* violence
al-'Azm family, 68

al-Bakhit, 'Abd al-Muhsin, 223–25, 238–39
al-Bakhit, Nahar: Ayn Suwaylih attack, 158, 164–65, 185; Ayn Suwaylih attack aftermath, 186–91, 193–94; as headman, 182–85, 217, 238–39; networks of, 163–64; simultaneous loyalties, 195, 196; wealth accumulation, 217
al-Bakhit, Naharayn Nahar, 217
Balkans: loss of, 16, 20, 138; loss

of and refugees, 165, 257; tent-dwelling communities, 43, 105, 133
Balqa district formation, *84*, 110–14, 122–23. *See also* bureaucracy in crisis; commercial capital in Syrian interior; land registration; taxation, property, and citizenship; tribes and property
Banaji, Jairus, 292n4
Bani 'Atiya, 231–35, 238, 268
Bani Hamida, 151–53, 302n85
Bani Harb, 238
Bani Haritha (Turabays), 48
Bani Hassan, 158, 186, 226, 301n55
Bani Mahdi, 49. *See also* Mahdawiyya
Bani Sakhr: administrative sovereignty usurped, 100; agricultural production, 13, 98–99; allegiance to Amir Abdullah and Hashemite regime, 268–69; attacks on pilgrimage by, 68–69; conflict over settlement of Karaki Christians, 153–54, 303n90; conflict with 'Adwan, 85–86, 87–88; conflict with Sardiyya, 51–54; designated nomadic by British, 267; *dira* of, 77; in Egyptian interregnum, 89–90, 112–13; Fawwaz Effendi's tent, *227*; land disputes in Madaba, 235–37; land registration by, 312n86; landed property of, 66; livelihoods, 10, 27, 81; migration from Hijaz, 288n63; migration from Najd, 50, 51–52; between Ottoman and Saudi spheres of influence, 64–65, 69–71; political privilege, 27; and politics of administration, 37–38; regional autonomy of elites, 73; seasonal mobility continued, 254;

of, 28, 116–22; and networks of communities, 163–64; in the North, 122–32; Ottoman state transformation, 3–8, 28–31; and rural populations, 78–80. *See also* headmen (*mukhtars*); men of property

Stolypin land reforms (Russia), 258

street-level bureaucrats, 24

subjecthood and citizenship, 25–26; contestations over nature and scope of citizenship, 29–30; in rural areas, 230

subsidies to Bedouin: administrative integration of Bedouin, 250–51; amounts of, 289n80; apportionment system, 60, 62; distribution within tribes, 285n3; neglect of, 68; payments in coffee, 34, 65; and pilgrimage duties, 34, 37–38, 50, 55–59, 57, 289n89; purchasing power of, 62–63, 290n100; and taxes to Saudi state, 70. *See also* sphere of submission (*ṭāʿat al-dawla*)

subsidy registers: data collection on Bedouin, 59–64, 61; network of human alliances, 72; payments in coffee, 65

Şukri Paşa: complaints against Cemal Bey, 199; disputes in Madaba, 237; investigation of Ayn Suwaylih attack, 186, 193, 197; opinion of Bedouin, 240

al-Sulayman, Hamad bin ʿAwad, 226, 228, 240–41

Sulayman Paşa, 70

Supreme Council of Judicial Ordinances (*Meclis-i Vala*), 93–94, 101

Syrian interior, 39, 42, 84, 177, 247. *See also* Bedouin; bureaucracy

in crisis; commercial capital in Syrian interior; taxation, property, and citizenship; tribal frontier and beyond; tribes and property

tābʿīn, 219

Talal Paşa, 235, 236–37, 238–39

Tanūkhī, ʿIzz al-Dīn, 71

Tanzimat (agrarian reforms). *See* agrarian imaginary

Tapu Regulation (1859). *See* Title Regulation (1859); title-deed (*tapu*) system

Tawqa (Bani Sakhr), 51–52. *See also* Bani Sakhr; al-Fayiz (Bani Sakhr)

tax collection: apportionment system, 60, 210–11, 221–22; rural taxation nature, 193–94, 196–97; from tent-dwellers in sixteenth century, 43–46. *See also* tax farming; taxation, property, and citizenship

tax farming: and administrative sovereignty, 54–55, 65–67; grain production expansion, 67–68, 291n124; provincial treasury funding, 50–51, 287n56; reforms, 105–6, 297n104. *See also* tax collection; taxation, property, and citizenship

taxation, property, and citizenship: headmen, taxation, and political representation, 25–26, 209–15, 260, 310n23, 310n25, 310n34; taxation conflicts, 29–30, 202–9, 230–37; taxation conflicts and subject rights, 237–42; tax-collection practices, 221–30, 311n61; wealth accumulation and inequality, 215–21. *See also* headmen (*mukhtars*); men of property

Printed and bound by CPI Group (UK) Ltd, Croydon, CR0 4YY

09/06/2025

14685890-0001